TAILSPIN

JEAN ZIMMERMAN

TAILSPIN

WOMEN AT WAR
IN THE WAKE
OF TAILHOOK

DOUBLEDAY
New York London Toronto
Sydney Auckland

PUBLISHED BY DOUBLEDAY
a division of Bantam Doubleday Dell
Publishing Group, Inc.
1540 Broadway, New York, New York
10036

DOUBLEDAY and the portrayal of an anchor with a dolphin are trademarks of
Doubleday, a division of Bantam Doubleday Dell Publishing Group, Inc.

No copyright is claimed on U.S. Government material quoted throughout this
book.

Book design by
Jennifer Ann Daddio

Library of Congress Cataloging-in-
Publication Data
Zimmerman, Jean.
    Tailspin : women at war in the wake
of Tailhook / Jean Zimmerman. — 1st
ed.
            p.   cm.
    Includes bibliographical references
(p.   ) and index.
    1. United States. Navy—Women.
2. Tailhook Scandal, 1991–1993.
3. Women in combat—United States.
4. Sexual harassment of women—
United States. 5. United States—
Armed Forces—Women. I. Title.
VB324.W65Z55   1995
355′.0082—dc20   94-45140
                                      CIP

ISBN 0-385-47789-9
Copyright © 1995 by Jean Zimmerman
All Rights Reserved
Printed in the United States of America
July 1995

First Edition

10   8   6   4   2   0   1   3   5   7   9

FOR GIL

Animae dimidium meae

Acknowledgments

I am grateful to all those whose names and words appear in the pages that follow. I would not have been able to enter the world of the U.S. Navy if not for the incredibly generous people I spent time with over the last three years. There is not space to name everyone, but I want to thank those individuals who shared their time and insights aboard USS *Abraham Lincoln,* USS *Cape Cod,* USS *Elmendorf,* USS *Samuel Gompers,* USS *Briscoe,* USS *Tortuga,* USS *Emory S. Land,* USS *Atlanta,* and at the San Diego Naval Base, North Island Naval Air Station, Miramar Naval Air Station, Lemoore Naval Air Station, Moffett Field Naval Air Station, Alameda Naval Air Station, Pensacola Naval Air Station, Oceana Naval Air Station, Treasure Island Naval Station, San Diego Recruit Training Center, the Naval Education and Training Command in Pensacola, the Orlando Recruit Training Center, Norfolk Naval Base, Little Creek Naval Amphibious Base, Naval Aviation Schools Command, the Naval Special Warfare Command at Coronado, the Chief of Naval Education and Training in Pensacola, the U.S. Naval Academy, the Navy Women's Bureau at the Pentagon and the Bureau of Naval Personnel at the Navy Annex. Special thanks to Rear Admiral Louise Wilmot, Rear Admiral (Ret.) Paul Gillchrist,

Commander Cathy Miller, Commander Byron Iverson and Lieutenant Michelle Dunne Iverson, Vice Admiral R. J. Zlatoper, Captain Kathleen Bruyere, Commander Deborah Loewer, Captain (Ret.) Kay Krohne, and Lieutenant Commander (Ret.) Walt Deckert—and others I cannot name—who gave me valuable background and context.

Without the support of the Department of the Navy, this book could not have been written. A number of individuals were especially helpful in arranging interviews and embarks, as well as pointing the way through the maze of Navy hierarchy, acronyms and bureaucracy. I am grateful to Lieutenant Lana Hampton in New York City, Lieutenant Taylor Kiland in San Diego, and Lieutenant Donna Hoffmaier, Lieutenant Karen Jeffries and Lieutenant Beci Brenton in Washington, D.C. Beyond their efforts on behalf of my project, they served as personal examples of strong, dedicated women within the Navy.

Major General Jeanne Holm flagged inaccuracies, as did Jean Ebbert. My indefatigable editor and good friend Betsy Lerner deserves accolades for her commitment to this project right from the get-go, and for her vision and skills in seeing it through. Thanks also to Betsy's assistant, Brandon Saltz, for acting as a capable go-between.

Kim Witherspoon guided this book along an unusually eventful path to publication, watching out for it at every step of the way. Her former partner, Dona Chernoff, was the initial angel who presided over its inception.

Lloyd Westerman read the manuscript and made invaluable suggestions.

On the home front, Alison Riley deserves mention for her organizational abilities around the home office. I am grateful to Peter Zimmerman, who provided research leads and first suggested the title, and Andy Zimmerman, who offered valuable suggestions. Stephen and Betty Zimmerman were, as always, endlessly supportive. Maud Reavill demanded pictures and play time at just the right moments, and was always there to recharge my batteries.

Finally, this book is a work of collaboration inasmuch as Gil Reavill served as my first and finest reader, editor, sounding board and general all-around helpmate throughout its long gestation—with minimal spilling of blood in the process. It is difficult to work hard and play hard with the same person, but being partners on this project made us stronger, me happier and the book far better than it would have been without him.

CONTENTS

Preface

I began research on this book in early June, 1992. The Secretary of the Navy had just quit his job over Tailhook, and the scandal was spreading, deepening, changing like some massive, subcutaneous bruise.

I planned to write about what happened at the Tailhook Association's 1991 symposium, why it occurred and about the ongoing efforts within the Navy to transform its culture so as to be less inimical to women. What I didn't realize at first was that there was another subject informing the events in the Las Vegas Hilton over the 1991 Labor Day weekend. That subject was the exclusion of women from combat positions in the U.S. military, which worked to relegate females to second-class status vis-à-vis their male cohorts.

As I got further into my research, I discovered a disturbing fact: there remained only one place in American culture that was legally closed to women, where they were specifically barred by legislative fiat. That place was combat—specifically, the cockpit of military warplanes and the combat ships of the U.S. Navy.

Tailhook and the legal ban on women in combat were linked, and that link forms the substance of this book.

As the ramifications of the scandal unfolded, a strange poetic symmetry seemed to show itself. If the combat exclusion for women had contributed to the events at Tailhook '91, then the scandal would eventually lead to the lifting of that exclusion. Given the opinions of the people I talked to, who were overwhelmingly negative about the chances of the combat ban being repealed in the foreseeable future, and given the glacial pace at which military reform is usually conducted, the lifting of the combat ban was an astonishing, even epochal, development.

Somewhat to my surprise, the Department of the Navy was supportive of my research. Navy leadership and the service in general proved to be not a monolithic entity, but one with many different elements (including reform elements), all struggling to come to terms with what *Newsweek* termed the Navy's "worst embarrassment since Pearl Harbor." I got a feeling there was strong curiosity in some quarters to know the truth about Tailhook, warts and all, and a growing impulse to treat the scandal as a watershed, to use it as a lever for constructive change.

All told, I conducted nearly 400 sit-down interviews, and many more informal discussions. With only a few exceptions, the people of the Navy were eager to say where they stood on questions related to Tailhook, how they felt about women in the Navy, where they thought things should be going in terms of women in combat. Men and women alike were forthcoming about their personal experiences. My sources included officers and enlisted personnel at naval bases and air stations all over the country. I arranged to go on board a number of Navy vessels, and thus I got to see what life was like on a tender, a destroyer, an amphib, a carrier, even a fast-attack submarine.

Most impressive during this long process were the women I met in the Navy, a small minority of the whole (a little over 50,000 in a 500,000-member service), who were clearly a great resource for the military and for the country overall. These women were strong-willed, tough and totally devoted to what they would invariably call "my Navy," even in the face of the various negative and demeaning responses to their presence. Their struggle to become established as part of a community where their welcome was uneven at best struck me as extremely poignant. I remember interviewing a young helicopter pilot at Florida's Whiting Field, where she and a male buddy were giving me a tour. He jokingly said to her, "Why would she want to talk to women in the Navy anyway?" "Because we're studs," the pilot replied.

Navy women's determination, as well as their skills, is a tremendous asset to the men with whom they serve, who must rely on their female colleagues daily, in life or death situations. It is their story that I most want to tell.

I don't want to slight the challenge that Navy men must now face, as women enter their heretofore closed culture in increasing numbers. The naval aviator is a tremendously strange bird, but the extreme circumstances of naval aviation exert strange pressures. I grew up believing in the glamorous jet-jock mythology, since an uncle of mine was a Navy pilot, a Top Gun of his day. He died as an ensign when the plane he was training in flamed out in the skies over Virginia, and within the family he was legendary ever after as a risk-taker. Did the risks of military flying make the excesses of behavior at Tailhook explicable?

I set out to find what motivated the men of the Navy, including the younger generation, the ones who blew it out at Las Vegas, and the older generation, the ones who helped the junior officers believe their behavior was acceptable. If I couldn't resolve the contradiction between an officer and gentleman and the beast of Tailhook, then perhaps I could better understand it.

Earlier in my professional career, I focused on the problems of women in another traditionally male environment, that of corporate America. Within the more arcane atmosphere of the U.S. Navy, the traditions and culture at times exhibited an even more entrenched enmity toward the presence of women. I spent many hours talking to the same junior officers who were held up as the villains of Tailhook. I sometimes had to make an effort to square what I saw with the credo of the Roman poet, Terence: "Nothing human is alien to me."

Nonetheless, I found much to admire in the courage and idealism of the men and women who volunteer to defend the country. The course of my research was filled with the unexpected, not the least of which was how fluid were the roles of men and women in the Navy. Nowhere in the civilian world, I knew, was it so common to find women in nontraditional jobs, working as jet mechanics and machinists and, yes, fighter pilots. That's something I found radical and exciting. The military may still have an "armor-plated ceiling" limiting women's advancement, but beneath it there lurked the beginnings of a gender-neutral workplace.

Soon after I turned in my manuscript, one of the central figures in this book, Lieutenant Kara Hultgreen, perished in a crash in the Pacific Ocean while on a training run. Hultgreen had flown alongside men and lost her life alongside men. That, finally, may be the bond between the men and women in our country's military service, and the final frontier of equality—the pledge they make to give their lives, if necessary. I can only hope that the book as a whole pays tribute to the tenacity, spirit and sense of adventure that women like Kara Hultgreen embody.

Part One

THE THIRD DECK

ANY TRUTH CREATES A SCANDAL.

—Marguerite Yourcenar

Chapter One

LIGHTING YOUR HAIR ON FIRE

GANDHI, LIKE HIS NAMESAKE, WAS A SENSITIVE MAN, AND HE brought his sensitivity to the practice of female leg shaving.

He loved the whole procedure, the bracing smell of Barbasol, the heat of the towels, the feel of the flesh afterward—firm, clean, slightly moist but above all smooth, preternaturally smooth, like warm marble.

Even the sound. There was no sound in the world like that of a woman's leg being shaved, the tiny *scritch scritch* of the razor. No matter how crazy the party grew around him, that sound brought Gandhi instantly back to the fact that he was the Man. The Barber of Seville. Lieutenant Rolando "Gandhi" Diaz, at your service.

It was September in the Nevada desert, and it was hot. The stink of sweat and beer and beer-vomit in the hotel room was terrific. Bodies crammed in together got slicked up in the heat like seals. A banner that read FREE LEG SHAVES hung outside on the pool patio over the door to Suite 303 of the Las Vegas Hilton. The 1991 Tailhook Convention was zooming and booming.

Sometimes, when Gandhi looked up from his work, the crowd would have suddenly grown enormous. They were pounding on the windows outside. The Animals were rattling the bars of their cages.

Everyone was there; they had flown in from all over, the Navy's elite, dropping out of the skies from Miramar, Oceana, El Toro, Lemoore. The third floor of the Hilton was as crowded as the deck of the *Titanic*.

He bore down and scrutinized the calf of the woman in front of him, handling it as tenderly as one man might hold another's infant. *Scritch. Scritch. Scritch.*

Crossed hairs, double hairs, hairs that imploded in the follicle. A lot of people had bad problems with stubble. Gandhi moved his fingertips along the leg and felt every hair, the strange way each one twisted from its pore.

The crowd howled. Women were lined up, begging for his ministrations. Not only the showgirls and dancers and hookers, either. There were plenty of professionals waiting for a shave, but filling out the line were party-girls, the kind who showed up whenever Navy aviators got together, who knew Tailhook to be one world-class bash. There were female industry reps and airline stews. Lieutenant Diaz hadn't brought his own wife, but some pilots had. There was even the wife of a Vegas-area police chief waiting her turn. Some of these women came to Tailhook every year, like a pilgrimage. He'd already done a couple of female naval officers.

There were times when Gandhi's art could move his audience to tears. He remembered the year before, he was shaving a legal secretary named Robin from Tempe, Arizona. She was leaning way back in the chair, clearly enjoying herself, when a drunken guy got in Gandhi's face and started weeping. Gandhi was going, "Dude, you okay?" Said the drunk, "My God, she's coming on your chair." "So?" said Gandhi. The guy was muttering, "You're a god, man, you're a god." "Would you relax?" said Gandhi.

He even got fan mail. This from a woman he had shaved at least four times:

If I have to choose somebody to go to war for me, it'll be you, because you were the perfect officer and a gentleman. Just what I would expect any Navy guy to be.

But he couldn't think about all that now. He tried to telescope the world down to the razor and the flesh, the blue Gillette crawling up the leg, leaving a neat twin snowplow trail, foam and colloidal trimmings of blond hair. He wanted to shut out the sound of the party —the roar of it, the "Woooooo!" of the assembled drunken Animals— so that he could concentrate on the delicate *scritch scritch* of the razor.

They weren't making it easy. The woman in the chair now, a stripper named Stormy, had already taken off her top ("Woooooo!"). She was now asking him, begging him for a bikini shave. She squirmed to her feet and began to tug her shorts down toward her knees. More hollering from the patio. Gandhi could anticipate the guys all around bursting into even greater mayhem when their collective gaze discovered what only he could see from the vantage point of his low bench: Stormy wore no panties.

The room had a crazy tilt to it, dense with a haze of tobacco and sweat and booze, the alcohol flowing so freely that it seemed to have atomized in the air. The carpet was thoroughly soaked with spill-over keg beer, frozen margaritas, "rhino spunk" (Kahlúa, rum and cream), "bushwackers" (rum and Kahlúa), "Cubi specials" (who knew?). A creamy fizz would squish up around the soles of your shoes when you walked.

Not that Lieutenant Diaz had walked anywhere. He hadn't gotten up from his barber's station to take more than a sip of beer or make more than a trip to the head all night. Gandhi was probably the only sober person around for miles. Hadn't circulated at all, hadn't seen much of the party, beyond his chair and the parade of female gams he presided over like some worker ant. The room was packed, the patio was packed. Most of the brass—flag officers, who on the job could be recognized by the yellow-gold braid known as "scrambled eggs" piled on their hat brims—most of the admirals and commanders and captains stayed out on the patio, but the action in the squadron suite was clearly visible to all.

Gandhi felt as if he were in a goldfish bowl. Earlier that Friday evening, he had even seen the Old Man himself, right outside his window, Admiral Frank Kelso, Chief of Naval Operations, the Navy's representative on the Joint Chiefs. Gandhi knew it was Kelso because the guy had a very distinctive pair of eyebrows. They had wagged at him like a couple of caterpillars predicting a long winter.

The smoke, the noise, the Scrambled Eggs. Everyone pumped from coming off the Gulf War. It wasn't the craziest Tailhook convention Gandhi had heard of—that would have to be '85, when eight Marines put their heads through the wall and a couch got ejected from an upper floor out into the Las Vegas twilight—but it was coming close.

"Shave me," Stormy commanded. The sight of her bare crotch drew a hoarse, desperate "Woooooo" from the patio.

It was hard for an artist to work with all the distraction.

AVIATORS CALLED IT "LIGHTING YOUR HAIR ON FIRE," BY WHICH THEY meant registering a party on the Richter scale, cranking it up from bacchanal to full-throttle blowout. It's what the carrier pilots of the U.S. Navy did for three days each year at the annual convention of the Tailhook Association.

"The Tailhook Association started as an old man's drinking club," said retired Rear Admiral James D. Ramage, one of the founders of the Tailhook Association. It was a curious comment, considering that the eight naval aviators who founded the organization were young in 1957, when Tailhook began. The founders called their first gathering a "reunion," and held it on the beach in Rosarito, Mexico, some fifty miles south of San Diego. They convened for a "young man's" ritual of self-obliteration by alcohol, attempting to prove, along the way, the truth of Chuck Yeager's famous equation, "flying and hell-raising—one fuels the other."

They named themselves after a piece of military hardware with a vaguely salacious nomenclature, the tailhook, made at first of tempered steel and later of high-tech metal alloys, and which basically consists of a pole with a barbed flange at one end. The hook drops from the belly of an aircraft attempting a carrier landing, in order to catch one of four steel arresting wires stretched across the deck. A carrier landing, or "trap," is a complicated, dangerous ballet, described by pilots as a "controlled crash." The tailhook is the only thing that halts a 60,000-pound plane's hurtling progress toward the edge of the deck and thus oblivion.

In the thirty-five years since Rosarito, the Tailhook Association had matured, solidified and developed several additional chins, as befitted a full-fledged professional organization. It had a corporate mission statement, a monthly magazine (*The Hook*), nonprofit status. There were lectures and symposia at its annual conventions now, and salespeople from Hughes and McDonnell Douglas displayed their wares in the exhibition hall.

But despite the trappings of respectability, Tailhook had never shaken off its rude and ragged beginnings, never outgrown its "drinking club" reputation. The "can you top this?" mentality, the competition for boasting honors that goes on in any fraternity, was partly responsible. Add the strange calculus of command, which held if you could outdrink other men they would respect you and obey your orders willingly, and the legacy came to life. Over the decades, Tailhook had developed a split personality, part respected professional organization and part wild-ass brawl. Eventually, another duality compounded this first: that of the old men versus the boys. Here were the aging admirals outside on the Hilton's third-deck patio, the Scrambled Eggs, carefully nursing their beers, peering in at the next generation, Lieutenant Rolando Diaz and company, shaving a naked stripper called Stormy.

Of course, the old bulls had all been there before. As young naval aviators, as junior officers, most of them had participated in brawls as drunken and sex-drenched as anything going down on the third floor in '91. Who were they to cast stones? They might have felt a vague uneasiness, a sense that it was all getting out of hand, but the essential impetus to step in and draw the line was absent.

There was something else at play in Las Vegas besides the generational differences. Peel back the onion of the Tailhook scandal far

enough, and there is an element that promised to upset the meticu-
lously balanced world of men at sea. Slowly at first, and accelerating
exponentially over the decades since the close of World War II,
women were entering the Navy, creating ever deeper inroads into the
exclusivity of the domain. They were showing up in support facilities,
coming aboard surface ships, flying helicopters and cargo planes and
every jet the Navy had. They were aggressor pilots, dogfighting with
their male peers on training missions over the lush jungles of the
Philippines. And now it looked as if women were about to enter a
world held exclusive to men since aviation began: air combat.

They were changing one of the most hidebound and traditional
organizations in the world, the U.S. Navy.

THE FIRST THING THAT HAPPENED TO KARA HULTGREEN WHEN SHE
hit the third floor that Friday of the convention was that she was
mistaken for a hooker.

The third floor was either legendary or infamous, depending on
who you were talking to. The "third deck" was where The Party happened, where the naval air squadrons that were attending the convention set up what were called, in a quaint-sounding phrase nowhere
near the reality, "hospitality suites."

Hultgreen was wearing a black blazer, a black leather miniskirt
and heels. She knew all about the third deck. But it was early, not
even nine o'clock, and she figured there wouldn't be anything up there
she couldn't handle. There wasn't much that Lieutenant Kara Hultgreen couldn't handle. She was one of the Navy's bright shining stars,
the mirror image to one of the most glorified figures of modern times,
the male fighter pilot. Numerous books, novels and movies had been
devoted to this elite class of high-flying, hard-partying warrior. Hultgreen worked with these guys, and looking at them, she had to admit
that their ineffable good looks, their hunkiness, was undeniably a de-
fining feature. It was as if the Navy were culling the ranks to find not
only the best and brightest, but also the prettiest. There they were,

square of jaw, bright of eye, taut of muscle. "Cut and buffed" was the California phrase for it, "squared away" was the Navy phrase, the term Kara Hultgreen used.

And she was their peer. Like the other aviators, Lieutenant Hultgreen was chosen, it seemed, not only by the Navy, not only on the basis of test scores and flying skills, but by biology itself. Nearly six feet tall, with a wealth of honey-colored hair, she had an unmistakable physical charisma that off-base and off-duty would be called full-blown beauty.

Ever since she was six years old, Hultgreen had known that what she wanted to do was to go fast. The course of her life thus far—she was twenty-five— had consisted of sorting out the options for speed. For a time she thought she wanted to be a race-car driver, then an astronaut. She finally came to the same conclusion as everyone else who was serious about velocity: that flying jets was the apogee not only of speed, but also of life itself. So she went into it and aced it. She'd been the only female to graduate in her class at Aviation Officer Candidate School in Pensacola, one of two or three women who received wings in '89 to "go jets," as they said, meaning she had entered the jet-training pipeline.

But on the third floor of the Las Vegas Hilton at the 1991 Tailhook convention, she was "a hooker." She heard the word float up above the din of the party as soon as she stepped off the elevator.

"That's no hooker," said a naval captain standing there. "That's an A-6 pilot." Hultgreen knew the captain. She'd been one of the junior officers under his command at Naval Air Station Key West.

The hooker comment hadn't bothered her; it even made her laugh. It was the kind of jerky, ignorant thing you heard. The carrier pilots who attended the convention expected, if they saw a woman at Tailhook, that she either wanted to get laid by an aviator (à la *An Officer and a Gentleman*) or she was a prostitute or dancer. And in 90 percent of cases that was true. But how stupid could they be? What kind of hooker wore a blazer?

Hultgreen came to the third floor that Friday night to look for a

few friends. She had known Tailhook by its reputation as a testoster-
one festival. But she had a very specific purpose in attending the
convention that year. Women still weren't allowed to fly tactical jets in
combat units. She was there to tug on a few sleeves, buttonhole a few
admirals. Lieutenant Hultgreen was determined to fight the regulation against women in combat, determined to take on the whole Navy,
if she had to.

By an order of Congress passed in 1948, twenty years before
Kara Hultgreen was born, she was prohibited from serving in the fleet
with the men she'd trained alongside. Some of these men were pilots
she had topped in the schools command—beat them, proved head to
head, toe to toe, stick to stick, that she was a better aviator than they
were. Yet they were out flying Tomcats and Hornets in the fleet, and
she was stuck flying a modified Intruder called a Prowler, an A-6
packed with so much electronic gear that its totem animal should have
been a mule rather than an eagle. Other EA-6B Prowlers had a combat mission; hers didn't, she was assigned to play the role of an aggressor in an electronic warfare squadron that trained combat pilots. Her
airplane wasn't a "real" Intruder, as the boys who flew the other ones
would say, because it didn't drop bombs, and it wasn't a "real"
Prowler, because it didn't fly in the fleet. But it was the only kind the
Navy would allow her to fly.

She had hit the proverbial glass ceiling, a particularly bitter metaphor when you were a pilot, made more bitter still because unlike the
glass ceiling in the business world, say, this one was official policy,
there for all the world to see. In fact, the cockpit of a military warplane, along with combatant ships and submarines, was the only workplace in America that was still legally off-limits to women. It was as if
one of the most mystical potions of all—the blood of the martyred
warrior—had been reserved by males for their exclusive use. Women
did not have the right to die fighting for their country.

Lieutenant Hultgreen was happy enough flying her EA-6B, even
though, as she told people, "It's kind of a pig—it's not pointy and has
no afterburners." She would be ecstatic when she got to fly a "real"
jet, one that had those two magical qualities—either the Tomcat or the

Hornet, in other words. At present those jets were reserved for the proud possessors of a penis.

Hultgreen knew that would change. "It's destiny," she liked to say grandly. "And I'm gonna be a part of it."

Her plan was to stand up at the microphone at the Flag Panel Saturday afternoon, and ask what was the future for women in tactical aviation. In other words, when were the girls going to get to play with the boys' toys? For all the tough, macho, battle-hardened men in attendance, the question was a time bomb. Hultgreen came to Tailhook as part of her determined, fierce and unrelenting campaign: it was like Sherman's March through Georgia for her. Her mission was nothing less than to convince the Navy powers-that-be to give her more and better flights, to let her prove that she could fly the Tomcats and Hornets her male peers took for granted.

Kara Hultgreen knew she could be a warrior. Other people were becoming convinced, too. Back in flight school they had hung a tag on her, "Hulk," or "The Incredible Hulk," from Hultgreen, certainly, but also because she was almost six feet tall and fierce as hell. Another time they nicknamed her "Fang," for a comment she had made when a TV reporter asked her if women were ready for combat: "Why not?" she had said. "My fangs grow as long as anybody else's."

The Incredible Hulk lobbied Congress with other female aviators. She submitted formal requests to the Navy's Bureau of Personnel, asking to make a career transition to tactical aircraft. Her mother, her father, even her mother's friends were writing their congressional representatives urging them to let women into the cockpits of combat warplanes.

Finally, it looked as if it might happen. Just a month before the Tailhook convention, on the last day of July in 1991, the U.S. Senate had followed the House in voting to lift the restriction on women in warplanes. Some of the wording still had to be worked out, and as was its wont, Congress also voted to create a commission to study the subject. It was a start, but there was a long way to go.

Hultgreen wasn't alone in her campaign, of course. The other women in the female flight-jock community were out there beating the pavement, too. They were a tiny minority, of course. The Tailhook Association was 96 percent male. Of 9,419 Navy pilots, 177 were women, and of these only 27 flew jets. The women aviators were all feeling good about the Senate vote. The *Navy Times* had reported their reactions in a story on the new combat role for women "It's like having the Berlin Wall come down," said Brenda Scheufle, an instructor with Training Wing 2 in Kingsville, Texas. Susan Still, a squadron-mate of Hultgreen's, told of her dream of going to test pilot school and then becoming an astronaut. An admiral's aide named Paula Coughlin, a helicopter pilot, said she hoped someday to command a squadron detached to a frigate or a destroyer.

Hultgreen knew, though, that no matter what restrictions were lifted, there were still hurdles to clear. One was the predominantly male attitude in naval aviation. It was a "guy" sort of place. You called aviators that instinctively—guys, not men—like they were members of one big frat. For the most part they were good guys. They were smart, and they had an excellent sense of humor. They were just like the guys you went to college with. And like the guys you went to college with, some of them acted like stone idiots now and then.

The night before, Thursday night, Hultgreen had been standing in the A-6 suite, talking with some guys she didn't know all that well. One of them was a Marine pilot from El Toro, and he was going on about women in combat, playing devil's advocate, explaining why women couldn't do this and couldn't do that. They were getting into a heated thing, trading arguments back and forth. The gist of it was the same as hundreds of conversations Hultgreen had had on the subject in the past year.

Suddenly she felt something land on her buttocks. A guy's hand, it turned out, when she half-turned in response. Two or three times, she swatted him away, continuing to make points with the Marine flier. She was revved up, demolishing his arguments one by one like so many matchstick soldiers. Finally, the fourth time Fingers groped her ass, Hultgreen took action. "Oh, shit," she said to one of the guys she was standing with. "Will you hold my beer a sec?"

She grabbed Fingers by the collar of his shirt and pushed him up against the wall. "Look," she said. "I'm an officer. I'm an aviator. You touch me again and I'll kill you." She collected her beer and resumed the debate. Then, as if all he heard was the "touch me again" part, Fingers was back, but this time, he's biting Hultgreen's ass. "Sharking," they called it, in lingua frat. Slide and bite. Butt rodeo.

Okay, Hulk said to herself. Flex those buns of steel, and teeth will fly. She once again asked the guy next to her to hold her beer. Then she elbowed Fingers in the back of his head with all she had, dropping him to all fours. She pushed him sideways with her leg so he couldn't get up, glaring down at him and saying, "Look. You idiot. I told ya. Get the hell away from me. I'll kill ya."

Finally, Fingers got the message and crawled out of the room, and Kara Hultgreen never saw him again. She reclaimed her beer, got back to her discussion. The Hulk had prevailed.

All around her now, on Friday night, she could see plenty of other guys gearing up to be as obnoxious as they could. None of it surprised her. She was just glad she was getting out of here tonight. If she could ever find her friends.

IT WAS THE LABOR DAY WEEKEND AFTER THE MONTH-LONG GULF War. This was before the revisionists had deconstructed the triumph, when it still seemed an astonishing, unmitigated victory. The picture that was fresh in everyone's mind was that eerie TV image of a Tomahawk closing on its target—footage that always had the same satisfying, Fourth of July finish. Apocalypse now, film at eleven.

The flush of victory was still on their faces as they flew in to Las Vegas, the naval aviators who had played such a large part in winning the war. The conflict had provided the bitter relish of martyrdom, too, since six of their own had not returned from the Gulf.

So the carrier pilots came to Las Vegas, ostensibly for a professional convention. "War is our business, and business is good," as the T-shirt slogan read. At Tailhook 1991, pilots were offered eleven and a half hours of symposia. Lockheed test pilot T. Morgenfeld spoke about "Advanced Aircraft Technologies." Rear Admiral Riley Mixson discussed the Navy's plans for carrier air wings. The presentation that really got the flight jocks' juices flowing, the first standing-room-only event at the convention, featured Navy Lieutenant Nick Mongello and Marine Captain Chuck McGill, giving blow-by-blows of their MiG shootdowns during the Gulf War. Afterward, three of the eight Navy and Marine fliers captured during the conflict in the Gulf described their experiences.

On Saturday, there was another standing-room-only event. The Flag Panel was the only venue anywhere in naval aviation where the Scrambled Eggs submitted to cross-examination by their juniors. Nine admirals on the dais, the top of the hierarchy in aviation, up in front of a packed house, taking all queries, on any topic. There was a sense of excitement at the panel, as there was throughout the fleet, because of what had just gone down in the Persian Gulf. But there was also an edgy sense of changes about to happen. Budget cuts were coming. Everyone knew the Navy was going to lose programs, carriers, personnel. Next year's Flag Panel might host seven admirals instead of nine.

Then, in the middle of the Q and A, a woman—not Kara Hultgreen, it turned out, but a C-2 pilot named Lieutenant Monica Rivadeneira with the same thing on her mind—got up and started asking about the future of women in tactical aviation. Nobody wanted to hear about it. These were guys who were trying to sort out their options, waiting to see if the Navy would have a place for them, if there were going to be enough slots for all the fliers who wanted to fill them—and then this . . . *female aviator* comes along, asking to get hers?

They hooted her down. Nothing special, just the usual bum's rush this audience gave to any fool. The flag officers let the catcalls go on. Vice Admiral Richard M. Dunleavy, the Deputy Chief of Naval Operations for Air Warfare, said primly, "The Senate has voted, and we will comply." But no one really heard him underneath the "Woo-woo!" of the crowd. The woman sat down.

So the party later on that Saturday night was powered by twin engines: residual Gulf War energy and anxiety over the changes the Navy was going through. Whatever was fueling it was sure enough supercharged. Things were getting crazy on the third floor.

Out on the pool patio, men spat out alcohol, ignited it, and breathed fire. In the pool, there were "chicken fights": girls tried to knock each other off the guys' shoulders. A woman stood on a step and teased the crowd, half lifting her shirt. An older guy, a commander, hopped up beside her. She pulled down his trousers and fondled him. When he started to grab her, she pulled away and disappeared into the crowd.

Women were getting "zapped": having squadron stickers slapped on strategic parts of their bodies. Some guy loped through the hallways wearing only a rhino horn, propped crazily on his forehead like a party hat. He was more or less a shill for Suite 308, the "Rhino Suite," where Marine pilots had imported the "rhino with a ding dong," from Trader Jon's bar in Pensacola. The five-by-eight mural of a bull rhinoceros was equipped with a spigot dildo that dispensed a cocktail of rum, Kahlúa and cream. Some women went right for the Spunk, going down on their knees in front of the painting. Others needed encouragement.

Late at night, the urge to strip grew contagious. Vegas "dancing girls"—no one ever called them strippers—were everywhere, up on a table in one suite, shucking duds to 2 Live Crew's "Me So Horny," or performing a lesbian pas de deux in another room. Men conspired to hang out their nuts in front of the admirals' wives. Or they tore off all their clothes and ran across the patio, trailed by hapless security guards.

Quite a few people simply disappeared for the whole weekend, holed up at private parties, serious stag affairs with skin flicks and dancing girls who didn't stop at dancing.

AFTERWARD, WHAT HAPPENED TO LISA REAGAN AND MARIE WESTON that Saturday night would take on an air of unreality. The two careful young women from Sacramento could trace the progress of the night for the lawyers' depositions, they could remember it all with absolute clarity. But they couldn't quite believe it had happened.

As far as the Tailhook Association was concerned, if Reagan and Weston had any status at all, they were simply guests. They weren't fliers, or members of the aviation community. They weren't part of the huge corps of Vegas working girls who descended upon the convention like modern-day camp followers. They were simply two single girls from Sacramento who came to Vegas for the weekend. Like about 99 percent of Americans, they had never even heard of the Tailhook Symposium.

But since they'd arrived in Las Vegas it seemed all they had heard about was The Party. They'd seen all the Navy guys in their white dress uniforms wandering around the lobby when they arrived to check in Friday afternoon. Other men, wearing blue polo shirts branded with the insignia of the Tailhook Association, rode the elevator with them up to their room on the twenty-eighth floor. They chatted them up: "Hey, what are you girls doing this weekend? You oughta come to the third floor tomorrow night."

Around the pool there were more invitations, more naval officers, now in their civvies, hanging out, swimming, drinking beer. They were rowdy and a little arrogant, but not at all out of hand, and nothing Reagan and Weston hadn't seen before.

Marie Weston had attended Chico, which *Playboy* magazine had consistently voted among the top party schools in the country. She'd been to frat parties there. Lisa Reagan had friends in the Navy. She loved to watch any war movie that had airplanes in it, especially, of course, *Top Gun*. She had been raised in the panhandle of Florida, flight-jock country, so she could relate to aviators. As a matter of fact, for the past three years she had been dating an Air Force pilot.

They had come on this package-deal mini-vacation from Sacramento to have fun and relax, not necessarily to meet men. They planned to gamble, snooze by the pool—laze around, really. Something they didn't ordinarily get to do, since at home they worked long hours, Reagan at appraising real estate, Weston as a computer engineer.

The guys around the pool were pretty obvious about checking out women. Reagan and Weston saw one girl stand up. She had a good-sized chest. In unison the voices of the men rose, higher and higher: Woooooo! When Reagan and Weston saw that happen, they moved back from the edge of the pool to the shade.

Larry, a Marine captain who escorted them to the party, seemed like a decent enough guy. They had met him on Friday, over the casino games. Lisa liked to play blackjack. Larry had invited them to dinner, and had talked to them about his wife, his two kids, his hobby (woodworking), his squadron at El Toro. He was their age, early thirties. He was insistent on paying for the meal, saying he'd won some money gambling. Lisa and Marie finally acquiesced. He was so polite and friendly it was impossible to refuse.

Saturday night they ran into him again in the lobby as Reagan was cashing in some chips. They had just walked around the convention hall, at the urging of a fellow they'd met the day before—he claimed to be an admiral—and found it almost empty, about to be shut down. A guard had told them they weren't supposed to be there. Larry asked what they were up to, and Weston told him they'd been invited to the third-floor party. No, of course they wouldn't mind if Larry escorted them.

Around eleven o'clock on Saturday night, the three of them stepped off the elevator and looked down the hallway. The place was crowded; men in shorts and slogan T-shirts milled around, drinking from plastic cups. Lisa went first, then her friend Marie, and then Larry, somewhere behind them. They had to single-file it as they worked their way toward a hospitality suite down at the other end of the hall.

It was odd, Reagan thought. The people around her seemed to be closing in, and she felt that someone might knock her off-balance.

Suddenly, there were hands reaching out at her, a frenzy of groping, touching and feeling. Arms were everywhere. They seemed disembodied, as if they were floating free of their owners. Reagan felt hands insert themselves under her blouse, yank up her skirt. She screamed, "Stop!" Nobody stopped.

Reagan was overwhelmed by panic. "If you've never been attacked by anybody before, and then you've got fifty or however many
people with their hands all over you, you don't know, if they're capable of doing that, what they are going to do next. Here there were five
or six guys with their hands up my skirt, grabbing my crotch from
different angles. I didn't know what was next. They're feeling me up.
They're pulling at my clothing. Are they going to pull my clothes off?
Because they could have overpowered us easily."

Weston was certain they were going to be gang-raped. She tossed
her drink in the direction of the hands. She was blinded by liquid
thrown in her own face. After that she lowered her head and didn't
see anything. She could feel the hands, pulling up her dress, reaching
to pull down her panty hose.

Most of all, she could hear the voices, so loud she didn't even
bother opening her mouth to scream above them. It was a chant like
the one she'd heard poolside that afternoon, except in this closed
corridor, eight feet across at its widest, the noise was deafening. A
deep, howling crescendo: Woooooooo! The sound was gigantic all
around them, louder than a football stadium after a touchdown, but
somehow inhuman.

Weston's face and hair and clothing were soaked. She could
barely think to tell her fists what to do, but she fought back instinctively, punching as hard as she could, anywhere she could. Sometimes
her jabs landed on flesh, and she would be vaguely aware of a body
that drew back. That was all the encouragement she needed to keep
throwing punches. The more she fought, the more alcohol was tossed
on her. She got one drink after another thrown directly into her face.
If something's going to happen, she thought, they're going to have to
kill me first.

There was a thick pink drink, like Pepto-Bismol, splashed over
the front of Lisa Reagan's white western blouse. Keep going, she told
herself, keep on your feet. Her eyes swept the crowd, trying to con-
nect hands with faces, but it was all moving too fast. She tried to look
back but she couldn't spot Marie. All she saw were the faces of men,
laughing.

The last punch Weston threw, she hit someone hard. Everything stopped. Then she saw yet another Marine Corps captain standing there, doubled over, someone they'd met by the pool earlier in the day. "You punched me!" he said to Marie. Now Lisa was standing next to Marie and she thought she saw the captain's lips move, heard him say something. "I'm sorry, I'm sorry," he repeated softly.

Reagan and Weston bolted. They found a door and staggered outside in their drenched, disheveled clothes. The patio was jammed with men and women. They felt it difficult, terrifying, to walk through a crowd, to be jostled by strangers. A couple of people looked curiously at Marie, who was crying. "Smile!" they said.

The two women circled around to the patio doors near the elevator, where they had arrived. Larry, their Marine captain escort, still followed them, and as they reached the elevators they were also joined by the second Marine captain, the one Weston had punched. Only three to five minutes had passed since they'd arrived at the party. The doors opened. "It's been a pleasure, ladies!" said Larry.

And then, for a long time, nothing happened.

Chapter Two

———

SIERRA HOTEL

THE FLYBOYS AND FLYGIRLS WENT BACK TO THEIR DUTY STATIONS, THE
Scrambled Eggs returned to their commands. The hangers-on and the
jet-jock groupies crawled back under whatever rocks they had crawled
out from. The general concurrence was that Hook '91 had been the
hair-burner to end all hair-burners.

One or two incidents might have been over the top. Even before
the convention ended, rumors circulated that "a young, fat girl" (she
was always described that way) had wound up stripped naked from the
waist down, passed out drunk in the third-floor hallway. A female
admiral's aide was supposed to have gotten hassled. People talked
about women slugging men, trying to get them to lay off—and the
men slugging back. Things on the third floor had gotten "a little
rough." Some guys had maybe strayed across the line.

But the line was so hazy. It was drawn that way. If there hadn't
been complaints, if there hadn't been a bill for damages slipped under
the Tailhook Association's door in the morning, they wouldn't be Naval Aviators. When flight jocks took a package tour of Vegas, mayhem
was part of the package.

Much later, a Navy lieutenant named John Loguidice, who was a

witness for the Department of Defense in a Tailhook-related disciplinary hearing, would explain, "We put up $20,000 prior to getting there
because—they love it—you know, because we trash the place. They
can rip up the carpets and redo the walls. You know, 'It's yours, guys,
have at it.' In the past walls have been destroyed. I mean, they didn't
mind because we paid for everything we did."

The Las Vegas Hilton had been the Tailhook convention's home
for twenty-three years, since 1968. The whole convention was a cash
cow for the hotel, with 1,000 guest rooms, the convention hall, and 22
hospitality suites booked by the Association for the three-day weekend. The drink tab alone (low-balled at $33,500 by Department of
Defense investigators) was worth all the trouble repairing the damages. The third floor of the Hilton was known among the gambling
community to be the newest, freshest place to stay in the hotel, because it was commonly understood to be rebuilt every year, post-
Tailhook.

The Hilton was actually a rather staid venue, by Las Vegas stan-
dards at least, located a discreet distance off the Strip, away from
downtown's Glitter Gulch. Its main claim to fame—before the film
Indecent Proposal was set at the Hilton in 1992—was the fact that
Elvis had performed his last seven concerts in the Grand Ballroom.
Next to a life-size bronze statue of the King in the lobby, there was a
glass reliquary holding the white, sequined jumpsuit and an ode to
Elvis by Colonel Parker.

Saturday night of Labor Day weekend, after returning to their
room, Lisa Reagan and Marie Weston tried to call 911 to report what
had happened to them on the third floor. Reagan got the hotel operator, who put her through to security instead.

"Can I help you?"

"No," Reagan said, "I want the police."

"What's the problem?" the security guard on the other end of
the line wanted to know.

When a security guy finally came up, mostly what he wanted to
know about was damage to their clothes. Was the white western

blouse that Reagan was wearing ruined? What size was it? Where'd she buy it?

His questions were bizarre. That's not what it's about, Reagan kept telling him, but the Hilton rep kept right on obsessing about how much the damned blouse had cost as he took their statements. All Weston could think about was five years earlier, when she'd been in Vegas on business and had her purse snatched in a hotel parking lot. That time the cops were there in fifteen minutes, asking questions, taking her statement.

The next morning the two women went to the lobby to get a copy of the handwritten statement they'd provided the night before. There they overheard a pair of Hilton assistant managers reading it and laughing: "Oh, look what those guys did last night." When Reagan and Weston confronted them, one of the men said, "Don't you girls know what goes on at these parties?"

So Lisa Reagan and Marie Weston took their complaint else-where. On Sunday, September 8, they became the first women ever to file a report with the Las Vegas Police Department after a Hilton Tailhook party. Even with the cops, though, things were not much better. Can you identify the suspects? No? They were told that the case was closed even before they left the precinct. If you're so upset, file a civil suit, the cops said.

Nothing was going to disturb the status quo. Twenty-three years was one hell of a long-running party, even in a town that made parties its business.

THAT SAME SUNDAY MORNING, A THIRTY-YEAR-OLD NAVY LIEUTENANT named Paula Coughlin stood in the Hilton's sprawling lobby, just off the Day-Glo jungle of the casino floor, waiting to meet her boss for breakfast. Coughlin was a helicopter pilot by training, doing a shore tour as an admiral's aide, or "loop" (so named after the distinctive gold-braided aiguillette that hung from her shoulder). Loops were up-and-comers; it was a much sought-after billet, and only people known to the community as "hard chargers" were chosen.

Coughlin watched her boss, Rear Admiral John Snyder, thread his way past the Elvis statue in the lobby. It was Coughlin's job to attend to all Jack Snyder's professional needs, to oversee his schedule, even to accompany him to the banquets and parties he attended.

What didn't come with the territory, Coughlin had decided in the wee hours of the night before, was getting groped by a cotillion of drunken aviators. "All I had in my mind's eye was that the little monsters in that hallway are going to be commanding officers of squadrons, and they're going to have their little monsters behaving the same way. And that is not the way *my* Navy operates. That man should not be in my squadron. That man should not be in the Navy. That man should be in *jail*. And you could probably diagnose it as some kind of denial, but this was still a professional issue with me. This was not a personal assault. I said, [confronting] this is just for the good of the Navy." It was enough that it was a "professional issue," since her job, her employer, her Navy, were as important to Paula Coughlin as any other thing she had ever known.

"I have no other way of life," she said later. "That's probably why I had to do what I did. Not just because I love the Navy and it was the organization I was born and bred into, but that was the mental conditioning that I've grown up with. Those were the heroes in my life. And those were the men who attacked me. And I said, That's not the way it's supposed to be."

So she decided she was going to say something about it. When Coughlin had called her boss on the phone at a quarter after eight that morning to arrange their breakfast meeting, she thought Snyder might ask her about the previous evening, and he did.

"So how was the third deck last night?"

"It stunk," she said. "I was practically gang-banged by a group of fucking F-18 pilots."

"It's so wild down there," Snyder responded blandly. "That's why I went, had one margarita, said hello to a few friends, and left." The admiral and his aide determined a time to meet in the lobby, and the conversation was over.

The phone call contributed to Coughlin's sense of frustration.

You tell your boss you were practically gang-banged and all he can do is tell you how his own evening went? What was going on? Had everything been in her imagination?

What had happened last night?

Coughlin remembered seeing the guys when she came in off the patio, passed by the elevators and entered the third-floor hall. There were about twenty of them lining the walls at the start of the long corridor. It could have been claustrophobic, if you weren't used to tight quarters, all those people crammed into the narrow hallway. Spillover from the hospitality suites, she recalled thinking. Rowdy and loud, but she had been to crazy parties before.

She had been to Tailhook before, too, in '85, when she was an ensign in flight training down at Pensacola, so she knew how wild it could be. She thought she'd seen some fairly outrageous aviator behavior. But "there was never any malicious act," she said later. "The worst I can think of is, 'So I scored last night, even though her husband was deployed.' That was the kind of behavior that I had become used to thinking was normal—you know, men are animals, they have no scruples. But in my mind, we're thinking something consensual." Certainly nothing to cause alarm. They were pilots, just like her. Family.

She had a purpose that Saturday night for making her way through the crowd. She was looking for a friend she'd promised to meet up with after the Tailhook banquet, but who, in this sea of fighter bubbas, was going to be hard to find. Plus, Coughlin was running late, having had to return to her hotel, the Paddlewheel, to dress down for the party. She chose a denim skirt and dark blue tank top. It was hot, much too hot even for the desert, and the hallway stank.

Glancing around for familiar faces, Coughlin reached the first two men in the hallway. They seemed to be posted like sentries in the middle of the corridor, their backs to her. She squeezed around the guy on the right, and out of nowhere he gave her a vigorous hip check.

"Excuse me," she said, turning to address him.

He was a tall guy, over six feet, but the thing she noticed about him was his coloring: his short-cropped hair was dark, his skin was light brown, he had pale eyes and a smile with a lot of brilliant white teeth. Mr. Teeth threw his shoulders back and his chest forward and grinned at her. It surprised her. So the hip bump had been intentional, she thought.

Then a blond guy to her left shouted something that startled her even more. "Admiral's aide! Admiral's aide!" he called. Astonished, Coughlin looked at him, but the guy was a stranger. This was all too weird. How did he know who she was? She didn't have much time to mull it over, because suddenly Mr. Teeth grabbed her up by the buttocks. The guy actually picked her up by her ass-cheeks and moved her forward a step. She was like his puppet, her feet dangling off the ground.

"What the fuck do you think you're doing?" she said, still more surprised than scared. Then another pair of hands grabbed her ass, and she parroted out the same vain question, putting a little shrieky spin on it this time. "What the *fuck* do you think you're *doing!!?*"

It was madness. Hands were coming out of everywhere at her, pawing her butt, pinching, hurting. Then Mr. Teeth was behind her with his breath hot on the back of her neck, bumping her forward, a crazy tango masher serving her up for the boys down the hall. They tore at her clothes, and she fought them off.

Suddenly, from behind, Teeth reached over her shoulders and grabbed both her breasts, reaching down for them inside her bra and the front of her tank top. Coughlin decided it was going to stop there.

She threw her body forward into a crouch. The guy went down with her, until she was kneeling in the middle of the hall and her attacker was draped over her like a bad mink. He still had hold of her breasts as if he thought they were handles. She bit his left forearm, clamping down on it with her teeth until she tasted something metallic, like sweat or blood. It was a pretty good bite, and for a moment his arm wriggled in her jaw like a hooked fish. Then it sort of rolled away from her. His right hand was loosening, and as it did she bit that, too.

As Coughlin came up off the floor she felt a hand make a quick grab under her skirt at her crotch, as if to pull off her underwear. Nothing penetrated her and the guy hadn't even touched skin, but at that point she was terrified. I am going to be gang-raped, she thought. In a public corridor, with hundreds of witnesses. She had no idea what was going to happen next.

All the time that baffling cry, "Admiral's aide! Admiral's aide!"

She staggered forward two feet to a doorway, fighting off the hands. Two of her attackers simply stepped in front of the opening, one from the right and one from the left, and grinned at her smugly. Uh-uh, girlie. No way out. They were still grabbing fistfuls of her. She was like a drowning person whose mouth was being forced back under the water, again and again. She was going to get to land, or she was going to die.

Coughlin saw another blond guy in a faded red polo shirt. He was walking away from the group—maybe because he didn't want any part of it?

"Help me," she called to him. "Just let me get in front of you. Please!" The man stopped and turned. He reached out to her. And put one hand on each of her breasts.

Nothing, she could expect nothing, no help from anyone.

Coughlin threw her arms across her chest, broke the man's grip, ducked, and dove forward three steps to the next open door. It was over.

She sat in the room she'd landed in, alone in the dark, when a guy she had met a few times before came in. Coughlin asked if he had seen what had just happened to her and he said he hadn't. She told him.

"I guess you've just been through the gauntlet," he said.

AS COUGHLIN WATCHED ADMIRAL SNYDER APPROACH HER IN THE Hilton lobby, she wondered if her boss had any idea what had gone on upstairs the night before. She knew he went way back with Tailhook. He had headed the organization for a few years in the mid-eighties. At breakfast, they were joined by another helicopter pilot, a guy she knew from North Island. Coughlin launched into a bitter description of her experience.

"The guys I ran into were completely out of control," she said. "It was really bad. These guys started grabbing at me and grabbing my rear, they were so out of line, I can't tell you how out of control. They knew I was an admiral's aide. They started yelling 'admiral's aide.' I just walked down the hall and these guys went to town on me."

"They probably would have pummeled me, but I would have given anything to get off one shot at those guys," the North Island pilot said.

Jack Snyder was shaking his head. "I know," he said. "That's what you've got to expect on the third deck with a bunch of drunk aviators." He repeated what he'd said on the phone that morning. "That's why I just go, walk through the suites, have one drink, say hello and go."

"Those guys were completely out of line," Coughlin repeated. "I mean, I had to kick and fight and bite my way out of there. I bit the crap out of one guy. It was really, really bad."

The admiral said something about the third deck always being out of hand, and that's why this thing with women in combat is so complicated, referring to the Flag Panel discussion the day before. And the talk at the breakfast table somehow segued into the filming of *Top Gun*.

Now Coughlin grew silent. She let her boss reminisce, as she tried to make sense of his reaction. It wasn't like the two of them were soul mates. They had been brought into intimate proximity by their jobs, but he personified the senior-ranking, decorated, battle-hardened jet pilot, while she was a mostly untested helo flier (completely off the prestige scale by traditional aviator standards) who had never gotten a chance to go in and mix it up where it counted, in combat.

The Navy custom is for admirals to handpick their aides, but Snyder hadn't chosen Coughlin. She was a hand-me-down from the previous commanding officer at the Naval Air Test Center in Patuxent River, Rear Admiral Donald Boecker, a man Coughlin considered the consummate officer and gentleman. The change of command,

Boecker to Snyder, had taken place just a few months earlier, in July. It was natural that it would take some time for Snyder and Coughlin to understand each other.

On the other hand, something wasn't right. She was beginning to have a strange feeling of alienation from the man who was her boss, and whom she couldn't help but want to see as her mentor, her protector. When she talked about the third floor to Snyder, it was as though her mouth was moving but no words were coming out. Somehow the horror of her ordeal became muted. She was like a girl in a glass bubble.

But maybe it wasn't Coughlin who was sealed in the bubble, but Jack Snyder. Him and all the men in the hallway last night. She had kicked and bit and begged, but they didn't help her because they simply couldn't hear her. They had been somehow separated from her, and remained untouched in a bubble as pristine, as impenetrable as the Plexiglas canopy of an F-14.

THEY WERE LIKE ANGELS, FLOATING DOWN FROM THE SKIES ABOVE the ships to accomplish their impossible landings. Here were the sailors, the squids, plodding along at ten, twenty, thirty knots, sweating over their meticulous chores just so they could be allowed not to drown for one more day—and abruptly the gods had descended among them. What could the sailors do but grudgingly acknowledge their superiority?

From the days when the British retrofitted the Italian passenger liner *Conte Rosso* (rechristened as the HMS *Argus*) to receive biplanes, aviators had gradually assumed a place at the top of the Navy hierarchy. As the planes kept getting faster and eventually transformed into jets, the successful carrier landing entered into a fantastic realm of hyper-improbability. The pilots themselves compared it in terms of difficulty (and excitement) to achieving coitus during an automobile accident. "Sex in a car wreck," the pilots called it, an unlikely image (Who would want to have sex during a car wreck? Or perhaps the sex *caused* the wreck?) that somehow conveyed the jaunty, sex-and-death flair with which they conducted themselves.

By the end of the second world war, Navy culture had split into two spheres, the surface warriors and the aviators, "black shoes" and "brown shoes," co-existing in uneasy suspension. The submarine fleet, of course, represented a third Navy subculture, but most submariners were so far removed (mentally, some might argue, as well as physically) from the rest of the mix as to not pertain to the hierarchy. No one ever talked about the color of a submariner's shoes.

The introduction of pilots into the maritime mix was to have enormous consequences for Navy tradition, for pop mythology, and finally for everybody who walked down that hallway on the third floor of the Las Vegas Hilton. For one thing, in a society as hierarchical as the Navy, being on top of the heap meant everyone else was relegated to second-class status. The aviators inspired awe, but their arrogance triggered resentment, too, especially among the poor black shoes below. After spending a month at Miramar, the Navy's elite West Coast master jet station, journalist Ehud Yonay wrote in a May 1983 article called "Top Guns" for *California Magazine:*

. . . There are few caste systems as elaborate and demanding as the one military pilots live under. Its dividing lines are drawn like circles around the bull's-eye of a gunnery target. On the outside is the mass of humanity that doesn't count at all—non-flying nonentities. In the outer ring, only slightly more significant, are the aviator's families, groupies, and hangers-on. Then come helicopter pilots, transport pilots, bomber pilots, and assorted prop-driven plane pilots, and next the attack pilots, whose planes have no afterburners and who charge at ground targets only. In the inner rings, where the fighter pilots belong, there are finer distinctions that only the pilots themselves can discern, until one tiny circle is left at the center, the bull's eye, where the elite of fighter elites stand in glorious isolation. The greatest of the greats, the makers of legends—the "shit-hots."

One of the pilots profiled in the "Top Guns" article was a commander named Jack "Gringo" Snyder, skipper of the "Wolfpack" Squadron, VF-1—the same Jack Snyder who, eight years later, as an admiral, was changing the subject raised by a nettlesome aide, talking instead about his glory days at Miramar. Back then, he was quoted to convey the romance of fighter-pilot mythology: "It's like in the old days, when one knight from each side would come out and they'd joust, one on a white horse, and one on a black horse."

Yonay was only extending and popularizing the hagiography of the jet pilot that had begun a decade earlier in Tom Wolfe's *The Right Stuff.* Wolfe started out writing about astronauts, but soon enough realized where the real story was: the cocky, swaggering world of the test pilot, of the fighter jock, of "military flying and the modern American officer corps."

Shit-hots. That's what they called each other, only they usually encoded it in pilot-speak. In the static-ridden frequencies of high-altitude flying, things have to be spelled out: "A-Alpha, B-Bravo, C-Charlie" and so on through the alphabet. "Shit hot," meaning great, superb, awesome, was abbreviated S-Sierra, H-Hotel. So they didn't even have to come right out and say it. They could just say a particular pilot's flying was "sierra hotel" and let it go at that.

A short time after the "Top Guns" piece was published, it came to the attention of a successful Hollywood producer named Jerry Bruckheimer, who with Don Simpson was responsible for hits like *Flashdance* and *Beverly Hills Cop.*

"I opened this page," Bruckheimer recalled, "and I saw this helmet streaking across the sky, and it said, 'Top Guns.' Don was on the phone and I flipped it to him and he said, 'We've got to buy this.' "

The world of naval aviation struck Hollywood the same way as it had appeared to the sea-bound legions of the surface Navy: breathtakingly dangerous, impossibly glamorous, downright sexy. "This looks like Star Wars on earth," Bruckheimer later told *Life* magazine.

The only problem was that Simpson and Bruckheimer could not exactly run down to Props and requisition a few F-14's. They wanted to make a realistic movie about elite fighter pilots learning the principles of dogfighting in the skies over the Imperial Valley (and China Lake in the Mohave, Nevada's Chocolate Mountains, the Pacific Ocean off Ensenada—*Top Gun* was a movable feast). It was absolutely essential that they win the cooperation of the U.S. Navy.

Which didn't seem all that likely to be forthcoming. The previous year, 1982, a film called *An Officer and a Gentleman* had been released. After protracted negotiations over content, its producers had been denied the Navy's support and cooperation. The result was a movie with countless niggling errors in costume and settings, which, if no one on the outside of the Navy noticed, and if the box office wasn't affected, contributed to a certain feel of ersatz cheesiness.

Less than rigorous attention to detail was acceptable in *An Officer and a Gentleman* because the focus of the film was aspiring aviators in training at officer boot camp. There was no hardware required. The main props needed to achieve any sense of realism, aside from vaguely military-looking uniforms, were sweat and mud. Anyway, who cared about realism when you had Richard Gere boffing Deborah Winger in slo mo? Simpson and Bruckheimer, on the other hand, couldn't repaint a leased Learjet and pass it off as an F-14. Only the real thing would do.

The ostensible reason the Navy declined to lend its support to *An Officer and a Gentleman* was that the Gere-Winger love story was a little too passionate, and some of the screenplay's language struck the brass as too raw (probably the first time on record that an R-rated film offended a sailor). While *Officer* bought into the "glamorous" Navy flier lifestyle, it also opened with whores in a Subic Bay fleabag. A particularly galling scene had to be one where the officers-in-training jog along a beach to the tune of a cadence call, taken from real life, which ended with the refrain, "Napalm sticks to kids."

That was a bit too much realism for Navy PR flacks to handle. And in a wider sense, after films like *Apocalypse Now* and *The Deer Hunter*, the old-guard military, Navy included, had come to consider Hollywood a hostile camp. But what Simpson and Bruckheimer didn't know, as they prepared to approach the government for approval of their project, was that *An Officer and a Gentleman* had sparked a 20 percent surge in Navy recruitment. The Department of the Navy was suddenly wide awake to the possibilities of Hollywood. The Reagan eighties were in full swing, and the Pentagon buildup underscored the need for top-quality recruits. The *Top Gun* project was greeted with open arms. A public affairs person for the Navy, Captain Nancy LaLuntas, called the movie *Top Gun* "an excellent opportunity to tell about the pride and professionalism that goes into becoming a Navy fighter pilot."

George Bush, then Vice President and a former naval aviator himself, gave his blessing to the project. Through Bush's good services, Simpson and Bruckheimer managed to secure permission to shoot on location at Naval Air Station (NAS) Miramar, north of San Diego, with actual Top Gun instructors performing dangerous stunt work. Paramount, the producers' studio, negotiated a complicated formula with the Navy by which the government would be reimbursed for use of jets, the aircraft carrier USS *Enterprise* and other hardware. What's an hour's flying time in an F-14 Tomcat worth? Exactly $7,600, the Navy calculated.

Writer Alexander Cockburn was on the set one day when *Top Gun* director Tony Scott was setting up a shot of an F-14 flying out of the sunset to a landing on the *Enterprise.* Scott noticed with dismay that the ship was changing course, and the shot would be ruined. The director rushed up to the bridge to speak with the commanding officer. Cockburn described for *American Film* magazine what happened next: "After a brief calculation, the captain remarked that it would cost Paramount $25,000 to resume the original course. Scott hastily scribbled a check to the Defense Department, and, in the nick of time, all was well."

The Navy's participation wasn't limited to contributing hardware and personnel. Navy reps and the film's principals sat around a table at the Pentagon and hammered out a plotline they could both live with. Although co-screenwriter Jack Epps, Jr., said, "I didn't feel the military pressured me to paint any sort of rosy picture," Paramount did make dozens of changes in the script at the behest of Pentagon public relations representatives. The cockiness of the Tom Cruise character had to be portrayed as a problem for him to overcome in order to succeed in the military. The Kelly McGillis character was originally a Navy officer, metamorphosed into an aerobics instructor, then finally wound up being modeled on a real Department of Defense civilian consultant. She was Christine Fox, known around Miramar as "Legs," who was brought into a Paramount meeting by the Navy as an example of a woman who fitted into this overwhelmingly male environment.

The degree of government cooperation and involvement is precisely what makes *Top Gun* more, historically speaking, than just a piece of popular entertainment. Here was a vision of the Navy fighter pilot that was officially and enthusiastically sanctioned by the Navy itself. Had there been some sort of Faustian bargain here? In the end, the Navy allowed Hollywood its fighter-jock love story, in return for a splashy cinematic recruiting poster. "The script was no good," said Vice Admiral Ed Martin, head of Naval Air at the time and the man who claims responsibility for *Top Gun* getting Navy cooperation. "The flying was superb."

The collaboration paid off handsomely for both Paramount and the Navy. The domestic box-office gross for *Top Gun* was more than $176 million, making it the most popular film of 1986. The Navy experienced record-breaking enlistment increases. Recruiters set up desks in movie theater lobbies, in order to take advantage of the post-film euphoria. And the film's influence didn't stop at the theater. *Top Gun* created an image of the naval aviator that reverberated through officers clubs and flight lines. More than a few pilots imagined themselves cut of the same cloth as Maverick, the fighter jock that Tom Cruise portrayed in the movie. But it wasn't exactly that the pilots wanted to be Tom Cruise. What they thought they saw, when they watched *Top Gun*, was Tom Cruise wanting to be them.

Five years after its release, the film can still be "read" for vital clues to the aviator's mind-set during Tailhook. *Top Gun* is part action movie, part coming-of-age saga. At center stage is Cruise as Pete

"Maverick" Mitchell, a feckless, reckless F-14 pilot who earned his reputation as "a famous MiG insulter" by inverting his jet over a Russian plane's cockpit and flipping its pilot the bird. Maverick's problem is that he is just too much of a lone wolf to be an effective squadron-mate. At the start of the film, he receives word that he and his backseat radar intercept officer, "Goose," have been chosen to enter Navy Fighter Weapons School, popularly called "Top Gun" after an old fifties-vintage gunnery contest.

At Miramar, "Fightertown U.S.A.," Maverick and Goose join the fraternity of the fighter-jock elite, a raucous, competitive, locker-room world where men are men and boys will be boys. The trainees are engaged in an elemental contest to see who will win the "Top Gun trophy" and have his name engraved upon a plaque as "the best of the best." In the starkly reductionist environment of *Top Gun*, the "plaque for second best is down in the ladies' room."

Women are not absent from this world, but by and large they divide into the traditional camps of wives and party-girls. Charlotte "Charlie" Blackwood, the Kelly McGillis character, is the lone female authority figure; she is quite literally a rocket scientist. But she winds up making a career-threatening compromise in order to bed a fighter pilot.

Top Gun's mating rituals are rendered in broad strokes. Maverick describes Miramar's famed "O Club" (officers club), packed with beautiful women, as a "target-rich environment." These women seem to delight in serving as the objects of a bar bet on the part of the fliers, the goal of which is "to have carnal knowledge on the premises."

Whatever covert homoeroticism is present among the flight jocks is held firmly in check by the overt sexuality of the skirt-chasing. But the camera lingers on the half-naked pilots in several locker-room scenes, and in an extended volleyball game, the primary function of which seems to be to show off the well-oiled torsos of the male stars. They claim to love women, but what the pilots really get off on is the image of themselves they see in each other. "This gives me a hard-on," one pilot declares during a briefing. "Don't tease me," his sidekick replies. Goose and Maverick address each other lightly as "honey" and "dear."

In this strutting, preening atmosphere, attitude is all. Maverick brashly announces he will be the one to win the Top Gun trophy.

INSTRUCTOR: That's pretty arrogant, considering the company you're in.
MAVERICK: Yes, sir.
INSTRUCTOR: I like that in a pilot.

The movie traces Maverick's bad-boy progress through Top Gun training, allowing for plenty of spectacular aeronautic acrobatics. Goose, Maverick's sidekick, is sacrificed along the way, killed attempting to eject when their F-14's engines flame out. ("It was very important for us to show death in the film," Simpson said. "We wanted to show reality. Up at Miramar, people die in Top Gun training. We're not interested in cartoon movies.")

Maverick's relations with Charlotte Blackwood are acted out against a background of raucous aviator hijinks. He woos her in the O Club, backed up by "a passel of drunk aviators" as he lip-synchs some jukebox Righteous Brothers. They engage in Bogie-and-Bacall-style double-entendre banter. Maverick's clichés conquer all.

"I just don't want anyone to know that I've fallen for you," Charlotte tells him, explaining why she sometimes says "no" when she means "yes." Through Charlie, Maverick learns to confront his fatal flaw, and to be less of a loner and more of a team player. But the world of women drops away at the climax of the film, which features a classic one-on-one duel with a MiG over an unspecified enemy's airspace. This is pure single-warrior combat, the kind for which F-14 pilots are trained. Maverick, demonstrating his newfound self-knowledge, triumphs.

Top Gun is crudely effective at doing what it sets out to do: provide a spectacular cinematic circus for the ticket-buying public. Along the way, the movie lends heroic dimensions to its fighter-pilot lead—although he's not a hero in a way the traditional Navy would recognize. Maverick was something new for the military, an MTV hero (the *Top Gun* soundtrack rocketed to number one on the Billboard charts).

"We always saw the pilots as rock 'n' roll stars of the sky," Bruckheimer said.

A MONTH AFTER THE 1991 CONVENTION, ON OCTOBER 11, THE president of the Tailhook Association sent out what was called, in the clipped language of the military, a "debrief." It began with a generic all-hands-well-done paragraph, thanking participants. "We said it would be the 'Mother of all Hooks,'" crowed Captain F. G. Ludwig, Jr., parodying a phrase of then-popular Saddam-speak, "and it was."

> All of our naval aviation leaders and many industry leaders had nothing but praise for the event. We can be proud of a tremendous Tailhook '91 and a great deal of thanks goes to all the young JO's in the various committees that made Hook fly.

So far, so good. But Ludwig continued by sounding an alarum about the future of Tailhook Symposium, if all this wild-hair craziness (he called it "unprofessionalism") continued.

> This year our total damage bill was to the tune of $23,000.00. Of that figure, $18,000 was to install new carpeting as a result of cigarette burns and drink stains. We narrowly avoided a disaster when a "pressed ham" pushed out an eighth-floor window which subsequently fell on the crowd below. Finally, and definitely the most serious, was "the Gauntlet" on the third floor. I have five separate reports of young ladies, several of whom had nothing to do with Tailhook, who were verbally abused, had drinks thrown on them, were physically abused and were sexually molested. Most

distressing was the fact an underage young lady was severely intox-
icated and had her clothing removed by members of the Gauntlet.

In journalistic terms, Ludwig had buried the lead. But there it all
was, laid out for everyone: the questionable conduct ("pressed ham"
meant bare buttocks flattened against a windowpane), drinking, the
gauntlet, the warning of doom.

Even so, it was nothing, nothing. Things like this had happened
before, letters like this had been written before (Ludwig even wrote
one *before* the convention, warning against "late-night gang mentality"). "Poetry makes nothing happen," as Auden said. All the letters
and high-minded talk and civilian complaints weren't going to change
long-standing tradition. Reforms had been attempted before. After
the debacle of the '85 Hook, for example, kamikaze drinking contests
(which made participants behave "like partial lobotomies" according
to the Tailhook Association's longtime executive director, Ron
Thomas) were curtailed. All-alcohol "specialty drinks" were outlawed.
A duty officer was assigned to control "rambunctiousness" in each
hospitality suite.

All that was nothing, too. It was like a Sunday morning hangover
after the Saturday night binge—and these convention-goers were
hangover cognoscenti. You always felt a little rueful unease about the
excesses of the night before. But if you waited it out, the air would
clear, the nameless dread would lift. That was the saving grace of
hangovers. They always went away.

And in those first weeks of fall, as the doubts about Hook '91
faded, the feeling among those who attended was that it was just about
the best party ever.

WAS IT POSSIBLE THAT TAILHOOK, WHICH HAD ASSEMBLED IN LAS
Vegas for how many years, had never once come under the scrutiny of
a reporter? The Hilton third floor was a public place. It wasn't as if the
media was barred. The wild-hair partying, the couches flying out win-

dows, the staggering alcohol consumption—no one thought fit to report on this?

Within the journalistic community, the U.S. Navy was not exactly
what you would call an A-list assignment. Not a coveted assignment at
all, in fact, since a reporter's attraction to a beat roughly mirrors the
public's interest in it. Despite their protestations otherwise, Mr. and
Mrs. Front Porch America weren't really much interested in the military unless there was a war on, and even if there was . . .

Who was keeping tabs on the Navy? Tom Wolfe, of course,
twenty years ago in *The Right Stuff*, profiling aviators from twenty
years before that. A few investigative mavericks, like Randy Shilts,
whose *Conduct Unbecoming*, covering the military's treatment of gays,
was in its research stage when Tailhook happened. A few journalists
for the major dailies and the wire services specialized in the military,
knowledgeable reporters like Melissa Healy at the *Los Angeles Times*,
Molly Moore and John Lancaster at the *Washington Post,* Eric
Schmitt at the *New York Times*. But unless there was a war going on,
editors tended to treat the beat as feature fodder, only occasionally
generating front-page news. Then there was the obligatory disaster
coverage, the carrion-eaters who descended every time a Navy jet
augered into the ocean.

For real nuts-and-bolts, meat-and-potatoes coverage on life in
the U.S. Navy, you had to wade through the writing of local reporters
from the small- or medium-sized dailies in Navy towns like Norfolk,
San Diego, or Pensacola. The *San Diego Union-Tribune,* for example,
extensively covered the Navy and the Marine Corps because a prepon-
derance of its readership were military personnel or had relatives in
the service.

Even if you lived in a Navy town, however, if you weren't in or
married to a uniform, you'd probably skip past all military coverage. It
was just all too . . . foreign. There was a wall of strangeness erected
around the military that was as impenetrable as fog, with layer upon
layer of acronyms and jargon and oompah bands and xenophobia.

By the same token, where were the feminists? To many of the
nation's feminist theorists, the military seemed to epitomize the en-

emy, a vast patriarchal death machine that women would do best to reject and avoid entirely. Feminism, of course, was not a monolith. But since so many in the contemporary women's movement had cut their teeth in the antiwar movement of the 1960s, it is understandable that the pacifist arm of American feminism gained ascendancy and that military women were thus given somewhat short shrift by activists. In the 1970s and '80s, these activists focused their most visible efforts on the issues of pay equity, abortion rights and the Equal Rights Amendment. There were some exceptions. *Ms.* had run a handful of articles on female military members, mostly in its first decade; Gloria Steinem wrote an editorial for the magazine in 1980 wherein she described herself as "a pacifist inexplicably proud of military women." The battle over the ERA in the late 1970s had provoked heated discussion about equality for male and female servicemembers. The prospect of drafting women alongside men (along with mixed-gender bathrooms) was used as a bludgeon by the right to kill popular sentiment for the amendment.

As far as it pertained to the military, the feminist agenda in the 1990s had concentrated on worthy issues, but ones which could appear less than central for American servicewomen: exposing the rape camps in Bosnia, for example. Lifting the combat exclusion did not rank high as a concern for most mainstream feminists. The war in the Persian Gulf—which many pacifist-feminists opposed on principle—exacerbated tensions between the feminist left and military women. Many servicewomen, who tended to embrace the same "Limbaugh-tarian" political philosophy as their male peers, were wary of liberals, including feminist liberals, and so contributed to the estrangement.

When news of the '91 Tailhook convention and the assaults on women there came to the fore, it pushed open the door a bit, allowing the Navy and the society at large a quick glimpse of one another's astonished faces. It was no small wonder that the occasion was marked by mutual misunderstanding, anger, recrimination and bafflement. A sudden shock convulsed both parties, like getting splashed with chilled ocean-water by Shamu at Sea World.

FOR FIVE WEEKS, PAULA COUGHLIN TRIED TO BREAK THROUGH. SHE made repeated conversational forays, some more fully articulated than others, attempting to get her admiral to understand what had happened. When anyone at work asked about Tailhook, she'd make comments. "Those jet pilots are disgusting, and they sure had a good time screwing with me."

By the time Admiral Snyder returned to Pax River from the convention, it was September 13. Coughlin joined him and his wife at his home on the base for a late supper, and the conversation wound back to Tailhook. Coughlin remarked again that those guys were way out of line in the way they treated her. And for the second time, Snyder's response was, "That's what you get when you go on the third floor full of drunk men." Coughlin didn't answer, completely frustrated by his attitude.

A week and a half after it happened, the lieutenant entered her admiral's office. "Sir," she began, "I don't think you understand how bad that thing was at Tailhook. It was the worst thing that has ever happened to me."

"Yeah," Snyder replied, "those guys get really wild." What did she have to do to get him to listen?

When later that day a colleague came by the desk and nonchalantly asked how Tailhook was, she gave her by-now standard reply. "It was terrible," she told him. "Those jet pilots are a bunch of animals."

Snyder happened to be walking past her desk just then, on the way out the door for another work trip. And for a third time, he denied her rage. "That's what you get when you go to a hotel party with a bunch of drunk aviators."

Something inside Coughlin snapped. She stood up and actually stuck a finger out at him: "That's not what I get! You better watch what you say!"

The people in the office were silent. A junior officer, a lieutenant, poking her finger in her admiral's chest? *He'd* better watch what *he* said?

Coughlin turned heel and walked into the office of Snyder's chief of staff, Captain Bob Parkinson. "That's it, I quit. I will not work for a man that tells me 'That's what I get.' "

Parkinson hurriedly scheduled a meeting with the boss for the next day. Coughlin gave a blow-by-blow description of her experience at Tailhook. Snyder sat through it grim-faced, silent, half-turned away from Coughlin in his chair. This was the first time, Snyder would maintain later, that he had ever heard the full story.

"Were you raped?" was the only question he asked.

In that September 19 meeting, the three of them agreed upon a course of action. Snyder would personally draft a letter to Vice Admiral Dunleavy, the head of naval aviation, demanding "some action" on what had happened to Coughlin in Las Vegas. Snyder would also telephone Dunleavy first to give him a heads-up on what had happened. He failed to reach him until the following Tuesday, September 24. It was now over two weeks after the Saturday night at the Vegas Hilton.

Coughlin couldn't understand why, if her boss finally "got" what had happened to her, his response still seemed to proceed in slow motion. By the twenty-fifth, Snyder had not drafted the letter. He went on leave September 26 and 27. Then the weekend. Coughlin was lying awake at night, trying to put on a good show at work. But her days of gut-wrenching worry over when some action would take place and what that action would consist of were just busy workdays for Snyder.

"This was a learning experience," the admiral told her at one point. "Now you know the hatred and chauvinism that exists in the TACAIR community." He voiced his concern—a warning which somehow came across as a threat—that Coughlin might be blackballed by her fellow aviators if word got out that she had raised the issue of culpability.

Several days later, Coughlin confided her fears that all this would be swept under the rug. "I don't want a witch-hunt," she told the admiral, then, in the same breath: "Yes, I do want a witch-hunt. I want to know who did this to me and let everyone know you can't get away with that type of behavior."

"You can't go off like a Roman candle," the admiral said, "and leave those people with burns on their hands that say 'Paula Coughlin.' " He told her he was confident that she would see action once his letter was received.

But the end of the month came and still no letter from Snyder. On September 30 Coughlin made a decision. She would go outside the chain of command. She realized it was the most serious action of her Navy career. But she felt she had no choice. Coughlin would write her own letter to Admiral Dunleavy. The lieutenant still believed that Snyder might eventually write his. But she couldn't wait until it struck him as a priority. She was going to send her letter up to Washington, but would show Snyder a courtesy copy first.

Snyder had told her he would endorse hers when she showed it to him on September 30, but after reading it, said he would prefer to write a letter himself. Finally, the following day, he did so, and on Wednesday, October 2, Snyder hand-carried both letters to Washington.

At the same time, however, Coughlin had covered herself by giving a copy of her letter to a friend who worked at the Pentagon. Snyder was discomfited to learn that the letters he had delivered by hand were preceded by a bootleg copy of Coughlin's letter, passed through her friend to Dunleavy.

It was Admiral Dunleavy who had so flippantly answered the question at the Tailhook Flag Panel about female pilots' entry into combat roles. It would seem that here might be yet another glass-bubble man, and Coughlin's complaint would again go nowhere. But Dunleavy took the lieutenant's allegations very seriously. He phoned her himself to tell her he was setting a formal investigation in motion. Coughlin was summoned to the Pentagon to meet with investigators, and reassigned to a staff job in Washington so she could easily aid in the probe.

On October 11, the same day Captain Ludwig of the Tailhook Association wrote his admonitory letter, over a month after the events of Las Vegas, the Navy finally rumbled awake.

Chapter Three

———

In the Company of Intelligent Animals

Annapolis, Maryland, home to the U.S. Naval Academy, is pretty and charming, if somewhat precious, like a historical re-creation that has been half-abandoned and allowed to take up modern ways. It is surprisingly Southern, in the way of certain border states. The town appears small for its function (it serves as the state capital, also). Along cobbled streets with names like Shipwright, Pinkney Dock, Prince George and Duke of Gloucester, three centuries of history have been lovingly preserved. Gambrel-roofed colonial cottages nestle beside Georgian brick mansions of the eighteenth century and elegant Victorian townhouses that date from the building boom when the Naval Academy opened in 1845.

Walled off between King George Street and the banks of the Severn River is the academy itself, likewise a relic from an earlier time. To the right of Gate 3, overlooking the "Yard," is the Cathedral of the Navy. In the chapel basement lies the crypt of John Paul Jones, the Revolutionary War hero whose "I have not yet begun to fight" first gave the U.S. Navy its spine.

The circular mausoleum is a strange place, its marmoreal chilliness only partially humanized by the precisely placed exhibits illustrating Captain Jones's life. (He led something of a strange one. A Scots immigrant and former captain in the British merchant marine, Jones made his American reputation as a commerce raider of merchant and cargo vessels. He wound up a long, journeyman naval career, in which he served under four flags, as a rear admiral in the Black Sea Fleet of Russia's Catherine the Great. After carrying an unrequited love for another man's wife to a scandalous—by Colonial standards, at least—conclusion, Jones died, destitute, "like a wine-skin from which the wine is drawn," in Paris.)

The crypt is a vivid symbol of the Old Navy. Death—noble and honorable—is enshrined by the central sarcophagus of Grand Antique des Pyrenees marble, while along the periphery, paintings and exhibits portray the meticulous activity of day-to-day Navy life: a gold-hilted sword, a parchment commission signed by Washington and Jefferson, dioramas of shipbuilding, the cult of tradition. All of it patrolled by a single solemn, smooth-faced Marine.

The world of the Old Navy, the surface Navy, exists proudly and stubbornly beyond the modern, secular, egalitarian society of today. Inherent in it, however, are elements that contributed to what happened at the Tailhook convention in 1991. To some degree, what those Navy brown shoes were doing in Las Vegas had a heritage as old as the seas.

From the end of World War II the military has become increasingly divorced from mainstream American life. Since the early part of this century, notes Tom Wolfe, "The rising business classes in the cities had been steering their sons away from the military as if from a bad smell." In the 1960s, the process accelerated. Military personnel were viewed as "baby-killers," not heroes. In the seventies, the draft ended, as did America's involvement in Vietnam. War-making became a specialized pursuit. The average American citizen no longer had a personal experience of the military, and thus the collective understanding of what it meant became attenuated also.

The Navy appeared consistently in headlines over the seventies and eighties, as diverse actions and incidents like the *Mayaguez*, the

Vincennes and the Gulf of Sidra muscled their way onto the front pages, but these days of the military were a far cry from Tolstoy's time, when the most brilliant match a young lady of society could make would be with a career officer. That was clearly no longer the case. In fact, the Navy might as well have been a separate, endogamous tribe, given how isolated its role in contemporary society has become.

A deep conviction of ostracism had developed in the Navy as American society withdrew its emotional support from those who serve. "They don't understand, they don't care, they don't appreciate," was the running plaint of sailors and aviators both. "Everyone hates the warrior when there's no war going on," a retired Navy commander commented. This was the "peacetime" military. There really weren't any wars anymore; they had become obsolete. Now there were conflicts rather than battles, embargoes rather than blockades. War was conducted covertly, behind a camouflage of euphemism. When it did come out from hiding, as in the Persian Gulf, America might hail the conquering hero. Otherwise, the warrior was left out in the cold. As for female warriors, the public did not seem to know they existed.

Even in peacetime, however, the "optempo," or operational tempo, of the Navy continued at a high pace. Ships deployed for six months out of every eighteen, and training workups were almost as grueling and dangerous as missions conducted during wartime. There was little public appreciation of this reality, partly because the official stance was to downplay everything that could be controversial, whether war games or small-scale "actions." Men—and women—continued to die in the military, occasionally in hostilities, usually in training accidents. The armed services had to exist in a state of perpetual readiness, and that meant perpetual risk. The exigencies of military life meant that the Navy developed different attitudes, different habits, different traditions from the rest of American life.

To the outside (civilian) observer, the 1990s' Navy might appear less like the cornerstone of a strong national defense than some vast floating maritime theme park, built and maintained by the U.S. government. Or perhaps a curious but long-running period melodrama, once popular, now playing to near-empty houses on an endless world tour. The Scrambled Eggs might bluster about readiness, but what it really seemed to be all about was keeping alive some bizarre, alien, throwback community, functioning separate and distinct from the mainland, like a cultural Tasmania, producing all sorts of evolutionary irregularities. The Navy was the modern social equivalent of an egg-laying mammal. Quaint maritime rituals flourished, Masonic-style secret-handshake affairs which appeared, to the outsider, almost surreal in their outlandishness. For all the Tomahawk missiles in the hold and nuclear reactors in the engine room, rum, sodomy and the lash still held sway. It was as if the Navy were a dotty old aunt who got packed off to a rest home, and with the years just got nuttier and nuttier.

"Rum, sodomy and the lash." You can't look too far into Navy culture without running into that line from Churchill. Writers and commentators love it. You can almost visualize old Winnie saying it, talking around his cigar, his mind pleasantly pickled by Krug. His words immediately written down because (like another of his shock-value aphorisms, "War is delicious") they sounded as if they were not meant to be written down. The quote surviving over the decades because it had the ring of a good mot: too improbable to be true, and too true to be forgotten. Churchill had earlier abandoned a military career, claiming he did not want to spend all his time "in the company of intelligent animals." But he bequeathed the trinity of rum, sodomy and the lash to all those who would try to understand Navy culture after him.

To an astonishing degree, the day-to-day life of a sailor has remained changeless since Churchill's time and before. On a modern warship, the preindustrial experience exists alongside the mechanized and computer ages. Navigation has been revolutionized, as well as the ways in which ships are powered. But people still sleep in narrow racks, stand the "midwatch" in the middle of the night and awaken to the boatswain's pipe.

The psychological burden of seafaring is no different for today's sailor than it was for Horatio Hornblower or, for that matter, Ulysses.

No matter how much their work is modernized, sailors still find themselves in the middle of an inhospitable ocean ("lost in its unshored, harborless immensities," Melville wrote). They get underway for ten days, three weeks, sometimes six weeks at a time, with no land in sight, working fourteen-hour days. When Navy people today talk about their experiences at sea, it is often with the same sense of bereft longing as the Ancient Mariner. "I don't know how many birthdays I've spent on the fantail," one petty officer said mournfully, "staring at the sunset, crying and wondering what I had gotten myself into." The sea is salty, the Greeks say, because of all the tears that have been cried into it over the years.

In the industrialized world, where existence is mostly at a remove from the strike-point realities of weather and food supply and simple survival, the seafaring world seems frighteningly close to the bone. Cold, wet, fear, loneliness—at a most basic level, these are precisely the things we have so busily constructed our civilizations in order to avoid. The traditional response to a harsh and unforgiving environment has been to more tightly prescribe human behavior. The Inuit in the Arctic, the Bedouin in the Sahara, the sailor at sea—each must follow exact dictates or die. Navy personnel enthusiastically adhere to their elaborate code of behavior, in part because their lives depend on it.

At the same time, being separated from the larger community engenders, in the Navy, a compensatory emphasis on courtesies, customs, honors and ceremonies. Rules of social intercourse are minutely rendered. The minimum number of paces (six) at which salutes are exchanged is exactly prescribed; in fact, one entire article of Navy regulations encodes the occasions for rendering salutes. Individual elements of dress are dictated according to season, rank and function.

Navy life is ordered to the inch and by the second. Its regimen is especially striking when compared to the modern hurly-burly. Navy personnel wake knowing where they will be at every moment, according to a posted Plan of the Day, which sometimes generously includes a Thought for the Day. Their duties (itself a jarring concept, in a world that has become largely dutiless) are extremely well defined, following regulations as inescapable and inevitable as the tides. Aboard ship, sailors are hedged by natural law as well. They are physically confined by the sea around them. No one goes AWOL during an embark.

The deck of a Navy ship is a place still informed by a draconian set of sea laws known as the Code of Oléron (so named after the island where they were drawn up). Originally promulgated by England's Richard I, and compiled, legend has it, by Richard's mother, Eleanor, some of these musty edicts ("a shipmaster shall have the power to raise a navy") dated back still further, to ancient Rhodes. Elements of the code found their way to the notorious "Black Book" of the British Admiralty. In 1775, it was passed to Colonial America, when John Adams used the Black Book as the basis for this country's first "Articles for the Government of the Navy." The Code of Oléron had thus been passed down like a particularly hardy gene sequence through generations of sailors.

It was a document of parched medieval harshness. "Anyone that should kill another on board ship should be tied to the dead body and thrown into the sea." A thief "should have his head shaved and boiling pitch poured upon it and feathers or down strewn upon it for the distinguishing of the offender; and upon the first occasion he should be put ashore." Blasphemers would be gagged and their tongues would be scraped, or burned with a red-hot iron. Flogging was the most commonly prescribed punishment.

For centuries, any change in the rules for shipboard life was fought tooth and nail. When Congress proposed to eliminate the practice of flogging with cat-o'-nine-tails in 1862, the Navy Department objected strenuously. "It would be utterly impracticable to have an efficient Navy without this form of punishment." Even today, a ship's captain in the Navy has the authority to put some offenders in the brig and feed them nothing but bread and water for three days at a time.

The bulk of the activities and terminology on a "modern" Navy ship date back several centuries or more. The "wardroom," for example, which refers to the compartment where officers eat and relax, derives from the "wardrobe" of the early 1700s, a locker to store valuables located near the officers' staterooms. Present-day officers entering for a meal must first ask the permission of the most senior-ranking officer present to "join the mess," and other customs of the wardroom are equally stylized.

Devotion to tradition has made the Navy one of the only places in America where people still exist within a feudal, heraldic society. Get underway with a Navy ship and you enter a universe that is still broken along the lines of nobles and commoners (here called officers and enlisted). The U.S. Navy's social interactions, like its regulations, derive explicitly from the nineteenth-century British example, which in turn evolved from the medieval model. Navy life is relentlessly class-oriented, rank-based and rigorously structured. Almost every human interaction within this sphere has been formulated and pre-scribed.

But as extreme as the rule-bound inheritance of the Navy can be, it is counterposed with the extraterritoriality of the seafarer. The di-chotomy was struck long ago by Plain Ned Ward, the British philoso-pher-seaman, who wrote of the sailor in 1707, "He's one that is the greatest prisoner, and the greatest rambler in Christendom." Con-fined, yet free. When the sailor sails away from port, he sails away from the laws of home, too. In foreign ports, all manner of taboo activity is available to him. Sea life and shore life break the sailor's existence in two. Long stretches of enforced sobriety alternate with spectacular, obliterating drunks. Sexual deprivation with brothel crawls. Claustrophobic confinement with the freedom of a port of call.

Alcohol has long been a prime familiar of Navy life. Early navies floated on an ocean of wine or rum. With water supplies unreliable, consumption of alcohol was a health measure. The history of the mod-ern American sailor has been the slow voyage toward shipboard absti-nence. "Anchors Aweigh," the Navy anthem composed in 1906, was grog-drenched: "Drink away, drink away, for you sail at break of day." "Grog"—rum or whiskey cut with water—was first weakened by fur-ther dilution, then rationed ("two dips" a day), then banned entirely in

1914 by a temperance-minded Secretary of the Navy named Josephus
Daniels.

There has always been some surreptitious drinking aboard Navy
ships, especially on the part of aviators. But by and large, what the
ukase against alcohol did was transform shore leaves into extended
binges. Heavy alcohol consumption is twice as prevalent in the Navy
as in the population as a whole. In 1987, the Department of the Navy
attempted to set a precedent with a liquor-free military club for underage sailors on the Norfolk Naval Base. Six months later the Wind-
jammer Club was in the red to the tune of $40,000 each month, and
base officials begged Washington to shut the operation down. "It's just
not paying off," said a base spokesperson.

However, it is sodomy, not rum, that may be the most problematic issue for the Navy male. For as much as he devotes himself to the
arts of the warrior (the most macho posture one can assume), the faint
intimation of homosexuality has always hung around sailors. The Village People, the campy, gay-identified singing group of the seventies,
were only expressing a preexisting notion in the culture with the sug-
gestive lyrics of their hit "In the Navy." There are strict regulations
against carnal relations aboard ship, with any homosexual act grounds
for immediate expulsion from the service. None of which prevents
(and may actually enhance) the raging sexual underground present on
every ship in the fleet. In Navy slang, it's called "sea pussy": supposedly straight sailors, taking a walk on the wild side during extended
cruises.

In an odd way, the homosexual notoriety of Navy men may help
drive the raucous, drunken binges for which sailors on shore leave are
famous. The proximity to men, the intimacy with men, can conceiv-
ably be the goad which drives some sailors to prove themselves as
studs with women. Homosexual panic is a great ice-breaker.

Plain Ned Ward continued his observation about "the wooden
world," as he called life at sea: "There is not a corner of the world the
sailor visits . . . but when he does get ashore he pays it off with a
vengeance; for knowing his time is short, he crowds much in a little
room and lives as fast as possible."

The sailor, cheated of a normal life, living a tightly controlled shipboard existence of sobriety and abstinence, must compress a month or more of sex, drinking and excess into whatever liberty period he is allowed. The binge-and-purge mentality is deeply ingrained in Navy life. It informs the wide acceptance by the higher-ups, the Scrambled Eggs, of the inalienable right of all sailors to light their hair on fire.

CROSS-POLLINATE THE MYTHOLOGY OF *TOP GUN* WITH THE NAVY'S traditional binge-and-purge mentality, and you get a strange, potent hybrid, a more virulent strain of rum, sodomy and the lash.

In the modern Navy of the supercarrier, the proud tradition of men at sea had been usurped by one of arrogant men in the air. They embraced the same frenetic party philosophy as their rum-sodden forerunners. A contemporary Tomcat pilot brought Plain Ned up to date: "As long as you didn't cause an international incident, you were probably okay. If they saw you drunk, dancing on a table in the bar down in Palma [Spain], well, there was no problem with that at all." A former Navy pilot described a group of pilots arriving at an overseas O Club: "They'd proceed to destroy the place. I mean, they'd eat the fish out of the goldfish tank on the wall. Destroy the furniture. One time it was $30,000 in damage. And it was 'Okay, let the boys have a good time.' There was a belief, 'Hey, we've done our time at sea, we have the right to go crazy.'"

And why not? The aviators were at the apex of the Navy hierarchy. They were like monkeys in a barnyard: the pigs and goats and other animals might stare up at them, awestruck, but stopping them, controlling them, was simply out of the question. It was the Top Gun Syndrome. Aviators had never been truly integrated or tamed by the rest of the Navy. There was a singular lack of effective checks on their behavior.

The outside world was accustomed to thinking of the Navy as a monolithic entity. Civilians were not attuned to the more subtle differences between black shoes and brown shoes, surface and aviation communities. The water-bound, straight-ahead sailors of the surface community unwittingly reinforced the Top Gun Syndrome by according Navy pilots instant hegemony. A naval flight officer stationed on the carrier U.S.S. *Abraham Lincoln* summed up the pecking order: "Everyone wants to fly something that goes fast, makes noise, drops bombs or shoots missiles. Those are the F-14, F/A-18 and A-6."

And the adulation didn't come only from the Old Navy. Everyone lionized the jet pilots. A Navy pilot: "All *Top Gun* did was walk in to Miramar O Club and turn the camera on. It's the same at Oceana. That whole mentality there, they just showed it in all its cockiness. It verified it. A lot of guys felt they'd been recognized. That's part of it too—the Navy pilot has finally been recognized as being this super-hot dude."

Throughout the Reagan-Bush era, as a series of limited engagements (Grenada, Libya, Panama) brought the military back from the brink of its Vietnam disgrace, the fighter pilot gained in stature. Especially after *Top Gun*, adulation from the outside matched that within the Navy. There were legions of women—they flocked to O Clubs every week—who didn't mind one bit being patted on the fanny by a Navy aviator.

A Navy commander who was stationed at the Pentagon in 1989 reported this exchange with a married female secretary also working there.

SECRETARY: You're not an aviator, so you're not going to Tailhook this year, are you?
COMMANDER: No, I'm not.
SECRETARY: Well, I'm going.
COMMANDER: Why are you going? What does your husband say?
SECRETARY: I don't care what my husband says. I'm going to Tailhook to get laid by an F-14 pilot.

In part, this adulation gained force from the idea of the single-combat warrior, a legacy from an earlier age when knights would be sent out, one on one, to prove the honor of their community. The contemporary fighter pilot, who straps on a high-performance jet and goes out to a duel in the sky, was but a late incarnation of this earlier icon. As a culture, wrote Tom Wolfe in *The Right Stuff*, we continue to enter into an agreement with the warrior, a pact whereby we give over the spoils of war even before the victory is won.

> . . . The honor and the glory were in many cases rewards *before the fact;* on account, as it were. Archaic cultures were quite willing to elevate their single-combat fighters to heroic status even *before* their blood was let, because it was such an effective incentive. Any young man who entered the corps would get his rewards here on earth, "up front," to use the current phrase, come what may.

The rewards were given in advance not only as an "effective incentive," but because the task of the single-combat warrior was so dangerous. It is hard to award a fighter pilot a medal when he is burned to a crisp. So you grant him ultimate license to act any way he wants when he is alive.

License. It became a part of the Navy pilots' equipment. There was a sense of entitlement that came with the territory, and it applied as much to off-duty life as active duty—maybe a little more. Partying was a tradition, not written down in all the official squadron histories, but very real nonetheless.

When the Top Gun fighter weapons school was created at Miramar in 1968, legendary parties were held out at Lafayette Escadrille, the La Jolla beach house once owned by actor Victor Mclaglen, which two Top Gun pilots rented. They called their bachelor pad a "snake ranch," because you would "invite a girl over and show her your 'snake.'" The tradition continued through the seventies. Writer Robert K. Wilcox captured the flavor of the era in his book *Scream of Eagles: The Creation of Top Gun—And the U.S. Air Victory in Vietnam.* He quotes a Top Gun instructor's description of the Downwinds bar in San Diego, which at the time was fighter-jock central:

Nothing in it was breakable—no glass. They gave you beer in a plastic cup. They'd pack people in and I guess the fire marshal or whatever only allows so many at one time. So girls would climb over the walls and guys would help them. . . . After about 30 seconds there was beer everywhere, and you'd be slipping and sliding and fights were generated just by everybody falling into everybody else.

W. C. Fields used to say that it was hard to know where Hollywood left off and the d.t.'s began. It was that way with the Top Gun pilots—hard to tell where the war fighting left off and the partying began. The two sectors of their life bled into each other. It was an incredible, body-draining regimen. Flight jocks who partied all night told of heading into Miramar without sleep, at 4:30 A.M., for an early briefing and a launch at first light. The best cure for a hangover, the pilots found, was the pure oxygen fed through their flight masks.

In their intensely competitive world, it wasn't surprising that the question of who could drink who under the table became a signifier of rank within the community. Thus, inevitably, partying, drinking, scoring—it all became wrapped up in what it meant to be a fighter pilot. To be good at it was as much a part of being a good Navy pilot as being a "hot stick." In an interview for the Department of Defense Tailhook investigation, agents pressed Lieutenant John Loguidice, one of their more cooperative witnesses, to give an account of the culture that spawned Tailhook. He said:

Naval aviation, to an extent, shaped a certain attitude, reinforced that attitude. . . . We were always taught in flight school to be . . . the first at the O Club, the last to leave the O Club, the ones to get the "chicks," . . . the wildest, most adventurous, both in the cockpit and out of it. It sounds like a lot of hogwash, but if you've been in naval aviation, you know that that's how it is. And you become leader of the squadron by being leader on liberty and a leader at the O Club and a leader at parties. . . . Naval aviation rewards those that are the wildest, and to an extent, we all conform, and not because we didn't want to. We enjoy that lifestyle, being able to go out and drink and have a good time.

A favorite motto of Navy pilots is the "work hard, play hard" equation. But somehow the two elements became fused, until playing hard had the same value as working hard, and could earn you comparable merit among your shipmates.

Most salient about this lifestyle—and the popularization of the fighter pilot through *Top Gun* increased this effect exponentially—was how incredibly attractive it appeared to those people just outside it. The aviation community had legions of wanna-be's. To those on the edge of the bull's-eye, looking in to where the fighter pilots dwelled in perfect isolation and isolated perfection, it was almost hypnotic. If a guy drove a transport plane, maybe, or a helicopter, he took his place outside the sacred circle and sat there with his nose pressed up against the glass.

He looked in and he thought, There I'd be, if it weren't for some twist of fate—less than 20/20 vision, say, or legs that were too long, or the tendency to "gray out" upside down at high altitudes. In flight school, everyone wanted to go jets, be a fighter pilot. Even those who were not at the top of their class, and therefore would not make it into the high-performance jet pipeline, could will themselves into the conviction that they, too, had the guts, the spirit, the moxie—they just didn't have the breaks.

If the Navy wouldn't allow them to drive an F-14, how could they show those lucky stiffs who existed in the center of the bull's-eye that they were worthy, too? By partying a little harder, drinking a little more, acting a little more crazed, scoring more with the babes.

That was part of what happened at Tailhook. Some of these wanna-be's lined the hallway of the third deck that night in Las Vegas, and they had to prove themselves. All the other elements were in place, also. The Top Gun Syndrome. Binge-and-purge. The apotheosis of the fighter pilot within the Navy and among the public at large. Homosexual panic. Hard partying as a status-enhancer.

Still, things might not have reached critical mass at Tailhook '91. Saddam Hussein had to play his part, too.

THE OFFICIAL SPOILS OF THE WAR IN THE PERSIAN GULF WERE EASILY grasped: 4 billion barrels of oil, an end to Iraqi lebensraum, restoration of Kuwaiti sovereignty. It was a "good war," as Studs Terkel termed World War II, meaning, essentially, that it was a popular one. For a whole generation of Navy pilots—those who had come into the Navy in the years since Vietnam, and thus had very little "purple time," or combat experience—the Persian Gulf represented a chance to do what they had been trained to do.

But as a war, Desert Storm fell short in one important respect. Along with the official spoils of war, there had always been more immediate booty that fell by tradition to the individual soldier. Prostitute camp followers had attended every previous conflict in American history. As recently as the Vietnam War, sexual favors, even rape, had been an off-record but widespread perquisite of the conquering U.S. soldier. Alcohol consumption likewise had quasi-official status as stress reliever and reward for combat service.

But the Persian Gulf was a dry war, a chaste war. Islamic society had stern prohibitions against alcohol, and Muslim women were kept strictly segregated. For R&R, Gulf War troops had to make do with the Cunard *Princess,* a cruise liner, rented for $31 million by the Pentagon and stocked with hamburgers and beer. It was a far cry from the alcoholic binges of previous conflicts, of the "hospitality women," also known as "Little Brown Fucking Machines Fueled by Rice," whose services cost five dollars a week at Subic Bay.

There is some evidence, not officially corroborated, that U.S. military authorities, in an effort to address this imbalance, installed a corps of prostitutes aboard the Cunard vessel and a smaller cruise ship also rented for R&R. According to Ninotchka Rosca, director of a Filipino activist group called the GABRIELA Network, around 100 women were imported from the Philippines for exclusive use by U.S. military personnel aboard the two luxury liners.

The Persian Gulf was, finally, the younger generation's chance for boasting honors. They had listened to the war stories of their seniors for long enough. It was time they got a war of their own, spoils of their own. Only when they did, it was a brutal disappointment. Two floating whorehouses could hardly equal the vast pleasuring grounds of Vietnam, especially in the imaginations of the junior officers who had never been there. Bill Hoover, a former Navy lawyer who spent much of his military career trying to open sea duty to women, offered this analysis:

> The last extended conflict we had ended in 1972. So from '72 to '91, that's nineteen years. Well, that's an entire generation . . . You have the young guys that have never had "their war," but they get a little bitty taste of it over there in the Gulf—but what kind of an environment did they have? The opposite [of Vietnam], where women are under lock and key—a chaste environment. No way to release the tensions built up. . . . It's a dry country. Okay, we're going over there, and we're going to bomb all those people down there, but you can't drink and you can't have sex. You can't do any of these things. So these people get to Tailhook, in Vegas, where you have nude women dancing on the stage, it's a party town. So you've got the old guys trying to recapture their youth, and the young guys trying to get a little . . . and there was just enough to allow it to get a little out of hand. You had two ends of the spectrum. You had the old ones, they'd tell the stories. Then you'd have the young bucks coming in, that were in a chaste, dry war, and there's a lot of stress builds up when you go out day after day and you're being shot at. And you have no traditional warrior stress relievers.

The Scrambled Eggs had had their war. They were beyond all that now, beyond the craziness of the third floor ("It's just too damned noisy for me," said Admiral Ramage, one of the Tailhook founders), certainly beyond the gauntlet. They were old men. For them, flight operations had given way to prostate operations. But the junior officers, the JO's, still had something to prove. The Persian Gulf, their war, had failed to supply what they knew to be, from listening to the stories of their senior officers, the full breadth of military experience. Somehow, they had been cheated.

One Tomcat aviator, a lieutenant stationed at Oceana Naval Air Station, articulated it. Tailhook, he explained, was the result of "the post-Vietnam mind-set, which was just a continuation of the post-World War II, "right-stuff" mind-set associated with the aviation community. The post-Desert Storm, Attila-the-Hun mind-set was that we had won the war, and the spoils are for us. What fostered it was not only the undercurrent of 'boys will be boys,' but now tacked on top of that was the fact that these 'boys' are warriors. You know: 'We survived getting shot at, and now we get to do whatever we want—because America owes us.' "

One recently winged young woman put it like this: "It's like a frenzy. It's like when sharks frenzy to eat. Because it's a fest, and people forget about human frailty. They forget that there's somebody in the world other than themselves. That's the big thing about aviators, in general. The majority of aviators are focused in on who they are and what they want. They are the center point. And when you're frenzied like that, it's ten-fold. It's all what *I* want: 'I'm going to get what I want. I want that. I want that person. I want to touch that person. I'm going to do it now.' And they see everybody else doing it so they think it's all right."

And up until Tailhook, it was all right.

Chapter Four

THE END OF THE WORLD

IT WAS ALREADY OVER. ONLY THE LIFE HAD BEEN SO GLORIOUS, SO goddamn much fun, that no one wanted to admit they were the walking dead. It was like Tibetan mythology, where the dying don't realize the actual fact of their death until long afterward, and continue with a sort of dreamy momentum to behave like the living.

Every male on the third floor that night, every guy standing around with a drink in his hand, wearing the off-duty uniform of the aviator—clipped hair, T-shirt, shorts and shoes without socks—had at least a dim awareness that the culture which had sustained his world for so long was undergoing a vast change. Their response was so automatic as to seem practically inborn.

Dead? How could they be? They were bulletproof. Naval aviators were selected, trained and groomed for invincibility. The ones who didn't believe, who had some niggling, secret flaw in their character that allowed Doubt to creep in, who didn't swagger out onto that tarmac every day as if they were immortal, those men were banished. Eliminated by official action or struck from the skies by a flick of God's little finger. The life they had chosen was so dangerous, so close to the edge—fliers have by far the highest casualty rate in the peacetime military—that whoever blinked in the face of it was immediately smoked.

The way to survive, the pilots would tell you, was not to turn away from the dangers, never to discount them. The most successful aviators learned instead to take their lessons from those who messed up, and, finally, to relish the risks themselves, to love the dangers as though they were life-sustaining. When you are focused like that, when you are immune and certain and self-contained, the world can change around you, but you yourself are never affected.

The jacket patch that aviators receive at the Top Gun training school at Miramar continued to feature a Soviet MiG centered in the middle of a set of gunsights. The world had moved on, with the collapse of the Cold War; anyone, even a civilian, could now rent a ride on a Russian MiG in Moscow. Every sign pointed to the fact that the role of warfighter as the Top Gun pilots had known it was outdated, sorely in need of revision. It didn't matter. They were bulletproof.

Likewise, Congress could legislate women in warplanes, the Secretary of the Navy could make male fliers train with females, they could even see women pilots with their own eyes enter and hormonally desecrate the sanctum sanctorum of the jet community . . . and they would still tell themselves it would never happen.

In the months after it became uncomfortably clear that something had gone wrong at Tailhook '91, a handful of women—Lieutenant Paula Coughlin, civilians Lisa Reagan and Marie Weston, an ensign out at Miramar named Kim Ponikowski and the Las Vegas minor who had been stripped of her clothes—told of the assaults they had suffered. Gradually, as their stories surfaced in the local news, and as local news stories grew into national headlines, people outside the military demanded explanations.

But what no one seemed to grasp was that Tailhook, an event that called out for change, was itself an aftershock of a seismic change within the aviation community. Women had entered and irrevocably transformed what had heretofore been a closed clique. No longer was naval aviation a place where men were men and boys would be boys.

But the men just kept clinging to their old world, and the boys went on acting like boys. What the whole affair really represented was a lesser Götterdämmerung. It was the happy hour of the gods.

When a species nears extinction, certain behavioral niceties drop away and its individual members begin to perform desperate measures — roaming huge territories in search of mates, for example, or senselessly attacking nonpredators. The more any group is threatened, the more it tends to lash out at enemies, real or imagined. So perhaps the threat of extinction was what made them party a little harder on the third floor that night, act a little crazier than they had in the past. It put a hysterical edge to the celebrations. The Feast in the Midst of the Plague.

For the naval aviator, there was something askew, something so fundamental and challenging to life's basic assumptions about a woman in a warplane cockpit, that it couldn't be talked about. Everyone knew that some part of the old order was gone, but no one knew what to do about it. So there was a sort of group-think agreement to act as if nothing had really happened at all.

The important thing was to maintain the aura of invincibility. Even though you are flesh and bone, insist that you are bulletproof. Even when the Naval Investigative Service comes to call, pulling your chain about the stuff that went down at last year's Tailhook, you don't have to worry. It's the end of the world, R.E.M. is singing, and you feel fine.

BARBARA POPE, THE ASSISTANT SECRETARY OF THE NAVY, WAS TROUbled by night thoughts.

It was early May 1992. The Navy's report on Tailhook had just been released.

They all saw nothing, Pope thought, they all knew nothing. It's ludicrous.

That the young officers had not cooperated with the investigation was bad enough. But what really disturbed her was the vacuum at the top. The senior officers, the admirals. If they had only used their command clout, they could have broken the case open. No one seemed concerned about the issue she had been hammering for the past six months: accountability. She had sifted through the reams of documentation produced by the Naval Investigative Service—the Navy equivalent of the FBI—and the true scope of what happened at Tailhook had appalled her.

The investigators of the NIS had started out believing the case was about one woman who was unlucky and got groped. But almost immediately, the scandal unfolded outward like some malodorous hot-house flower. Victims multiplied, from one to twenty-six; witnesses reported behavior that went further and further beyond the pale. It was clear, even in the first few weeks, that Tailhook was not about an isolated incident.

Someone had to be responsible.

The men in charge of the investigation kept telling Pope to just hold on, they were going to get it together, they would nail the cul-prits. But now the reports were out, and they were giving up only two names. You've got to be kidding, Barbara Pope thought. That's the best we could come up with?

But there it was: 270 field agents involved, 2,193 interviews, over 20,000 man-hours invested, $400,000 spent. After the full weight of government bureaucracy had leaned upon the events of September 5–7, 1991, on whose shoulders did the stern hand of blame land? Two dudes. It was like those old Richard Pryor jokes, which always started out, "Two dudes, two dudes . . ." and you instantly knew that those two dudes were the lowest, unluckiest dudes in the world. The Naval Investigative Service accused two men of committing indecent assault at Tailhook. One was a Marine Corps pilot, Gregory Bonam, and the other was an Australian exchange flier, the "biter" who went around drawing gluteal blood whenever the urge struck him.

There were over 2,000 pages of investigative exhibits, catalogs of malfeasance that read like St. Patrick's Day police blotters. People were carting around the NIS report in cardboard boxes, on hand

trucks. It weighed over fifteen pounds. But it provided only two criminal cases the NIS could recommend.

Barbara Pope's anger supposedly carried a lot of weight, at least
inside the Navy. It was coming from the E-ring at the Pentagon, that
literal inner circle of power where the paint is fresher and the carpet
deeper, where if someone sneezes, someone else on a ship halfway
around the world says "Bless you!"

But Assistant Secretary Pope had so far been ineffectual. She
had been talking to anyone who would listen about everything that
galled her on the subject of Tailhook. And nothing she said had made
a bit of difference.

To begin with, she had been brought into the loop late. The
Tailhook "problem" had actually been in the system for over a month
when, one evening the previous October, she had been called into
Dan Howard's conference room. Howard was the undersecretary of
the Navy, her direct superior, and he had filled the room with senior
officers, legal advisers and public affairs flacks. Pope had the uncomfortable awareness of joining a party already in progress. They were all
sitting around the table, planning a media strategy. Howard explained
that the Tailhook story would break in the *San Diego Union-Tribune*
the next morning. Senator John McCain, the Republican from Arizona
who was a former pilot and POW from a distinguished Navy family,
was getting ready to make a statement about the incident on the floor
of the Senate. Already, the NIS had begun its investigation into Paula
Coughlin's complaint. The whole debacle was in fact already careering
at full tilt when the assistant secretary of the Navy was called in.

"At first I was angry," Pope recalled, "that as the ASN [assistant
secretary of the Navy] I knew nothing about this. Because we had had
[sex scandals at] the Naval Academy and [at the Navy enlisted training
center in] Orlando. I had people actively looking to change policies,
behavior. We had made personnel changes.

"But nobody had mentioned it to me—I suspect because they
thought I would overreact. The idea was that they could contain it,
that they could investigate it and find out the truth before I went off

the wall. . . . So they pulled me in for whatever reasons—I don't
know, damage control, having a female involved."

Barbara Spyridon Pope came to the assistant secretary's job via a
Vanderbilt education, a position on the staff of Barry Goldwater, a
stint at the Small Business Administration in the Reagan years, and
finally a position at the Department of Defense. She was the first
female assistant secretary in the Navy's 217-year history, and its highest-ranking nonuniformed woman.

Pope had been parked in the "soft" jurisdiction of personnel
(officially, her title was "Assistant Secretary of the Navy for Manpower
and Reserve Affairs"). She was perceived by some government conservatives as nontraditional, if there could be such a thing as a nontraditional Reaganite. To the stiff-upper-lips inside the Navy, she was over-
emotional. Her operating style was informal, passionate, impulsive.
Sometimes she seemed like the only warm body in a sculpture park of
frozen-faced generals and admirals.

Even though personnel was traditionally something of a backwater, in an era of downsizing, "manpower" issues were hot-button topics. Pope was well positioned to make her mark. She was small, five
two, around forty, and talked volubly and quickly. She was the kind of
woman to whom the term "fireplug" is applied. In debate, she could
drown you with sheer volume of words.

They always called her "Mrs. Pope." In the title-laden world of
the Pentagon, where everything was "Admiral" this and "General"
that, "Mrs." was the only honorific anyone could come up with. Somehow it tied her to the image of a Bethesda hausfrau.

In fact, her swearing-in as assistant secretary had taken place on
the due date of her second child. The idea was that the next morning,
if she didn't check into the maternity ward, she'd come in to assume
her duties. At a good-bye party they threw for her at her old office at
the Department of Defense, she'd been handed one of those corny
bouquets of helium-filled Mylar balloons, which she was carrying out
to her car at the end of the day. Crossing the Pentagon parking field,
Pope had run into a Marine Corps general whose face was familiar,
though they'd never been introduced.

He seemed to recognize her, too. "Just have a baby shower?" he asked, being friendly.

"As a matter of fact," Pope said, feeling kind of bad about having to clue him in, "I was just sworn in as the first female assistant secretary of the Navy and Marine Corps." Standing there, hugely pregnant, with those ridiculous balloons, she watched the chagrined general waltz off between the cars. For a long time after that, he seemed to avoid her.

"Mrs. Pope." There was no easy pigeonhole for her in the vast concentric dovecote of the Pentagon, certainly not in the E-ring. And it had gotten worse since October, when she had gone down to Dan Howard's office and listened, with incredulity and anger, to the first reports of Paula Coughlin's complaint. Since then, she hadn't held back in giving them her opinions.

There were a lot of angry women in the fall of 1991. The Clarence Thomas–Anita Hill hearings brought the issue of sexual harassment onto the front burner and then turned up the heat. In retrospect, it seemed astonishing that the issue had been dormant for so long. The daughters of the middle class had been in the workforce for three decades, and only now there was an outcry raised to provide a safe working environment for them? The appearances of Anita Hill and Clarence Thomas before the Senate Judiciary Committee monopolized the airwaves like nothing since the Watergate hearings. As with Watergate, there was an uncanny sense that the whole nation was watching.

And perhaps that's why no one paid much attention as Tailhook began to unfold. At the start, the Tailhook affair played like a poor-relation melodrama against the backdrop of Anita Hill's testimony. The scandal might have gotten more press if it had not been knocked off the front pages by Hill-Thomas. But synchronicity cut both ways. Anita Hill prepared the way for Paula Coughlin. And in the atmosphere generated by the Hill-Thomas hearings, even a Goldwater girl like Barbara Pope could not help be affected by the angry mood of her sisters.

Every week from November through April, she attended a

Tailhook briefing in the office of the "Under," Dan Howard. Pope would look around at all the faces, a lone woman in a room full of men. Rear Admiral George W. Davis, the Naval Inspector General. Rear Admiral Duvall "Mac" Williams, Jr., the commander of the NIS. The Navy Judge Advocate General Jack Gordon. Commander Peter Fagan, the Navy secretary's Special Assistant for Legal and Legislative Affairs. Through the close of the old year and the opening of the new, the dimensions of the story slowly expanded. Eventually, Pope found herself sitting around with the others discussing dildos and vomit.

From the beginning, the men in the room with Barbara Pope couldn't seem to grasp that what had happened to Lieutenant Coughlin at the Las Vegas Hilton was much more than a public relations problem. It made Pope crazy, their insistence that Tailhook was a minor, isolated issue. She couldn't believe she had to spoon-feed these guys. Some of them saw the whole Tailhook episode as a joke. They failed to grasp the basics, i.e., what it was like to get physically assaulted. Pope remembered asking some admirals, What if it were your wife? What if it were your daughter? What if it were your girlfriend making her way down that corridor and getting assaulted while hundreds of men looked on? But she could not elicit from them the outrage that existed among some of the women who had been abused, the outrage she shared.

"Imagine that you attended a Navy-sponsored party," she finally said, "and you happened to get off the elevator at the wrong floor, walk into a drunken brawl of homosexual aviators—and you got assaulted."

The reaction of the flag officers was unanimous. The perpetrators would be dead.

"You wouldn't need an investigation, would you?" she asked them. "You'd go in and find out somehow, any way you could, who screwed up."

Mrs. Pope made a few recommendations: Ground them. Don't let them fly. Stop their promotions. The admirals had refused, and always with sterling rationales. In this case, they cited the danger of "unlawful command influence," the Navy term for tampering with due process.

Do a stand-down, said Pope.

They had argued over that one. Shut the whole Navy down so we can talk about what's going on, about the seriousness of the investigation. For Pope it seemed simple enough. Whenever there was a rush of accidents, it was standard procedure to hold a "safety stand-down" --a total, worldwide halt of operations—in order to see what was causing the problem and to focus on it as an entire organization.

Do a stand-down on sexual harassment.

That's too radical, they said.

"We've got a radical situation here," Pope said. She proposed measure after measure, and they weren't even considered. They told her that the investigation would run its course, and that it would be all taken care of when the reports came out.

What agonized her now was that the whole thing seemed to have come to nothing. The reports had been released on April 30. They settled nothing, just tossed gasoline on the fire. Congress was up in arms, the media was howling, the public was disgusted. They were all saying the things Barbara Pope had said over and over in those weekly meetings. What she eventually came to see was that the men responsible would not be punished, and the senior officers would not be held accountable.

She wasn't going to stand for it.

ANY INVESTIGATION MOUNTED BY THE UNITED STATES GOVERNMENT will have certain common characteristics, but alacrity and perspicacity are not chief among them. An Internal Revenue Service audit, say, or a General Accounting Office investigation is lethal not because it floats like a butterfly and stings like a bee. It kills by grinding its subjects down, like a steamroller stuck in low gear.

The Naval Investigative Service shared with its government cohorts the same dogged, detail-drenched, exhaustive and exhausting approach to determining the truth. Formed in 1915 as the Office of Naval Intelligence, the NIS was a supposedly independent arm of the military justice system, charged with providing the Navy's prosecuting attorneys with the raw materials out of which they would fashion their criminal cases.

In the civilian world, the same function would be served by investigators assigned to a district attorney's office, and in fact an overwhelming majority of the 1,050 agents in the NIS were civilians. Many of them came out of the forensic culture of local police departments, others performed lateral career moves from investigative bureaus in the Defense Department, Justice or the GAO. The NIS might not have been a glamour posting—its operatives were nowhere to be seen in the hit Broadway/Hollywood melodrama of military justice, *A Few Good Men*—but it was a steady one. The NIS was the apparatus that the Department of the Navy employed to determine what had happened in Las Vegas at the beginning of September 1991. The huge, clanking, investigative bureau approached Tailhook like a hybrid between a dinosaur and a bloodhound.

The NIS had one characteristic which would prove an immediate boon in the Tailhook investigation. Generously supported in the way of all Pentagon duchies, the NIS had offices all over the globe, with hundreds of agents at its disposal to track down leads. The day after the probe was opened, agents were able to conduct screening interviews with fliers in Brazil and Japan. The civilian equivalent would be if local police had detectives to spare for every neighborhood, every block.

But almost immediately, another hound was put on another scent. On October 29, the day after Barbara Pope first sat in on a Tailhook strategy meeting, Secretary of the Navy Lawrence Garrett directed the Navy Inspector General's office to examine the "cultural" context of the Tailhook convention. The Inspector General (IG) would search not for criminal wrongdoing, which was the NIS's bailiwick, but for noncriminal violations of the Navy's code of conduct. Since this code covered an immense range of behavioral constructs—from adultery to spitting on the sidewalk—the IG would necessarily have to cast a much wider net than any criminal investigation.

Dan Howard, the Under, had the unenviable job of supervising the combined efforts of the NIS and the IG. His job was made more difficult by the notoriously bad relations which stood between the two agencies. Most recently, the IG had turned in a critical report on the NIS's mishandling of the USS *Iowa* gun-turret explosion.

Nor did the IG come along willingly. We don't have the people, said the IG to the Under. And indeed, the IG's office would be able to assign the Tailhook investigation to only a half-dozen agents, and even then it termed the duty "collateral"—a favorite word of the military, usually applied to jobs you don't want, don't have time for or can't figure out anyway.

Finally, a compromise was reached. The IG would piggyback its inquiry on the NIS findings. The Navy's investigation into the events of the Tailhook convention was thus bifurcated from the start. Or maybe bifocal is the better image—the NIS would closely examine criminal cases, with the IG looking up to see the big picture. The bloodhound had gone cross-eyed.

Even with two entities in pursuit of the truth—perhaps because of it—there was a pervasive sense of pessimism as the NIS/IG started work. One point that beleaguered NIS operatives were quick to raise, when their report was later assailed for its shortcomings, was the extremely onerous conditions under which they operated. Tailhook was what detectives call a "cold case." The convention had been over for a month when the investigation began. The crime scene had been effectively obliterated, every bit of forensic evidence Hoovered up by Hilton cleaning crews. A new carpet had even been laid down—of necessity, since the old one had been thoroughly trashed by the combination of overimaginative mixology and careless cigarette etiquette.

A cold case with no crime scene. Anyone who has even a glancing familiarity with forensic science will recognize that this situation represents an almost insurmountable handicap for investigators. Many DA's in the civilian world would toss in the towel immediately, knowing that to build a case on the recollections of witnesses months after the fact is a fool's labor.

"We were first informed of this case more than 30 days after it occurred," said Rear Admiral Williams, commander of the NIS. "The party was attended by thousands of people, many not associated with the Navy and probably unidentifiable by us. Heavy alcohol use was prevalent. These are not ideal circumstances." As Williams put it, Navy-style, the NIS didn't have "a fart's chance in a whirlwind" of assembling viable criminal cases.

Speaking specifically about Coughlin's case, the civilian head of NIS's criminal division said, "As soon as it came to our attention, we jumped into it. But the odds against solving the crime were just tremendous. The problem was that the only evidence was Coughlin's ability to identify her assailants. And therefore time became crucial."

The NIS was running up against a quandary that increasingly angered and frustrated those mobilizing against sexual assault in the society as a whole: the difficulty in proving the crime in a court of law. What at first seemed simple—string the buggers up!—immediately became entangled in legal thickets. Moreover, the witnesses that the NIS would have to rely upon were literally scattered all over the globe. Lieutenant Coughlin told NIS agents she thought she could identify three of her assailants, all of whom she described as junior officers. But where were they now? They had dropped from the skies to Las Vegas that September, and then they had climbed back into the skies and disappeared.

By October 11, when the NIS dinosaur-bloodhound groaned into action, the Navy officers who had been at Tailhook had dispersed to an absurd number of venues. But again, with NIS offices around the globe, suddenly weeks later all those aviation JO's, posted to Norfolk's Oceana air base (or the one at Rota, Spain, or Adak, Alaska), their Las Vegas hangovers long cleared, were tapped on the shoulder by the NIS. "Lieutenant K., we're here to talk to you about the events of last September . . ."

The odd thing about all those junior officers, it almost seemed as if they were prepared for it.

———

NOT DIRECTLY, OF COURSE. NOT COACHED OR PREPPED OR WARNED
in any way that would constitute suborning a witness. But the majority
of the aviators involved in Tailhook, men and women both, were specifically and thoroughly trained how to react to hostile individuals
approaching them and asking a routinized series of questions.

Depending on your appetite for irony, considering that both
sides were running on the taxpayer's dime, it is either deeply awful or
darkly humorous, the face-off of the initial Tailhook investigation as it
attempted to sniff out a cadre of officers specifically schooled in techniques to dissemble and deceive, through a curriculum known as
SERE training. Like Miramar's Top Gun school and other practices
and strategies of the modern Navy, SERE school was shaped and
honed in the wake of a particularly miserable showing early on in the
war in Vietnam. Those who saw them will never forget the shivery,
black-and-white images supplied by the North Vietnamese of Navy
fliers, broken by advanced techniques of torture, testifying to America's perfidy in mounting a war against the blameless proletariat
masses of Vietnam.

SERE training—the acronym stands for Survival, Evasion, Resistance and Escape—is designed to give captured Navy flight crew
members at least rudimentary tools with which to defend themselves
against the increasingly sophisticated battery of modern interrogation
techniques.

The basic counterinterrogation strategies learned at SERE
school are simple. Give out only direct replies to specific questions, do
not embroider, volunteer nothing, limit the amount of information
that changes hands as much as possible. Trainees are abandoned in
trackless wilderness, allowed two jugs of water, a survival knife, an
optional roll of Lifesavers. They wind up eating anything, everything,
or more commonly, nothing, for eight days. "Rabbits and trees" is how
one female SERE graduate characterized her diet. Exhausted,
starved, hallucinating, they are taken as "prisoners-of-war." They are
beaten and humiliated. When American forces "liberate" the camp

and the SERE prisoners are released, there is a grandiose (and classi-fied) patriotic ceremony. Everyone weeps.

Of course, it's just another brand of brainwashing, using some of the same techniques that the Vietnamese were fond of using. For the individual who undergoes SERE training, however, it is described as one of the formative experiences of his or her life. SERE training becomes internalized until it is as much a part of the naval aviator's psychic survival kit as the revolver is a part of his or her flight bag. (Apart from Navy police and couriers, only aviators are allowed to carry sidearms, and only flight personnel receive SERE training.) The SERE program is grueling physically, but it is designed to be particu-larly challenging emotionally. It provides for a set psychological re-sponse that fliers can fall back upon in times of stress.

It also seems to feed a cockiness that has been shaped and honed through Aviation Officer Candidate School and in the primary and secondary aviation training squadrons. The conviction of tribal superi-ority combines with an inculcated toughness that makes fliers believe they can withstand anything. Bulletproof.

What the NIS agents were running up against was the "Resis-tance" part of the SERE acronym. One lieutenant described the tech-niques used in the NIS Tailhook interviews as "classic SERE school garbage, where they try to trick you into saying things. You were instantaneously guilty." He continued:

> There was no question about it. I don't think a lot of guys didn't tell everything they knew, but I guarantee none of us went in there and spilled our guts. I answered specific questions. You're looking at your fraternity being beaten up. And it's like, I'm going to protect my fellow frat brothers. It's not a matter of evading and hiding things, but we're all aviators and we've all been to SERE school and had the crap beaten out of us for a couple of days, and we know what these guys are doing. They tell us at SERE school: find your limit. Tell exactly what's asked. Well, I answered exactly what was asked of me. I did not volunteer information. If they

wanted me to spill my guts, they would have had to ask the right questions.

When the press or Congress suggested, later on, that Navy avia tors had perhaps conspired to deceive their interviewers about Tailhook, the accusation was the product of a fundamental misapprehension. The fliers didn't have to sit down in some wardroom somewhere and plan out how to react—although, it must be said, there was plenty of that. Even if they did conspire to perjure themselves, the point was that SERE-trained Navy fliers didn't have to. Resistance was bred in the bone.

All through fall and winter, the unstoppable force met the immovable object. In the far-flung offices of the Naval Investigative Service, officers of the equally far-flung tribe of naval aviators trooped in, one by one, to receive the third degree about what had happened the previous September at the Las Vegas Hilton.

Most of them didn't talk, but enough of them did.

CONSIDERING THE OUTRAGE IT IGNITED, THE FINAL REPORT ON THE NIS investigation is an unlikely document.

Released on April 30, 1992, the NIS Tailhook report is impenetrable, unwieldy, impossible. There is no title page, no index, no table of contents. The blocky sans-serif print is difficult to read, its computer-generated characters soft, gray and broken, created by a photocopier with toner levels at low ebb.

The report is made up of the rawest of raw material. Its features all seem to run together: the prosecutive summaries, the complaints of the victims, the reports of interviews with suspects, the sworn statements of witnesses. Dates are jumbled.

The text consists simply of interview after interview, all "redacted," as the government calls it, which means edited for privacy of the individuals involved. The heavy blue pencil of the government censor gives the pages a gap-toothed, jack-o'-lantern effect. Some pages show more gap than text.

"No, we didn't put out a big PR thing," said Bill Hudson, an ex-El Paso, Texas, cop and head of the criminal division at the NIS throughout the Tailhook investigation. Which was putting it mildly. The NIS report was a clay-tablet-and-cuneiform text for a computer age. As an attempt to lay to rest the myriad questions about Tailhook, it failed miserably.

There was plenty of dirt, however. The lurid party practices of the naval aviators were trotted out for national display. Witnesses described the flier wrapping his "crank" in a woman's waist-length hair, the minor "left on the floor at the location where she was stripped . . . totally naked." A bartender remembered a woman who was "visibly upset and her clothes were stretched and torn"; she was being chased by three men, who "were laughing and urging the woman to come back to them." There were detailed analyses of the gauntlet's properties, what it was and wasn't: "not constant but more a flowing thing," "a good-natured, fun practice which was conducted with a jocular-like [sic] attitude."

But what the NIS report didn't have, what it lacked in spades, was names. There was no payoff.

Later on, the NIS would insist that the report probably should not have been released at all, that it was an internal document, about as suitable for public consumption as a police blotter.

The Naval Inspector General's office released its piggyback report at the same time. Summed up in a media-friendly six pages was the IG's gloss on the NIS findings: a terse catalog of sexual assault, stonewalling and systemic hostility toward women in the naval aviation community. Faced with the daunting prospect of plowing through the NIS report itself, many people in Congress, in the media and in the Navy itself opted for the streamlined IG version.

The IG noted a "marked absence of moral courage and personal integrity," "a gang mentality," "a sense in the TACAIR community that what happened on the third floor was acceptable social conduct."

It also noted that the gauntlet had existed at least for the past two years at Tailhook conventions, probably for the past five. It concluded that much of the behavior examined fell into the category of "conduct unbecoming an officer." But the IG, too, failed to identify any suspects.

Dirt, but no names. Crimes, but no one held responsible. It was a lethal combination, one which was to twist the spine of the public response to Tailhook from that point on. The media stepped in to act as purveyors and packagers of the information. And the press quickly decided that what it had on its hands was a travesty of justice. Eric Schmitt of the *New York Times* pegged the most dramatic tally (on page 14—Tailhook wasn't yet front-page news), the proportion of indecent assault suspects to number of victims:

> A Navy investigation into sexual abuse at a convention of naval aviators last September has found that dozens of women, rather than the five or so who initially filed complaints, were assaulted.
>
> Further, the investigators have been able to identify only two suspects despite evidence that scores of officers took part in the assaults. The investigators attribute that outcome of their inquiry to the refusal of many pilots, some with senior rank, to cooperate with them.

A consensus quickly formed. For a press corps that had cut its teeth on Watergate, the behavior of the Navy pilots targeted by the investigation was instantly recognizable.

"When investigators questioned the pilots, they ran into a stone wall of silence and lies," reporter David Martin told Dan Rather in a lead segment on the "CBS Evening News." Twenty-six women, he stated, testified they had been assaulted or molested at what he somewhat disingenuously labeled the Tailhook "cocktail party."

Rather also featured the electronically altered voices of Lisa Reagan and Marie Weston, and quoted Navy Undersecretary Dan Howard, who explained the failure of the investigative process he had managed by saying that some of the pilots interviewed had flat-out lied.

Such was the overwhelming image communicated to the public in the wake of the NIS report. Male sexual transgression linked with female innocence, victimization and accusation. A stone wall of silence in response to a botched investigation, and a lingering smell of cover-up.

What left the deepest impression was the assault on justice itself. Whatever the merits of the he-said-she-said Tailhook testimony, there was a blatant imbalance here that offended what was customarily identified as "the American tradition of fair play." The sense of outrage over this state of affairs would become the engine that would drive the Tailhook scandal for many months to come.

TAILHOOK'S "MAN-BRUTE/WOMAN-VICTIM" EQUATION ALIGNED ITSELF neatly with prevailing cultural mythology, now electrified by the currency of the Anita Hill–Clarence Thomas hearings. As a broad-brush characterization of reality, it was reasonably accurate. But it wasn't necessarily the whole truth.

While the press could characterize the NIS findings in a thoroughly black-and-white manner, in substance the report contained not only shades of gray, but a crazed sort of herringbone.

A central paradox concerned the accounts given to the NIS by women who attended Tailhook. One would have expected to find anger, resentment, or at the very least, an eagerness to see justice done. Again and again, these expectations were confounded.

NIS's Bill Hudson: "If you read through the statements, you can find that they described approximately fifty women who went through the gauntlet. And many of these women were described by the people standing there as willing participants. They said some of them went through a second time or a third time. We would have liked to have identified some of them, because they might be able to recognize some of the gauntlet participants. But the only victims that we were able to find were the ones that were identified by boyfriends or people that were interviewed. None of these people were coming to us. They weren't lined up coming in to report assaults."

Sexual assault victims who are unwilling to come forward represent a familiar paradigm for investigators. What perplexed the NIS agents more was the almost surreal gulf that existed in women's perceptions of the Tailhook convention in general and the gauntlet in particular. There were women who were haunted by being assaulted, and others who professed to enjoy, even relish the experience.

One woman told investigators that she had traversed the hallway many times on Saturday night. She remembered walking down the corridor with two girlfriends at one point and seeing ten to fifteen men standing on both sides of the hallway. She and her friends, according to the report, "were carrying beer in their hands as they walked down the hallway."

As she went past the group of men—a trip of some twenty feet that took her less than a minute—some of them "reached out and pinched her on the buttocks." She "stated she was laughing the entire time and was not offended by the situation." They didn't even spill their beer, she said. The woman "strongly stated that at no time was she touched or grabbed in any of her private areas, and she did not observe anyone being touched or grabbed in such a manner."

A golf course attendant from the Marine Corps air base at Fallon, Nevada, was asked to tend bar in one of the hospitality suites. She staunchly defended the behavior of the men at the convention, and told investigators she had walked down the hall by herself many times without being bothered or touched.

"She said that a few comments were made but she said that they were regular comments and they did not bother her at all," read the NIS agent's summary of her interview. "She said that everyone she came in contact with treated her very nicely. She said that she was even in the hot tub with 10 men and no one made any advances toward her." In fact, she stated that "she had received worse treatment from persons at the golf course!"

The exclamatory gloss suggests a deliberate mind-set on the part of the NIS agent receiving the woman's testimony, and brings up the question of objectivity, which lingers in the background of the entire document. The effect of the observer upon the observed is less than clear-cut here, but the image of the prototypical NIS agent that comes across in these interviews is not of a person attempting to cover up or deny the existence of serious wrongdoing.

That said, there is throughout a flavor of the Puritan's double standard. The report is full of hearsay evidence by women about women, describing a female who "strutted" through the gauntlet "wearing only a USN member's white hat, a Sinatra T-shirt and panties pulled up to expose most of her bottom"; another, a groupie who "stripped to her thong"; others who "wear enticing dress, and readily go down the gauntlet whooping and hollering," who "incite the male behavior."

Some of this fit all too easily into the stereotype of the party-girl. However, the cumulative impression of the NIS report was undeniably one of a wide spectrum of female experiences at Tailhook, much wider, at any rate, than was portrayed at the time of its release in the press.

That was true of men too. While many male aviators were assaultive during the convention, and presented a stone wall to the investigation, others actively intervened in the assaults and were more than forthcoming afterward. One officer, for example, eventually led NIS agents to Lieutenant Gregory "Goose" Geiss, identified as one of the instigators of the gauntlet. This witness and a friend had stationed themselves at the gauntlet's head, "about 10 feet from where the guys [had] organized themselves." They leaned against the wall and waited. The officer told investigators that, "A woman approached the gauntlet and she was hesitant to go through the crowd. She leaned against the wall near us and I told her that if she went through she would get touched and if you really need to get to the other end of the hall I would take an alternate route." He told this to two women, and both went the roundabout way.

Then the two men were approached by Geiss, an aviator who, like them, was assigned to the naval air station at Whidbey Island. Geiss "got very close to our faces," the witness related to NIS agents.

He said if we didn't like what was going on to leave, that we didn't deserve to be on the third deck. He asked if this was our first Tailhook. We both said yes and he replied with "that figures." He said the gauntlet was a Tailhook tradition and we were going against tradition and made us feel that we weren't players, real aviators or one of the guys. We tried to talk to him and confronted him about violating the women. He said the women knew what they were in for when they came to Tailhook. He didn't seem concerned with how the women felt about being touched. We stood there and listened to him for about 10 minutes. It was obvious that he had been drinking. He told us that a girl had passed out in the hallway earlier and her clothing was removed. I don't really know what happened. He was really proud of the behavior of the guys in the gauntlet. We thought we got through to him because he seemed to understand our point. We reminded him that we were naval officers and this type of conduct was unbecoming of a naval officer. We didn't want to be associated with a group of men that attacked and molested women and treated women so rudely. He kept defending the gauntlet tradition. He said we would be here in three years doing the same thing.

THE FIRST TIME KARA HULTGREEN WENT UP SOLO TO DO "AERIAL combat maneuvering" ("ACM," or dogfighting) in an A-4, as part of the Navy's routine flight training program, her instructor was another woman. "Like a big catfight—meowr! I'm like, 'I thought there was a rule against females flying together.' Because I'd never flown with her the whole time I'd been in the squadron."

What jet pilots love to do more than anything else is describe their aerial encounters. On these occasions, they break from their usual laconic prose style and rise into only slightly less laconic poetry. Intent and gesticulatory, they mimic the high-altitude maneuvers of jet aircraft, until their hand motions resemble complicated Indian mudra. The specifics of the flight stories differ. Always, though, they feature spins, dives, flame-outs, with remarkable, miraculous recoveries each time. Again, just beneath the surface is the unalterable moral of every jet-jock lesson. I'm invincible. Look at this, I can fly in the face of death—and come out alive!

Female pilots are just as likely to buy into this as the males. Hultgreen and her female A-4 instructor were doing some "nose-high" maneuvers that day, pointing the front part of the jet toward the sky. Following behind the instructor, Hultgreen suddenly realized her plane was out of control, "departing" (entering a spin) violently. "I did all the procedures to recover, and still we're tumbling out of the sky, end over end. I'm getting smashed up against the canopy, just all over the place. I'm like, 'What the hell?' I'm checking my altimeter. The first time I looked we're at 18,000 feet, and then it's winding down like you wouldn't believe. I'm getting thrown all over the place trying to keep the controls neutral and make sure my ailerons were neutralized, because in an A-4 that's real important, your ailerons will put you into a spin—they're the surfaces on the wings that make you turn. So I'm looking in the mirror at my ailerons, making sure they're level, and looking at my turn needle and my airspeed and my angle of attack to check to see if I'm actually in a spin, because then you have other procedures to do.

"At 10,000 feet if you're out of control you're supposed to eject. So, I'm tumbling out of the sky, I'm waiting for this airplane to recover. Usually the nose points down and you accelerate and you fly away and it's not such a big deal. All of a sudden I hear '14,000 feet. Check your ailerons,' and it was the other airplane just sort of following me down. And I'm like, 'What do you think I'm doing in here, filing my nails? Of course I'm checking my ailerons, you idiot!' Then I looked at my altimeter, it's going to 11,000 feet. I'm like, 'Oh man, the next time I look at that gauge I'm supposed to eject.' I thought, I don't want to have to eject. I'm not going to be able to get my wings on the fourth of August. That was July '89; I was on my last couple of flights before graduation. All these things go through your mind in a nano-second: 'I'll have to call my dad, he'll have to get his plane reservation changed' I'm just like, 'I can't eject out of here! Jeez!' I'm scope-locked on the airspeed, because I didn't want to look at the altimeter anymore, because then I'd have to eject. We'll wait till it gets to five— to hell with 10,000 feet, we'll give it an extra couple of thousand, see what happens.

"Suddenly my airspeed went from zero to like 200 knots, boom. I pulled out of it at around 7,500. The heart's going a mile a minute. So I went right back up on the lead plane and we just went and did some more dogfighting. It was so funny, because I kept thinking, I don't want her to think that I'm going to be less aggressive now. So I do this max performance turn to join up, we did some more engagements and then we went home. The thing is, I never departed the A-4 again, I never made that same mistake. I made sure that my airspeed was in my scan."

It was strange, but the same attitude of invincibility influenced the Tailhook investigation when the NIS agents began to make calls on female aviators who had been in Las Vegas. Hultgreen was visited by NIS investigators, and duly gave them a full account of her encounter with a butt-biter. But the attitude of the NIS investigators infuriated her. "They called me a victim!" she said, indignant. "Certainly nothing happened to me that I didn't handle. Nobody maliciously tried to assault me. So the guy was just being an idiot. Once I made it per-fectly clear that I was not receptive to his advances it was over."

Hultgreen rejected the NIS characterization because it would challenge the very core of her self-image—a self-image based on the same feelings of bulletproof invincibility that existed in the hearts and minds of male aviators. It was such an essential component of being able to walk out to the flight line every day. *Nothing will happen to me that I can't handle.* You had to believe that, or you couldn't function.

There was a crucial difference between the male and female

versions of being bulletproof. Kara Hultgreen could still summon a
fiery anger about the physical assaults in Las Vegas. Just because she
refused to let anyone term her a victim did not mean she withdrew
compassion from others. "They say, 'You see, Kara, it didn't happen to
you because you were smart enough to leave the third floor.' Or, 'You
were smart enough not to go in there alone.' Or, 'You were smart
enough not to go near that hallway.' Now, does that make it right? No.
I don't agree with that attitude. That attitude really pisses me off."

If flying jets taught arrogance, taught invincibility, there were
also other lessons to be learned from it, too, lessons that were closer to
humility. A close friend of Hultgreen's in flight school had crashed his
plane and died. This was the guy who had turned her on to the whole
idea of flying with the Navy to begin with, when they were in ROTC
together at the University of Texas. But just before they were to go to
the boat to qualify in A-4's, he had made a mistake from which he
couldn't recover.

"It's not that big a deal that he died—the hard part about all that
is when you have to go to the funeral and see his parents. And you just
sit there and you think, 'That could be my parents.' The mother's in
tears, and everyone's crying. You're like, 'That would be bad.' But I
don't feel half as bad for him, because he died doing something that
he really liked doing."

Don't cry for me, Argentina. The guy knew what the risks were.
If this attitude seems cold and unforgiving, there was a purity to it,
also, a clear-eyed sense of life's possibilities, both terrible and courageous. And it was an ask-no-quarter attitude that fed the reactions
toward what happened on the third deck, on the part of Kara Hultgreen and a lot of other female fliers who had been there.

"When I went to Tailhook I certainly knew what Tailhook was all
about. I had heard about the third floor, and I knew that I probably
didn't want to be up there after about nine. I wasn't going there
fearing for my life, but I certainly went there realizing exactly what
goes on and taking precautions so I wouldn't get caught in a situation I
wouldn't want to have to deal with."

———

IN MAY 1992, A WEEK AFTER THE NIS TAILHOOK REPORT HAD BEEN made public, Barbara Pope met with Secretary of the Navy Lawrence Garrett. Justice clearly had not been served by the NIS report, Pope told him. How was it possible, she demanded, that so much money and time had been spent and so little fruit borne from the two investigations?

Pope strongly recommended that the people who hadn't come forward but who obviously knew something—the operational, senior-level folks, the commanding officers of the squadrons who sponsored party suites—had to be called on the carpet. And she told her boss that she would have no choice but to resign rather than stand by the report that was now in the hands of the public.

Faced with a horrendous public affairs hemorrhage in Tailhook, Garrett could ill-afford to lose Barbara Pope now. Her resignation would be a devastating blow. The Navy was already suffering from a public image that characterized it as brutish, anarchic and sexually Cro-Magnon.

At the beginning of June, Garrett sent a memo to his operational commanders, the two men who represented the Navy and Marines on the Chiefs of Staff: Chief of Naval Operations Frank Kelso and Commandant of the Marine Corps Carl E. Mundy, Jr. Consciously or not, the memo revealed that Garrett had aligned himself with Barbara Pope's vision of a broader, more systemic response to Tailhook.

Not two but seventy Tailhook suspects, the memo stated, would be referred to the chain of command "for appropriate action." The files now included six assault suspects, fifty-seven people who had "been at the 'gauntlet' or other areas where inappropriate conduct occurred," five who had allegedly "violated standards of conduct" and two more who had impeded the investigations.

In the memo, Garrett used conventional military rhetoric to condemn the conduct of "certain of our naval aviators," which, he said, had "stained the fabric of this institution." Other comments even more directly reveal the influence of Mrs. Pope.

> We cannot—and will not—tolerate the demeaning and insensitive behavior and attitudes of the past. Our goal in the Department of the Navy must be to cultivate through education an environment where actions demeaning to women are as a matter of course considered unacceptable—and, even more, where behavior and attitudes reflect respect for women and the valuable contribution they make as an integral part of the Navy/Marine Corps team.

On Barbara Pope's favorite subject of accountability, Garrett went further. He directed that a group of Scrambled Eggs be assembled, headed by Admiral Frank Kelso, to dun the squadron commanders who had been at Tailhook and find out what they knew and when they knew it.

"The leadership responsibility of squadron commanding officers," Garrett stated ominously, "[must] be given particular attention."

Garrett's June 2 memo also created a working group called the Standing Committee on Women in the Navy and Marine Corps, which would report directly to him, to make recommendations on initiatives that would enhance opportunities for and eliminate bias against women. The Standing Committee would be chaired by Barbara Spyridon Pope.

The best-laid plans of Larry Garrett and Barbara Pope were suddenly swept away, however. There was no time for the punitive actions and disciplinary measures outlined in Garrett's message. Suddenly the secretary himself was sucked into the Tailhook maelstrom.

THE BIZARRE THING ABOUT THE FIFTY-FIVE-PAGE "SUPPLEMENTAL REPORT" to the original NIS investigation was the way it just materialized. Questions about why it had not been attached to the original report seemed to baffle everyone to whom they were put. It was a ghost report.

Its content, however, was real enough. New material placed Larry Garrett on the Hilton patio, in proximity to the most outrageous of the party suites.

The Secretary of the Navy, read the sworn testimony of a Marine captain interviewed by NIS agents, had made an appearance in the infamous "Rhino Suite," the same room occupied by the Kahlúa-and-cream-spewing rhino that served as the mascot for a rowdy Marine squadron. Many senior officers, stated the officer, had "made it a point to drop by the suite" in the course of the convention.

Perhaps most awkward for Garrett, the NIS had known of this information as early as mid-February, but had not seen fit to release it with the April 30 report.

The material contained in the supplemental report was collected by the NIS agent in charge of the Tailhook case. Because none of the testimony indicated criminal wrongdoing, the control agent, employing the NIS "just-the-facts" mind-set, did not deem it germane to the investigation.

When Garrett's June 2 memo widened the purlieu of Navy's response to Tailhook to include "leadership responsibility," interviews placing him at the scene suddenly became very relevant indeed. The Secretary of the Navy, as the military metaphor goes, was hoist by his own petard.

In a statement released on June 16, Garrett belatedly acknowledged having attended the party after delivering his keynote banquet address on the final night of Tailhook. He admitted to socializing for forty-five minutes on the hotel patio. He claimed to have seen no "inappropriate or offensive" conduct. But witnesses asserted they had seen Garrett enter the VMFP-3 suite to get a cold beer, which would put him no more than thirty feet from where the worst of the sexual assaults were taking place.

Garrett, saying "the Navy's ability adequately to investigate itself in this instance has been placed in question," called in a bigger gun. He requested the Department of Defense Inspector General (IG) to conduct yet another probe into the entire Tailhook incident.

Suddenly, it seemed, the Navy was back at square one.

Part Two

IN HARM'S WAY

I WISH TO HAVE NO CONNECTION WITH ANY SHIP THAT DOES
NOT SAIL FAST, FOR I INTEND TO GO IN HARM'S WAY.

—John Paul Jones

Chapter Five

———

SEASON OF THE WITCH

FOR EIGHT MONTHS, FROM SEPTEMBER 1991 TO MAY 1992, THE Tailhook affair had managed to survive lacking a basic food group in the diet of sensationalism, red meat. Students of the contemporary school for scandal name certain necessary qualities in the making of a bona fide national fiasco. Sex helps, of course. A convenient, media-friendly handle. A colorful cast of characters. Something real at stake, preferably jail, or perhaps a Senate confirmation. There've been so many recently that they tend to blur, but a few rise out of the weird cavalcade of our sequential obsession and manage to speak to the Zeitgeist in some indefinable but undeniable way.

What Tailhook had so far failed to supply was that sine qua non of scandal, a warm body. The public had gangs of rogue aviators, females run like prisoners through a gauntlet and perhaps most importantly, a still nameless "admiral's aide" who had started the whole thing.

For seven months, Lieutenant Paula Coughlin had remained anonymous to the press while she endured the slow burn of the NIS investigation. She was interviewed by agents a half-dozen times. She had duly performed the surreal, mechanical tasks that are assigned to the assault victim, had advised the police artist who put together the composites of suspects and paged through photo lineups. Some of the process was a nightmare itself. A Naval Investigative Service agent named Laney Spigener, one of a small team originally assigned to work with her, had invited Coughlin for a drive in the country, pestered her with late night phone calls in which he asked her height and weight, offered to bring over Chinese takeout. He called her "Sweet Cakes" while she was reviewing photos of aviators who were assault suspects.

But a full eight months after the Tailhook convention, after the NIS and IG reports had run aground, Paula Coughlin still had not been named. The Byzantine social protocols surrounding sexual assault are such that the press could not decide unilaterally to identify her; when New York's *Amsterdam News* decided to name the victim in the "wilding" attack on a Central Park jogger in 1989, the newspaper had unleashed a torrent of scorn upon itself.

Tailhook might never have been launched into the public consciousness if not for Coughlin filing an official complaint. And it might never have made the front pages had she not decided to go public with her story. There were already quite a few in the Navy, especially in the insular aviation community, who knew who she was. There was some localized support for her actions, but it was accompanied by a steady and widespread campaign of vilification. She was a poor sport, a lousy pilot, a slut who had asked for it.

"Little Miss Paula Coughlin," as a Miramar Tomcat squadron commander put it, "wasn't so innocent, either."

Rumors about her spread through the Navy. Paula was a party-girl, a "player." She had "teased" the men in the hallway the night before; she "was doing . . . guys" in the party suites. Gandhi swore he shaved Paula Coughlin's legs, not once but twice and once while she was in uniform. She was doing "body shots"—sucking tequila out of a man's navel, or getting sucked. What she wore that night was soberly reported as increasingly fantastic variations on the scarlet lady's attire: a "red tight dress," a "leather miniskirt," a "mini leather skirt and halter top," a "short miniskirt that doesn't cover much and a very low-cut shirt."

Classic blame-the-victim stuff. It was easier to paint Paula Coughlin in lurid colors than to try to fathom what was going on between men and women in the Navy. Coughlin was a whistle-blower, too, and whistle-blowers have had decidedly uneven fates everywhere, but most especially in the military. Eventually, all this became part of Coughlin's reason for allowing her name to be used in the press. There was no such thing as the safe haven of anonymity. If she was going to put up with garbage being thrown her way, she might as well step forward. She was tired of feeling as though she should be the one with something to hide. Plus, she still thought of the Navy as "her" Navy, as something that could be, should be, fixed.

"I love the Navy," were Coughlin's first words on "ABC World News Tonight" on June 24, 1992. "The Navy's my life. I'm thirty years old, and I have a dog, but I'm in the Navy—*that's* my family."

When the NIS and the IG released their reports at the end of April, Coughlin had waited for something to happen. All she saw were Navy officials banging their drums about their "zero tolerance" policy —the same one that had been in place the night she was assaulted in the corridor of the Hilton. They were "saying, 'It's fixed, it's fixed, it's fixed.' " But she knew it was not. In coming forward, Coughlin wanted something fairly basic: to get the Navy to make it so its men could no longer do what they had done to her.

So, after consulting with the Navy PR reps and after spending the long weekend of June 20 searching her soul, she decided to come forward. She was helped in her decision by the righteous indignation and justifiable anger of her mother, Rena, the wife of a career Navy flier. The staff at CHINFO, ever the picture of bureaucratic efficiency, even provided Coughlin with media training so that she could, in effect, fire a bullet into the heart of the Old Navy.

"I was attacked by naval officers and Marine Corps officers who knew who I was. And it was a sport for them. It was a good time," she told ABC. "It was the most frightened I've ever been in my life," she told John Lancaster of the *Washington Post*.

American women could relate to the Paula Coughlin they met on the news that night. Baby boomers saw in her cropped hair and forth-right manner someone they recognized, although in military guise—a nineties career woman. There was something else evident in Cough-lin's face, too. Here was a woman irreparably harmed, but here also was a victim who had bounced back, a victim with a mission. She was Anita Hill's little sister.

"My message to women," she said, "is don't tolerate it."

Coughlin had managed to do what the scores of government agents and pages of government reports had failed to do. She put a human face on the victims of the Tailhook gauntlet.

She convinced an old Navy pilot in the White House, George Bush, that the case was not simply about a party that had gotten out of hand. Two days after Coughlin "came out" as a sexual assault victim, between an end-of-day policy briefing and the black-tie wedding-re-hearsal dinner of his daughter, George and Barbara Bush met with Coughlin at the White House. The President wept as Coughlin de-scribed her experience at Tailhook. He assured Coughlin that this time around, Department of Defense investigators would succeed in finding the men who had assaulted her.

That same day, June 26, 1992, H. Lawrence Garrett III took "full responsibility" for the scandal and resigned as the Secretary of the U.S. Navy.

THERE WOULD BE NO DANCING GIRLS AT THIS YEAR'S TOMCAT Follies.

So came the word down the chain of command at Miramar in that Jacobean summer of 1992. Every year the Top Guns of "Fight-ertown, U.S.A." held a little mini-Tailhook convention, limited to Pacific Fleet F-14 guys only. None of the random A-6 and F/A-18 pilots, the P-3 fliers and civilian hangers-on, the Johnny-come-lately helicopter guys who had recently polluted the annual Tailhook Sym-posium. This was pure, unalloyed fighter-jock stuff. For a full week, the Grumman sales reps came to curry favor. There was a lot of golf, a lot of beer, a lot of epoxy-style male bonding. All culminating in a no-women-allowed mummer's show called the Tomcat Follies.

"Historically, it's been just the guys and they tape the windows shut and they do all kinds of pornographic stuff," said one woman stationed at Miramar who had observed the progress of the Follies over the years. The dancing girls were the most visible emblem of the unreconstructed, smoker-style nature of the event. They didn't even get naked, usually—just came on stage between skits and performed their fifty-dollar no-frills routine.

But this was the new, improved, post-Tailhook Navy, so the bump-and-grind got bumped. The F-14 jocks saw themselves as martyrs on this issue, but they knew how to obey orders. Their credo was "Semper Gumby"—Be Flexible. They'd cede the dancers.

Strippers weren't the real point, anyway. What's most apparent to outsiders about the Tomcat Follies—and numerous events like it which seem to infest every sector of Navy life, such as the "Fo'c'sle Follies" at the end of a cruise, the "Wetting Down" to celebrate an officer's promotion, the "Dining In" feast that represents every wardroom's stab at elegance—is how strangely square they are. There is something about them of Judy Garland gushing "Let's put on a show!" to Mickey Rooney. That, and a dash of Sally's Hideaway, the transvestite circus in New York's Times Square, since drag at these events is de rigueur.

At the Tomcat Follies, the real point was the roast. Squadrons competed to come up with the foulest skit, the more insulting, the better. No one was exempt. "In aviation, nothing's sacred," said one A-6 bomber pilot. "If you're the fat guy in the ready room, they're gonna give you hell. Anything you do. You've got to have a thick skin and just press on."

The Tomcat Follies were watched over by a curious totem object, a statuette that had been brought back from Japan by Navy fighter pilots in 1961. A male raccoon with a bulging belly, eyes that lit up and a glowing navel, it resembled the Tripmaster Monkey of Bud-

dhist mythology, a trickster or a dybbuk. The fighter jocks called him
Tanuki. He sported a natty coolie brim and clutched a ceramic bottle
of sake. He was the patron saint and familiar of bars and pubs across
Japan, the original party animal. The aviators nicknamed him
"Mutha."

Winning the Mutha trophy in 1992 turned out to be less important, in the long run, than one skit which demonstrated the prickly
atmosphere of the Navy early that summer. This particular production, put on the boards at the Miramar Officers Club by Fighter
Squadron 51 ("the Screaming Eagles"), targeted not the fat guy in the
ready room but a female congresswoman who, due to her outspoken-
ness as a member of the House Armed Services Committee, was often
adopted as the military guy's prime nemesis.

All the more so in the summer of '92, when the prospect of a
Democrat in the White House had many denizens of the Pentagon in
a cold sweat. The unfathomable might happen: Pat Schroeder might
end up the nation's next Secretary of Defense. The Colorado member
of the House of Representatives had the track record. As a senior
member of the House Armed Services Committee, she had champi-
oned issues such as better housing, improved child care, higher hazardous duty pay for military members sent on dangerous assignments.
But she had also introduced legislation to overturn the ban on gays,
and to open combat jobs to women. She had been vociferous on the
subject of Tailhook. In Navy demonology, Schroeder dwelt close to
the fire.

The Tomcat Follies skit started by lampooning the ban on strippers. "They started playing music and five guys came out dancing with
these posters of women in bikinis," said one Tomcat squadron commander who was in the audience. "These were going to be our dancing girls."

Then the curtains opened on an elaborate Rube Goldberg con-
traption, with connecting gutters that angled gradually down to the
stage. A Screaming Eagle placed a bowling ball doused with lighter
fluid at the top of the tableau. The great ball of fire lumbered down

the first gutter. As it hit a hairpin turn, it tripped a flag. "Hickory," read the banner's one-word message. The ball continued on its fiery path until it tripped two more banners, reading "Dickory" and "Dock." When the bowling ball neared the bottom of the display it flipped up a last sign. Given the company, it was curious that the punchline was bowdlerized: "Pat Schroeder can suck my c---k." ("It could stand for clock," interpreted the Tomcat CO, "but also had the other connotation.") Then the ball rolled on to crush a clay effigy of Mutha.

Apart from giving the impression that Navy aviators might have too much time on their hands, the skit seemed "vanilla" enough to fall within the boundaries of the acceptable. The only response, recalled the Tomcat CO, was "the senior guys there rolled their eyes and looked [at each other] like 'that was pretty close.' " The Tomcat Follies were over. The debris from the skits— including the juiced nursery rhymes of the Screaming Eagles —were cleared from the stage and stashed out on the patio of the O Club.

That evening, June 18, a retired Navy Nurse Corps captain named Edna Peters dined with a group of friends at the Miramar O Club. En route from her table to the Mongolian barbecue buffet, she looked out the windows and noticed the detritus of the Tomcat Follies on the patio. She read the suggestion the Screaming Eagles had made to Pat Schroeder. And her response was killer swift. On June 21, after trying in vain to contact base commander Curtis Schantz by telephone (he was away on business), Captain Peters sent her letter of complaint directly to Washington, D.C., to Admiral Frank Kelso, the Chief of Naval Operations. On July 1, the Department of the Navy announced that two senior officers would be stripped of their commands for the duration of a formal inquiry. The two were Commander Dave Tyler of the Screaming Eagles and Captain Robert F. Braden, a twenty-four-year-veteran who just happened by the Miramar Officers Club for a drink that afternoon and was the senior-ranking officer present.

"I was really amazed," Pat Schroeder commented mildly. "They have a whole group of people who don't believe that things have to change." Ultimately, over the course of the summer of '92, the Tomcat Follies would take down more officers to date than had Tailhook itself: five senior officers removed from command (two were later reinstated, including Braden); eighteen junior officers disciplined.

The whole incident was a barometer of the New Navy, circa summer 1992. There would be others.

ONE OF THE MOST IMPORTANT SECRETARYSHIPS IN THE U.S. NAVY'S two-century history was also one of the briefest. When J. Daniel Howard assumed the post of Acting Secretary of the Navy upon Garrett's resignation, he lasted less than three weeks in the job. George Bush quickly replaced him with a second Acting Secretary—Sean O'Keefe, a Defense Department bean-counter who was a protégé of Secretary of Defense Richard Cheney. Howard was booted back down to Under.

But Dan Howard's brief tenure atop the Navy civilian hierarchy was crucial because he provided the single ingredient that had been lacking in the official reaction to the Tailhook affair. It was a mea culpa of sorts, but one that went beyond the company line thus far. Three days after he was appointed acting secretary, Dan Howard got up in front of the Army auditorium at the Pentagon. The auditorium was overwarm. The Pentagon had been built by General Leslie Groves, the same man who would go on to build the atomic bomb, but the huge building was notorious for its temperature control problems. It was freezing in the winter and sweltering in summer. Howard turned the heat up even further when he told 300 Navy and Marine Corps senior officers—generals, admirals, captains, colonels and commanders—that something had gone wrong not only on the third floor of the Las Vegas Hilton, but in the Navy as a whole.

His aim, he told the assembled officers, was "to dismantle a decaying culture, a residual fabric of counter-productive and unworthy attitudes." And he spoke directly of what would befall those men who refused to get with the program:

Anyone still wasting time disparaging women, fighting their integration or subjecting them to sexual harassment is a dragging anchor for the entire Navy and Marine Corps. Anyone who still believes in the image of a drunken, skirt-chasing warrior back from the sea is about half a century out of date. If that's you, we don't need you because we've got places we need to go, and not much time to get there.

Howard had come out of the world of public relations, which accounted for a little of the rhetorical punch of his words. A Tennessee native and former Marine, he had his crisis-management skills honed as a State Department spokesperson in the early eighties, where he handled the Beirut Marine barracks bombing, then the fall of the Marcos regime. He'd been a Reagan White House spokesperson and chief Pentagon spokesperson under Defense Secretary Frank Carlucci. So like Barbara Pope—with whom he had shared those weekly status meetings as the Tailhook scandal unfolded—Howard was a dyed-in-the-wool Reaganite, and thus an unlikely bearer of bad news for traditionalists. But he had also ridden herd over both the NIS and IG investigations into Tailhook, so here was a man who knew whereof he spoke.

"These things happened right under our noses," said Howard of the Tailhook assaults. "They were committed by a few, but, ladies and gentlemen, they were excused by far too many, and by all the leaders over the years who turned a blind or bemused eye to the crude, alcohol-inspired antics of a few idiots in our ranks."

Howard outlined a five-point plan designed to rid the Navy of its "stone-age" attitudes. He said there would be no delay in the daylong, service-wide "stand-down" first proposed by Barbara Pope the previous winter, and ordered by Garrett before he decamped. Howard endorsed the formation of the Standing Committee on Women in the Navy and Marine Corps, called upon the Tailhook Association to disband and proposed making sexual harassment a separate offense under the Uniform Code of Military Justice.

He also let Navy and Marine Corps pilots know that now was the time to come forward and tell all they knew about what actually happened in Las Vegas: "I can expect you to search your conscience, to uphold your standards of professionalism . . . I can also ask you to recall the face and the words of Lieutenant Paula Coughlin and realize that this was not some kind of victimless lark. People were hurt, and the institution was hurt. Now is the time for honor, and honor means honesty."

Reporters were barred from Howard's tongue-lashing, but the acting secretary ensured that his comments would reach beyond the Beltway. On July 2, the Chief of Naval Information released a transcript of Howard's remarks to the major media. Then Howard took one step further out of the bunker by inviting a handful of journalists for an intimate one-on-one in his office. Rumpled, hound-faced, Howard was clearly a different-style Navy leader. During this audience, he used the Tomcat Follies as another opportunity to put the Old Navy on notice. "What it tells you," he told the *Times*'s Eric Schmitt, "is that we're an organization of almost one million people, about 700,000 in uniform, and that on any given day you can be absolutely certain that somebody is doing something stupid somewhere."

"Idiots." "Stupid." These characterizations were not what Navy personnel were used to, especially coming from their civilian head. Dan Howard was soon enough replaced, by Defense Department Comptroller Sean O'Keefe. Dick Cheney was O'Keefe's mentor, yet could offer him nothing more than a post as another acting secretary. There was an election on, and no one relished the prospect of a confirmation hearing at this particular juncture in time. But clearly, there was a retrenchment going on, as both Cheney and O'Keefe tried to soften Howard's hard-ball stance. Introducing O'Keefe at a news conference the morning of July 7, Defense Secretary Cheney was careful to put on the Tailhook hair shirt—calling the events of Labor Day weekend 1991 "outrageous . . . behavior that is absolutely unacceptable"—but his remarks just as carefully avoided the global urge toward reform expressed a few days earlier by Howard. Tailhook, Cheney assured news reporters, was an "isolated incident that should not reflect on the Navy as a whole."

"I think it would be a mistake to look at these events as somehow indicating there's some kind of fundamental problem with the United States Navy," said Cheney, contradicting what his own acting secretary had said weeks previous. "For the nation, or the press, or anyone else to judge men and women in uniform based upon what a handful of individuals did in Las Vegas would be absolutely, totally unfair and irresponsible."

Two weeks later, Sean O'Keefe seconded Cheney's idea. While "a handful of junior officers . . . somehow have forgotten the term 'officer and a gentleman' didn't come from a Hollywood script," O'Keefe said, too many people in the Navy "have been tarred with a brush they don't deserve." O'Keefe, sounding like all of Richard Nixon in the throes of Watergate, promised to move the issue of Tailhook off the center stage, to focus on what he presented as more pressing, but more mundane concerns of his job.

Too late. The condor was already out of the closet, as Hunter Thompson would say, and Dan Howard's vision of the Navy as a sick beast could not be so easily erased. The titular head of the Navy had proposed that Tailhook was not an isolated occurrence, not an aberrant swerve from a tradition, but an excrescence of some deeper failing. Howard effectively transformed Tailhook from an event to a symptom.

It was this view of the scandal that would prevail in the press, in the public at large and, eventually, in the Navy itself. It was to be underscored by a cavalcade of Navy sexual transgressions, almost ludicrous in scope, which would come to light over the summer. Finally, it changed Tailhook from a problem of a specific institution, the U.S. Navy, and raised it into something capable of transforming women's status in society as a whole.

As OF SUMMER 1992, THERE WERE FOUR SEPARATE GOVERNMENT RE-
ports completed or being prepared on Tailhook. In addition to those
of the Navy Investigative Service and the Navy Inspector General, the
Department of Defense Inspector General and the House Armed
Services Committee had opened their own probes.

Congress had asserted its clout before. In a move calculated to
madden an institution dependent on Capitol Hill patronage, the Senate Armed Services Committee had frozen some 4,500 upcoming
Navy and Marine Corps promotions until all of the junior officers
under consideration were cleared of any involvement in the Tailhook
affair. The senators were just being careful. As one committee staffer
told a *Navy Times* reporter, "We don't want to approve an officer and
see him up for court-martial the next month."

Now it was the turn of the House. Two Democrats, Wisconsin's
Les Aspin and Beverly Byron of Maryland, promised the House
Armed Services Committee's report would concentrate on Tailhook as
a symptom, not an event. They wanted to examine contributing cultural issues—the Dan Howard open-choke approach to Tailhook, in
other words.

"At the root of sexual harassment is a series of cultural beliefs,
attitudes and perceptions about women," Aspin and Byron intoned.
"Unless we can change stereotypical thinking, sexual harassment training programs will likely prove ineffective." They examined two other
"watershed moments" in recent Navy history—the racial crisis of the
1970s and the drug crisis of the 1980s—to find out how to use
Tailhook as a lever for reform.

By far the most serious investigation of the '91 Tailhook incident
itself was being conducted that summer by agents from the Department of Defense Inspector General's office. The DoD IG probe was
initiated by Lawrence Garrett in one of his last actions before becoming a scandal casualty himself. It was mounted out of the general
dissatisfaction with the government's first two attempts to make sense
of Tailhook, the NIS and the IG investigations.

The DoD agents were more aggressive than those of the Naval

Investigative Service. Their inquiries, charged their subjects, were not so much interviews as humiliating interrogations in which the agents flouted procedures designed to protect the constitutional rights of military criminal suspects. According to fliers they questioned, the agents physically menaced subjects, forced them to undergo illegal polygraph tests and posed questions about topics unrelated to conduct at the convention, such as their preferences regarding masturbation and oral sex with their wives.

The atmosphere was particularly strained at the Marine Corps Air Station at El Toro, located in the parched tablelands north of San Diego. The infamous Rhino squadron, VMFP-3, was based in El Toro. Gregory Bonam, the Marine F/A-18 flier ID'd by Paula Coughlin as one of her attackers, had been stationed there the previous year. The DoD agents at El Toro gave off the determined sense of junkies working a collapsed vein. Five Marine aviators were under especially close scrutiny for offenses ranging from indecent assault to obstruction of justice.

Four separate government probes, and the Fifth Estate conducting an assault of its own. Summer 1992 had developed into the season of Tailhook for the media, with *Newsweek* and *Time* both doing cover stories, and wide-ranging play in the tabloids, televised and otherwise. Part of why the gentlepersons of the media became so impressed with Tailhook, throughout the long hot summer of 1992, was because of its now-demonstrated ability to bring low the mighty, like Navy secretaries and flag officers. Blood on the tracks.

The media also now had an element of which it had been sadly deprived in the immediate aftermath of Tailhook. Suddenly, in late July, there were visuals. Snapshots, really, grainy high-speed Ektachrome that could have been shot anywhere, at Navy parties from Virginia Beach to Treasure Island. Or, for that matter, as Tailhookers were fond of pointing out, at any large gathering of inebriates, from the Shriners to the American Medical Association. But these photos had been shot at Tailhook in September of 1991, and had eluded the concerted efforts of four government investigative bureaucracies for almost a full year. Throughout the NIS probe, interviewees had insisted that bringing a camera to a Tailhook convention was, by popular consensus, verboten. Now, at Miramar, a series of pictures—given over to agents, according to one source, by fliers who'd "had a bout of conscience"—showed the pale form of a naked young woman being led by Hilton security guards down the third-floor hotel corridor. The image was that of the inebriated seventeen-year-old who had gone through the gauntlet to be stripped, passed overhead and dumped in a heap on the floor.

Also in July, two Las Vegas civilians identified only as Kim and Stacey made their party snapshots available to Fox-TV for airing on "A Current Affair." Reporter Mike Watkiss said that the two women, who had been invited to the Hilton party by two fliers they met in a local restaurant, "knew what they were getting into." Despite the generalized rowdy behavior, the two said they didn't feel harassed by the male partygoers.

That wasn't what made the news. The image that found its way into print was of two sunburned men in alcohol-spattered shorts and T-shirts. They gave out heavy-lidded, "we've got wood!" grins to the camera. Their genitals, which hung outside their shorts, were electronically scrambled in the "family newspapers" and magazines of America, via a new computer process that effectively replaced the censor bar.

Suddenly it seemed the whole seagoing service was, like the Village People's seventies disco hit "In the Navy," dedicated to "find[ing] pleasure." In mid-July, a Navy commander who had received three Purple Hearts during Vietnam was tried in a general court-martial at Camp Pendleton for his actions at the birthday party of a female subordinate. He had spanked her "21 times with a wooden oar and hand to gratify his sexual desires."

"Unfortunately," Commander Steven C. Tolan said soberly in his closing statements to the court, "I set my professional demeanor aside and participated in the rough-housing with my troops. In retrospect, I should not have, nor would I in the future."

At the Naval War College, a civilian clerk announced her intention to sue a Navy captain who she said had written her in December 1990 to ask that she pose nude for photographs which would be used in a "fun but outrageous project" to improve sailors' morale on a Navy ship deployed to the Persian Gulf. "I will be right up front with you," read the captain's letter. "Regretfully, we don't know each other yet. I visited your office recently and was impressed! I returned and observed again. Even more impressed."

The skipper of a Navy salvage ship, USS *Safeguard*, based in the South Pacific, was relieved of duty after allegations surfaced concerning fraternization, sexual harassment and general misconduct (specifically, nude, co-ed swim parties on board). The male executive officer and a female petty officer, who were allegedly having an affair, were also removed from the ship.

The commander of Naval Hospital Bremerton, just outside Seattle, was relieved of duty in the aftermath of a case where a Nurse Corps lieutenant alleged she had been sandwiched in between two male petty officers, who then simulated sexual intercourse. The two men, maintained their attorney, were simply giving the nurse a "power hug" to reassure her after a reprimand from a senior officer. A subsequent investigation into "discipline problems" at the hospital brought forth nine additional allegations of sexual harassment.

All these incidents took on more weight in the wake of Tailhook. By Labor Day, everything the Navy touched seemed to turn ugly— even something as harmless as a Howie Mandel routine. The stand-up comic "invited women in the audience to perform oral sex on stage" during a performance at the Naval Academy. School officials subsequently demanded that Mandel return his fee. Academy Superintendent Thomas Lynch offered a public apology "for what he called Mandel's excessively profane and vulgar performance." Mandel's road manager, Nick Light, protested that Academy officials had signed off in advance on the show's material. "What is the first thing [the Navy] is fighting to protect?" he asked. "The First Amendment, freedom of speech."

It got to the point where even the Navy's West Coast hometown paper, the *San Diego Union-Tribune,* would portray the canceled '92 Tailhook convention with the following sly commentary. "With hard times depressing the local hotel industry, scandal has deprived [San Diego] of a major convention. . . . But all is not lost. Another lively group, Lifestyles, is expected back. That's the regional convention of swingers and swappers . . ."

"What was playing there up in the Pentagon scene," remembered Jack Fetterman, one of the first admirals to be disgraced in the wake of the Tailhook affair, "was the female issue, the sexual harassment issue, and all of a sudden, bang, the Inspector General's report —and the homosexual thing had the potential to get big. The media would have jumped on it."

There was something of a lion in winter quality to Jack Fetterman. He was at home in Pensacola, in his den. The world of admirals is largely a world of dens, offices and studies which, like his, represent the end result of every middle-class male's dream—total access to wood shops and engraving tools on ship after ship. It is an environment that is not decorated so much as it is bedecked, with photographs, plaques and memorabilia of a long Navy career, so that the walls lose their architectural meaning to become souvenir support systems.

On Fetterman's walls, there were "cruise plaques," fashioned of rosewood and brass, to commemorate overseas deployments. A baize-mounted collection of rifles and pistols. A pair of stained-glass wings. Shadow boxes and ship models. Fetterman could gaze around at the objects on the walls of his den and realize that while they might not mean anything to anyone else, when he looked at them he saw the faces of a great many people, all of whom he had served with, many of whom had died.

From this vantage point, with the purple Johnny-jump-ups out in the yard and the barbecue-scented sea breezes stirring the curtains, all that is going on "up in the Pentagon scene" seemed very far away. But it had reached out and snapped up Jack Fetterman as if he were no more than a between-meals snack. One of the crueler neologisms of the military is the antiseptic phrase "collateral damage," and Vice Admiral John H. Fetterman, Jr., could well be considered a collateral casualty of the Tailhook scandal.

"It's a good thing to kill an admiral from time to time," wrote Voltaire, but in Fetterman, Tailhook had claimed a strange victim. He was the author, chief proponent and overseer of something the Navy called its "core values" program, an attempt to educate its recruits in ethics, to screw their heads on right, morality-wise. Fetterman had done this while serving as Chief of Naval Education and Training in Pensacola, a billet that was going to be a suitably philosophical cap to a sterling career.

Fetterman had, as Navy people phrased it, "gone through all the wickets" to become one of the Navy's very top Top Guns. For thirty-seven years, he had served as an attack pilot in a career that encompassed a Naval Academy commission in the mid-fifties, fleet tours in the Korean and Vietnam wars and command of a combat squadron. He'd amassed 7,000 hours of flight time in twenty different types of naval aircraft, and accomplished 960 aircraft carrier landings. He'd done a stint at the Naval War College, a staff tour with the CNO and one at the Navy liaison office at the Senate. At one point or the other, Fetterman had led the aviation community on both coasts, most recently as the commander of the Naval Air Force, U.S. Pacific Fleet.

Fetterman was a traditionalist, but he was also a strong backer of women in the military. The Chief of Naval Education and Training, or CNET, as Fetterman's last command was known, is based in sedate, campuslike quarters in Pensacola. It was there that Fetterman oversaw the development of the core values program, a five-hour training course for all new recruits, to be reinforced periodically throughout a Navy career.

Core values was a response to an uneasy feeling, in Fetterman and among Navy higher-ups, that the moral underpinnings of American society had somehow become undone. In a July 1992 interview with the *Navy Times*, Fetterman listed among the reasons that an ethics curriculum was needed such factors as "absence of firmly founded goals," "no self-respect," "racism," "alcohol and drug abuse," "teenage pregnancy" and "self-indulgent sexual activity and concomitant ills."

Tailhook was not specifically named, but was the impetus behind the Navy's accelerated adoption of Fetterman's program. In the spring of 1992, Secretary Lawrence Garrett and CNO Frank Kelso had announced that the entire Navy would undergo a day of sensitivity training in sexual harassment. That would be the quick fix. Core values represented the long-term repair job on the Navy's moral compass, targeting sexual harassment as one of a quartet of social issues that also included violent crime, racial discrimination and fraud.

The scandal also transformed Fetterman's core values from a pet project to a crusade. Having come up in the aviation pipeline, he knew how wild fliers could get. Still, the younger generation clearly needed a serious, upside-the-head moral reawakening. "I don't think we'll ever ask anybody to be choirboys," Fetterman said. "But there's no excuse for conduct that is bizarre. There's no excuse for drinking until you fall down." The core values training would in effect rolf the consciences of everyone within its reach. It would hammer home the importance of honesty, honor, responsibility, competence, teamwork, loyalty, concern for people, patriotism and courage. Bedrock values, which somehow had come to be called "old-fashioned" in today's brave new world.

"No matter what you do with your workforce, your workforce is only as good as its people," Fetterman observed. "And your people are only as good as the values they bring to the workforce. So if you have Old Charlie here, who beat up on his wife his whole life, and his father beat up on his wife his whole life, and he's in your work place, and you've got somebody over here that's always been padding his income tax, his father did too, I mean, you don't know what you have."

As Fetterman spoke, his earnestness about the subject was unmistakable. His gnarled, arthritic hands folded in upon themselves like puffy prehensile claws. He looked around the study as if momentarily baffled he should be there, instead of at his post at CNET.

Among the catalog of Navy embarrassments during the summer of 1992 were the events surrounding the early retirement of Jack Fetterman, its core values guru. Just as Fetterman's accomplishment in reshaping the Navy was being trumpeted, the incident that ended his career was uncovered. Among the press and outsiders, there was an irresistible irony in watching such a moral arbiter take a fall. Within the Navy, however, Fetterman's dismissal was a sobering measure as to just how far things had gone.

Sobering, too, was how it all came about. Over Thanksgiving of 1991, Fetterman's executive secretary, a chief petty officer named Edmond Bonnot, was housesitting for the admiral, taking care of his dog, Mac. Bonnot asked a friend over to the "compound," and they shared a six-pack of MacGuire's Red Ale, a Pensacola favorite. Bonnot played host, and boasted to the friend about how much money Fetterman made.

"We went up there and took the Admiral's dog out to the kennel that they have out back for it," the unnamed friend recalled to Navy IG agents. "We had a few beers, and Bonnot showed me around the Admiral's house and told me the history behind the Admiral, and you know, how long he had worked for him. Some of the items he had in the house, Bonnot told me about the history of them."

The Fettermans were in Jacksonville visiting their daughter. It is almost spooky, imagining the two sailors roaming the empty house, sipping their beer, reading the plaques in the den. At some point during the evening, after they'd proceeded to a local bar, Bonnot came on to the friend, who refused the advance. The evening was sodden enough that Bonnot's lawyers would later argue the real issue was alcoholism, not homosexuality.

Bonnot had been on the admiral's staff a long time, had come with him from an earlier posting in San Diego. When Bonnot's friend

made formal charges concerning the evening, Fetterman was con-
flicted. He thought he was acting properly when he referred the matter to Bonnot's supervisor, Commander Wayne Hurst, who discovered
enough merit in the complaint to order the military equivalent of a
grand jury hearing, known as an Article 32. Twice earlier, it turned
out, once in 1987 and again in 1989, similar charges had been brought
against Bonnot, but both times had been dismissed as groundless.

At the conclusion of the Article 32, in February, it was recommended that Bonnot be court-martialed, not for homosexual acts but
for fraternization with other enlisted men. Commander Hurst overturned the recommendation, instead ordering alcohol counseling and
a reprimand. Trusting Hurst's judgment, Fetterman seconded the suggestion and took no further action.

Then, in April, the Pentagon Inspector General's office received
an anonymous hot-line complaint about Fetterman's handling of the
case, and opened its inquiry. When agents discovered that Fetterman
had heard of the charges in question as early as January and had not
directed a Naval Investigative Service inquiry—as protocol would ordinarily dictate—the IG concluded that Fetterman had not reviewed
the case impartially. (A year later, Bonnot would receive a general
discharge under other-than-honorable conditions after he agreed to
plead guilty to two indecent assault counts and three lesser charges
rather than face a court-martial.) The admiral would be relieved of his
command and transferred to the staff of Admiral Kelso at the Pentagon. But Fetterman would not tolerate the ignominy that accompanies
such a transfer. Instead, the following day, he asked to be retired
immediately, a move which was approved by Secretary O'Keefe. He
left the Navy at a reduced rank of rear admiral. O'Keefe directed that
a letter of censure be placed in the admiral's file. Replacing Fetterman would be his deputy, Rear Admiral Louise Wilmot, at the time
one of only three female admirals in the Navy.

The news of Jack Fetterman's forced retirement spread through
the fleet, amplified by Fetterman's refusal to go away quietly.
Throughout the weeks following, the admiral took interviews with re-

porters in which he spoke persuasively of his massive, worldwide support network, throwing around figures like 950 supportive telephone calls, 800 fan letters. Two days after his removal from command, Fetterman wrote the chief of naval operations a letter in which he denied the allegations against him and urged Navy leadership today and in the future to "rise above the current climate of suspicion and innuendo."

The admiral with the brilliant career had been retired to his wall relics and his ruminations.

"I've been in those rooms," Fetterman said about the Pentagon office where his fate was decided. "The lawyers are talking: we've got to deal with it fast, we've got to deal with it punitively. We've got to get it on and off the hook as fast as possible, so it will go away. And I was just a victim."

Fetterman's experience impressed many in the Navy community as the confirmation of their worst nightmare, a clear indication that even paranoiacs have enemies.

"He always tried to do the reasonable thing when applying strict rules and regulations," said Fetterman's inspector general, Captain Jack Ensch. "Right now, the Navy's hemorrhaging internally, and I'm afraid we'll end up with a Navy with muscles and bones, but no heart."

"They are going after the wrong admiral," said one female chief petty officer. "This shows you the whole world is upside down."

WHATEVER ELSE JACK FETTERMAN WAS, TO MANY HE REPRESENTED the best of the Old Navy. As such, he articulated an old salt's lingering concern about what might be lost as the service rushed pell-mell into the new, post-Tailhook age. Fetterman observed, "The whole purpose of what the taxpayer invests in a tactical pilot flying off a carrier is that if called upon, that person can put his life on the line and get the job done, whatever it takes. Some of that stuff you have to train very high, but the end point is always the psyche of the person and how he's going to go into harm's way. So if you create a different culture—if you say, Nobody drinks anymore! Nobody parties anymore! Nobody harasses anymore! Nobody! Nobody! Nobody! then that type of person you get—is he the type of person that will be able to do that? We need that bonding, we need that interface. You've got to be sure that that person that's flying on your wing or in those three airplanes with you are not only trained but they're disciplined enough that they're not going to let you down, that they're not going to cause you to die. And to do that there's not only training on the job, but there's a certain amount of bonding off the job."

Most of the old-line Navy reacted to post-Tailhook developments with a lot less equanimity than Fetterman. Outright horror was common, as they watched Tailhook broaden from a simple blot on the escutcheon into a scandal that challenged a whole way of life.

One of the main forums in which Navy defenders chose to voice their concerns was the letters column of the *San Diego Union-Tribune,* the paper of the company town, to be sure, but nonetheless a somewhat ironic choice. The *Union-Tribune*'s military affairs writer, Gregory Vistica, was the reporter who had scooped the Tailhook scandal back in October. Vistica had set his terrier teeth in the Navy's hide and refused to let go. Day after day, month after month, he managed to fetch up new details about the Tailhook Association, the '91 convention and about other instances of Navy misconduct. He became the sounding board of every disgruntled sailor in San Diego County. If there was a journalistic cabal out to destroy the Navy, Vistica was the ringleader.

Other media outlets with a special military interest also probed deep into the Navy's wounds that summer, first among them the *Navy Times.* Despite their reporters' determined muckraking, or perhaps because of it, these newspapers' letters and op ed pages attracted Navy apologists of every stripe. The writers were retired Navy, or active-duty folk with dwindling outlets for their views within the service. They echoed elements of Fetterman's measured analysis in more florid prose, but their collected texts represent a window into the Old Navy.

What they were concerned about, in the summer of 1992, was

the assault on their traditions. A writer named Mark A. Peterman complained of being ordered to take down a "mini-poster of Heather Thomas" from his work space on an all-male frigate.

Valvoline and Snap-on calendars are being torn down throughout the ship. Even autographed Bud girl photos and Raiderettes (who, by the way, visited our ship, sponsored by MWR [Morale, Welfare and Recreation] and sold us the photos!) are not spared. Is art to be banned in the fear of offending some narrow-minded, misguided souls? Does this mean I can no longer attend the Hawaiian Tropic bikini contest sponsored and held on my base without fear of reprisals?

"Betrayed," "misunderstood," "scapegoats" and "witch hunt" were some of the locutions favored by these upholders of tradition. Their chosen villains, in approximate order of frequency of mention, were Paula Coughlin, Pat Schroeder, Barbara Pope, radical feminists and the weak-livered, mealy-mouthed Navy hierarchy.

"Woman is God's finest creation and is to be loved, honored and cherished," wrote one *Union-Tribune* Tailhook correspondent. "To degrade her is unacceptable. But, in this case, is she also a dark avenger who presses for the ultimate punishment . . . ?"

As the Navy's troubles deepened over the summer, a mood of desperate defensiveness set in. The first evidence of this was a subtle change in the image of Paula Coughlin.

QUITE WITHOUT ANY DESIGN ON HER PART, COUGHLIN HAD ACCOM-plished one of the mythical transformations of our age, from simple victim to a grander and more compelling creature, the Victim Avenger. A new figure on the cultural landscape, the Victim Avenger was a modern archetype that appeared with the advance of certain empowerment philosophies into the center of American civic debate. She gained power from oxymoron, from her position as a walking paradox. She was powerful and terrible exactly because she combined the innocence and righteousness of the weak with the vengeful fury of the wronged. She was particularly impervious to attack, for to battle with her immediately cast one in the role of those who victimized her in the first place. She gave conservatives and members of the right wing fits.

Ever since Paula Coughlin came forward and told her story to the press, those who sought to discredit her were careful to avoid frontal attacks. Coughlin was simply the victim of her own lousy judgment, of what was called, in the language of the Navy, "bad headwork." ("Smart people," ran one critique, "don't go to a hotel where there are a few hundred drunken men in attendance and not expect to get grabbed and hit upon.") But Coughlin was also guilty of transgression herself, of straying out of powerless victimhood into a more assertive role. She was only a lowly helo pilot. Who was she to take on the Navy? To go on television in her uniform whites? Said one lieutenant commander, "Paula Coughlin is empirically right. I mean, how can you argue with what she's talking about? But how does a male aviator perceive her? She's allowed herself to be elevated to this position far beyond what her stature otherwise would be."

And what was her goal? What was the mythical harpy after? The thing that distressed those with an investment in the Old Navy was the possibility that Coughlin could somehow become an agent for change —stop the good times from rolling, disband the Tailhook Association, take down the Snap-on Tool girls. Fine, they seemed to say, give her justice. Bust the guys who did this to her. But keep the Navy the same way it always was.

"Now it is the fashion to 'unman' the Navy," wrote a *Union-Tribune* correspondent. "You begin by singling out one drunken brawl, then accuse the entire military establishment of debauchery. Next you take, as holy grail, the innuendo and suspicions, blend them with those who are disgruntled with their lot and then force out of service every breath of masculinity."

What these communiqués had in common—apart from the purplish tint of their prose—was their tourniquet approach to Tailhook.

Navy Lieutenant Paula Coughlin came forward in June 1992 to put a human face on the burgeoning Tailhook scandal. (*Margaret Thomas*—Washington Post)

Secretary of the Navy H. Lawrence Garrett III (right) resigned on June 26, 1992, over his handling of the Tailhook affair. Sean O'Keefe (left), the Defense Department comptroller, assumed the role of acting secretary after J. Daniel Howard, Garrett's undersecretary, served in the position for less than three weeks. *(Harold J. Gerwein)*

Dan Howard vowed to "dismantle a decaying culture, a residual fabric of counter-productive and unworthy attitudes." *(Doug Pensinger—Army Times Pub. Co.)*

Barbara Spyridon Pope, the first female assistant secretary of the Navy in its 217-year history, was one of the Navy officials charged with overseeing the Naval Investigative Service (NIS) Tailhook probe. (*Steve Elfers—Army Times Pub. Co.*)

Rear Admiral Marsha Evans headed the Standing Committee on Women in the Navy and Marine Corps. Formed in the summer of 1992, it had a mandate to make the culture of the Navy more hospitable to women. Here, Evans accepts the "No Nonsense American Woman" award for May 1993. (*Department of Defense*)

Navy jet pilots see themselves as "bulletproof," not least because their day-to-day job includes the feat of landing a 60,000-pound plane on the pitching deck of an aircraft carrier. Here, an F-14 Tomcat prepares to "trap" aboard the USS *Abraham Lincoln*: the jet's lowered tailhook will catch one of four steel arresting cables strung across the carrier's flight deck. *(Navy Photo by PH2 Dennis Taylor)*

Top Gun fueled the bad-boy reputation of the naval aviator. Its potent combination of breathtaking flight photography and jet-jock romance (Kelly McGillis and Tom Cruise) made it the top-grossing Hollywood film of 1986. *(Courtesy Archive Photos)*

The deprivations of seagoing life can lead sailors to self-obliterating binges on liberty— or to seek out available intimacy while embarked. In the late 1890s, photographer Frances Benjamin Johnston captured a moment of same-sex entertainment on board a U.S. Navy ship. *(Courtesy of the Library of Congress)*

A World War II submariner in his rack aboard the USS *Capelin*. *(National Archives)*

"But, honey, I haven't got a girl in every port I ain't BEEN in every port!"

The sailor's randy reputation was well established by the time cartoonist E. Simms Campbell lampooned it in 1941. *(King Features Syndicate)*

During World War II, a series of classic photographs by Edward Steichen and his Navy unit further glamorized the daredevil world of carrier aviation. *(National Archives)*

By Tailhook '91, the naval aviator's license to party was a given. Squadrons vied with each other to come up with the most outrageous hospitality suite décor—including, as a central attraction at the party thrown by Marine Corps Tactical Reconnaissance Squadron 3, the "rhino with a ding dong," imported from Trader Jon's bar in Pensacola, Florida. *(Department of Defense)*

Party hijinks: igniting alcohol on the Hilton's pool patio —an evidence photo from the Department of Defense Inspector General's 1993 report on Tailhook. *(Department of Defense)*

Tailhook T-shirt slogan: WOMEN ARE PROPERTY. *(Department of Defense)*

Rhino headgear worn at Tailhook '91; the photo has been "redacted" (edited) by the Department of Defense for privacy. (*Department of Defense*)

A stripper displays a flight squadron "zapper" during her performance in a hospitality suite. (*Department of Defense*)

After the party came the hangover, when investigators descended on Navy air bases in the summer of 1992. West Coast aviators sidestepped an official injunction against wearing the Bart Simpson Tailhook patch by sewing it inside their flight jackets.

Lieutenant Paula Coughlin in July 1992, at the height of what many Navy fliers were by then terming the Tailhook "witchhunt." *(Ann States–SABA)*

One year after the convention that spawned the Tailhook scandal, the Women's Action Coalition organized a protest that led to a brief closing of the main gate at Miramar Naval Air Station. (San Diego Union-Tribune—*Jerry Rife)*

Stanch the bleeding. Don't let a localized wound hemorrhage into a life-threatening rupture.

Old-line Navy supporters watched with horror as Tailhook mutated into a force that might "unman" the Navy, transform it into "a bunch of 'pantywaists,' sailing around like members of a yacht club." They found themselves talking less and less about what Paula had wrought and more about the feminist and congressional assault on the male-only domain of combat.

"Congratulations to Rep. Pat Schroeder," wrote one correspondent. "She is accomplishing what the Soviet Union couldn't achieve in the past 40 years—destruction of our military forces, 'man by man.'" Schroeder, Representative Beverly Byron, Barbara Boxer, et al.—the new evil empire. Again and again, "naturalness" and "nature" were cited as ultimate arbiters of what should be, with the image of the woman warrior held up as some sort of Darwinian horror story. "The success of any operation," wrote a World War II veteran, "depends on its operators being in their natural places. Segregation is a fact of life. For society to promote pugnacity in women is an outrage. What is there to come home to if the women are not there?"

The last sentence here, the cry of the latchkey child, gives it all away. A woman's place was up on the widow's walk, scanning the horizon for the return of the warrior. At times, the emotional insistence of these letters could achieve almost an elegiac tone, a fantasy mantra wishing for a time that never was, an idealized relation between the sexes that never will be. In mid-July, San Diego resident Patrick Groff penned the following *cri de coeur* in the Letters column of the *San Diego Union-Tribune:*

> In times better than these—I think—it used to be the dangerous duty of men to put themselves in harm's way as warriors for the nation at times of crisis. Women took on the personally life-threatening responsibility of bearing children. Women perpetuated humankind; men defended its culture and politics at war.
>
> To become bona fide warriors, men passed through funda-

mentally important rituals that bolstered their courage, honed their killing prowess and strengthened their bond with their peers. There also were ceremonies silly and informal enough to lessen the perpetual specter overshadowing warriors—unpredictable death at an early age. The preparations women followed for their birthing ordeals were different, but were equally complicated.

This age-old scheme now is under intense fire from government bureaucrats pressured by certain women who want to upset the archetypal arrangement. The ancient order must be turned on its head, they demand. Women will become brood animals, the nurturing of children turned over to strangers, the venerable code of the warrior will be rewritten. He, and now she, must be asexual, supersensitive to derisive banter, and given to open expressions of guilt. Bonding will be quashed, due to ominous sexual implications.

Tradition says it won't work. Honor finds itself insulted. The peculiar needs of the nation are poorly served.

In harm's way. It was an old formulation, traceable all the way back to that hero-mercenary, John Paul Jones. The phrase stepped lightly through bravado to reach for the aura of the martyr, and Navy people loved to quote it, drop it in conversation, work it into their speeches. "I wish to have no Connection with any ship that does not sail fast," Jones said, "for I intend to go in harm's way."

Tailhook was proving itself to be a two-headed dragon, a sex scandal and a rallying cry. Paula Coughlin's sin, in the eyes of the Old Navy, was also twofold. She had, either by mistake or design, put herself in harm's way on the third deck of the Las Vegas Hilton. It was foolish on her part, bad headwork, or maybe a perverse flouting of the rules of the tribe.

But worse—much worse—was her desire, her insistence, her pronounced intention—casually stated, as if it were her right!—to proceed into harm's way as a combat aviator.

Chapter Six

CHIMNEYS IN SUMMER

ROSEMARY MARINER IS A STRIKING EXAMPLE OF HOW BEDROCK CON-
servatism and feminism need not be mutually exclusive. Captain Mariner is the Navy's second most senior female aviator. She is on staff at
the Joint Chiefs, and in line to become one of the few female admirals. She subscribes to a brand of Libertarian-flavored political philosophy that is so popular within the Navy it comes off as quasi-official
government issue, right along with the ball caps and ditty bags. She is
given to Nietzschean pronouncements ("Being female is not an excuse
to be a coward"), which sound as if they would more readily roll off
the tongues of talk-show provocateurs. Mariner is unshrinking in her
advocacy of equal opportunity for women in aviation.

She is a fiercely intelligent woman, but at the same time there is
something of the fishwife in her blunt manner, her imperfect teeth,
her weathered face. Mariner grew up as a 1960s California girl, but
she didn't fit the stereotype. She wasn't a Beach Boys' girl with
bleached hair and a Corvette, or an acid-addled Summer of Love day-
tripper. A military brat, her home turf was the Orange County/San
Diego County nexus that still remains a firmly buckled belt of Southern California Republicanism. She spent the Vietnam era in a flag-

waving community next to Miramar Naval Air Station. The war was not abstract here; there were two Vietnam POW's whose families lived on Mariner's home street.

Her own father was gone permanently, an Army Air Force pilot killed in a crash when she was three. Her mother had been a Navy nurse during the Second World War, and there was no doubt in Mariner's mind growing up that her mother "had had the time of her life" while in the service. Her childhood experience presented the Navy, flying and strong women as a single complementary package.

Mariner was in the ninth grade when she decided to be an airline pilot. Her Catholic girls' school was more an extended philosophy class than anything else. That's where she first read Plato, marking his words in the fifth chapter of the Republic about women and men defending the Just City side by side. But this was 1968, and there were no women military pilots. There weren't any women airline pilots, either, but that goal seemed slightly more accessible. Mariner announced her career plans to the principal of the school. "She didn't blink an eye," Mariner remembered. "Nuns were the original career women."

Mariner persuaded Fred Priest, the owner of the flying service at Gillespie Field, to let her wash airplanes in exchange for flight time. Priest had been an instructor for the Women Airforce Service Pilots (WASPs) who trained at Avenger Field in Sweetwater, Texas, during World War II. By the time Mariner picked up her private pilot's license, on her seventeenth birthday, she was steeped in WASP lore.

During World War II, the WASPs had been created to help address a desperate shortage of pilots. Women—"air Janes," they were called—were put to work ferrying military airplanes, and almost 2,000 women flew every type of aircraft in the military inventory, including the heaviest bombers. With makeshift uniforms and only perfunctory martial training by the Army Air Corps, the WASPs were classified as civilian. But they proved that women could fly planes. Specifically, military planes.

Women had been a part of civilian aviation since the late nineteenth century, when the first crazy aircraft were put together out of patchwork substances like silk and bamboo. When flying became a reality, it was as much a fad as a serious business, a fad in which women avidly took part. The best known American aviatrix, of course, was Amelia Earhart, whose reputation was largely the creation of her ace promoter husband, publisher George Putnam. Among the coterie of serious women aviators, Earhart was seen by some as less than perfectly practiced. She always had the latest aircraft and equipment, and yet, for a long time, she was unable to win a race. Her spirit and her risk-taking were always more impressive than her flying skills, and she might not be known to the American public today if not for her last, ill-fated voyage across the Pacific.

It was Jackie Cochran rather than Earhart who captured Mariner's teenage imagination. She devoured the stories about Cochran, speed demon and cosmetics queen. Cochran spent her childhood largely barefoot, wringing the necks of chickens to make money as a preschooler and, at the age of seven, hiring herself out to help local women bear and care for their babies. She worked in a Georgia cotton mill, delivering spools of thread to the weavers, and so earned enough to buy her first shoes (predictably, a pair of high heels) from a traveling salesman.

It was her love of the elaborate mechanics of female beauty—specifically, cosmetics and hairstyling—that first led Cochran at age fifteen to Alabama, where she became a beautician, and later brought her to Pensacola. She operated a beauty shop and attended dances at the Pensacola Naval Flying School. There, dating future captains and admirals, she first heard about the glory of flying. Cochran earned her pilot's license for a crudely practical reason: to make better money peddling cosmetics on cross-country jaunts. Later on, after breaking this or that world speed record (she set some for both women and men), she would never step out of the cockpit without first freshening her face.

For Rosemary Mariner, Cochran and her peers were a formative influence. Mariner knew that Cochran had won the Bendix trophy in an otherwise all-male race in 1938, and in 1953 (the year Mariner was born) had broken the sound barrier in an F-86, with Chuck Yeager chasing her. Cochran was still setting Mach 2 speed records in the early 1960s.

WASPs were all over Mariner's personal pantheon of aviation greats. It was Jackie Cochran who almost singlehandedly formed the WASPs. Mariner earned her multiengine rating under a former WASP named "Mac" Huntington, who had flown the B-29 Superfortress, the enormous silver monster that had carried the first atomic bomb in its bay. And when Mariner went to college—the first woman to enter the aviation program at Purdue, and the only woman out of 200 in her department—she studied with Jill McCormick, another former WASP. Mariner was the type of person to self-mythologize, to self-consciously link herself with the greats of the past. Already, as an undergraduate, she was readying herself for a dazzling career as an aviator.

Suddenly, in Rosemary Mariner's last year of college, a man she had never met, Chief of Naval Operations Elmo Zumwalt, effectively changed the course of her life. Arguably the most visionary CNO ever, Zumwalt ushered the service through its difficult post-Vietnam adjustments. He would later endure (and write a book about) the heartrending personal tragedy of seeing a son die from Agent Orange exposure —after Zumwalt himself had ordered the exfoliant dropped on the Vietnam jungle.

Another element of Zumwalt's Vietnam experience would perhaps shape his attitude toward women in the Navy during his later tour as CNO. "The most vicious, ruthless, cunning enemy I ever had to fight," said Zumwalt, "were the Vietcong women, who had the stamina to keep up with their men in the jungles and marshes and who were very capable of suckling their babies by the roadside and then dropping the baby and picking up a rifle and shooting a sailor in the back."

In the autumn of 1972, Mariner's mother sent her a clipping from the *San Diego Union-Tribune* that was like a bolt from the blue. It was difficult for her to grasp at first. The airlines hadn't opened up, but the Navy, the hidebound, traditionalist Navy, was going to begin training women pilots. Touched by the ERA-, equal opportunity-

driven climate of the early seventies, nervous over projected manpower shortages with the advent of the all-volunteer armed forces,
Zumwalt had sent forth one of his famous "Z-GRAMs," number 116,
outlining unprecedented opportunities for women in the Navy.
Z-GRAM 116, which went to the fleet in August 1972, announced that
Zumwalt had "established a task force to look at all laws, regulations
and policies that must be changed in order to eliminate any disadvantages to women resulting from either legal or attitudinal restrictions."
It said that effective immediately, enlisted women could enter hith-
erto-closed Navy jobs, and that a pilot program on a ship called the
USS *Sanctuary* would bring nonmedical women on board Navy vessels for the first time, in anticipation of legislation that would ease the
1948 ban on women at sea. Finally, Zumwalt suspended the restrictions on women serving in a command capacity at shore stations.

Finishing up her last semester of Purdue early by taking the final
exams over Christmas vacation in 1972 (thus graduating from college
at age nineteen), Mariner prepared to go to Pensacola to join the first
class of female naval aviators in what was being called the "WAVY
Navy." The term was a tongue-in-cheek reference to the acronym
WAVES (for Women Accepted for Volunteer Emergency Service),
which was applied to the Navy women's reserve in World War II.
Although the term had long since outlived its usefulness, it was not
officially deep-sixed until 1972.

The first women pilots in the Navy received their share of sudden celebrity. All the major networks and news services came calling.
"There is nothing like watching the Johnny Carson show and hearing
yourself mentioned in the monologue," Mariner recalled. But getting
national media attention was one thing, surviving Navy flight school
was another.

"While the newspapers were making heroines of us," Mariner
said, "our male counterparts were not so impressed. The first burst of
criticism dealt with that old bugaboo, physical standards. The supposed logic was that if the women could not do the same number of
chin-ups as the men, then they were not strong enough to fly airplanes.

"It wasn't enough that women had been flying since the beginning of aviation, that they had flown all the airplanes of World War II without benefit of hydraulically boosted flight controls, that the Russians had had three squadrons of women fly in combat during that same war, or that by this time the airlines had hired women pilots."

The men of the Navy, in fact, tended to exhibit a convenient amnesia when it came to recalling anything women had done in aviation. "One commander told me that women were physically incapable of flying high-performance jets because 'they can't wear G-suits.' When I informed him that Jackie Cochran had broken the sound barrier in 1953 in an F-86, and that Cochran and Jackie Auriol had volleyed speed records back and forth in excess of Mach 2—both while wearing G-suits—he looked at me as if I were an outright liar. Such criticism and attitudes were our first indication that maybe we weren't the Navy sweethearts that the papers pictured us to be. For the first time in many of our lives we were disliked by some people solely because of what we were; unwelcomed outsiders invading a fraternity."

Of that original class of six women fliers who received their commissions in the spring of '73, Mariner was one of two still on active duty in 1992. Perhaps the dropout rate could be attributed in part to the career limitations. Female fliers learned during flight training of the long list of prohibitions that, despite Zumwalt and his Z-GRAM, effectively circumscribed the brave new world of women in the Navy. Females were still legally banned from all Navy vessels aside from the rare hospital ship or transport. "The fears about women in ships were almost hysterical," recalls Mariner. Women were not allowed to even hover in a helicopter above the deck in port. All they were allowed to do was fly out of the Navy's shore bases.

The rules resulted in some weird paradoxes. While female Navy pilots such as Mariner faced a near universal shipboard ukase, civilian women, contractors, scientists and government officials could readily land on ships as passengers in Navy planes. But a woman naval officer could not step on board a ship unless she was on leave, in civilian clothes and accompanied by a male officer.

Later, when Mariner was approached to join a 1978 class-action suit brought by seven Navy women—the suit that eventually pushed the Navy to assign permanent sea duty to women—she refused. "I was doing very well in those days," she admits. "I went to a squadron where I was basically well supported—Oceana, the fighter community, A-6 guys—and I had things going very well. I was asked to join the lawsuit, with [helicopter pilot] JoEllen Oslund, who was a very close friend. And I basically wimped out. Because I had it good, I didn't want to get in trouble with the Navy. And I consider that moral cowardice on my part."

Mariner's squadron at Oceana was a "jet composite squadron," comprised both of the old, Vietnam-era jets called A-4's, as well as the S-2 propeller plane, which Mariner had trained to fly. She towed targets for ships to shoot at in gunnery practice, but she was surrounded by A-4 bomber pilots. Their experience of Vietnam was still so immediate that Mariner couldn't help but believe "the average lieutenant commander must be twenty-four years old and have a chestful of medals."

These men were different from the jet jocks who preceded and came after them, the ones who were so insistent that women could not fly airplanes in combat. "People who have actually been to war are very sobered by that experience. They're aggressive and they're warriors, but they understand that there is a gulf of difference between myth and reality. You know, it was not John Wayne that earned the medal of honor, it was Audie Murphy, little five-foot-four Audie Murphy. The things that distinguish warriors when the chips are down and people are really shooting at you are issues of character, not of macho image. What the bomber pilots cared about was performance."

Mariner, the only female aviator on the base, received the benefit of this hard-earned wisdom. Sure, there were detractors, but "the ones that were the worst, the ones that would be openly hostile toward women and would do a lot of the petty insipid things that you hear about, were the guys that were the most insecure. And invariably, they were the ones that had never been anywhere near a war."

But it was Mariner's commanding officer at Oceana, Captain Ray

Lambert, who made the decision that changed her fate. When the squadron needed more jet pilots, Lambert chose the most junior aviators in the group—the ones who had the longest careers ahead of them, including Rosemary Mariner—to go jets. The other pilots' approval came back in two weeks. It took Mariner's transition eight months to be okayed, but ultimately it came through. It was in 1975, a full seven years before Navy women were officially allowed to complete the full jet syllabus, that Mariner first flew a tactical jet, the single-seat A-4E/L Skyhawk.

Rosemary Mariner learned many lessons at the feet of Captain Lambert, who had joined the pre-Zumwalt Navy as a young black officer. This was before the early seventies race riots and wildcat strikes on the aircraft carriers *Kitty Hawk* and *Constellation* led to a newly rigorous emphasis within the Navy on equal opportunity. At that time, says Mariner, "the Navy was a tremendously racist organization and they were very overt in their attempts to drive people out."

Mariner, a self-described "middle-class white girl who had never been discriminated against and didn't understand what it meant to be questioned, from the beginning, on your abilities," saw in Lambert's experience a paradigm of "some of the things that I would be up against." The strength of the Navy, when confronted by issues of social inequity, was that it was a rank-based, authoritarian culture. How many stripes on your sleeve mattered more, in the end, than the color of your face—or your gender. During the early 1970s, the Navy had decided to change its policies about race, and had simply gone ahead and done so. In this way, the military actually had a leg up on the messy, sprawling civilian world, where changes could be endlessly debated, resisted, undermined.

From Captain Lambert, Mariner also learned the importance of forming a network with others in the same position. He had a folder that contained a list of the names of every black pilot on active duty in the Navy. The senior officers were mentors for the more junior ones.

This rich mentoring tradition was something Rosemary Mariner would help create for female aviators—a military old-girl's network, rudimentary and severely limited by the numbers of women involved, but real enough to draw the scorn of men who felt shut out. Instead of joining a class-action suit, and perhaps motivated in part over guilt for "wimping out," Mariner would work from the inside. As the Navy's first female squadron commander, in 1990–91, she worked tirelessly to make sure that the female junior officers who served under her got every opportunity to train in ordnance and procedures that were supposedly closed to women. "I decided somewhere along the line that it was payback time. And the area I got into for that payback was opening up the jet pipeline for women."

Lambert had at an earlier, crucial juncture in his aviation career been persuaded to accept what was billed as a plum job, teaching chemistry at the Naval Academy. Lambert's peers were racking up combat time in Vietnam, but the powers that be wanted a black professor at Annapolis. As a result, Mariner saw, Ray Lambert's career had suffered. From that, she learned another key lesson: stay operational, do not get derailed into the equal opportunity career ghetto. Mariner had remained in the cockpit for over eighteen years.

All told, she had logged 3,500 flight hours in fifteen different naval aircraft. Mariner dropped bombs, fired guns, tested new weapons systems in the Mojave Desert. She had served aboard the training carrier *Lexington,* been a flight instructor and maintenance officer in the Navy's largest jet-training squadron. Ten years into her career, she'd finally been allowed to "carrier qualify," prove that she could land a jet on an aircraft carrier, making her one of the first women to do so.

Mariner knew women could be warfighters alongside men. She had no patience for those who complained that readiness would be impaired or camaraderie damaged by the inclusion of women. "The idea that women will destroy cohesion is nonsense. Cohesion is not homogeneity."

She should know. In the Navy, and especially among the women of the aviation community, Mariner was legendary for being the first female (of only two so far) to serve as commanding officer of a jet squadron. The achievement of this could perhaps be fully appreciated only within the hierarchal world of the military, where command was all. Mariner's example was still clung to by a whole generation of Navy women being trained to fly Navy aircraft. She had been the vanguard, the pioneer, the point person. They were all Rosemary's babies, the 400-plus female pilots who came after her.

In January 1993, some fifteen months after the Tailhook convention in Las Vegas, they were running scared.

LEMOORE, CALIFORNIA, IS IN THE MIDDLE OF THE STATE'S CENTRAL Valley, the great, vast San Joaquin, a breadbasket in shape and function, cornucopia to the nation, pouring out grapes, soybeans, safflower and cotton. The present-day Central Valley is a place so fecund and intensely agricultural that it's easy to forget it was called—before the irrigation schemes of twenties and thirties—the Central Desert.

Lemoore still has something of the unforgiving nature of the desert. January is what passes for a wet season here, dank and cold, when the fields darken with moisture. Red-tailed hawks hunch on the fence posts, grounded and sullen. All winter, thick, miasmic fogs roll through this section of the San Joaquin almost nightly, making traffic on Interstate 5 a movable hell. The fogs usually recede by mid-morning, when road crews administer to the carcasses of cars that litter the muddy shoulders like so many overturned turtles.

The Navy, drawn to marginal land like some prospective real estate swindler—for the simple reason that there are fewer people in deserts, swamps and wastelands to complain about air traffic noise— settled into Lemoore in 1961, when it commissioned a huge air station ten miles out of town. Highway 198 west from Lemoore is four lanes until it passes the gates of the air base, where it reverts to its more likely status as a sleepy country two-lane. The local joke is that the Navy fliers need every one of those four lanes to get back to base after a night on the town.

Naval Air Station (NAS) Lemoore is what the Navy calls a "master" jet base. It is to the deadly strike-fighter hybrid, the F/A-18, what

Miramar is to the fighter jet. If Miramar is Top Gun, Lemoore is top bombs, top drop. The people from Lemoore are the people who flew Vietnam.

In the lobby of the main entrance building, just inside the front gate, there is a mini-museum of sorts, displaying squadron insignia, vivid, incendiary artwork featuring various naval air engagements, and the ubiquitous plaques and framed letters which form such a vital part of any Navy decorating scheme. Also on display are three tailhooks, samples of the military hardware used to halt a screeching Navy jet on the truncated expanse of a carrier runway. Tailhooks all resemble en-larged crochet needles, but their proportions vary considerably from jet to jet. The ones mounted at Lemoore represent the three major airframes that have flown out of the base since its founding. The squat, flat tailhook is from the now-extinct A-7, one of the planes most likely to bomb Vietnam. The spindly barber pole of black-and-white stripes comes from the A-4, still used extensively in the Navy for advanced jet training. The third tailhook on display is six feet long, about the thick-ness of a forearm, painted in gray stripes, with a flange on one end and a universal joint on the other. It belongs to the F/A-18 Hornet, cur-rently the Queen Bee of Lemoore and of naval aviation in general. "F" stands for "fighter" and "A" for "attack," the Navy's vaunted hiero-glyphics being surprisingly transparent here. The sleek, twin-engine, swept-wing Hornet "combines the strike and air-to-air all in the same mission," said one flier currently stationed at Lemoore. "That's what it's like in the real world, where you have to fight your way in, drop the bombs and fight your way out."

Pentagon planners bet the future of Navy aviation on the Mc-Donnell Douglas Hornet, which was notorious for its initial bugginess and the extreme expense of keeping it in the air. It was the prize everyone came to Lemoore to fly. The strike-fighter jet even elicited envy from the Navy's F-14 Tomcat pilots—though the envy usually came out as a sneer. The Hornet was known as a cakewalk kind of jet, so technologically adept that landing it on a carrier was almost simple, especially compared with the squirrelly F-14.

Lieutenant (jg) Loree Draude was one of those who had come to

Lemoore in the fall of 1992 looking to fly the F/A-18. The "jg" means "junior grade," just a step up from ensign, which is the initial rank all officers receive upon commission. Coming off flight school and electronic warfare training, Draude was inching her way along the Navy's jet-pilot pipeline—not really a pipeline at all, of course, but more of a bureaucratic obstacle course. Being assigned to NAS Lemoore represented a chance to do what she desperately wanted—fly jets, the fastest and most powerful jets the Navy had to offer.

At that point in time, in fall 1992, only 400 women had ever flown for the U.S. Navy. The naval aviator as a species was already an anomaly, a tiny demographic blip—1 percent—in the vast Navy population. So Draude and the eight other female fliers at Lemoore that season were anomalies within a larger anomaly—1 percent of 1 percent. This was driven home in a number of ways, not the least of which was the fact that of the fifteen squadrons which flew out of the base, only two were open to women, and these were the only two that never deployed. One was VFA-125, a training entity, officially the Fleet Replacement Squadron (FRS) but known almost universally by its older acronym, the "RAG," which had stood for Replacement Air Group. The other was VAQ-34, oddly named "the Flashbacks," a support squadron that was used to play-act as adversary in electronic warfare training. This was the squadron that Rosemary Mariner had commanded, from 1990 through August 1991.

Despite its cachet, training in the F/A-18 was essentially a dead end for the Navy women stationed at NAS Lemoore. No matter how well they did, because of the combat exclusion, they would never be assigned to the fleet squadrons, which spent six months at sea for every year they spent at the Lemoore base. It was as if Draude and her peers were locked in a closed loop where their cohorts could travel at will. All they were allowed to do with their Hornets—a fifty-million-dollar flying machine designed for the most dazzling aeronautic acrobatics—was fly the thing straight and level. It was like being given the keys to a Porsche and then told not to go over 35 mph. Loree Draude had never performed—never would perform—a carrier landing in the F/A-18. There was no need to train women pilots to "trap" in the jet, since they would never be stationed out in the fleet. If you looked at it simply in terms of hours, the women at the RAG got about 25 hours' worth of Hornet training, and a fleet-bound aviator got 110 hours. Draude and her female peers were not trained in weapons, bombing, dogfighting, in-flight refueling. "That's the meat of the syllabus," she said. "The stuff we did is just kind of the fluff."

If Loree Draude performed well in the RAG, the only move possible for her was next door to VAQ-34. The pecking order was very distinct. The perks, the advancements, the brilliant careers went to those who went "behind the boat," who performed that sine qua non of naval aviation, the carrier landing. And if the boys really wanted to stick it to you bad, they'd start talking about their night carrier landings, the most dangerous maneuver of all. On vehicles around the base, it was still common to see bumper stickers that read "Proud to be a Tailhook Member." The tribe had been threatened, but its members were holding their heads high.

Draude felt her second-class citizenship when she came up against the attitude of the male instructor pilots, or IP's. "There's this whole 'I'm an IP, worship me,' kind of attitude," she said. "They're like, 'If you haven't been behind the boat at night you're not shit.'" Draude felt like saying to these guys, "You know, you've got your wings, I've got my wings. All that's separating us is a tour of duty that I can't get. I mean, great, you've been behind the boat at night, but there's some guy out there in the world that's developing a cure for cancer, so who the hell do you think you are?"

The symbolism was almost too perfect. The tailhooks showcased in the air station's front lobby, the grimly mechanical, wholesomely phallic objects of war that represented an aviator's slender-thread link to earth, to home, to the mother ship—these were denied, both symbolically and literally, to the handful of female aviators at Lemoore. You don't even have to ask what Freud would have said about that. It was all so . . . bald.

Loree Draude was not the type to dwell on such things. She was a modern, energetic, straight-ahead person, like Rosemary Mariner a daughter of California's golden age. In the style of a lot of Navy women, she kept her hair—a striking shade of auburn—not in a careerist bob, but wavy and long. Required by regulations to wear it up, she did so with a coiled braid, as if she were a skating champion or ballerina.

When Loree Draude talked you heard the California girl, and also the beginnings of the aviator's flat, monochromatic tone of speech, used to artfully downplay the hyperkinetic world of supersonic flight. Things could be "cool" or "awesome," but the emotion she invested in the words seemed remote, as if she were reserving her passion for some unforeseen future moment. This is how she described her advanced jet training: "I really liked air-to-air, the aerial combat maneuvering, because it is so dynamic. Every little thing you do counts, and every thing your bogey does counts. It's really neat. Bombs were fun, too. My favorite part was low levels—I like flying close to the ground. All that tactical stuff is just really neat."

"Fun." "Neat." Just as Draude's speech was not particularly expressive, her intellect was keen without being particularly analytical. Her major complaint about being stationed in snoozy, cultural-backwater Lemoore was the lack of decent shopping opportunities ("no Victoria's Secret!"). In conversation, she tended to float on the surface of things. Her speech was peppered with pop references, from Rob Reiner to Seinfeld to Bill Murray. It was either the Navy way or the style of her generation. Her call sign at the RAG was "Flounder," off an old *Animal House* riff.

At Lemoore, a long avenue called Enterprise runs straight through the heart of the base, leading from its front gate to the airplane hangars at the northern end. For all the time she was there, Enterprise Ave. was Loree Draude's main drag. She would drive down it and gaze over at the farmers raising dust in the fields. A naval base is one of the more insular communities in the world, surrounded by fences both real and metaphorical. Inside those fences, there were stores, machine shops, night clubs, gas stations, a dry cleaners, a car wash, a bowling alley ("Tailhook Lanes"), a driving range. Loree and her friends spent almost twenty-four hours a day with people on the base, socialized with them, went to all the Navy barbecues and functions. There were a lot of community outreach programs, to be sure, but most of the time all she saw were Navy people.

Draude was twenty-five when she came to Lemoore. She wasn't a star—she was "average." There is no grade inflation in the Navy, so the modifier "average" implies a rigorous level of competency. Nevertheless, Draude was Everywoman, not Superwoman. If there was to be a place for women in naval aviation, it was the experience of pilots like Loree Draude at air bases like Lemoore that would provide it. But her experience thus far made her doubt that the Navy she called 'my Navy" was really hers after all.

This was not the first time Draude had encountered problems. Like other female Navy pilots, she'd been given a mixed reception in her three training squadrons. Her first carrier landing, flying a T-2 trainer—"the baby jet," she called it—had been a study in ecstasy. Afterward, out on the carrier deck, watching a San Diego pink-sky sunset with little dolphins skipping in and out of the water, she was filled with exhilaration and pride. Though she was less than thrilled with the printed T-shirts the guys in her training squadron printed up, featuring a picture of a cherry and a slogan, "You'll never forget your first time." The aircraft carrier upon which pilots performed their first trap—in Draude's case, it was the "Ike," the USS *Eisenhower*—was always referred to as the "cherry boat." Fine, Draude thought. What's my shirt have on it? A banana?

Little things, but they added up. In the training pipeline, she had felt she was always being made to try out for the team—even after she supposedly made it. Still, Draude went on to her next posting, at NAS Lemoore, hoping it would be somewhat more professional. But nothing quite prepared her for the level of hostility she encountered when she entered the Lemoore ready room in fall 1992, after her second training flight at the RAG, to find an eight-page article from the *Marine Corps Gazette* tacked up on the bulletin board, covering nearly half the cork. The two Marine pilot authors argued, point by point, why women should not be allowed to go into combat. The pages had been heavily underscored and highlighted in red ink.

Draude found some of the points made in the article insulting. She went up the chain of command to the head of her department. "What's with the board?" she asked. "I thought it was meant for official notices and ads for houses for rent, that kind of thing. I didn't know it was a soap box. Does that mean I can bring my own stuff in?"

"Well, I don't know," the officer replied. "Let me check on it."

He came back about an hour later and said he couldn't take down the clipping, because the person who put it up on board outranked him. A small chill ran through Draude. The only two people who outranked her department head were the XO and the CO—the executive officer and the commanding officer of the RAG. These two are god and god's flunky in any squadron. A junior aviator under their command would question their authority only in the rarest circumstances. The following day, the clipping was down, and the day after that, Draude was summoned into the XO's office.

"I didn't put it up to insult you or anything," the XO said to her. It was merely a tool to stimulate discussion, he said. When Draude asked that she be allowed to offer some clips, maybe "stimulate discussion" on her own, the XO said he was all for it.

"Bring 'em in, submit 'em, we'll put 'em up," he said.

Draude didn't want to get into a straight, point-by-point bulletin board debate. Instead, she brought in a copy of a letter she'd clipped by somebody who was arguing in favor of the legislative ban on women in combat. But the reasons the writer gave were so ludicrous that the whole thing read like a parody. The letter came out sounding funny, and Draude thought posting it would inject some humor into the subject, as well as make some points of her own. The XO was good as his word. The letter went up on the cork. But he had penned a disclaimer to it: "This is from Lieutenant (jg) Draude. This is not my opinion."

Draude felt some sort of personal violation here. Her name had been posted. It is difficult for an outsider to imagine what this kind of singling out meant within the clannish, hermetically sealed world of a flight squadron. To take an individual stand on anything was grounds for ostracism. Draude hadn't been at RAG for a week, and this was how she had been introduced to her peers, by a scrawled ID at the bottom of a polemic.

"The talk in the ready room was that I was going in and complaining to the skipper that the XO was putting up articles," Draude said. "I was supposedly asking to have his taken down and mine put up."

The men she flew with were nice enough to her off base, when they met at social functions and barbecues. Very polite. But from the moment that letter went up with her name on it, in the ready room they treated her to stony silence. She had been cut from the herd.

It wasn't only the ready room. Things got very tense in the air, too. "A lot of my flights, I didn't feel my instructors were really trying to teach me. We'd go up and fly and they simply wouldn't instruct. It was more like they'd wait for me to make a mistake and then chew me out for it. It got to the point where I was so nervous about making any kind of mistake . . . It was like I was teaching myself how to fly this jet, which is kind of tough to do." She kept getting disciplined for things that other student pilots got away with. "Because I had spoken up about something, now I'm getting slam-dunked."

The only consolation for Draude was that she wasn't alone in all this. The other women at Lemoore, whether at the RAG or at VAQ-34, were all terrific, awe-inspiring, really. They were so damn competent, which made their status there all the more infuriating. It drove Draude up the wall to see someone like Pam "Dandy" Lyons, with 1,500 flight hours, having to argue, day after day, telling some bull-headed jet guy that yes, women really were ready to fly combat aircraft.

But if that's what they were, that's what they were: emissaries. The ones who came first had to prepare the way for the others. If they had to spend hour after hour enduring Neanderthal logic in the ready room, so be it. They had gotten used to it in three years of flight training. It wasn't their primary problem.

Nor was their main concern the Tailhook scandal, though some people in the press made it out to be. They'd have preferred it if the reporters and the sympathetic D.C. types would get a life, stop nattering on about Las Vegas and figure out where the real battle was. The women pilots at Lemoore basically agreed that Tailhook was a gigantic pain, way overblown and hyperinflated. That the public and the media and Congress kept dwelling on it made it far more difficult for female fliers to be accepted among their peers.

Draude and the rest of the women at Lemoore had an insider's view of the scandal. It was their community, the aviation community, that had gotten stigmatized by the affair. Brenda Scheufle, one of the pilots at VAQ-34, had been in flight school with Paula Coughlin. She knew Paula was a serious person who wouldn't make a big deal about something if it wasn't warranted. True, Brenda acknowledged, Paula was a partier, but that didn't make what happened to her any less horrifying.

Tailhook had made its presence felt in the ready rooms at Lemoore, but not as a topic of discussion. What was there to talk about? The scandal permeated everything, like the fogs out on Interstate 5, sending certain lines of conversation spinning into the ditch. In frontline places like Lemoore, it had what First Amendment lawyers would term a "chilling effect" on dialogue, on mood. Call signs, the slangy, shorthand ID's fliers use over the radio, were being "reevaluated." Long-standing aviation terms were now suspect, like the one used to describe a certain high-pitched alarm that sounded in the F/A-18 cockpit, which used to be known as "bitchin' Betty." Relations between men and women grew even more strained.

"It's caused a lot of reluctance on the part of the male aviators to joke around with the female aviators," Draude said. "They're afraid they're going to get slam-dunked somehow. And I'm sorry to see that, because I kind of miss that joking around stuff."

Sobering, too, was the Navy's botched response to the incident.

Part of what was haunting Lemoore the fall Loree Draude was in training at the RAG was the official fallout from Tailhook. There was a sense that the people in Washington who were supposed to be leading them through this quagmire didn't really have it together. In September 1992, the Department of Defense Inspector General's office had issued Part 1 of its two-part report on Tailhook, titled *Review of the Navy Investigations*. The report pilloried every official in the Department of the Navy who had overseen the two probes at the start of the investigative process, accusing them of sabotaging the effort out of their own hostility toward women.

The commander in charge of the NIS was singled out for special criticism. Rear Admiral Duvall "Mac" Williams, Jr., was portrayed as a sexist jerk who shied away from interviewing senior officers who had ignored the behavior at the convention. Williams commented on Paula Coughlin's use of profanity in her statements to Navy investigators, saying any woman who would speak like that "on a regular basis would welcome this kind of activity." Williams also, said the report, at one point engaged in a "screaming match" in a Pentagon corridor with Barbara Pope, in which he "made comments to the effect that a lot of female Navy pilots are go-go dancers, topless dancers or hookers."

Acting Secretary Sean O'Keefe had called a press conference and led with the mea culpa that had been inherited from the Hill/Thomas debacle: "I need to emphasize a very important message," he told the assembled press corps. "We get it." Williams, along with Rear Admiral John E. Gordon, the Navy's Judge Advocate General, were taking early retirement, said O'Keefe, while Rear Admiral George W. Davis, the Naval Inspector General, would be reassigned (the three of them denied all wrongdoing in 200 pages of blustering rebuttals). Because the DoD report had portrayed the Navy as unable to conduct a competent investigation, O'Keefe also announced plans for restructuring the department in order to exert more civilian control over the Navy's investigative agencies.

Then there was the ongoing DoD investigation, which would lead to Part 2 of the report. Agents were still flying regularly in and

out of NAS Lemoore. Some of the base's star jo's were getting summoned to Washington for further interrogation. Even though the hospitality suite at Las Vegas sponsored by the Lemoore RAG had not
been implicated the first time around, who knew what the second
probe would bring?

All this led to an atmosphere of unease and foreboding around
the base. No one could say when the roiling instability caused by the
scandal would finally end, how far it would go, or whom it would drag
under. With Bill Clinton getting elected, a new Navy secretary would
be appointed, and a new Secretary of Defense. People were saying
that women were going to run the military.

Out here on what passed for the frontlines in the Navy, it
seemed that most of the measures that had been taken, post-Tailhook
—the service-wide stand-down included—had the effect of upping
the anxiety level while not actually addressing the problems concerned. At Lemoore, everyone was walking around on eggshells. Just
months before Draude had reported to the RAG, there had been an
incident that still threw its shadow across the whole air station. A male
instructor had been hit by a sex discrimination complaint, brought by
a female student after the instructor graded her poorly on a flight
simulator check ride. The student said her grade was the result of the
IP's view of women aviators, which she saw as biased.

The male pilots at Lemoore were shaken by the sex discrimination imbroglio, which ended up with the IP being given a nonpunitive
letter of censure. His "crime" had seemed to them so illusory, so
much a matter of how you interpreted things. The IP had spoken out
on his views about women in combat, and then later he had happened
to give a lousy grade to a female pilot. Suddenly that was enough to
put your career in jeopardy?

Listening to the IP, it was easy for the men of Lemoore to place
themselves in his shoes. A lot of them held similar views, views they
would staunchly defend. "It's difficult for me to visualize a woman
being on my wing going into combat," the instructor pilot said later.
"Whether the fact I was raised in the Midwest has anything to do with

it or not, my religious and spiritual feelings are [that] it's my job to
protect my mom, my sister and all the women and all the children in
this country. That's kind of old-fashioned, I know, but that's the way I
feel. It's going against a very basic instinct in me to have a woman go
along with me into combat. I just don't understand it."

There was a lot more along these lines. The instructor pilot held
these views and articulated them, and the female student knew about
it. When it came time for them to work together, she thought that his
opinion about women interfered with his clarity of judgment. The
Navy, reluctantly, after a great deal of hemming and hawing, agreed.

The whole incident was extremely scary to a large percentage of
the aviation community at Lemoore. A great many of the pilots there
held opinions similar to the instructor's; some were less charitable
toward women, some were out and out inimical. But what happened
in the Lemoore case, a lot of them thought, was that the guy had tried
to be honest and open, only to have his personal opinions thrown up
in his face and used against him. It was, by their lights, unfair and
somehow distinctly un-American. Maybe you couldn't even walk on
eggshells. Maybe you couldn't walk at all.

For Loree Draude and for the other women jet pilots at
Lemoore, though, Tailhook and bulletin boards and free speech issues
paled next to the more basic concern of where their careers headed.
As the men who had come up with them in flight school went on to
carrier training, the women were being left behind, dead-ended because of the combat ban. Every aviator in the military is locked in a
fierce competition with the other members of her generation. The
competition is for flight time, training, advancement. Loree Draude
and Brenda Scheufle and Pam Lyons and Tammi Jo Schultz and the
rest of the woman aviators at Lemoore were desperate. Congress, the
Navy, the new President—somebody had to do something that would
allow them the same chances that all their male counterparts had.
They had to be allowed to land their jets on carriers.

It was like being on a merry-go-round and seeing the gold ring
being awarded to everyone else but you. There was a phrase for mi-

norities in the military—women, blacks, Hispanics, everyone but live white males. They called them "chimneys in summer," and that fit the female jet jocks at Lemoore to perfection. Everyone had the sense of being ready, willing and able—and of standing by unused.

Change was supposedly coming. Congress had voted to end the military's combat exclusion policy, which kept women out of warplanes and off carriers. But when was it going to actually happen? The clock was ticking. To be of any use for the women at Lemoore right now, the combat exclusion had to be lifted, like, yesterday.

And if the ticking career clock wasn't enough, there was another animal waiting in the wings, ready to eat Loree Draude's dream for lunch. Draude was here at Lemoore to get the training she needed to fly F/A-18 Hornets. She wanted to fly fast and low, "in the weeds" they called it, to dogfight and drop bombs. If she did well in the training squadron—and Draude was grimly determined to do well— then she had a chance to be posted with the Flashbacks of VAQ-34. They were the only other squadron in the Navy that admitted female F/A-18 pilots, and they were being disbanded, probably as early as the following October, when their function would be handed over to the less costly reserves. The snapping beast called "downsizing" had showed up at Lemoore, and VAQ-34 was being sacrificed to Pentagon budget cuts. To the female pilots in the squadron, it was a bitterly ironic example of "last hired, first fired."

Personally, Draude found the whole situation bizarre and frustrating. She was being trained, but the one place she could use her training was about to disappear. The last dead end that had been available to her was being blocked off. "Wasted Time," that old Eagles tune, could have been her theme song.

Was there a place for the female jet pilot in the U.S. Navy? And if there was, where was it?

ACROSS THE CONTINENT, VARIOUS BODIES OF GOVERNMENT WERE grappling with the same question, and getting cumbersome, uneven and occasionally risible results. Congress was of course involved, most notably in the person of that prime blade runner for the nontheoretical arm of American feminism, Representative Pat Schroeder of Colorado. George Bush had empaneled a commission on the subject. Members of the bar were sniffing around, producing tracts and generally champing at the bit to argue the unconstitutionality of the combat exclusion.

The goad acting upon policy-makers, during the summer and fall of 1992, was the superb showing that American military women had recently made in the Persian Gulf War. Here was a concrete example of rudimentary gender equality in action. Some 41,000 women had served in the combat theater, with nearly 6,000 women in the Navy and Marines taking part, deploying with hospital ships and tenders, fleet reconnaissance air squadrons and other units. The Saudis, strict segregationists themselves when it came to the sexes, were astounded by the female presence in the American military, solving the challenge such female soldiers and sailors presented by declaring some of them to be "honorary men."

But there was a problem with women during the Gulf War—just like men, they had a tendency to get shot at. The line between combat and auxiliary roles in the modern theater of war was more blurred than ever. Women who had been assigned to "support positions" were bombed, shot down, wounded and killed—most notably in the Dhahran barracks attack of February 25, 1991, when three Army enlisted women died. Laws could relegate women to sideline positions in the military, but laws could not protect them from the vagaries of a Scud missile. During Operation Desert Storm, eleven American women were killed, five in action, and two were taken prisoner.

The obvious question became, as a *Washington Post* headline writer put it, "In the War, Did Combat Laws Save Women from Death or Promotion?" If the combat exclusion wasn't keeping women out of harm's way, as it was intended to, what, exactly was it doing?

Congress first got involved in telling the military what to do with the women in its ranks relatively recently, in 1948, when it passed the

Women's Armed Services Integration Act. This package of regulations made women an official part of the Army, the Navy and the Air Force, but levied severe restrictions on how many there could be, what rank they could hold and in what functions they could serve. It did not age well. Gradually, provision by provision, the act was dismantled, until the only restrictions left, by the time the Gulf War rolled around in the winter of 1991, were the ones disallowing women from serving on combat ships and aircraft. Indeed, one feminist theoretician identified these as "the only remaining official restrictions on women in American life." There were others, of course, but they were de facto. This was de jure.

If there was a natural target for Representative Schroeder to level her sights on, as a way to recognize and honor American military women's not inconsiderable contribution to Desert Storm, the combat exclusion was it. As a senior member of the House Armed Services Committee, Schroeder was in a position to do something about the creaky, leftover provisions of the 1948 law. Rather miraculously, for an issue that was mainly abstract for most Americans, Schroeder prevailed in beating back opposition that included the old-line military and its congressional backers. The House passed her version of the bill in May 1991, and the Senate, after tumultuous hearings and much hand-wringing by the service chiefs, passed a companion version on July 31.

But the new legislation simply *allowed* women to fly combat aircraft, it did not actually require the Navy to place women in the cockpits. The military, as always, was left free to make its own policy within the framework of congressional "intent." There was little rush, since the Senate's right wing had succeeded in forcing a compromise which allowed George Bush to form a presidential commission that would study the subject. His defense secretary, Dick Cheney, let it be known that any action the service chiefs took would have to wait until the commission made its recommendations. This was an obvious delaying tactic as conservatives within government tried to marshal forces to keep the combat exclusion in effect. Nevertheless, women like Loree Draude, for whom the combat ban was not at all abstract—

women who were in the jet-pilot pipeline, women whose careers hung in the balance—were ecstatic.

The presidential commission turned out to be another example of that odd amalgam, the political animal. George Bush was careful to pack its membership with conservative think-tankers like Elaine Donnelly, a Phyllis Schlafly protégé who headed up an advocacy group called Coalition for Military Readiness, which lobbied to roll back female involvement in the armed services. Donnelly was the most visible member of a five-person conservative bloc within the commission that included a vice president of the Heritage Foundation, a female master sergeant in the Air Force who was affiliated with the ultraconservative Concerned Women for America and a retired one-star general and Marine Corps veteran named Ronald Ray. "As a military historian and as a Christian," Ray would write of his work on the commission, "I sought direction from the Bible. I am keenly aware that these two world views, feminism and Christianity, are in opposition."

The conservative Gang of Five dominated the proceedings, staging elaborate walkouts when testimony was not to their liking. Mimi Finch, a U.S. Army captain, recalled later, "My service on the Commission was . . . one of the most challenging and frustrating experiences of my life, which includes my days as a plebe at West Point." Donnelly and her cohorts ensured that the investigation into the question of women in combat would be carried on in strictly political terms. Hearings of the commission, conducted in Navy towns across the country, took on the flavor of a crusade. Once, during a televised demonstration, Donnelly used a tower of wooden blocks to show the threat to the nation's military in opening combat positions to women. "Gender norming," she said, pulling out one block. "Quotas," "different standards of training," "deployability problems"—Donnelly went on, removing a block each time.

But the tower refused to fall. Donnelly removed block after block, naming fraternization, sexual relationships, the cost of child care, the problems of single parents and female POW's, and still the tower retained a precarious integrity. The assembled media reps held their collective breath, and Donnelly became flustered as the tower remained upright, through some seemingly impossible fluke of gravity. "She was trying to show how these things would weaken the military, not necessarily cause it to collapse," a commission staffer gamely explained later.

The *Report to the President* passed by the Presidential Commission on the Assignment of Women in the Armed Forces to lame duck George Bush on November 15, 1992, takes its place among the more impenetrable documents ever offered to (and sponsored by) the taxpaying public. The report is a muddle of conflicting opinions, its main body of recommendations followed by a section called "Alternative Views" to accommodate the jeremiads of the Gang of Five. There was also room for each commissioner to render his or her opinions individually. Out of such a welter of voices it was incredible that any single view prevailed, but not surprisingly, given their bellicose attitudes, it was that of the conservatives. The commission approved the recommendation that women be allowed to serve on surface combatants by a margin of one. But it decided at the same time that the ban on women flying combat aircraft should stay in place—and, astonishingly, that Congress should act to render the warplane exclusion into law once again. In other words, turn back the clocks.

One commission member had a more personal investment in the proceedings than the others. Marine Corps Brigadier General Thomas Draude, the report duly noted, had "a daughter who was a jet-pilot." Loree Draude's father had experienced a change of heart over the issue of women in the armed forces. During his three tours in Vietnam, he said, it would have been difficult for him to imagine wanting women in his unit. But during the Gulf War, he saw that women in the military "performed superbly."

"I have changed my views based on what I have seen and experienced, not just what I heard," Draude wrote, in a not-too-veiled jab at the think-tankers. For Draude, the questions involved here were in no way rhetorical. "Would you let your daughter fly in combat with the possibility of her becoming a POW? The answer is yes. I believe we have to send our best. If that means it is my daughter or my son, they should go."

"HE WAS REALLY DISAPPOINTED WHEN THE COMMISSION VOTED against women in combat air," Loree Draude said of her father. He had encouraged her during her whole military career, recommending the Navy over the Marine Corps because the opportunities she'd find there were better, suggesting she go for an NROTC scholarship, encouraging her aspirations to fly jets. In fact, his daughter's example contributed to Thomas Draude's dramatic shift in his feelings about women in war. He was an old-style Marine, and you could expect his opinions to be shaped by the macho culture in which he had been immersed ever since he was young. But more than anything, he was a fair man. And at the bottom of this issue, for Loree Draude and for all the women she talked to, it was a question of fairness.

Loree Draude not only had a father sitting on the committee, but her boyfriend, a Navy F/A-18 pilot she had met while in flight training, was attached to it as a staff member. Lieutenant (jg) Harry Hirschman had been with her the first time she sat in on the commission proceedings, when she was stashed briefly in Washington between postings. She was proud to see her father up there, interested in her boyfriend's backstage view of it all, but finally frustrated at some of the things she heard being said.

"There were times when I wanted to raise my hand and say, 'That's complete bullshit!' but I couldn't. I had to just sit there in the audience. If Harry were around, I'd whisper something to him and he'd say, 'Chill, chill.' "

Brenda Scheufle and Pam Lyons, VAQ-34 squadron-mates, had given spirited testimony in front of the panel when the commission members held hearings in Los Angeles. They'd flown in early and positioned themselves in the back of the hearing room as they listened to the testimony of the Top Gun pilots from Miramar.

"Of the 23 instructors we have at Top Gun," an instructor pilot named John Clagett told the committee, "I'll just tell you that I think we have 21 of them that decided that they wanted to sign this paper, and we'll give this to the panel, and it pretty much falls along with being a J.O. I'm going to say that it mainly is the lieutenants out there, and the captains in the Marine Corps, that are screaming that, 'No, we don't want this to happen.' And our big reason for it is that we need to have those units act as units.

"When you are out there in your fleet squadron, it is very important that you act as one, and you believe and you share your experiences with each and every member, and you expect a lot out of that person, and you have to act as a unit. And if you can't do that—and we don't believe that you can act as a unit unless you keep it the way it is, where it's the bonding—it's that intangible, the bonding, that makes a squadron good, better, and we don't believe you can have that go on if we have females in aviation."

Scheufle and Lyons were stunned by the depth of feeling against them. "It was the first time I've heard such open hatred and hostility from fellow aviators," Scheufle recalled later.

The commission members were spending $4 million gathering facts, but somehow they were missing the point. Politics was getting in the way of reality. There was a sense of dislocation, a sense that decisions being made out of Washington were too far removed from the people they affected.

Let the commission members come and sit in on the ready room bull sessions once in a while. That was where things were really being hashed out. Every point of contention, every subject being taken up by the commission, had already been aired in the ready room by the jet bubbas and flygirls for whom these regulations would apply. Some of the more articulate female pilots, Brenda Scheufle especially, and wisecracking Pam Lyons, both of whom had served in the squadron under commanding officer Rosemary Mariner, had their counterarguments down cold. Pipe up with some horseshit about the cost of pregnancy leave or the effect of G-forces or unit cohesion, and one of Rosemary's babies would be ready to answer, chapter and verse.

Refuting the b.s. was made that much easier because the objections they encountered around the base were so lame. The women of Lemoore heard endlessly about The Wall. At the Navy's flight school in Pensacola, there was an obstacle course that all students must run, and it featured an eight-foot wall for men to climb and a five-foot wall for women. The Wall was the current incarnation of the same "bugaboo" about physical standards that Rosemary Mariner had had to face twenty years earlier. This was a pet peeve of Elaine Donnelly's too, the one she'd termed "gender norming." Female aviators, went the conservative line, were being brought into flight training who were inherently less qualified to fly military aircraft than men, because they were not required to match men in this rudimentary fitness test.

Brenda Scheufle's answer: "If you can do everything the plane asks of you, then you have passed the test. If you can pull the G's in the plane, you're strong enough." Loree Draude said: "If you can show me how being able to climb over that wall is related to being able to fly an F/A-18, then okay, I'll climb over the wall for you."

What about women being taken as POW's? As one instructor pilot expressed it: "What would this country do if we had a female being raped in the streets of Baghdad being shown on CNN? We'd go into an uproar. And we should!" He had a real concern that the United States would tailor its rescue efforts to get back any captive woman, without regard for larger strategic objectives.

Loree Draude's response came in part from her SERE school training the previous April, where she'd been the only female officer out of eighty students. When the simulated "enemy" truck with its red flag and star rolled up, Draude was pulled out of the group and made the "senior officer." "They slapped me a lot and I didn't cry at all," she recalled. At the end of SERE training, some of the Marine Corps corporals going through came up to her and told her how impressed they were that she didn't lose control. That made her "feel really good, kind of like, 'Oh, wow, I did a good job for womankind.'" Afterward, she reflected: "No one can really train you to deal with rape, but it's like, guys having their fingernails ripped out is probably just as bad as being raped. It's just a different method of physical torture. And I cannot believe that no male POW has ever been raped."

The guys in the fleet squadrons at Lemoore, like those at Miramar and Oceana and everyplace else, were still concerned that women would ruin their "unit cohesion." Said Scheufle: "Basically what they're saying is that they can't perform when there's a woman in their squadron—that they are not professional enough to be a pilot if there's a woman in the plane next to them. To me, that sounds like, if you can't handle that in the air, then you don't belong in combat. Because combat is a lot more stressful than just having a woman on your wing."

"It's the leadership and respect for one another that make a unit cohesive," said Draude. "If there are females there, it'll be an extra challenge for the leadership. But it's definitely doable. Once people see that each person in the unit is carrying their load, then they won't have a claim . . . other than their own self-confidence or some other personal problem."

The male fliers had gall, the things they brought up. Living in close quarters with "girls" seemed to be a big deal. One jet pilot said, "The whole flavor of the ship would change. Like, I come out of my stateroom with a towel wrapped around me headed to the shower. 'Cause all that's gonna see me is a bunch of other guys. Now I'm gonna have to get dressed, go to the shower, get dressed, come back out of the shower. That sort of thing." But the women at Lemoore's VAQ-34 had bunked with the guys in the squadron plenty of times—on a cross-country detachment, they always shared one room, flew together, went out, got blasted, and crashed out together, and it was no big deal. Why would a fleet squadron be any different? Pam Lyons had once actually heard a male flier publicly state he didn't want to smell perfume in the ready room. "I wanted to tell him I don't want to smell his ugly socks either, but I put up with that every day."

The most deeply engrained views, though, were not the subject of ready room conversation. "It seems to me that usually the guys that don't want to have women flying with them are the ones that are here for the shit-hot-fighter-jet-jock kind of thing," said Loree Draude. "Because a woman is going to detract from that image. Most guys don't feel a woman could be studly enough. But it's like, Hey, I went through all the training you did, so why should I be less of a stud than you are? Just because you go out and scam all the chicks, that makes you a stud? You're the big jet jock?" What it all came down to was simple. "None of the boys want to share their toys."

WOMEN HAVE ALWAYS KILLED. THEY HAVE KILLED INTRUDERS WHO threatened their children. They have killed family members, parents and husbands and siblings, in anger or in self-defense. They have gone on criminal rampages, murdering strangers in the panic of theft gone wrong. They have murdered their own babies, in extremes of madness or desperation.

The fact that women have killed with much less frequency than men is apparent statistically, from the demographics of penal populations and other objective evidence. It also may be inferred from the transubstantiated mystique of woman as sustainer, nurturer, life-giver. There are times when this template slips a bit—allowing a glimpse, for example, of Kali, Hindu goddess of destruction. But in most societies and in most periods it is held firmly in place by elaborate socialization.

And of course, women have always killed in war, too. The story of female involvement in warfare is so widely ignored, yet so richly documented, as to number among what Michel Foucault terms the "secret histories" of the human race—aspects of experience so profoundly challenging to reigning taboos and archetypes that they must be instantly erased from the historical canon. To anyone familiar with the long and venerable tradition of women warfighters, the debates of George Bush's presidential commission—or the contentious disputes in the Lemoore ready room—take on the bizarre flavor of proceedings among members of the Flat Earth Society.

Throughout most of history, it is true, the woman warrior has most often been the odd, the excepted or the dissembled reality. But just because they have rarely been allowed to do so legally, in the normal course of affairs, does not mean women have not always fought in wars. When they have done so it was arresting enough to achieve the status of an icon. When Pliny mentioned the Amazons, he did so among a list of other historical oddities of the ancient (mythologized) world. But the image of woman as warrior hit a deep chord in the human imagination, and it was the Amazons who survived most prominently among Pliny's bizarre menagerie of one-eyed cyclops, fire-breathing giants and goatlike satyrs. The symbolism was close to the surface: the Amazons mutilated their breasts (i.e., removed themselves from the traditional feminine role of nurturer) in order that they could draw their bows (i.e., participate in the male-only realm of warfare) more easily.

Qualifying primarily as oddities, also, have been the warrior queens, the limitations of their gender subverted by their rank. Cleopatra, Boadicea, Elizabeth, all used variously as object lessons to signify the limitations of the female in war. Cleopatra, ruled by her passions, followed her heart into defeat. The terrible Queen Boadicea, who led the Anglo-Saxons in a victorious revolt against the Romans, has most often been pictured as a harridan, a madwoman rumbling breakneck toward death in a chariot heavily festooned with knives—a figure too extreme to qualify as a model. With Elizabeth, commentators concentrate most notably on her sacrifice of sexuality ("the Virgin Queen") in exchange for Britain's imperial gains.

Joan of Arc, another great exception to prove the rule, also has been effectively marginalized by her status as a historical oddity. After her military career she was excommunicated by the churchmen of the Holy Inquisition, who abjured her as much for her insistence on male dress as for claiming that the voices that guided her came directly from God. Her perhaps too simple rationale was that "it was more lawful and convenient . . . since she was among men, than to wear women's dress." Earlier, however, when her natural military prowess and inspirational leadership were desperately needed by France, there were few complaints about her aspirations or about her choice of clothing. She led her contingent of men (and women?) into the battle-weary city of Orléans, where she tipped the balance of the battle against the English, thus paving the way for Charles's coronation at Rheims. When she was needed as a warrior, she was given free reign. Afterward, she was punished as a transgressor.

This has been the plight of female combatants throughout the history of warfare. In times of general desperation, when the survival of the state might be in question, all able bodies are deployed, gender notwithstanding.

The most impressive example of this particular last-resort variety of female warrior is the Russian experience in World War II. There is a double reason why this particular history might be dismissed by the American military, since it challenges not only gender rules but nationalistic ones as well. One cannot learn from the enemy—especially not social science from the Evil Empire.

But if such cultural blindness could be remedied, it would be interesting to see what the jet guys in the ready room might make of Lily Litvak, a "free hunter" with the Soviet air force during the dark days of the siege of Stalingrad. Charming, girlish and deadly, a trademark wildflower tucked into the brim of her military visor, Litvak piloted her single-seat Yak-9 in solo search-and-destroy sorties against the Luftwaffe.

Lieutenant Litvak, romanticized at the time as "The Rose of Stalingrad," was one of more than 200 pilots enlisted by the Soviet Union in fall 1941 to form three all-female regiments of aviators. She had come up through the flying clubs that were the rage for Soviet teenagers in the 1930s. Knowing her parents would disapprove, she told them that she had joined the school drama society.

Her personal history was less disjointed than that of earlier women warriors, who either sacrificed their sexuality or were defeated by it. Litvak the warfighter drew strength from Litvak the lover. Her great passion was for one Alexei Salomaten, a tousle-headed fellow fighter pilot whose plane entered a fatal spin during a dogfighting exercise as she watched from the airstrip below. "Lily had always shown the sort of aggression you need to be a good fighter pilot," a close friend recalled later. "But her love for Alexei was the thing that turned her into a killer."

There is a recorded incident in Lily Litvak's history which might approximate the meeting of a modern-day jet bubba with this nightmare incarnation of a twentieth-century Amazon. After her tenth kill —out of twelve total in a warfighting career of just over one year— Litvak was brought face to face with her opponent, the man she had downed in single combat. Just over five feet tall, gray-eyed, wasp-waisted and big-bosomed, her long blond hair worn loose, "bursting with good humor and excitement . . . like a beautiful little animal, straining at the leash," Litvak confronted the tall, dour, middle-aged German ace, his chest covered with decorations. Well, said one of the Soviet pilots in the room to the prisoner, how do you like your victor? We promised to introduce you to the pilot who shot you down. The German ace did not like the Russian sense of humor. He wanted to meet the real pilot.

It was not until Lily motioned the German officer to his feet and, with pride and precision, employing the hand poetry of fighter pilots everywhere, demonstrated each maneuver and countermaneuver of their recent altercation that he was forced to believe he had been bested by a female who wore a blossom in her cap. The pilot's eyes dropped; he could not meet his victor's gaze.

Litvak was not alone. By the end of the war the "night witches," as the nighttime female bomber contingent was called by Germans who suffered under it, flew 25,000 sorties, and dropped over 30,000 tons of bombs, sometimes making as many as twenty trips a night against murderous German antiaircraft fire. Although they were excellent pilots once they got in the air, some female dive bombers who flew daytime missions in unwieldy PE-2's lacked the strength to get the aircraft off the ground. In such cases, the flier's navigator would have to physically stand behind her shoulders as she sat in the cockpit and help her pull on the stick. In the exigencies of war, the tyranny of gender was discarded.

While the U.S. War Commission officially closed the front lines to all American women during the Second World War, the ranks of partisan groups and resistance movements throughout Europe were filled with females. In Poland, 35,000 women received military training and served in sabotage, weapons building, assassination and armed combat, including teenaged Girl Guides who would creep into the homes of German officials to shoot them in their sleep. There existed regiments in the dense forests of eastern Poland that operated entirely without male input, including one named for Emilia Platter, a famed Polish heroine of the eighteenth century. In Italy, one tenth of all partisans were women.

The United States has from its inception similarly used the capacities of women in combat—but only during times of extreme duress. During the Revolutionary War, over 20,000 women served in a branch of the Continental Army known as the "Women of the Army" —not camp followers, as has sometimes been surmised, but women who performed support jobs, usually attached to the medical corps or the artillery. Although it was against regulations to recruit women into the Continental Army itself, female soldiers who adopted a man's name and clothing were common. Margaret Corbin, the only female Revolutionary War veteran buried at West Point, enlisted under her own name and served with her husband in an artillery battery during the Battle of Washington Heights in November 1776.

"If the woman was a good soldier," writes Linda Grant De Pauw, a preeminent historian of U.S. women's military experience, "it was not in anyone's interest to become a stickler for regulations and make an issue of gender. After all, the 12-year-old boys were not supposed to be in the army either, but in a time of extreme manpower shortages no one wanted to send them home." With the majority of able-bodied males off fighting with the standing army, the task of self-defense on the American frontier fell largely to women, who fought either with local militia or as irregulars. Abigail Adams wrote in 1777: "We are in no wise dispirited here. If our men are all drawn off and we should be attacked, you would find a race of Amazons in America."

One of the most famous regularly enlisted women was Deborah Sampson, from Plymouth, Massachusetts, who took the name Robert Shurtleffe and volunteered for hazardous duty in October 1778. Shot through the shoulder, feverish and in desperate need of medical attention, her sex was inevitably discovered. George Washington presented her with an honorable discharge, after which she married, had three children, and later supplemented her Army pension by going on stage in her infantry uniform to perform a musket drill and deliver patriotic addresses.

The Civil War likewise provides abundant evidence that, as one military historian puts it, "what men and women are arguing about in the twentieth century, women already did in the nineteenth, under more primitive conditions." Memoirs by women who had served disguised as men in the Civil War were common enough to comprise almost a sub-genre of writing about the conflict. "No man on the field that day," stated Loreta Janeta Velasquez of her participation in the first Battle of Bull Run, "fought with more energy and determination than the woman who figured as Lt. Harry T. Buford."

It is a particularly bitter form of hypocrisy, given the mortal stakes involved, to withhold recognition from women who have earned it in battle, but it is one routinely practiced. Similarly, Randy Shilts has noted that the U.S. military's ban on homosexuals was honored more in the breach than the observance during World War II, when all able bodies (especially able-bodied gay doctors) were needed. Only afterward, when personnel needs diminished, did the assault against homosexuals in the military begin in earnest.

Institutionalized hypocrisy aside, however, the primary point here is that the questions regarding females' performance in war have already been "asked and answered," to use the language of jurisprudence. This truth obtains not only to the small percentage of women currently assigned to combat aircraft, but to the more traditional purlieu of the Navy, the wine dark sea.

Chapter Seven

———

LEAVING THE BEACH

TO GO DOWN TO THE SEA IN SHIPS, EVEN IN THESE DECIDEDLY NON-Homeric times, still warrants the status of spectacle. A 90,000-ton aircraft carrier pulling out of port, a 60,000-ton battleship or even a noncombatant vessel can trigger a surreal sense of disproportion: there is simply no way something that large could move, much less float.

The USS *Cape Cod*—the prefixed abbreviation stands for "United States Ship," traditional Navy nomenclature inspired once again by the British—is by no means the largest ship in the Seventh Fleet. But lying in dockside, over eight stories high, it looks enormous: displacing 22,500 tons, it measures 644 feet long, with an 85-foot beam. The ship is powered by twin boilers, its steam turbines linked to the 30-foot screw by a single driveshaft. A practice actively discouraged by the command is "shaft surfing"—attempting to maintain a precarious balance on the greasy, spinning propeller shaft in the engine room.

The *Cape Cod* is a destroyer tender, which means that it is a sort of floating machine shop for the repair of ships—not only destroyers, but cruisers and other craft that are known as "small boys" in Navy

slang. Its high-bosomed, blocky silhouette, the consequence of an extremely tall freeboard, gives it the look of a freighter more than a
military ship. More tubby than sleek, the huge vessel tends to lumber
through the seas.

A tender's appearance, together with its ancillary function, rele-
gates it to the bottom of the Navy's big-boat hierarchy. But because
tenders are among the few ships that, since 1978, have been open to
female sailors on permanent assignment, they are targets of other
slurs, too. More than a few of them (the U.S. Navy has twenty-two
tenders) have been labeled "the love boat" over the course of the last
fifteen years, most recently in a *Wall Street Journal* article after the
Gulf War, causing a good deal of resentment both on the part of
official Washington and among the crews of the tenders themselves.
Shipboard pregnancies stigmatize not only the crews but the whole
class of ship. Even the name, "tender," has a soft, feminine feel to it,
which cuts against the military's masculine grain. When a tender is at
anchor, with its destroyers and cruisers nested alongside, it resembles
nothing so much as a queen sow suckling her farrow.

On January 11, 1993, USS *Cape Cod* was preparing to leave the
beach. The Southern California sun would burn off the clouds around
noon, but it was a chilly, overcast morning. The ship was moored at
Pier 7 at the San Diego Naval Base, while families and friends said
final good-byes to crew members. Steaming west out of the harbor,
she would clear the long bony finger of Point Loma, pass the wind-
pocked gravestones of war dead topping its promontory and head into
the open Pacific. The *Cape Cod* would then be "haze gray and underway"—a phrase that celebrates the slate-colored paint used on almost
all U.S. Navy vessels.

Just like the old children's rhyme, the sailors embracing their
families dockside that morning "wouldn't come back until the Fourth
of July." The *Cape Cod*'s "Westpac"—for Western Pacific—would be
a six-month deployment. It is more than 10,500 nautical miles from
San Diego to mid-Indian Ocean, a twenty-one-day transit for a ship
steaming at twenty knots. The cruise would take *Cape Cod* to her final

destination of Bahrain via Pearl Harbor, Guam, Singapore, Panang, New Delhi and Jabal 'Ali. Once in the Persian Gulf, and at stops along the way, the tender would park in the harbors and offer "availabilities" to all vessels in need. She could do this because her workshops were self-contained, down to the ability to manufacture their own nuts and bolts.

Since the *Cape Cod* was one of only ten ships in the Pacific Fleet open to women (out of forty-seven in a five-hundred-ship Navy), and since sea duty was a crucial element to every Navy career, a billet here was plum duty for the females on board. There were 1,515 people in the crew, and a third of them were women. Many of the sailors on the broad wooden pier were mothers saying good-bye to their infants, wives giving husbands embraces that would have to last a half year or girls who were still teenagers taking leave of their parents.

Sea captain James Hooper IV, the *Cape Cod*'s commanding officer, was not at all reticent about his paternal feelings for his crew. "Being a commanding officer is a lot like being a super-parent," Hooper said. The feeling could flow the other way, too. Hooper was "like a big Dad, just a lovable person" said an enlisted woman in his command. Hooper's father was a sea captain, and he had always wanted to be one: "I made my decision when I was seven years old and I never deviated from it." He had a long Navy career behind him, but this would be his first deployment with a mixed-gender crew.

Scattered among the lower decks were *Cape Cod*'s berthing areas for enlisted personnel, each designated male or female. Likewise, bathrooms and shower areas—heads, in nautical parlance—were segregated. There were times in the workday when a female might have to pass through a male berthing area, on which occasions it was the custom to announce, "Female on deck!" Up above, in the hushed, courtly precincts of "officer country," there was the same tight-quarters attention paid to the issue of gender. Male and female officers might have staterooms side by side, but the heads were segregated.

In a post-Tailhook Navy, these "habitability" issues—"heads and beds" as the question was shorthanded—had suddenly been thrust to the fore. Backwater commands like tenders, oilers and salvage ships, noncombatants, the only platforms open to women, were being examined under a magnifying glass. When the presidential commission made a fact-finding trip to the West Coast the previous summer, the ship it chose to visit was the *Cape Cod.* As much as VAQ-34 was a proving ground in Lemoore, so was the *Cape Cod,* even if a less prestigious one, on the lower-rung "squid row" of Navy fleet hierarchy.

On Pier 7 that morning, final, private good-byes were said. The last of the crew reported for duty. A short time later, under the bone-white skies of a San Diego winter, the tugs nudged the prow slowly away from the slip toward the deeper channel, and the sea behind the fantail began to churn black to dirty gray. A few family members still remained on the shore, waving fitfully at the ship until she was lost in the traffic of the harbor.

THAT WOMEN ON THE SHIPS OF THE U.S. NAVY WAS STILL AN ISSUE at all in 1993 was largely due to a historical fluke bequeathed to the country by a wily Southern congressman in the aftermath of World War II.

In February 1948, forty-five years before USS *Cape Cod* steamed toward the Persian Gulf, a House Armed Services subcommittee was conducting hearings on S. 1641, the Women's Armed Services Integration Act. The committee sat under the shrewd stewardship of Carl Vinson, Democrat of Georgia, large-featured, vigorous, the prototype of Southern lawyer turned congressman, a one-man argument for term limits. He had spent his whole adult life in the House, since 1914, before his grand-nephew, Senator Sam Nunn, was a gleam in anyone's eye.

The Swamp Fox, they called him, a nickname not so much in reference to geography—Georgia's Sixth District, from which he hailed, was made up of loamy farmlands—as to character. In his half century as a congressman, Vinson dominated the discussion of naval affairs in the House of Representatives, to the degree that the postwar service could be called, with no overstatement, "the Vinson Navy" (in appreciation, the Navy would name its fourth nuclear aircraft carrier after him in 1982). This from a local military-college graduate who had never served at sea, never served in any armed services capacity at all, but simply made the U.S. Navy his legislative hobbyhorse. Vinson first was the chair of the House Naval Affairs Committee, from 1931 to 1946, endured a short interregnum as the Democrats lost their plurality, then picked up again as the sachem of the powerful House Armed Services Committee, over which he reigned from 1949 onward. Vinson finally retired to his farm in Milledgeville, Georgia, in 1964, gifted by committee staffers with "the finest television set money could buy," having left an enduring impression on U.S. postwar and Cold War military policy

As the subcommittee hearing began on that February morning in 1948, the Swamp Fox had a problem. He didn't like the bill that had been sent over from the Senate: the Women's Armed Services Integration Act. To a Southern congressman, that word "integration" sent up a whole host of red flags. Vinson was accustomed to shaping any legislation pertaining to the U.S. Navy pretty much to his whim. Ordinarily, if he didn't like the elements of a Navy bill, they were as the Moabites before David, smitten and vanquished in a cloud of smoke.

But Vinson knew there'd be difficulties with the witness before the subcommittee that morning, the most popular man in America, General Dwight D. Eisenhower. This was not a man who could be bullied or dismissed. His opinions on the bill before the committee were likely to be problematic and, in Vinson's eyes, heretical. The Swamp Fox would have to handle Eisenhower gingerly, allowing him a hearing, but not a soap box.

Unlike Vinson's, Eisenhower's views on women in the armed services were formed in the crucible of war. There was no established constituency in favor of opening the military to women, but after Pearl Harbor, personnel shortages forced the government's hand. Each branch of the armed services formed a component of female reservists. Eisenhower had extensive experience working with soldiers of what was at first called the Women's Auxiliary Army Corps (WAAC), and later termed the Women's Army Corps (WAC)—a change that reflected the group's new, full military status.

Representative Edith Nourse Rogers (the only female in the House at the time) had sponsored the bill in 1941 to create a women's military component. Congressmen—Carl Vinson among them—asked for and received assurances that women would not command men, that the numbers of women would be limited and that they would be excluded from dangerous situations. Those assurances, coupled with the belief that women would excel at such traditional jobs as switchboard operator, typist, laundry operator, dietitian and clerk, allowed the legislators to support the bill. Eventually, 140,000 served with the WAC, 100,000 with the WAVES and 23,000 with the Marine Corps Women's Reserve. An additional 60,000 women joined the Army Nurse Corps and 14,000 the Navy Nurse Corps. While most women did not serve in anything near a combat capacity, nurses (and some WACs) saw hazardous duty in every theater. They dug their own foxholes and cared for wounded soldiers under enemy fire.

Of all the service branches, the Navy was perhaps the most guilty of foot dragging in setting up its women's branch. The reluctance was aided by a convenient lapse of communal memory: close to 12,000 women had served in the Navy during World War I, the vast majority of them in a secretarial capacity known as Yeoman (F). Secretary of the Navy Josephus Daniels—the Navy Secretary who earlier had banned alcohol at sea—enlisted women in the Reserves in response to a severe personnel crisis in 1916, and there was no language in the Naval Reserve Act to prevent him. That changed in 1925, when the act was amended to limit the Naval Reserve to "male citizens of the United States" (a rewording that provoked a lively skirmish on the floor of the Senate between female World War I veterans and senators). By the time the Japanese bombed Pearl Harbor and military leaders realized that they were dangerously undermanned, the precedent of the World War I Yeomen (F)—the "F," of course, for Female —had been effectively expunged.

High-ranking Navy planners at the start of the Second World War actively resisted the idea of pressing women into service. One of the people eventually hired to advise the services on how to set up female service components was Dean Virginia Gildersleeve of Barnard College. "If the Navy could possibly have used dogs or ducks or monkeys," she later recalled, "certain of the older admirals would probably have greatly preferred them."

Joy Bright Hancock, who would become the Navy official in charge of plans and policies for women after the 1948 Integration Act, had been a Yeoman (F) in the First World War, and served as a commissioned officer in the second. When the first auxiliary legislation was in preparation, Hancock was working as a civilian in the Navy's Bureau of Aeronautics, one of the few areas of the service whose leaders could envision a place for women in the wartime Navy. Later, she wrote that when the men in charge of the Navy's various bureaus were surveyed on the subject, their response was practically a stone wall of disinterest. The assistant secretary of the Navy wrote that he saw no place for a women's reserve: any jobs for which the Navy might need women could be filled under Civil Service procedures. The reactions of the rest of the Navy departments followed suit:

> Office of the Judge Advocate General: "No use for the services of the Women's Auxiliary is seen at this time."
> Bureau of Medicine and Surgery: "Do not visualize a need."
> Bureau of Supplies and Accounts: "It does not appear that the establishment of a Women's Auxiliary Corps would be desirable."
> Bureau of Yards and Docks: "Such a corps is unnecessary to assist this bureau in carrying out its functions."
> Bureau of Ships: "As clerks, typists and stenogs," thought it "probable" but deemed such use was precluded because it would invade the province of Civil Service.

One of the few exceptions, interestingly, was the Bureau of Ordnance, which said that based on "the experience of other nations in this war, it is entirely possible that combatant naval service (limited to zones of interior and continental Naval Districts) may be desirable in the case of women." But the support of one bureau was not enough to topple the resistance of high-ranking military men. Congress delayed the inception of the women's naval reserve until 1942. Another Barnard academic, Professor Elizabeth Reynard, came up with the acronym WAVES while keeping one eye on possible congressional and military objections. She described her main concerns in a letter to Gildersleeve:

> I realized that there were two letters which had to be in it: "W" for women and "V" for volunteer, because the Navy wants to make it clear that this is a voluntary service and not a drafted service. So I played with those two letters and the idea of the sea and finally came up with "Women Appointed for Volunteer Emergency Service"—WAVES. I figured the word "Emergency" could comfort the older admirals because it implies that we're only a temporary crisis and won't be around for keeps.

Now, six years later, Eisenhower began his testimony, recalling his initial trepidation to the idea of women in the armed services: "When this project was proposed in the beginning of the war," he told the subcommittee, "like most old soldiers, I was violently against it. I thought a tremendous number of difficulties would occur, not only of an administrative nature, and, of course—there are bound to be a few of those when you incorporate women into a military organization— but I thought there would be others of a more personal type that would occur that would be real difficult to handle, that maybe we were exposing people to various types of temptation and other things that would get us in trouble. None of that occurred." There had been no problems at all with the performance of the women under his command, Eisenhower concluded, only benefits.

The general had firsthand knowledge of women's success in non-traditional jobs. At the start of the war, Eisenhower had heard that British women had acquitted themselves well in antiaircraft units against the Luftwaffe, and so had suggested to General George Marshall that an experiment might be conducted to see what antiaircraft artillery duties could be performed by American female reservists. During the top-secret project that ensued, women were assigned to over half of the jobs in two mixed-gender antiaircraft batteries, as part of a program at Bolling Field and other East Coast locations. They were not supposed to actually fire the guns, and they were not trained in small weapons, but nonetheless the results were persuasive. "To the amazement of senior officers," writes a historian of the period, D'Ann Campbell, "the experiment showed that units that were mixed 50-50 performed better than all-male units, and had high unit cohesion or 'bonding.' "

Caught in a double bind, however, Eisenhower did not mention Marshall's experiment specifically during the 1948 hearings. He would alienate conservative legislators like Vinson if he was overly gung-ho. But the military, recently reverted to an all-volunteer basis, desperately needed personnel at the start of the Cold War. "Enormous offices and record headquarters must be run," Eisenhower told the committee, "otherwise the whole thing would collapse. They demand men and we do not have the men. We are 100,000 short. There are no people to send General MacArthur and to General Clay. There is no way of doing it."

Under these exigencies, and in spite of the political consequences, Eisenhower struck a tone that was aggressively positive about women's presence in the armed forces. He went further to confront a conservative bugaboo—their induction. "I hope that there would be a few [women] coming in young," he told the committee members pressing him on the question of retirement benefits for women service members, "that a few would stay with us, because they would be the ones who would study and develop the policies and methods by which you would use women in large numbers in the war, and I am convinced that in another war they have got to be drafted just like men. I am convinced of that."

The Swamp Fox had to go on the offensive. Delicately—very delicately in the face of Eisenhower's fulsome praise of women's mili-

tary worthiness—he raised the issue of whether noncombatant females might "be given rank not commensurate with responsibility."
The men were facing bullets, Vinson implied, while the worst a
woman could expect was to smear a carbon.

Eisenhower bristled. "I should like to say this, sir, I have met
[Army women] first in war. I never saw them at home. They joined my
theater of operations. We were horrorstruck, almost, at the idea [of
military women overseas]. In all the war I never had a woman ask of
me a favor except the one of service to the front. I had men say they
would be better fitted back home as instructors. I never had a woman
say that to me."

As Eisenhower's testimony concluded it had been abundantly
established that, in his eyes, arguments against women's permanent
participation in the military simply had no merit. "I can see no objections to the bill. Everything is on the favorable side."

To military professionals in 1948, the question of personnel
shortages was not theoretical; the next war seemed imminent, and it
would be total. In a statement to the subcommittee by the director of
the WACs, five-foot-tall Colonel Mary A. Hallaren, the service's ranking woman, made apparent just how terrifying and acute this Arma-
geddon-like vision of the next war could be. Nicknamed "the Littlest
Colonel," she demonstrated a pugnacious willingness to fight legislative battles. "When the house is on fire, we don't talk about a woman's
place in the home," said Hallaren, presenting a homey metaphor of
woman's natural combativeness in defense of the hearth. "And we
don't send her a gilt-edged invitation to help put the fire out."

General Omar Bradley, the Army Chief of Staff, spoke in the
same vein as Hallaren and Eisenhower, as did General Hoyt Vanden-
berg, Vice Chief of Staff of the fledgling Air Force. But it was Secretary of Defense James Forrestal, a Navy flier in World War I and Navy
secretary during World War II, who pronounced the most viable rationale for according women full status. It is a line of argument with
special relevance to what happened at Tailhook, and to the post-
Tailhook Navy. "No business, no governmental organization, and especially no military force, can accomplish its objectives where individ-

uals working side by side, doing identical work with equal degrees of responsibility, are classified differently as to status, prerogatives, or emoluments. Women in the services have proved their value and their capacity. They should be given equal rights with male enlistees and male officers . . . If we are going to use women in the armed forces, we should go the whole way and give them identical status and benefits as men." Forrestal went on to declare that "there are some aspects of war, such as . . . aerial photographic reconnaissance, the identity of targets, of contours, in which [women] are highly proficient and sometimes better than men."

The debate before the subcommittee that February seemed to cleave along lines of ignorance and experience, a pattern seen down to the present day, in the tug of war over women at war. Those military professionals who had served alongside women were in favor of being able to continue to do so, while civilians on the subcommittee questioned the whole idea.

As the hearings progressed, it became clear that simply on the basis of personnel imperatives, women would be permanently integrated into the U.S. armed services. The experience of the recent war, and the records of women who participated in it, served the proponents of integration well—foreshadowing the example of the Gulf War a half century later, when women's role in the military would again be transformed. But, for the time being, the committee members succeeded in capping the number of women in the military at 2 percent, and limiting the rank they could achieve.

Congressman Carl Vinson, who had served for years as a "long, loud, and lonely proponent of a big Navy," could not find room in his pet fleet for females. If he was not able to keep women out of the service entirely, or relegated to the Reserves, where they belonged, then he would do the next best thing: relegate them to the beach.

> Vinson: I propose an amendment, if somebody will draft it. I am just throwing it out for what it is worth . . . I think it will strengthen the bill to have it positively understood by Congress that ships are not places to which these women are going to be

detailed and nobody has any authority to detail them to serve on ships. Let them serve on shore in the Continental United States and outside of the United States, but keep them off the ships . . . I would not want to restrict it to combatant vessels. Put down "serve in sea duty." Just fix it so they cannot go to sea at all.

It took Navy women thirty years to overthrow the decree pronounced by Vinson in that single sentence: "Just fix it so they cannot go to sea at all." Public Law 625 prohibited the assignment of women to any vessels other than hospital ships or naval transports—two ship types that were effectively mothballed from the close of World War II to the Korean War. As the Cold War progressed, there would be repeated moves to liberalize and further integrate the military, and they were always opposed by the argument that such measures were against "the intent of Congress," when really they were against the intent of a small-town Georgia congressman who watched over the U.S. Navy as if it were his own.

WHAT PEOPLE TALK ABOUT WHEN THEY TALK ABOUT WOMEN AND MEN together on ships: Do they screw? What happens when they do? Can the women handle the hard work and rough conditions? Do they get preferential treatment? Do they get hassled by the men? How much does shipboard culture have to change to accommodate female sailors?

Captain Hooper of the *Cape Cod* would be confronted by all these questions over the long six-month cruise to Bahrain and back. Part of his job was to become a sort of cultural ombudsman for women. "The ship is a reflection of the captain," Hooper said. "So I have to get to them and say, 'Open your minds. You've got to make this work. You've got to integrate these women into your all-male society, and get on with it. Here are some of the problems and some ideas about how you might deal with them.' "

Hooper had had personal doubts about his first mixed-gender

command. "I was concerned about how I would deal with this. And what I discovered in a very brief time was that the people here are wonderfully competent. They're proud of what they do. They don't know this is extraordinary by comparison with other ships. They think this is better. And they're right. I've lost sight of the fact that it happens to be a woman who is my writer and a woman who is my cook, that my officers who are driving the ship are women, that my master helmsman on here is a woman. It doesn't make a difference."

If, as the old adage goes, the fish rots from the head, the *Cape Cod* exhibited no visible signs of decay in Hooper's character. It was a trim ship, spotless in the way only a constantly attended environment can be. It's an old maritime truth: an easy way to judge a commanding officer is on the cleanliness and order of the physical plant itself. Venture onto a ship with grimy, cluttered passageways, and you can be fairly certain there are deeper problems in the command. In Navy parlance, the USS *Cape Cod* was "squared away," as were its crew members. It showed up in performance, too. The *Cape Cod* was the first tender that anyone could remember actually getting underway on time for Westpac. The ship's no-nonsense approach to matters of gender relations also seemed to flow naturally from the commanding officer down. Sexual assault and harassment, for example, were dealt with in a direct, almost matter-of-fact fashion, as if to say, it might happen between people, but if it ever happens on the *Cape Cod,* it will be in spite of a determined official effort against it, and not in an atmosphere of neglect and ignorance. A self-defense course for women was offered by the *Cape Cod* as it got underway for Westpac.

The ship had eight decks below the weather deck, where all enlisted people slept and most of them worked, and four levels in the beetling superstructure, where the officers' staterooms were, along with the wardroom and the bridge. Down a short ladder from the pilothouse was the captain's office-cum-stateroom, palatial in comparison with the other personal spaces on the ship, more well appointed than the others, with views all around and a sliding door between the main office area and the sleeping quarters. Unlike the faintly greasy rails found throughout the rest of the ship, those leading up to the captain's cabin were wrapped with bright red rope. There was a jar of atomic fireballs on Hooper's desk, a collection of fifteen souvenir hats from ships he'd either crewed with or commanded, an old-fashioned spyglass, through which the skipper would sometimes actually look. From the Olympian perspective of the captain's quarters, the presence of women on the ship could take on a roseate glow. "People behave better," Hooper said of having women on board. "There's a natural softening, if you will. Nothing to make us less effective, it's just that the language tends to be better, and the conduct and courtesy are better."

Immediately below officer country, where enlisted personnel were forbidden to go without a specific job or special permission, were the weatherdecks, the most exposed areas of the ship. They were the domain of the boatswain's mate, a term always elided, in ancient tradition, to "bo'sun." On the *Cape Cod*, the 130-member deck crew was evenly split between men and women. The "Deck Department" retained the most proximate connection to the tall-ship seagoing past. "The last of the pirate ratings," was how it was put by one boatswain's mate third-class, smoking a Newport on the signal bridge. He meant that the deck crew still did the swabbing, rigging and hauling that all sailors have been doing for centuries. "There are no technical schools for this rating," *The Bluejackets' Manual* dryly states of the boatswain's mate. The weatherdecks were the realm of the bo'sun's pipe, the thin, melancholy notes of which still marked the day's activities. But the Deck Department was also where the Navy dumped the rawest seaman recruits, out in the elements, its informal apprenticeship program. On the *Cape Cod*, you could immediately spot members of the deck crew by their freckles, muscles and sunburn—and by their slightly retro swagger. "I like being out on the salt," said a boatswain's mate first-class who supervised many of the young seamen on the decks. He had been on the *Cape Cod* for nine months, and was accustomed to the integrated crew. "Working with all men, you get your temperamental people. The morale here is more together. Some of the men think that women can't pull their load. My attitude is, if you can't pull the load, let me know. I'll get somebody to help you. But you'll do the same work."

In every department of the ship, there were questions asked and answered about women's physical ability to do the assigned tasks. A female petty officer third-class in engineering was less taken with her colleagues' receptivity: "On a tender, you have to listen to the guys go, 'I'll be glad when I go to a real ship.' They don't consider it a real ship because it's males and females. You'll hear just about every guy on the boat say that at least once. Even the ones who say, 'we're not prejudiced against females,' you'll hear them say something derogatory at least once. It's not that they hate us. It's just that you get into situations where they go, 'a female can't do this, she's too weak.' Especially in engineering. Most of the time you hear it from people that are lower than you. A lot of times they don't like taking orders from females."

The berthing compartments of the enlisted personnel were warrened away throughout the ship, on every deck, in odd-angled, claustrophobic situations. At ten o'clock in the morning, the midwatch sailors could be seen sleeping under the fluorescent lights, their cheeks still pink from windburn, nestled in their gray wool Navy-issue blankets. Outside of the berthing areas, the rest of the *Cape Cod* belowdecks was essentially an industrial environment. In the passageway outside the mailroom there was a cash machine and machines that sold what the Navy called "geedunk"—junk food and soda. But the same space was also a staging area for damage control, with a collection of battered red hard hats stored in a webbed sling against the wall.

The lounges attached to the berthing areas were largely deserted, sailors instead preferring the society of the mess decks, which had the approximate atmosphere—raucous decibel level, steam table funk—of a high school cafeteria. Though there was a lot of "skylarking," fooling around, as the ship headed into its six-month cruise there was an underlying serious mood, centered around the same topics that dominated the discussion in the wardroom and weatherdecks up above: pregnancy, loneliness, men and women coping together. But usually the talk was about the work at hand. There were widespread high spirits and enthusiasm for going to sea. These were, a lot of them, small-town people, and they were on their way to exotic ports-of-call.

Only very obliquely would anyone address changes in the "new Navy." How, for example, would women take to one of the oldest and without a doubt most overtly macho traditions of the sea, one which goes back to the Vikings—the "crossing-the-line" or "shellback" ritual? The ceremony, which marks the crossing of the equator might seem nearly unfathomable from the sober-minded perspective of shore. The crew divides into two groups: shellbacks, who have already "crossed the line" and been initiated into the "mysteries of the deep," and pollywogs, or simply "wogs," who must undergo a series of rites in order to be transformed into shellbacks.

To an outsider, the shellback ritual appears not so much sleazy as cheesy, an amateur pageant featuring Neptunus Rex, Davy Jones, the Devil and various subfunctionaries dressed up to play the roles of the "royal baby," the "royal doctor," the "royal dentist," the "royal chief bear," as well as barbers, demons and police. A drag beauty pageant the night before the ritual crowns the best-looking sailor as Her Highness Amphitrite, the Queen, who is allowed to avoid the more rigorous aspects of the ceremony.

Sailors treasure their ornately illuminated shellback certificates, if only as a ticket out of further humiliations on the next voyage. Almost all Navy personnel have gone through a line-crossing hazing, either at the equator or the International Dateline (the Vikings, whose crossing-the-line ceremonies were murderous endurance trials, used the thirtieth parallel as their demarcation). Senator Joseph McCarthy would afterward claim his gimp leg was full of Japanese shrapnel, but the injury was actually sustained in a Navy crossing-the-line ritual, when McCarthy was made to walk down a ladder with a bucket tied to his leg. Ross Perot, Richard Nixon and John F. Kennedy also went through the shellback ceremony as Navy men.

"The discomfort of a good dousing in the tank," note the authors of the most comprehensive book on naval ceremonies and traditions, "a slight shock of electricity from the fork of the 'Devil,' and the slap-happy shaving ceremony comprise the most unpleasant features of the initiation." But everyone in the Navy had heard of "features" that were much less pleasant. During the tenure of the last *Cape Cod* skipper, for example, a wog lost his fingertips by getting a watertight door shut on his hand. There was some question if the *Cape Cod* under Hooper would even allow a shellback ceremony.

Beyond everyday pranks and "grab-assing," other traditions were equally problematic for the "new Navy." Chief's initiations mark the transition of a petty officer to a chief petty officer, and, though modified in the last few years, were traditionally binge blowouts. "Frocking," when a sailor receives new "hash marks" or stripes in a promotion, usually meant "tacking on," with shipmates each allowed a good punch to the bicep. "Dining ins" were formal affairs presided over by "Mr. Vice," or "Ms. Vice," the officer in charge of entertainment that Navy leadership would almost certainly have "zero tolerance" for. "Blanket parties" were informal punishments meted out between sailors, and involved pinning someone in a rack and pummeling them beneath a blanket. (Aviators had their own potentially injurious rituals, including those associated with receiving "wings," the pin which indicates qualification as a Navy flier. "Drinking your wings," meant the pin was placed in a glass of beer and downed, to pass through the aviator's system with its point unsheathed. "Blood wings" referred to the practice of pinning the wings directly onto the flesh.)

The presence of women in the Navy complicated such matters, and not only because of the blood sport involved. Many of the shellback rituals, for example, had overt homoerotic qualities. The event began with a drag contest and by its end a lot of men had wound up naked, getting hosed down with firehoses. Wogs were challenged to eat a cherry or oyster out of the grease-smeared navel of the diaper-swaddled royal baby, usually the oldest, most grizzled chief petty officer, the one with the most impressive beer gut on the crew. There were reports that in times not too far removed, wogs were raped by shellbacks during the ceremony.

Hooper had let it be known that he wouldn't stand for brutality on his ship. "There's no need for any of that crap that degrades and humilates someone," he said. The *Cape Cod* might forgo the more severe crossing-the-line traditions, such as wogs being whipped with "shillelaghs"—lengths of canvas firehose—and other traditions which had over the years resulted in injuries and even deaths. But if the coming ceremony would be anything like that on other tenders, wogs would still go through the "garbage chute"—get put in a commode filled with applesauce and have to fish a grape out of the stuff with their teeth. The women on the *Cape Cod* didn't seem worried. "It's a silly little game," said one of the female officers, a Naval Academy grad. "Like a birthday party." Almost universally, the women as well as the men on board agreed they wanted the traditional ceremony with all its trappings. But again, until it happened, if it happened, no one knew what form it would take.

There were a few pockets of unreconstructed, old-time Navy on the *Cape Cod,* sectors where the acceptance of women was more remarkable because it was hard-won. "One of the reasons I joined the Navy was to get away from women," said Bill Breznau, the *Cape Cod*'s chief engineer. "So here I are," he mused, Popeye-like, "going out to sea with them . . ." Chief engineers were always called by the collapsed title of "Cheng," and their domain was a series of sprawling compartments deep within the ship. It was a hot, greasy, chthonic world, tremendously loud, where Cheng played Vulcan to Hooper's Zeus. Neither man ever got more than four or five hours of sleep a night. Cheng would prowl down below while Hooper was up in the pilothouse.

Breznau was an ex-"bubblehead," a submariner, from a Navy community that was not yet integrated by gender, where the subject of female crew members had barely been broached. He was "pretty upset" when he heard about his assignment to a tender. He was afraid of "saying the wrong thing to a female, looking the wrong way at a female, being aware of all these females all over the place." But after the first day or so, he said, that self-consciousness went away. He was used to "the typical sailor attitude—you talk *about* women, you don't talk *with* women. And then all of a sudden you're working side by side with them. You're in the same environment as everybody in the rest of the world. And it's more normal. At this point in time, I wouldn't have it any other way."

Before the *Cape Cod* left San Diego, it had gone on an evaluation run in the harbor, when the main steam boiler went down and the emergency diesel, which powers the steering gear, the conveyers and elevators, the air conditioning and refrigerator and galley equipment, did not kick in properly. The ship "secured general quarters," meaning crew members assumed their assigned emergency stations. There was a line of people passing down five-gallon jugs of water to fill the boiler tank. The temperature was extreme; two people passed out from heatstroke. "It got very ugly," Breznau recalled. The sailors pulled off a miracle, starting the main engines by hand. "The crew pulled together after that point. You could feel it. That night, there were no men or women on board. There were no blacks, there were no Filipinos. It was just the crew—everybody working together."

Breznau seemed unsure if the egalitarian ideal presented that night would, over the long run, be strong enough to replace what the Navy used to have, the camaraderie of homogeneity, the shared traditions of the same tribe. Cheng was the type of person who saw a deeper value in traditions like the shellback ceremony, such as the kind of bonding necessary to cohere an outfit. "Our purpose is to go out and kill people. That may be redefined now by President Clinton and Congress, as the country heads into the twenty-first century, but up until now, our charter for existence has been to go out and kill people. We didn't train to 'deter' people or do crowd control. Everything we trained for was to go out and . . . brutally, physically, explosively gain control of geography. When you put it in that context, some of the other stuff begins to make sense. When you ask someone to march off to a situation where they could kill or be killed it requires a different sort of motivation and control. You can't just take a bunch of civilians who get together once a month at the local 'Y' and have a little philosophical discussion about what they'd like to do. In an environment where you're expected to walk into the jaws of death, it takes a certain mentality and camaraderie and peer group that you won't get simply by having civilian standards of conduct."

As the *Cape Cod* got underway for Westpac, though, the main concern on board was not the jaws of death, but simply getting through the workday. For a variety of reasons, the *Cape Cod* would leave the beach without its full crew contingent. Service-wide, pregnancy was not the major cause for absenteeism—studies had shown that women had less down time than men in the Navy, and sports injuries accounted for more days lost than pregnancy. But somehow, pregnancy had become the primary complaint against women sailors on the *Cape Cod*. They had a suspicious tendency to get knocked up right before a cruise, or so the apocrypha had it. They were using their biology to shirk their duty. The reality was that Navy women were allowed only forty-two days of maternity leave. They could be asked to return to sea duty four months after having the baby—so any shirking was relative. Shop talk didn't reflect this reality.

Alice Smith, the command master chief aboard ship and the senior enlisted person, estimated that "somewhere in the neighborhood of twenty-five or so crew members are not going to deploy with us, and it's all because of pregnancy. Now tell me that's not going to hurt a ship." In a meeting of the ship's department heads shortly before deployment, she was blunt: "Just about every division has been decimated by the number of pregnancies." But this has to be put in perspective. Out of a crew of more than 1,500, there were 200 who could not deploy for various medical or personal reasons, including the 25 pregnant women. Pregnancy, in other words, accounted for only an eighth of the predeployment departures. But even the relatively enlightened Hooper saw the problem as serious enough to recommend (in a memorandum to his superior) that pregnancy during deployment should mean automatic suspension from the Navy.

An unspoken aspect of the Navy's pregnancy equation was the almost total lack of abortion services in military facilities around the world. Since 1988, American military hospitals had been specifically prohibited from providing abortions to service personnel and their dependents, a ban that Clinton was quick to reverse two days after taking office. However, many military doctors continued to refuse to perform the procedure on moral or religious grounds. In the Navy's official pamphlet on pregnancy policy, those interested in medical options other than pregnancy are advised first of all to "seek counseling," adding that abortions "must be done at a civilian facility," be performed while on leave or liberty and are not covered by the Navy's health plan.

The ship's doctor, Lieutenant Sympharosa Williams, said she considered mandated Norplant birth control one plausible solution to the high rate of pregnancy. "But what's worse," she said, "is the risk of AIDS out there. Because any woman who comes to me pregnant is telling me she hasn't used a condom. And any woman who doesn't use a condom is playing with death. So I just can't stand to have them come in here and say they're pregnant." Born in New York and raised in Ghana, Williams was short, black and female—"so that's three disadvantages right there," she joked. The Navy had paid for her Yale medical school education, and she was now paying it back with the required four-year commitment.

Pregnancy is not only a medical concern, but one which the Navy sees as a discipline problem, since it can furnish embarrassingly concrete proof that sex is taking place on Navy ships (equally illicit homosexual fraternization, on the other hand, had no concomitant red flag). Fraternization did occur, of course. Hooper himself had found a man and woman having sex behind the closed and locked hatch of a conference compartment, and had taken them to mast ("captain's mast" is the disciplinary action one step below a court-martial) side by side. Since tenders were the primary Navy billet for women, they had the highest-profile incidents of fraternization and pregnancy both.

And while the focus on sexual matters aboard tenders appeared to Navy people to be overplayed, the bigger rub was that the press, in its usual lurid way, passed over the extraordinary contributions made by female crew members in favor of sexier copy. "During the actual hostilities period we had women manning gun mounts," said Captain

King, the commanding officer of the USS *Acadia* during the Gulf War. "It's cold and dark and you're surrounded by sand bags, wearing all kinds of heavy-looking, goofy gear, with flak jackets, and that's not a lot of fun. But we had a lot of women doing it. It wasn't considered combat duty because it was self-defense. The person who handled the burnerfront—it's a hard job, a dirty job. I had one of the finest burnermen in the entire Pacific fleet. She really shocked a lot of people."

With all the focus on fraternization and pregnancies, the emotional toll of parenthood in a seagoing environment was relegated to background static. "Deploying and leaving my daughter is the hardest thing I've ever done in my life," said Julie Robbins, storekeeper first-class, remembering her previous Westpac. "I didn't have as much difficulty leaving my husband. I figured as an adult, he can take care of himself. But I remember when my daughter fell off her bike—how many stitches did she have today?—baby-sitters in a week?—who's going to pick her up at school today? You can't drop a letter in the mail and get an answer back. It's that detachment that is very difficult. . . . A couple of weeks is forever." In the female berthing compartments, after lights out, it was common to hear the soft sobs of sailors crying themselves to sleep. Lieutenant Williams, the ship's doctor, had been speaking with one or two sailors a day who told her they were considering killing themselves. It was hard to judge if a person was serious. "But all it would take is one person," Williams said. The chaplain on board, Lieutenant Deb Mariyah, a former war protester now engaged to an Academy graduate, had witnessed the state of emotional turmoil into which a whole crew could plunge upon leaving the beach. "The first two weeks of deployment, you have an entire ship that's grieving." The *Cape Cod*'s half year at sea was just beginning.

Rear Admiral Marsha Evans devoted her whole career to opening doors to women, but they were doors that she herself would never walk through. "Marty" Evans was an example of a career Navy woman who never went to sea. A landlocked sailor sounds somehow improbable, like a vegetarian cannibal, but Evans was one. When Carl Vinson wanted to just fix it so women couldn't go on ships, Evans was one of those he fixed. Yet she survived and prospered.

Looking at her, you might have the thought cross your mind that perhaps Evans wouldn't much like sea duty, anyway. Not that she couldn't do it. There is a cast of permanent determination to her face, the product of years of battling an obdurate bureaucracy, that makes you conclude she could stand up to anything the sea threw at her. It's just that Captain Evans appears just about as far from the image of a squid as you can get and still remain Navy. There is a slight frostiness to her manner that might recoil at the gregarious rough-and-tumble of shipboard life. Approaching fifty, she looks thirty-five in a way that is not at all girlish. The promoters of No Nonsense panty hose once named her No Nonsense American Woman of the Month.

Evans would never be assigned to a ship, but she would campaign throughout her career to open all ships, combat platforms included, to all Navy personnel. She had joined the Navy before anybody believed the Naval Academy would ever be integrated, but she would make damn sure that Annapolis was a place where female midshipmen could get a fair shake.

Evans had, in fact, joined the Navy in 1968, when female service members were still customarily referred to as WAVES. The widespread though unofficial use of the term would not be banned until 1972, and even into the nineties it was possible to find some red-nosed relic at a Navy social event musing about how nice it was to have some WAVES around. In the late sixties, military recruiters were not wearing their uniforms to work for fear of being hassled or spat on by antiwar protesters. The woman in mufti who met a young Marsha Evans at the recruiting station was an "absolutely striking blond woman with a huge diamond ring on her hand who was dressed more elegantly than anyone I'd ever seen." The vision turned young Evans's head permanently. "I wanted to be like her. I joined because of the image."

It was Vinson's Navy she was joining, which was still ten years away from allowing women aboard its ships. Instead, recognizing that sea duty was central to the promotion of its male officers, the Navy constructed an elaborate alternative track for its female personnel, with special job categories created specifically for them. The effort attained new urgency when the American military went all-volunteer in 1972, and there was thus an actual imperative to attract women to the ranks. The Navy redid its personnel charts, making distinctions between what it considered "unrestricted line" jobs in "warfighting specialties" and something called "general unrestricted line" positions, created to accommodate the huge influx of women. In a spectacularly infelicitous turn of jargon, the Navy called the general unrestricted line officers like Marty Evans by the acronym of GURL. There were a few other specialty fields that women might join, and there were always nurses, but for the most part, if you were a female officer in the Navy, you were a GURL. No matter that the ranks of general unrestricted line officers always included a few men. The term gained instant currency as a facile synonym for female, one which could easily be worked into phrases such as "an attractive GURL," "the workday is so much more fun with some GURLs" or, pejoratively, "she's just a GURL."

Evans came in before the flood of females boosted the number of women in the Navy from its Vinson-ordained 2 percent, to 5 percent with the all-volunteer force, and eventually, by the nineties, to a full 11 percent. By the time these women entered the force, she was well established. As her career developed Evans took her place among the small number of high-profile Navy females (Rosemary Mariner among them). She became the designated administrative expert on "the woman problem." If there was a scandal or some other sort of egregious situation pertaining to the mixed-gender Navy, the call went out to "get Marty Evans." And get her they did when, in July of 1992, the Navy tapped Evans to be the operational head of its Standing Committee on Women in the Navy and Marine Corps, the uniformed counterpart to its civilian chair, Barbara Pope. Pope and Evans—it sounded like a brand of chicken—but together they were ferocious.

Post-Tailhook winds were sweeping through the whole department, the whole country.

Rumor and myth grow up readily around sources of cultural anxiety, and seldom have they tapped into deeper imaginings than with regard to women at sea.

The figure of the female sailor has always inspired colorful legendry. In spite of the obvious symbolism of the ship's figurehead, women were also said to be bad luck at sea, another hex in a dangerous environment of ghost ships, curses and superstitions. The female sailor became a stock figure in folk tunes and chanteys throughout the imperial maritime expansion of the European countries during the sixteenth to nineteenth centuries: a girl, almost always in disguise, who finds herself at sea. "We'll dress her up in sailor clothes, her jacket will be blue," runs the traditional eighteenth-century English folk song "Canadee-I-O." Other examples proliferate, celebrating both sailors and pirates—"Polly Oliver," "On Board a Man-of-War," "The Female Smuggler," "The Female Warrior," "The Rambling Female Sailor."

Evidence of actual seafaring women is scattered, anecdotal, but nevertheless robust. In the British Navy, they served as nurses, carried powder, worked as sailmakers. A black woman who called herself "William Brown" held the rating "Captain of the Maintop" in a British warship; she convinced authorities of her eleven years of service aboard the *Queen Charlotte*. As late as World War I, Kathleen Dyer was recorded in the books of HMS *Calypso* with the rating of "Captain's Servant." In March 1907, an American sailor serving under the name of "John Wilkinson" aboard the U.S. battleship *Vermont* had her true sex discovered while at her bath.

Just as they were to the seagoing male, allegations of sexual excess were often attached to the seagoing woman. Some of this characterization of lustiness had loose basis in fact. In the eighteenth and nineteenth centuries, it wasn't unusual for a man of war in port to have hundreds of women on board while the ship was docked. Few except officers were afforded shore leave out of fear they would desert, but a sailor's need for feminine company was recognized and accommodated. Wives and daughters joined prostitutes in boarding "bumboats," (at the traditional levy of three shillings) for transport out to the warship. HMS *The Royal George* had 300 women on board, reports military historian Linda Grant De Pauw, when the ship sank in Portsmouth Harbor in 1782. "It is surprising that the ships did not sink more often," De Pauw adds, "because the women's boarding was the signal for the beginning of a wild party during which virtually all shipboard discipline broke down. First of all, the women supplemented prostitution with bootlegging. At sea, the consumption of alcohol was tightly rationed, and the bumboat owners were not permitted to sell it to sailors in port. But the women took advantage of their voluminous skirts to conceal containers filled with gin, rum, or brandy."

Some women might not only board a ship in harbor, but remain on it when it got underway. Of these, some were prostitutes, but a greater proportion were guests, wives, servants of the captain, or women who were themselves warfighters married to marines or soldiers in transport. Women gave birth while in passage on military ships. Wrote one Captain W. N. Glascock in a nineteenth-century ship's log:

> This day the surgeon informed me that a woman on board had been laboring in childbirth for twelve hours, and if I could see my way to permit the firing of a broadside to leeward, nature would be assisted by the shock. I complied with the request, and she was delivered of a fine male child.

The spaces between the broadside guns were in fact the preferred spot for a woman in labor (De Pauw fixes this circumstance as the etymology for the phrase, "son of a gun").

The complex mythology associated with women at sea carried over into the World War II experience of the WAVES and other female military components. Immediately upon their formation, a virulent whisper campaign broke out in the ranks, to the effect that WACs and WAVES were only newly minted versions of "captains' doxies," that they were nymphomaniacs and hookers assigned the task of servicing whole ship's companies. Part of this was simple wishful thinking on the part of an enlisted force constantly beseeched to resist temptation. Naval commander (and ex-heavyweight champ) Gene Tunney stumped the naval bases, decrying the "rouged challenge" of prostitution. But the intensity and duration of what would come to be termed a "slander campaign" went beyond jokes and fantasy. It represented a fervent challenge to the perceived trespass of women in the military.

It started in 1942, with barracks humor, lampoons and caustic commentary printed in anti-Roosevelt newspapers (the administration was perceived as pushing the creation of the women's reserves). Cartoonists raised to the level of fetish the odd symbolic object of the khaki or camouflage brassiere. Hundreds of letters, oftentimes read on the air by Southern radio evangelists, circulated around the country, purporting to reveal what was really going on with women in the military.

At Camp Lee, Virginia, rumor had it that any soldier seen dating a WAC would be seized by Army authorities and taken in for immediate medical treatment. At Hampton Roads, the whisper was that 90 percent of WAVES had been found to be prostitutes, while 40 percent of them were pregnant. In one command, word circulated that physicians who screened female applicants rejected all virgins. At the Daytona Beach training center, it was said that the military hospital was overflowing with ob-gyn and venereal disease cases. Gangs of WAVES were supposedly abducting and raping sailors. Hundreds, then thousands of pregnant reservists were supposedly being shipped home from Europe. A "War Department Circular" made the rounds in Philadelphia, complete with the reservists' anatomical "specifications." A copy of the circular was found halfway around the world, in a New Guinea foxhole.

Oddly, the rumors contained shreds of twisted truth. Strange reports of hard-drinking, brawling uniformed women began to reach official Washington, WACs and WAVES who were soliciting soldiers outside the gates of military installations. It had become fashionable for civilians to mimic the female reservists, and replica uniforms from the WACs and WAVES were widely available in clothing stores. It turned out that streetwalkers had bought their own uniforms in an attempt to pander to sailors' fantasies. Known as "Victory Girls," they plied their trade in Harrisburg, Newport News, Hampton Roads and Baltimore, proudly wearing the khaki.

A few more serious incidents did not stop at slander, but broke into open sabotage against the female presence in the military. After a number of WASP planes had gone down in suspicious mishaps, Jackie Cochran visited Camp Davis in North Carolina to investigate. She was shaken to discover after one fatal crash that there were traces of sugar in the downed plane's fuel line, "enough to stop an engine in no time." On other occasions, women fliers assigned to tow targets complained they were deliberately shot at by the gunners-in-training down below. Some WASPs were so rattled that they resigned.

Eventually, after a syndicated columnist for the McCormick newspaper chain printed the charge that women recruits were issued prophylactics "according to a supersecret agreement reached by high-ranking officers of the War Department and the WAAC Chieftain, Mrs. William Pettus Hobby," official Washington deemed the slander campaign serious enough to warrant a response. Both Franklin and Eleanor Roosevelt mounted spirited public defenses of the morality of women auxiliary service members.

But the impression of scandal lingered around women service members throughout the war and afterward. The beast might have gone underground, but it didn't die. The military has always been the province of raw jokes, of course—but this shaded into something else. In the "Love Boat" rumors of the Gulf War, the same heady mix of wishful thinking, slander and misogyny was again at work. And soon after Tailhook, when the rumors started about Paula Coughlin—that she was seen in Lieutenant Rolando "Gandhi" Diaz's leg-shaving booth, or that she was administering blow jobs on the third deck of the Hilton—the same beast would surface once more.

JUST AFTER LABOR DAY 1992, ON THE ANNIVERSARY OF THE LAS Vegas convention that had brought the whole thing about, the first meeting of the Standing Committee had been called. For three days straight, its members, including Marsha Evans and Barbara Pope, had huddled—without uniforms, and for armed service members, that was the same as going naked—in the corporate bunker of the Xerox Convention Center in Leesburg, Virginia. It was "a monastic type of place," recalled Evans later, "where you have a little cell for a room, and then you have these meeting rooms that have no windows. You'd break for meals, which are right in the building, and the discussion would continue over the table, and then you'd go right back."

Marty Evans had sat on a lot of women's committees before. The difference here was that there were admirals involved as well as lieutenants. As a result of their work, the Standing Committee ended up presenting eighty recommendations to Sean O'Keefe, ranging from a sexual harassment hot line to alcohol education, and the Secretary of the Navy had astounded them by approving the whole list.

Six months later, in January 1993, as a tepid, border-state winter settled on Washington, the Standing Committee had completed what Evans considered an even more important task. It had convened with the acting secretary (O'Keefe) and the CNO (Frank Kelso) and gone through the list of recommendations from George Bush's Presidential Commission on the Assignment of Women in the Armed Forces, ticking them off one by one. Together, Pope and Evans and O'Keefe and Kelso and the rest of the committee had answered the threat to Navy women dissembled within the commission's report. It was incredible. It was exhilarating.

Part of the reason they could afford to be proactive—aside from the fact that both Kelso and O'Keefe seemed genuine in their commitment to liberalization of the Navy—was that by and large, the presidential commission had become irrelevant, with George Bush on his way out and Bill Clinton as incumbent. He had promised on the campaign trail to remove the last vestiges of discriminatory policy from the armed services, going so far as to say he would end the military's ban on homosexuals. The coming of the new administration, together with the lingering political effects of Tailhook, would furnish an opening for reform as never before.

The Standing Committee's work was not the only thing in Marty Evans's life in the winter of '92–'93. Evans had just been promoted to the rank of admiral. She was about to get the command of her career, as the head of all Navy recruitment. But the lifting of the ban against women in combat was of paramount importance to her. She knew that the Clinton people would examine the presidential commission report some time in the new year. "I just wish it would happen this week," she said. All she could do was sit back and wait.

If there was one thing Marty Evans had become familiar with during her quarter-century in the Navy, it was the systolic nature of reform. Bad conditions led to scandal led to change, which was inevitably followed by a lapse into bad conditions, which started the whole process over again. Tailhook was more egregious, more far-reaching in its implications than other scandals she had bumped up against in the course of her career, but it prompted the familiar feelings of ambivalence: it was dispiriting because things like it had happened so many times before, exciting because it presented such a clear opportunity. For her, the bottom line was obvious: "The root of discriminatory behaviors, including sexual harassment, is an undervaluing of the contribution that women are making. They're not seen as full team players. You don't harass a full-fledged member of the team. There's a direct relationship between respect and acceptance and those behaviors."

Evans had shocked people in the War College, where she was stationed at the time of the Gwen Dreyer hazing scandal, by practically chortling with glee when the case hit the front page of the *New York Times* and the *Washington Post.* A female midshipman at the academy was chained to a urinal during a hazing incident and Evans was *happy?* But it was the giddiness of rapture of the deep: it just showed how far gone she was in her involvement with women's issues. Sitting at her tiny study desk in the seminar room at the War College, reading the *Post,* she blew right past the private pain and personal embarrassment of Gwen Dwyer to seize upon what it meant for all women. That it was "the best thing that could happen to the Naval Academy, to get this nasty story all over the front page," was all she could think.

"Because now they're going to be forced to look at the issues. Nothing in the normal order of things was going to cause the place to do the kind of true introspection that needed to be done, or make the academy's leadership get emotionally involved. Now they were not going to get away with saying, 'Well, boys will be boys, and that's the way it is.'"

Evans knew whereof she spoke. It had been one of her first hatchet jobs, critiquing and recommending changes at the academy to bring it into the vague vicinity of the twentieth century as far as women were concerned. She had taken it on herself, soon after arriving at the academy in 1986, its first-ever female Battalion Officer.

"When I got there in August, I was absolutely aghast at what I found. It was the worst place. It was horrible. Women were treated badly, after ten years of being there—there were still major problems. I came in as a commander, with my own command. I couldn't believe the sexism, the lack of respect for me as a woman." If there was one thing Evans personally had a problem with, it was that she "was not a white male, there's no way I can be a white male, I don't want to be a white male. I want to be appreciated for what I bring to the table, and thank you, no, I'm not going to remake myself in somebody's expectation of what a white male should be like."

Evans confronted the Naval Academy superintendent, Rear Admiral Ron Marryot, with her three-and-a-half months' worth of observations, highlighting the appalling lack of respect for women officers, and voicing her primary concern that graduating midshipmen were not ready to be officers in today's Navy.

In the time-honored bureaucratic response to all complaint, the admiral convened a study to look at the status of women after ten years at the Naval Academy. Under the leadership of an associate professor of history named Jane Good, Evans and six other faculty members, staff personnel and students produced the first study of its type. They found that the rate of attrition for women at the academy was significantly higher than that of men, largely due the level of sexual harassment, which two thirds of female midshipmen believed posed a significant problem. Such harassment might take many forms, including obscene electronic mail messages, porn movies in the company gathering areas and some of the academy vernacular, in which dating a female midshipman was called "going over to the dark side." The report received national attention, mostly for its laundry list of academy problems. It was also "overflowing with substantive recommendations," Evans said later. But there was no follow-up, no implementation. Ultimately, Marty Evans left the Naval Academy "happy to go, mentally exhausted from pushing this rock uphill the whole time."

But the experience had one lasting effect. As the result of her helping turn in such a "beautifully researched" report on conditions at Annapolis, the Navy began to consider Evans its designated hitter on women's issues. A year after her experience at the academy, in August 1987, there came yet another installment of the ongoing Navy gender crisis, when the Pacific outposts of the U.S. Navy were visited by the Defense Advisory Committee on Women in the Services, more commonly known as the DACOWITS. On August 26, 1987, a memo from DACOWITS chair Dr. Jacqueline K. Davis to Secretary of Defense Caspar Weinberger presented a scathing catalog of day-to-day Navy intransigence halfway across the globe. Davis complained of behavior "that is at best inappropriate and at worst morally repugnant" at each installation the DACOWITS visited. This time the call went out for Marty Evans within thirty-six hours.

For the Western world's navies, the Pacific Ocean has always been somewhat more wild and woolly than the Atlantic, its vast expanses less mitigated by the blandishments of order and authority. The Atlantic might be Nelson and Hornblower, the Pacific was Con-

rad with flashes of Gauguin and Brando. For the U.S. Navy, the Pacific's wide open spaces were ruled by the aviator (whereas in the
Atlantic, the submarine was king). Pacific fleet aviators had long had
carte blanche, not least because they were physically so distant from
official Washington, D.C. Thus, no one could have predicted the culture clash or public reverberations that resulted from the findings of
the DACOWITS, especially as the committee had been for much of
its existance a somewhat supernumerary body, officially appointed and
then ignored.

The DACOWITS had been founded in 1951 as a bipartisan committee of fifty prominent women—academicians, former wartime di-
rectors of the women's military components, professional women from
the arts, business, the law and politics. The mandate of the organization was indicated at its inaugural dinner, when the female Assistant
Secretary of Defense for Manpower addressed the gowned and coifed
committee members: "We expect counsel from this group to help us
evolve policies that will make military service an attractive duty and
that will assure parents that we are genuinely interested in the welfare
of their young women in the services." *Dulce et decorum est pro
patria mori*—as well as *in loco parentis.*

The DACOWITS's bluestocking reputation was upheld by its
membership roster over the decades. These weren't the fashionable,
media-savvy, Coast-based intellectuals of the left, no Gloria Steinems
or Letty Pogrebins, but rather the powerful, usually conservative,
successful-but-somewhat-anonymous   women   of   the   heartland.
DACOWITS members during the 1980s, for example, included the
president of an organization called American Agri-Women (she also
was the wife of Frank Perdue), the provost from the University of
Oklahoma and a past president of the National Federation of Republican Women.

As time went on, the advice the DACOWITS offered Pentagon
leaders on expanding women's military role grew sterner, more influ-
ential. In 1967, the DACOWITS had taken a stand on removing the 2
percent ceiling on female service members. It successfully lobbied to

remove the grade restriction, paving the way for women to become generals and admirals. It had urged the assignment of women to Minuteman and Titan missile crews. It had come out in favor of integrating the military academies in 1974—two years before it actually happened in 1976. But the organization's research, its influence, and its activities were still not always taken seriously. At times the military simply refused to produce documents that the DACOWITS requested or answer its queries. Seemingly simple issues could drag on for years, such as convincing the Army that women needed a substitute for the baggy, revealing gym trunks worn by the men.

Then, in the late eighties, the committee made official its regular inspection visits to U.S. military bases, both domestic and abroad. It was one of these trips, in 1987, to Navy and Marine Corps installations in the Western Pacific, that broke the organization out of the white-glove ghetto and into the public consciousness.

The furor over the DACOWITS tour was all the more surprising since the sites had been carefully vetted to showcase what the Navy felt represented a positive working environment for female personnel. The members of the committee, primarily civilians, with some military officials in tow, were not out hunting for misconduct. One woman present, according to one historian of the DACOWITS, "was known, prior to the trip, to have dismissed such issues as sexual harassment as a problem that women themselves invited."

Nevertheless, the DACOWITS was not at all amused by what it found in the Western Pacific. The most serious case was that of USS *Safeguard,* where a majority of the ninety-four women aboard the salvage ship accused their skipper of sexual harassment and misconduct. Lieutenant Commander Harvey's offenses included "public sex, attempts to 'sell' female sailors to the Koreans . . ." as well as " 'fraternization' with enlisted female sailors." The problems weren't just aboard this one ship, however. The sprawling base-and-bagnio combination at Subic Bay in the Philippines came in for especial examination. The Davis memo described such traditions as " 'peso-parties' (Subic Cubi terminology for the liberal and routine public 'use' of

Philippine females at places such as the enlisted, NCO and officers clubs), noon-time burlesque shows and 'dining-ins' that emphasize sexually-oriented entertainment, with the alleged participation of audience members." The climate was one in which sexual harassment and gender discrimination were endemic. Navy women in the Western Pacific told DACOWITS observers that they were routinely ignored when they complained about these matters to their commanding officers. In some cases (as with the USS *Safeguard*), it was the commanders themselves who were perpetrating the harassment.

The Western Pacific tour was to prove a turning point in the effectiveness of the DACOWITS, a sea change in more ways than one. The organization's president, Jacquelyn Davis, made sure that her memo was leaked to the *New York Times*. The organization's new activist profile now merited the scorn of right-wing ideologue Phyllis Schlafly, who labeled the DACOWITS "the feminist thought-control brigade of the U.S. military." Davis begged to differ. "I don't view this as a women's rights organization," she told the *Air Force Times*. "I'm not a feminist. I view this committee as being supportive of the national security structure." Not for the last time, conservative revulsion over moral inturpitude would vector with the feminist agenda to produce an unlikely dynamic for change. And the Navy once more lurched forward on the path of reform.

Marty Evans was there to coax it along. Another scandal, another study. Reagan-appointed Secretary of the Navy James Webb placed Evans at the head of a study group that recommended changes in Navy policy. And Webb made a curious move on his own, one which implicitly recognized the relation between the combat exclusion and the DACOWITS horror stories. He redefined the term "combat mission" in a way which opened more than 10,000 additional Navy jobs to women.

The secretary could redefine it, but he couldn't get rid of it without Congress. Still stuck in the craw of reform efforts was the seemingly indestructible legal provision known as Title 10, Section 6015, which kept women out of combat aircraft and off surface combatants. It was the last remnant of Carl Vinson's special bequest to the U.S. Navy. Yet another study group report, this one from 1990, attempted to meet the devil head on.

"There is no doubt that this legislative provision limits women's assignment opportunities, both directly and indirectly. In the view of all Navy members the law also profoundly influences both the acceptance and quality of treatment accorded women since they are perceived to be distanced from the heart of the organization and its primary mission-achieving units. Not surprisingly, many women see section 6015 as the genesis of all their assimilation problems . . ."

The 1990 study group also faulted "the Navy institutional character," which it described as implying that "women don't belong because they haven't the physical strength and stamina, the psyche, or the 'killer instinct' to willingly and ably confront aggressors who would threaten freedom of the seas or our other national interests. This mentality often rejects women as 'distractors' from the business at hand, and as 'time takers' who burden the system either with their aspirations for equality or their inability to handle their 'personal problems' (e.g., pregnancy). 'It would be a lot easier if women weren't here' is a favorite expression of the traditional image upholder, as is the alternative pronouncement that 'Women are to be protected, not to sail in harm's way and any woman who would want to do the latter is abnormal.' "

Scandal, attempts at reform, lapses into inaction. The recommendations of such reports "were not aggressively carried out," Evans said, and the reports themselves were "put on a shelf and forgotten about."

To a woman of Marty Evans's experience, who had seen incremental change, small pulses of progress, the question in January 1993 was not about policy. All the policy papers had already been produced —she herself had helped produce them. The Navy knew what it had to do if it was to transform itself into a truly democratic institution. The issue became one of willingness to change. Tailhook, the scandal to beat all scandals, might be the hammer blow that would force the

Navy finally into new age, but Evans had been disappointed too many times to count on anything. She was heartened by a speech that Sean O'Keefe had made at Annapolis earlier that January.

> The Presidential Commission that reported out in late November recommended opening some combat specialties and leaving others closed. I don't think they went far enough. Based on my discussions with our own Standing Committee on the Role of Women, I believe we should expand the role of women in combat in all the armed forces, including permitting women to fly combat missions, as well as serve in all naval vessels. I also believe we should rescind the current Department of Defense "risk rule," and require the registration and potential conscription of women on an identical sociological basis as men.

An astonishing statement, really, coming from a sitting Secretary of the Navy. If implemented, it would transform the United States Navy into the most progressive military institution in the world—transform American society itself.

Rear Admiral Marsha Evans could be forgiven if she remarked under her breath that she would believe it when she saw it.

Part Three

SEA CHANGE

IF THE FEMALE SEX TOOK THE FIELD WITH THEM, I AM SURE THAT THEY WOULD BE ABSOLUTELY INVINCIBLE.

—Plato, *Republic*

Chapter Eight

GOOD TO GO

IT WAS ONLY A "MINOR" CASE OF SEXUAL HARASSMENT. IT OCCA-
sioned no media attention, and was largely lost in the mix of a
525,000-person Navy. When men and women work together, there
are bound to be cases like these, instances of she-said, he-said that
complicate the work environment tremendously. How the Navy han
dled the Tailhook investigations was the stuff of front-page, prime-
time news, where scandal led to policy changes. But how it dealt with
the run-of-the-mill, quotidian sexual harassment cases would prove
more important, in the long run, to the question of whether the Navy
was able to create an environment in which women could work.

What happened between aviation machinist's mate second-class
Karlene Dent and one of her superior officers over the course of a
deployment on the island of Diego Garcia, in the Pacific, was the
substance of a general court-martial proceeding that transpired in San
Francisco in mid-January 1993. At the time, both Dent and the man
she accused, Lieutenant Commander Carl Edmond Bailey, were
based at South Bay's Moffett Field. Dent had joined the Navy late,
just before her thirty-fifth birthday, having first had a career as a heavy
equipment operator, running "paddle wheels and 'dozers and back-

hoes, on irrigation canals in Arizona, power plants in Utah, freeways in
Utah, just about everywhere." Dent is small and compact, with long
dark hair and a round, expressive face. There is a toughness in her
speech and manner, an ease with the physicality of the traditionally
male environments she has labored in. Describing the cross-examination the defense put her through during the court-martial, Dent said,
"They tried to rip me a new one," meaning, in the language of both
the Navy and the construction trade, they tried to provide her with a
new asshole, i.e., they fucked with her good. Dent said she was "prepared" for the Navy after suffering "verbal and physical abuse" at the
hands of her fellow construction workers. "I just about went home in a
pine box a couple of times," she recalled of her experiences. Nevertheless, when she joined the Navy in 1987, "I had so much faith in the
system. I thought, you put in a hard day's work, you go home, you feel
good about yourself, and they'll stand up for you."

It didn't work out that way. Dent first was propositioned by
Lieutenant Commander Bailey in December of 1990. Bailey had been
in the Navy for almost twenty-five years, first as an enlisted man, then
as an officer. "He's gone through all the hard-knocks," is how Karlene
Dent put it. He was old-line Navy. According to Dent, Bailey approached her in December of 1990 and said, "I've been watching you
for a while and I find that you're very mature. My marriage is on the
rocks. Would you consider having an affair with me?" Dent told him
no, that she didn't get involved with married men. Over the course of
the next year, Bailey approached her with comments such as "Have
you changed your mind?" or "You sure are missing out on a good
thing."

Bailey's attentions intensified when the P-3 squadron they were
both attached to left for deployment overseas in fall of 1991. "It just
started getting out of hand," said Dent. The P-3 is the Navy's work-
horse sub hunter, and it's land-based, which makes P-3 squadrons
open to women. The atmosphere around P-3's is much more relaxed
than, say, a jet fighter squadron. According to Dent, the laxity extended to the Navy's rules against fraternization, and increased when

her squadron was deployed on Diego Garcia. "I found out about deployment before we went. Oh, they said, it's a free-for-all. Fraternization. You could almost hear the wedding rings clink to the floor when we got on that airplane to go over there. It didn't matter if you were a chief or an officer or what. If you were married, as soon as you got on the plane you were not married."

Her daily contact with Bailey increased on Diego Garcia, a remote, dusty island full of bars and donkeys. Bailey began singling her out for work details, keeping her late, engaging in the niggling behaviors of a boss determined to make an underling's life miserable. Finally, in February 1992, Dent said, Bailey broke down and begged her for "a sympathy fuck."

Upon the squadron's return to the States, Dent initiated a formal complaint against Bailey, following Navy protocol to the letter. Her complaint went up the chain of command and the ensuing investigation was handled by an officer outside of Dent's immediate group The NCIS—the Naval Investigative Service had been recently renamed the Navy Criminal Investigative Service—sent agents to take statements. It turned out that Carl Bailey had a history of sexual harassment complaints against him. A woman had asked him for a job reference, and (according to testimony) Bailey had replied, "I certainly will if you undo your coveralls and let me touch your breasts." Then he reached over and started to unzip her, before the woman backed away and left. In his court-martial, Bailey faced four charges: one count of "maltreatment," one of indecent assault, one of solicitation and one of conduct unbecoming an officer. After Dent and two other women testified against him, Bailey was found guilty of conduct unbecoming an officer. He received a relatively light form of punishment, an official reprimand.

"We were kind of numbed," Dent said of herself and her fellow accusers. "Of course his conduct was 'unbecoming.' But let's get down to brass tacks and say, look, you actually touched somebody, you were actually unwelcome. And I told him, 'I do not get involved with married men.' How exact can you be? And the [defense team] said, 'You probably led him on with your humor.' Well, everybody has humor. I'm just as guilty as the next person for telling dirty jokes. Because I worked construction, and I enjoy it. You know, you mingle with the guys and rub elbows. That doesn't mean, 'Hey, baby, come to my place.' "

For years, the Navy had emphasized its "zero tolerance" of sexual harassment. In the late eighties, various studies targeted sexual harassment as one problem among a constellation of issues that prevented equal opportunity for women. In 1989, there was a new "instruction," or set of guidelines issued to all Navy personnel, on sexual harassment, revised to strengthen the Navy's position against it; in 1990 and 1991 similar instructions were issued.

The actual definition of sexual harassment remained confusing, and even with the added emphasis of the one-day stand-down in the summer of '92, there was still a sense that the message wasn't getting across. When Barbara Pope and Marty Evans convened the Standing Committee on Women in the Navy and Marine Corps, the agenda included the development of a new, comprehensive sexual harassment instruction. The penalties for aggravated sexual harassment, which includes any touching, had been promulgated even before that, in the previous spring, by CNO Frank Kelso, in the aftermath of Tailhook. They involved immediate punitive discharge from the Navy. Prosecutors in Bailey's case decided on the lesser charge of conduct unbecoming, they explained to Karlene Dent, because they thought the chances were better they could make the lesser charge stick. The improved guidelines might make a difference somehow down the line, but they had no practical import for Karlene Dent.

If the daughters of the American middle class were going to feel safe in the Navy—and by extension, in the working world as a whole— this humdrum, everyday brand of sexual harassment was exactly the kind that would have to be addressed. The case against Lieutenant Commander Bailey never entered the realm of violent sexual assault or rape, never reached the level of egregiousness of the Tailhook gauntlet. But it stemmed from the same root cause. Like the WACs of

World War II, like Paula Coughlin on the third deck, Karlene Dent was still considered in some quarters a modern-day version of the camp follower. Because women were seen as marginal, because they were excluded from crucial prestige positions, this kind of sexual dynamic prevailed.

Dent would later feel hounded by a sense of reprisal for her actions against Bailey. She was Little Miss Moffett, a troublemaker in the victim-avenger mode, the woman who had brought down a twenty-three-and-a-half-year veteran. "Since the court-martial," Dent said, "since I've been treated the way I have, let me tell you, I don't want to stay in a corporation where they don't back me up." She paid a personal visit to the office of the senator from her home state of Utah, Orrin Hatch, to register her dissatisfaction, and she contemplated leaving the Navy. In the end, she resigned herself to waiting for the transfer to her next duty station—far away, in Millington, Tennessee, where she would teach jet mechanics—in the hope that she'd be able to put the whole thing behind her.

By winter of 1993, an enlisted woman's complaint of sexual harassment seemed of little consequence. Tailhook and the issues it had brought to the fore—sexual harassment and women in combat, among others—were rapidly becoming overshadowed. The Scandal That Wouldn't Die suddenly found itself buried alive by a debate over another kind of military outsider. As Karlene Dent left Moffett Field to drive to the court-martial proceedings at San Francisco's Treasure Island Naval Base in mid-January 1993, she passed banks of television cameras set up just outside the gates. But the media wasn't there to interview her. Its prey was a pale, sandy-haired Navy sonar instructor who was assigned to the P-3 training squadron at Moffett. His name was Keith Meinhold, and he was battling to remain in a Navy uniform after declaring publicly he was gay.

IN THE EARLY MONTHS OF 1993, THERE WAS NO SHORTAGE OF PEOPLE willing to assure anyone who would listen that the issues of gays and women in the military were two absolutely separate, totally disjunct subjects. Among the disestablishmentarians were some of the most vocal and visible advocates of women's full participation in the Navy. No one, it seemed, had a taste for the larger fight.

One reason for this, of course, was tactical. The issue of gays in the military had become the first policy crisis of the Clinton administration, and it had blindsided the new President. What was, on the campaign trail, a mild if fully articulated declaration of principle ("there [is] no real evidence that homosexual status, per se, disable[s] people from distinguished service in the military") became, in the harsh realities of Washington, a much more explosive issue. Bob Dole warned that ending the ban could "blow the lid off the Capitol." The conflict would become the first cut in a series of wounds that the Administration would suffer. This first cut was also the deepest, since the gays-in-the-military controversy set the pattern which the Administration seemed to follow in subsequent crises: bold policy initiative, concerted and effective attack by the opposition, indecision and retreat by Clinton.

"The way it was reported and the way it was talked about was all in screaming matches, where everybody had a temperature of 105— on both sides," Clinton later recalled to a religious gathering about the contentious atmosphere of the gay debate. "Everybody's neck was bulging. Steam was coming out from everybody's ears."

Much of the President's response to the gay issue was determined not politically but viscerally, through such examples as the no-nonsense figure of Colonel Margarethe Cammermeyer, a middle-aged military nurse with a twenty-seven-year gleaming record. In June 1992, she had acknowledged on a routine questionnaire the fact of her sexual orientation. It had earned this Bronze Star veteran from Vietnam an immediate discharge, on the grounds that she was a lesbian. But such personal stories were lost in the fury of the right-wing backlash, which came complete with audiovisual aids. A videotape called *The Gay Agenda,* a sort of *Protocols of the Elders of Zion* for the homophobic produced by a Christian fundamentalist organization, was in fact distributed widely in military circles. General Carl Mundy, Jr., Commandant of the Marine Corps, thoughtfully forwarded copies to the Joint Chiefs.

If voices from antiquity were to be believed, the U.S. military was missing out on a vital resource by shunning gays within its ranks. Plato extolled an army "composed of pederastic lovers and their boys," where men would draw courage from their passion for each other. Hundreds of years later, Plutarch praised the valor of the Sacred Band, the mythic unit of 300 homosexuals that conquered the Spartan army: "A band that is held together by erotic love is indissoluble and unbreakable. . . . Eros is the only invincible general." But it could be argued that the United States already had an armed forces that at least partially conformed to Plato's model. Once the debate over homosexuals in the military began, gay and lesbian pilots, soldiers and sailors began announcing their presence in droves. The irony of the situation was brought home by a gay travel guide published around this time, *Betty and Pansy's Severe Queer Review of Washington, D.C.*, which noted the busiest cruising grounds among the Pentagon's 284 bathrooms. Everyone was squabbling over "allowing" gays in the military—but they were undeniably already there.

The U.S. Navy had always conveyed mixed messages about homosexuality. Known to some as the world of "sea pussy," it was also a place where investigators spent millions of dollars each year to ferret out and discharge gays within its ranks. Homosexuality is such a loaded subject in military circles that questions concerning women— sexual harassment, women in combat, issues that had recently plagued the Navy—now took on a comparatively less sinister aspect.

Lin Hutton, along with Rosemary Mariner, was one of the most successful female Navy aviators and the only other woman apart from Mariner ever to command a squadron, the VRC-40 "Rawhides." Hutton, a C-2 "Greyhound" transport plane pilot, had been tireless in her efforts to get the combat ban lifted. Not for her own career (it was way too late for that), but to help the younger women coming up after her.

("How I wish I were in their shoes!" Hutton wrote in a *Newsweek* op-ed piece in favor of the end of the ban.) When Captain Hutton went out on the stump to Congress, to the DACOWITS, to the brass, pleading, cajoling, strong-arming, the people she was doing it for were the next generation, the Kara Hultgreens and Paula Coughlins of the new Navy.

In the late eighties, Hutton had been Frank Kelso's aide when he was commander of the Atlantic fleet surface forces, and she had filled the future CNO's ear with the rationale for getting rid of the combat exclusion. With her bedrock confidence and distinguished performance record to back her up, she would have been a hard woman to ignore. Some of the thoughts she planted in Kelso's mind turned up in his thinking years later, when he would be the chief of naval operations responsible for dropping the combat ban. Even within a bureaucracy as immense as the U.S. military's, there is still something to be said for being able to tug on an admiral's sleeve and talk to him one on one.

However confident and resolute Hutton was with regard to the combat exclusion, she was equally forceful in her views on gays in the military. "Here we are spending all this time on a small percentage of people who are very vocal," Hutton told a hearing of the Senate Armed Services Committee, convened in Norfolk that spring to consider the Clinton proposal. "We're here to tell you today this is a grave, grave error at this time in our history." The senators were receptive. Ninety-year-old Strom Thurmond, his hair flaming orange, asked one of the few openly gay witnesses at the hearing if the young man had "taken any steps to get help from a psychiatric standpoint." Sentiment of those who appeared before the committee and those in the audience ran overwhelmingly against allowing gays to serve openly in the military. At Norfolk and at other hearings, the most vocal Navy women adamantly opposed lifting the ban on gays.

Navy and civilian women both. In mid-February 1993, Barbara Pope addressed a meeting of the Navy's Women Officers Professional Association. She listed some of the issues she felt would top the Navy agenda for the coming year. First was the combat exclusion. "Obviously, the issue of gays in the military is going to be important. My concern is how the gay issue is getting rolled up with the women's issue. The timing was lousy. All of a sudden, women and gays were getting rolled up together. Which of course isn't the same. We're both in uniform—but being female is not the same as being gay." What was especially interesting was the reaction of the WOPA audience. Not just a ripple but a wave of nervous laughter followed Pope's words. It could have been that the mere public mention of homosexuality was enough to set off the WOPA members, or else that there were enough female gay officers (present that day or in the ranks) to make Pope's denial unintentionally ironic. Perhaps the audience members couldn't help but recognize that the situation of military women and that of gay servicemembers were in almost every sense identical, from their innate marginality to the types of discrimination suffered.

Yet even in the wake of Tailhook, most Navy women refused to align themselves with anyone outside the official order, whether that meant Paula Coughlin or homosexuals. Navy women and their erstwhile opposition, Navy men, came together to battle against their perceived mutual foe, the homosexual interloper. It was an infernal alliance, born either of short-term political expediency or stubborn moral conservatism. For a brief moment, all the hatred and mistrust men had for the Other that was Woman was redirected onto the Other that was gay. As the military's women awaited some decision from the White House on the recommendations made by the Presidential Commission on the Assignment of Women, men began to feel that serving alongside women seemed almost normal—at least in comparison with the troubling image of "fags in the showers." Some of the tension remained, of course, but it was tempered, less hysterical. There was now room for discussion about women's roles. Conservative military women and men had a new sense of unity, of shared purpose.

The almost complete lack of women's support for embattled gays could perhaps be laid to historical precedents. While the current debate mainly centered around male homophobia, the accusation of homosexuality had long been used as a weapon against women in the military. "Many men still don't think women belong in the military," said Margarethe Cammermeyer; "the [gay] ban is the perfect mechanism to get us out." Navy women knew this all too well. "We fought long and hard to not be characterized as whores or lesbians," one lieutenant commander in San Diego said. "If we throw the door open, it will adversely affect all of us. I have nothing against homosexuals, but I prefer not to be characterized as one."

The Navy was notorious for its lesbian witch hunts. At Parris Island, South Carolina, where all women Marines received basic training, a 1988 investigation targeted seventy suspected lesbians; fourteen members of what the NIS characterized as a "nest" of lesbians were discharged. Three who refused to name names landed in the brig for sodomy and "indecent acts." In the same year, thirty women (including every black woman on board) were investigated aboard the destroyer tender USS *Yellowstone;* eight were discharged. A 1980 probe aboard the USS *Norton Sound* led to charges against eight women and dismissal of two. The cost to taxpayers of such probes was enormous. A 1984 congressional report estimated the Pentagon spent an astounding $336 million on homosexuality investigations in 1983 alone.

According to varying estimates, Navy women were three, five or eight times as likely as men to be discharged under the military's ban on gays. A politically outspoken woman might be labeled gay as a way to silence her; a sexually unresponsive female might be called a dyke in an attempt to coerce her into having sex. Representative Patricia Schroeder had in 1992 sponsored legislation calling for reprisal protection for whistle blowers. Accusations of homosexuality are "a way of fighting back" for men accused of sexual harassment, Schroeder said. "They're saying to the woman: 'How could you turn down my advances? You must be gay.'"

The link between homosexuality and women in the armed forces might have been too thorny an issue for military consumption. In intellectual circles, however, such connections had long been drawn. "Males," the poet Robert Bly stated in a *New York Times* op-ed piece on the gay ban, "are an experiment toward 'the masculine.' " The military helps some young men reach their long-quested-after goal of secure masculinity, wrote Bly. "But when a 20-year-old unfinished warrior notices a gay man walking across a parade field, he may some-times—not always—see a feminine walk, a feminine gesture, a feminine spontaneity, a feminine radiance, and feel instantly afraid." The young man thus feels cheated out of his promised "incontrovertible stability." Senator Sam Nunn, the most outspoken proponent of the gay ban, was in Bly's eyes "caught in an incomplete warrior phase, oppositional and polarized. Many military men want all shining of the feminine in the soldier to be invisible, not seen and not spoken of. . . . The men need not fear . . . The sky will not fall."

One of the most cogent analyses of how the homosexual exclusion and combat exclusion overlap comes from UCLA law professor Kenneth Karst. "The belief that power rightfully belongs to the masculine," Karst wrote, has two corollaries. "The first is that the gender line must be clearly drawn, and the second is that power is rightfully distributed among the masculine in proportion to their masculinity as determined not merely by their physical stature or aggressiveness, but more generally by their ability to dominate and to avoid being dominated. Both parts of the ideology contribute to the subordination of groups."

The ideology, he noted, "by making anxiety into an everyday fact of life . . . leads nervous men to seek reassurances of their masculinity through group rituals that express domination over other groups." Karst also wrote about the need for men to see other people who are not white males as abstractions, as labels: blackness, femininity, homosexuality. "To a great many white heterosexual men these masks of the Other are frightening; when we police the color line and the gender line in the world around us, we are policing the same line in our own minds, defending our senses of self. The fear of members of subordinated groups is more than a fear of competition, or even retaliation. No spectre is more terrifying than our own negative identity."

Peggy Reeves Sanday, a feminist anthropologist, investigated in-

cidents of fraternity gang rape at the University of Pennsylvania. Substitute the closed order of naval aviators for fraternities, and the Las
Vegas Hilton for the college campus, and some of Sanday's analysis
could as easily be applied to the gang-bang mentality that was opera-
tive during Tailhook. Sanday acknowledged the universality of her
subject when she stated "the specific location is not relevant to the
subject of this book. The kind of behavior this case [of fraternity gang
rape] illustrates appears to be widespread not only among fraternities
but in many other exclusively male contexts at colleges and universities in the United States, such as organized sports. It or its equivalent
is also found outside universities where men band together in clubs,
work groups, athletic groups, athletic teams, military units, and business conventions—in all settings we associate with the term 'stag
party.'" Sanday described the practice known as "pulling train"—
fraternity slang for gang raping a drunk or unconscious woman—as a
way for men to validate their heterosexuality through the unspoken
implication that those who do not participate are unmanly or homosexual. For a group of military men, the need to expunge the "feminine" seems to fuel the ritualized behaviors which have at their core
homoerotic underpinnings. Recall the shellback ceremony, for example. According to Sanday, "In the sociodrama that is enacted, the idea
that heterosexual males are superior to women and to homosexuals is
publicly expressed and probably subjectively absorbed." The men who
participated in the Tailhook gauntlet were similarly bolstering their
sense of superiority to women, and through participation denying any
possible latent homosexuality. The Navy fliers might have been expressing some sublimated form of homosexual panic, in which the
Navy male's reputation for sodomy and inversion was challenged and
violently repudiated. The junior officers publicly assaulted women in
order to establish that they were not guilty of desiring men. In a
purely reductive way, groping Paula Coughlin in a crowded corridor is
vindicating and validating, especially if you've recently sucked a cherry
out of the greased belly button of a chief petty officer during a crossing-the-line ceremony. They formed the gauntlet to prove their mem-

bership in society's dominant group, that of male heterosexuals. They did it precisely because it separated them from the despised "other": gays, or women.

In the midst of the national debate over the military's gay ban in early 1993 came news of a horrific homosexual hate killing near a U.S. Navy base in Sasebo, Japan. Even though the actual murder of radio-man Allen Schindler had occurred months previous, in October 1992, media interest was not generated until a roommate of the victim wrote to President Clinton advocating removal of the homosexual ban ("It is absolutely senseless for someone to die because of who he is," wrote the sailor. "Al didn't choose to be gay, but he did choose to serve the country he loved.") The details were suitably grisly. Schindler's body was so battered his mother had to identify it by the tattoos on the forearms. "The only thing left of his face," she said, "was his nose." His attackers had surprised Schindler in a public rest room on the grounds of a park known as a gay cruising ground, kicking him bloody and slamming his head against the urinals. The two killers, only one of whom was later court-martialed, stopped to tear off the blood-soaked hems of their trousers, then faded into the crowds in Sasebo's tiny "Sailor Town."

Climactic, emblematic, serving to polarize the whole issue, the Schindler murder took center stage in the ongoing debate on homo-sexuals in the military. Both sides sought to use the incident. Those in favor of the gay ban solemnly cited it as an object lesson on what might happen to the military if openly gay personnel were allowed to serve (Schindler had declared his homosexuality a month before he was killed). But the brutality of the incident probably had a mitigating effect on the antigay forces, and in effect there might have been some softening in the hard-core opposition to women in combat as a result. In the face of such bloody evidence of tribal bigotry, compromises had to be made somewhere. It was easier, at that point in time, to make them vis-à-vis women than vis-à-vis gays.

Again, such flights of theory would not play extremely well in the wardrooms and ready rooms, the lounges and mess decks of the Navy.

What mattered most there—and what would prove crucial for the fate of women in the Navy as a whole—was that over a watershed span of three months in early 1993 the issue of homosexuals in the military would dominate, dilute and distract from the issue of women in combat. In strategic terms, Clinton's proposal to end the gay ban opened a second front. Those military men seeking to keep the armed forces an exclusive preserve of the dominant culture, a self-contained tribe where only male heterosexuals need apply, now had to fight two battles at once. And so the ferocious debate over gays in the military sent up an all-encompassing smoke screen, behind which women would steal into the cockpits of combat aircraft and onto combat platforms virtually unopposed.

IT WAS IN THIS OVERHEATED ATMOSPHERE THAT THE DACOWITS, the ladies who launch, came together for their semiannual conference. From April 18–21, they met at the Tysons Corner Marriott in Falls Church, Virginia, just inside the orbit (but barely) of the beltway.

As was commonplace for recent DACOWITS conclaves, the event got underway in an atmosphere of high expectation and high dudgeon. Frank Kelso had just announced a sort of good-news, bad-news development that fed the buzz mightily. The Navy was decommissioning more than twenty ships, among them training frigates and the USS *Forrestal,* the Navy's sole training carrier. That was bad news for Navy women, since these ships represented many hundreds of difficult-to-get seagoing billets. The *Forrestal,* a ship that never went on full-length deployments, was the only aircraft carrier open to women. Rosemary Mariner had served as a member of the ship's company on a training carrier, and a whole generation of Navy females, enlisted and officers alike, had counted on such a ship to get crucial carrier experience. To counter this blow, Kelso announced a broad reclassification of Navy ships, opening 2,000 more shipboard jobs to women. The large print giveth, and the small print taketh away.

Kara Hultgreen prowled the sanitized "salons" of the Marriott like a pissed-off poltergeist. None of Kelso's moves were going to help

her. Time was running out, and it was either going to happen for
Hultgreen or it wasn't. Practically the whole female jet-jock community was at the conference that spring, showing the colors, working the
rooms, making sure there was no falling away from the hard-line stand
the DACOWITS was taking on the combat exclusion. The fiery debate
over gays in the military was making everyone jumpy. People were
hoping, praying, that the two issues didn't get, as Barbara Pope had
said, "rolled up" together. There was no question of solidarity with the
estimated 250,000 gay rights advocates who were to march on the
capital the next weekend. Two groups of barbarians were banging at
the gates of the military, but without much concern for one another.

Hultgreen and her cohorts in the female aviation community
would appear at formal functions in their service dress uniforms,
nylons regulation shoes, in the heavily coded femininity of the military. Then they would go up to their rooms and change into their
flight suits for the cocktail receptions, shouldering their way through
the crowds of uniformed military advisers and folder-toting civilians
like a gang of Dead End kids.

In the time since Tailhook, Lieutenant Hultgreen had become
more aggressive. She was still in Key West, still at VAQ-33, still flying
her pig. Every three months like clockwork she would send off a
transition packet to BuPers in Washington, requesting a change in her
status so she could transfer to TacAir. But it was like throwing coins
down a well. The Bureau of Personnel would note it had received her
request, and after that, nothing. It got a little frustrating, and the
frustration showed up once or twice in a couple of uncomfortable
incidents. The worst was when she nearly came to blows with a squadron commander at the base officers club in Roosevelt Roads, Puerto
Rico.

"The CO of one of the A-6 squadrons that was there came over
to the guy I was talking with and said, 'Scally, I thought I'd come over
and get introduced to the prettiest girl in the club.' I'm the *only* girl in
the club. This guy, he was kind of drunk, and I was feeling no pain,
drinking Coronas. And Scally goes, 'Yeah, she's an A-6 pilot in 33. She
was a student at the RAG when I was an instructor there.' This CO

goes, 'Well, that just makes me sick.' He's pointing his finger at me. 'There is no way that a woman could do what I do. There's no way that you could do my job.' He just went on and on about how I couldn't handle the boat at night, blah, blah. So I insult not only him and his leadership abilities but his mother. I was saying, 'You dirtbag, I'm glad I'm not in your squadron, 'cause there's nothing worse than poor leadership, and you'll never make CAG with that attitude.' I'm putting my finger in his chest and saying, 'And another thing, pal!' "

Her friend Scally tried to drag her away. " 'We gotta go, Kara, we gotta go, we gotta go!' Because you just don't do that to a skipper. It was this big scene in the club. I'm screaming at this guy. I'm just furious, like, 'Can you believe he said that?'

"And Scally goes, 'He's an asshole. Everybody knows he's an asshole. But you just don't do that.'

" 'What am I supposed to do?'

" 'All you do is say, "Oh, excuse me, I'm going to go to the bathroom." And then you don't come back!'

"And I'm like, 'Oh. I never thought of that.' "

For a year and a half after that incident, "especially after the Presidential Commission on the Assignment of Women came down with its recommendations," Hultgreen "just sort of refused to talk to people about the whole issue." She began to take a perverse pleasure in pranking the male aviators she talked with, those men she considered overly concerned about sharing their squadrons with women.

"All these guys would say, 'Well, when do you think this is going to happen?' I'd just spit out some answer that was really ridiculous: 'Oh, it's about to happen. According to all my friends, everyone I know in D.C., it'll happen quite soon. As a matter of fact I'm expecting orders tomorrow. Yeah, I'm going to get my syllabus. I think I might even be in your air wing—so I'll see you out there, hmmm?'

"They'd all go, 'What? What?'

"Then I would say, 'Could you hold my beer? I'm going to go to the bathroom.' And then I'd leave and I wouldn't come back."

The whole strategy contained a large dollop of wishful thinking, and it was a little bit sad, but such was the fate of the women caught in

the circa 1993 limbo of the Navy's policy toward female pilots. If Kara
Hultgreen had a chip on her shoulder, it was understandable. At the
DACOWITS that spring she finally got up to ask the question she had
wanted to pose back at the Tailhook Symposium. There was General
Merrill A. McPeak, the Air Force chief of staff, delivering the welcoming remarks and then laying himself open to questions. Hultgreen
asked about the assignment of women to combat aircraft. It was now a
year and a half after Congress had voted to lift that ban, and still there
was no movement on the part of the services.

"It's a mistake to open up bombers and fighters to women," the
general responded. Then, hearing mutterings from the audience, he
continued, "It's hard for me to explain . . . I just can't get over this
feeling of old men ordering young women into combat . . . I have a
gut-based hang-up here. And it doesn't make a lot of sense in every
way. I apologize for it."

The women of the aviation community were disgusted. "Women
are invisible to him," Rosemary Mariner said of McPeak. "They're not
in his scan." The whole thing was all the more outrageous in that the
Air Force had already betrayed its female fliers. It had decided that
placing women pilots in the jet-pilot pipeline was useless, since they
would never get to fly combat. So the Air Force was simply aban-
doning plans to train women for jets. "June is our pumpkin time," said
Kelly Hamilton, the most senior female flier in the Air Force, meaning
that was the month when the Cinderellas of the Air Force were going
to turn from princesses back into drudges.

DACOWITS had grown increasingly vociferous on the issue of
lifting the combat ban. In the 1992 DACOWITS brochure were listed
"current issues pertaining to military women and of concern to
DACOWITS." Topping the list was "impact of combat exclusion."
Three female images appeared on the pamphlet's cover. One showed
a uniformed woman typing at a computer workstation, another a head-
set-equipped woman at a high-tech console. But the third image was
of a woman in fatigues, crouching out in the field, holding a machine
gun. Locked, cocked and ready to rock, as they would say in the Navy.

The combat ban was the only topic of interest to the female

aviators at the Marriott in late April 1993. The issue was aired out at a symposium, early in the conference, about the impact of the Presidential Commission's report. Lin Hutton, Mariner, Hultgreen and other members of the aviation community had converged upon Salon III to make sure everyone heard them. "We are being sent to Reserve squadrons," Hultgreen said. "That would be permanent duty. It's basically a career killer for all of us. If we don't act on this now, we're going to lose a valuable resource. We've been there, we've done it, we're ready to inject a little leadership into this transition. If we don't do this now, people like me are going to have to leave the Navy."

FOR MILITARY WOMEN, THE LAST WEEKS OF APRIL 1993 WERE packed almost too full. It was like those strange days in the summer of 1969, when the moonwalk, the Manson murders, Woodstock and Chappaquiddick happened during a single dizzying four-week stretch. Now the logjams and inaction of the past months (years? decades?) ended in a sudden rush of activity.

For six months, the people of the Navy had been waiting for the other shoe to drop, for Part 2 of the Defense Department Inspector General's Tailhook investigation. It wasn't that they burned to know what the Inspector General's agents had discovered, or they felt a sense of justice delayed and denied. It was like waiting for a boil to be lanced. You didn't look forward to the scalpel, but to the relief after. Most Navy people thought that only when the report came out would they be allowed to return to "normal," to life as they knew it before Paula Coughlin opened her mouth. Promotions had already been held up a year and a half now. Enough was enough.

The report was supposed to have been released in December 1992, then January 1993. It was now April. The primary reason given for the delay was the shuffle at the top. Sean O'Keefe departed from the office of Navy secretary on January 20, 1993. Before he left, O'Keefe did manage to set up something called the Consolidated Disposition Authority, Grand Inquisitors for the Tailhook affair, their

Women have always fought in wars, including those on American soil. Loreta Velasquez, pictured here, disguised herself in order to serve in the Civil War as an officer of the Confederate Army.

Legendary Soviet fighter pilot Lily Litvak accomplished twelve confirmed kills before perishing in an air battle over the Donbass in July 1943. *(Archival Files of the International Women's Air and Space Museum)*

Myth: Howard Chandler Christy's Gibson-flavored World War I recruiting poster. *(Office of Naval Records and Library—National Archives)*

Reality: World War I Yeomen (F) in full-dress uniform undergo inspection by Rear Admiral Victor Blue on the grounds of the Washington Monument. *(Navy Photo)*

Joy Bright Hancock was in charge of plans and policies for Navy women after the Integration Act of 1948. She had previously served in World War II as a commissioned officer and as a Yeoman (F) in 1918. *(Navy Photo by Portrait Studio, Bremerton, Wash., courtesy of Mrs. Joseph A. King [née Fitzgerald])*

A hundred thousand Navy WAVES served in World War II. Here Lieutenant (jg) Ballou holds a signal light at the Naval Air Station in Anacostia. *(Navy Photo)*

Jackie Cochran, Bendix trophy winner, speed demon and cosmetics queen. In World War II, Cochran headed the Women Airforce Service Pilots (WASP), which employed 2,000 female pilots to ferry every type of plane in the military inventory, including the heaviest bombers. *(San Diego Aero Space Museum)*

Congressman Carl Vinson, Democrat of Georgia, at the 1980 launching of his namesake nuclear-powered aircraft carrier. Vinson's 1948 decree—"Just fix it so they cannot go to sea"—left Navy women on the beach for thirty years. (*Navy Photo by Phan E. G. Noociolo*)

Admiral Elmo R. Zumwalt, Jr., pictured here during a ready room briefing on board the USS *Forrestal*, ushered the Navy into a new era for women as Chief of Naval Operations in the early 1970s. (*National Archives*)

One of the first women permanently assigned to sea duty, Ensign Linda Day of Gallipolis, Ohio, reports aboard the submarine tender USS *L. Y. Spear* on October 31, 1978. (*Navy Photo*)

Captain Rosemary Mariner (at left, when she was Ensign Rosemary Conatser) in a 1974 portrait of four of the Navy's first female aviators. (*Navy Photo by PH2 R. A. Meadows — National Archives*)

Boatswain's Mate Third-Class Robin Eckel, armed with an M-60 machine gun and 7.62mm ammunition, maintains her post aboard a port security boat during Operation Desert Shield. The war in the Persian Gulf proved to many Americans that military women could pass muster. (*Navy Photo by PA1 Chuck Kainbach, USCG*)

Navy Lieutenant Loree Draude inspects her F/A-18 on the flight line at Lemoore Naval Air Station in California's Central Valley. (*Jon Anderson — Sygma*)

Good to go: Secretary of Defense Les Aspin (flanked by Chief of Naval Operations Admiral Frank B. Kelso II, Air Force Chief of Staff General Merrill A. McPeak, Army Chief of Staff General Gordon R. Sullivan and Marine Corps Commandant General Carl E. Mundy) announces the plan to end the air combat exclusion for women at a press conference in May 1993. (*Steve Elfers--Army Times Pub. Co.*)

In August 1993, Lieutenant Paula Coughlin finally faced her alleged Tailhook attacker in court. Captain Gregory Bonam, a Marine F/A-18 pilot, would see his case dismissed for lack of evidence after a pre-court-martial hearing in Quantico, Virginia. Bonam is shown with his attorney, Patrick J. Mackrell. (*Steve Helber--AP Photo*)

Admiral Frank B. Kelso II sits with Navy Secretary John Dalton on October 6, 1993, the day after Les Aspin decided to retain Kelso as CNO—against Dalton's recommendation. (*Doug Pensinger—Army Times Pub. Co.*)

Admiral Kelso had urged Les Aspin to overturn the combat ban. He became a scandal casualty when he was forced to announce an early retirement so the Navy could "finally close this difficult chapter" of Tailhook. *(Shayna Brennan—AP Photo)*

Democratic Congresswoman Patricia Schroeder of Colorado (center, pointing) and other female House members show solidarity in a march to the Senate side of Capitol Hill on Tuesday, April 19, 1994, opposing Admiral Frank Kelso's retirement at four-star rank. By a 54–43 vote, the Senate determined that Kelso would keep his stars. *(John Duricka—AP Photo)*

Even in a gender-blind Navy, some cultural issues remain. How will women deal with such ancient sea traditions as the crossing-the-equator ceremony? Illustrator Robert Cruikshank published a lithograph depicting a "Neptune party" on board a British ship in an 1844 book titled *Old Sailor's Jolly Boat*. *(Print Collection, Miriam and Ira D. Wallach Division of Art, Prints and Photographs, The New York Public Library, Astor, Lenox and Tilden Foundations)*

Sucking the cherry from the navel of the "Royal Baby" during a Neptune party on board a U.S. destroyer, circa 1982. *(Navy Photo by McManus)*

An old-line Navy tradition: plebes scaling the lard-coated Herndon Monument at the U.S. Naval Academy. *(Collection of the United States Naval Academy Archives, 89-711-9)*

Paula Coughlin and her mother, Rena, leave the Las Vegas courtroom on October 31, 1994, after the settlement of Coughlin's civil suit with the Hilton. (*John Gurzinski*)

The first Navy warship with women permanently assigned as crew members deployed out of Norfolk, Virginia, in the Fall of 1994. Here, Lieutenant (jg) Joy Adams of Strike Fighter Squadron 105, one of the Navy's few female combat pilots, conducts preflight checks on her F/A-18 Hornet prior to launching off the USS *Dwight D. Eisenhower*. Her mission is to enforce the no-fly zone over Iraq. (*Navy Photo by AN Charles Beaudin*)

Navy Lieutenant Kara Hultgreen died at sea when her F-14 Tomcat crashed into the ocean off the coast of San Diego in October 1994. (*Photo Courtesy Sally Spears*)

names kept secret. O'Keefe evidently fell into a philosophical frame of mind as he was leaving. "I have no easy answers for the new secretary, except to observe that judgment is the hardest of human tasks, and that my successor must look deeply into the human heart, attempting to see what is good and true—and, sadly, what is not—before making the best decisions possible."

A deeply ironic statement, it turns out, given that O'Keefe's temporary replacement, the man to whom this plea for justice was addressed, was Admiral Frank Kelso. With O'Keefe gone, Kelso was in the awkward and, many felt, politically treacherous position of wearing two hats ("covers," Navy people would say). He would be CNO, chief of naval operations, and acting SecNav, Secretary of the Navy. Keeping such a high visibility would ultimately make Kelso the logical target of Tailhook fallout. Even with its temporary eclipse by the gay ban debate, the scandal was proving remarkably evergreen. As the months went on with no report, no new facts or names, the story still didn't seem to dissipate.

Much of what had kept the scandal alive over the winter and into the spring could be traced to the media charisma of Paula Coughlin. Year-end wrap-ups all over the print and broadcast media and television featured her prominently—she was one of "The Women We Love" in *Esquire*, a '92 Woman of the Year (along with Carol Moseley-Braun, Hillary Clinton and Susan Faludi) in *Glamour,* one of "A Few Good Women" in December's *Vanity Fair.* As one Navy flier put it, Coughlin was everybody's "sexual harassment poster child of the year." She also brought a civil lawsuit against both the Tailhook Association and the Las Vegas Hilton, asserting that the organizer and the host of the convention "created, fostered and indulged an environment" that degraded and threatened women.

Of course, to some of her peers in the Navy, Coughlin's willingness to appear in these magazines and her decision to litigate were interpreted as further examples of bad headwork. In the flight squadrons and ships of the line, people who had never met Paula Coughlin felt free to assail the purity of her motives. The woman was a money-grubber and publicity hound, it was said, out for her own gain rather than the Navy's good.

Coughlin concerned herself less and less with what her peers might think. She was back in Norfolk that spring, back near the Virginia Beach haunts of her adolescence, stationed at the naval air station with Helicopter Support Squadron 2. At least she was flying again. After coming forward the previous summer, she had been grounded for six months, prevented from flying her CH-53 Sea Stallion because she was supposedly suffering from too much "emotional strain." But she hadn't exactly been welcomed with open arms at the squadron. The more she thought about it—and try as she might, she couldn't think about much else—the more she grasped new nuances in why she was now being ostracized. It was too bad that the Standing Committee on Women in the Navy and Marine Corps didn't include among its recommendations a support group for victims of sexual harassment and assault, so that Coughlin could have met and offered some insights to Karlene Dent and others like her. Coughlin now recognized that, in coming forward, she violated some of her community's cardinal rules. Arcane, but still cardinal.

The most sacred rule was one that Dent had also alluded to, and in strikingly similar language. "What goes on det stays on det," was how Coughlin put it—"det" short for a "detachment," a deployment of part of a flight squadron. "That means whatever goes on when you're deployed with your buddies stays there and doesn't come home. Whoever you pick up in a bar, however drunk you get, if you get arrested, if you get busted, any of that—it doesn't come home with you. Those are the rules. You know, the '2 Tac N Rule.' The 2 Tac N Rule means, if you are two navigation stations away from home, you can take off your wedding ring and you're a new man. A lot of aviators just don't wear wedding bands. They say it's too risky, it could get caught in the flight controls. That's Navy-wide, that's aviation-wide." The Tailhook party, Coughlin now realized, as much as the kind of no-holds-barred scene you might find on deployment, was inherently 2 Tac N. No one was supposed to mouth off about it later, much less complain about it. In the cold, bright winter of 1993, Coughlin was being punished for her transgression.

"The guys in my squadron [at Norfolk]," she said, "there are some coneheads, some Fred Flintstone types that just will never get used to the idea of me bustin' up the boys' club." Yet she was beginning to see changes in the mentality of her peers. "There are guys maybe a little younger than me—you know, their wives all work. This is a new generation, and the world is full of two-income families. And a guy starts to think, 'You know, if that had happened to my wife in the workplace, I'd kill the bastard.'" Some of the guys even would go out of their way to say that to her, and some women would pull her aside. But at Norfolk, there was little public support for Coughlin. "I have women that come up to me and say, 'Off the record, I support you.' I'm like, why off the record? I didn't break any laws, okay? Those guys did." But she could understand why so many Navy women turned on her: "Women . . . just hear too many horrible things said about me. They go, 'Wow, I just couldn't handle that.' And I don't blame any woman that has seen what ugly things have come out . . ."

Over the winter she spent at Norfolk, walking along some of the same beaches she lifeguarded at as a kid, Coughlin had the opportunity to reflect on a lot of things she'd never given much thought to before. Like Marine mentality. "A lot of the guys in that hallway were Marines. And the Marines make a tradition out of treating women like shit. You know what the acronym for a female Marine was? A 'BAM'— 'broad-assed Marine.' That was something that a general could turn to his aide and say: 'Who's that BAM?' Up until, like, yesterday. That's something so simple, you could bring that point up to a man and he'd say, 'Oh, what's a name?' But what if I called you something nasty?"

She'd tried to find acceptance at her new squadron, but it was hard to create a welcome for yourself when you had the kind of loaded reputation she did by now. "It puts shock waves ahead of me," she said. "I know that I probably have a very tenuous working relationship with 60 to 70 percent of the guys I work with." She described one of the senior officers in the squadron as "a real numbnuts"—he couldn't deal with her. Nor could one of the enlisted men she supervised; she'd criticized him one day and he would never let her forget it. She did have supporters in the squadron, including one lieutenant commander in her chain of command, a black officer with twenty-three years in the service.

Few people could understand how hard it was for her. "I have some basic fears, of walking into a group of men in a room, a bunch of naval aviators. I don't want to be there. No thanks. You're having fun, you're having a meeting? Uh-uh. I don't like it. But my fears are founded on something concrete, something bad that happened to me."

By that time, Tailhook revisionists who saw it as their crusade to "set the record straight" were also starting to make themselves heard in the mass media. One of these was a civilian named Beth Rudd, who described herself as "the bite girl" of the Navy Inspector General Report. Rudd appeared on "Hard Copy" the last week in February for a segment titled, *I Ran the Tailhook Gauntlet.* She was coming forward, she said, in order to clear the names of her Navy friends ("I hurt for them because their reputations have been damaged"). Contrary to popular belief, the '91 convention was "very much a celebration . . . not a twenty-four-hour sex orgy for five days." Paula Coughlin was "a disgrace to the Navy." Rudd also announced she was getting into the T-shirt business, with a design that read "I Won't Press Charges."

If the Navy leadership was still hoping that Tailhook would somehow disappear from public consciousness, its chances looked bleak. After a while, the failure of the Department of Defense to release its report grew embarrassing. Fifteen congresswomen, led by Pat Schroeder, signed a letter to the newly appointed Secretary of Defense, Les Aspin, stating that "delaying the release of the final report sends a message to the nation that sexual assault and harassment of women are not sufficiently important to warrant immediate discipline." Former CIA director Stansfield Turner, himself a retired admiral and hardly among those out to "get" the Navy, wrote a *Washington Post* op-ed piece calling for the report's release. "We do not

need . . . to know which lieutenant pinched which women to take
the corrective actions needed . . . The fact that no senior officer has
been held accountable for the progressive deterioration of conduct at
the Tailhook conventions is undermining the concept of accountability."

So the other shoe finally, at long last, had to be dropped. In
keeping with the faint air of cheesiness that surrounded the Navy's
handling of the whole Tailhook affair, the DoD report finally came out
on a Friday. It's an old public relations ploy to release bad news just
before a weekend to give the muddy waters two days to settle. The
April 23 release date worked, since the impact of the report was buff-
ered by the massive gay march on Washington. But in another sense,
the Department of Defense could have handed the thing out in Me
dina the first day of Ramadan and it would still have made news. True
to Paula Coughlin's prediction, it read "like an X-rated novel."

In a sense, the DoD report was a demonstration of the power of
packaging. It covered much of the same ground as previous Tailhook
investigations, the drinking, the assaults, the disturbing image of a
stripped, unconscious teenager. It differed in that it offered up cul-
prits—files on 117 officers had been sent to military commands for
possible disciplinary action, compared with the two aviators accused of
serious offenses the first time around. The number of women assaulted at Tailhook climbed from 26 to 83, with 7 men thrown in for
good measure. (It would be difficult to interpret their complaints as
much more than disingenuous afterthoughts supplied by male officers
eager to even the score.) A cover memo attached to the report had it
that the thirty-five Scrambled Eggs who attended Tailhook would also
have their cases reviewed, by whom it was not yet clear. The Department of Defense had spent nearly a million dollars (an unheard of
sum for a single-incident study) on the investigation. All told, the
report was the result of 60,000 hours of labor—30 work years,
crammed into 10 months.

But the real reason the report cut through a lot of apathy was
that it was, for a government publication, surprisingly sprightly. Usu-

ally the documents emanating from the huge government printing combine in Pueblo, Colorado, were intrinsically dull. The activities that had gone down at Tailhook '91 had all received their due in the NIS report put out almost a year earlier. But they had never been cataloged so exhaustively, highlighted so prominently, given such memorable names ("ballwalking," among other terms, instantly entered the language) in an easy-to-skim table of contents. There were reproduced photographs, (most heavily censored), lavish graphics, fold-out full-color artists' renderings (produced at a cost of $10,000) of the scene of the crimes. It was, in publishing parlance, a beach read.

In fact, the report became exactly that. St. Martin's Press published the book—sans its salacious but legally problematic photos—commercially as a trade paperback. The faceless government wonks who authored the text (for Derek J. Vander Schaaf, DoD Deputy Inspector General) were so editorially deft that St. Martin's had little more to do than wrap the report in a new cover. From the vantage of mass appeal, it was already perfect. The chapter headings were a social satirist's dream. "Ballwalking." "Belly/Navel Shots." "Butt Biting." "Mooning." The contrast with the sober governmental imprimatur was jarring. Sections of the report were read nightly on the new cable channel, Comedy Central, probably a first for a taxpayer-supported publication.

THE EVOLUTION OF FRANK KELSO STOOD AS AN EXAMPLE OF WHAT can happen when an injustice repeatedly presents itself to a fair and logical mind. It finally didn't matter that Kelso was the product of a traditional conservative Tennessee childhood, that he had spent much of his Navy career in the environment that has proved most inimicable to women, submarines, that his peers at the top of the other service branches were dead set against any change in the status quo or that there was tremendous political and organizational pressure upon him to limit action. In the end, Frank Kelso went against all that.

It had been a bumpy ride. As recently as June 1991, two months before the Tailhook Symposium in Las Vegas, Kelso was in front of the Senate Armed Services Committee telling the committee members why he didn't think lifting the combat exclusion for women was a good idea. He invoked the statements of General H. Norman Schwarzkopf, then one of the most popular men in the country, after Desert Storm. "[Schwarzkopf] said that changes in this area must be made in the interest of military effectiveness, not as an issue concerning equal opportunity. On this question, as in most others . . . General Schwarzkopf and I are in total agreement."

Kelso also cited the favored "neutral" argument against expanding women's role in the military, "heads and beds," or habitability, which allowed him effectively to sidestep messy questions of gender equality. From the cramped perspective of a former submariner, it was the most potent line of reasoning against dropping the combat exclusion. He later analyzed his frame of mind. "I guess I was looking at it from the standpoint of people being together for long periods of time. You're out there on a submarine for two months, three months, standing watch every night together. How do we deal with this? I'd always agreed that females in the Navy didn't have equal opportunity from the standpoint of promotion. You simply cannot have that, we as an organization, if you go to a promotion board and the promotion board asks how you performed—if you haven't had that job, sooner or later it's going to affect your chances for promotion. The issue was whether the living problems associated with [full integration of women] were less of an evil than the other."

So at the hearings that June, he toed the official line. "It's my personal view that the law should remain as it stands," Kelso said. He admitted to his "worry about the young woman who wants to fly an airplane in combat or wants to ride on a ship. I understand the anguish it might give her."

Such empathies were out of synch with the statements of the other service chiefs, some of whom were openly scornful of women serving under them. General Merrill McPeak of the Air Force was asked by Senator Cohen what he would do if he had to choose be-

tween a female pilot "of superior intelligence, great physical conditioning, in every way . . . superior to a male counterpart vying for a
combat position." McPeak said that he "would pick the male over the
female under those circumstances. I admit it doesn't make much
sense, but that's the way I feel about it."

But the truth was that the evolution of Frank Kelso had probably
already occurred, and the June hearings were merely evidence of a lag
between thought and action. Frank Kelso eventually found it impossible to work with women, to be a father of daughters, while continuing
to say that he felt it necessary to relegate them to secondary status. "I
don't think there's any one day lightning struck and caused me to have
a different view," said Kelso. "When I came into this job, I'm not sure
I thought I would be on the side of changing [the combat exclusion].
I'd lived a life in the Navy for thirty-four years primarily where we
didn't have to deal too much with women. In most of my career, I was
not living on a day-to-day basis where I had to have many women
working under me or working with me."

When he came out of submarines and began to work in the
administration of the Navy, however, Kelso began to work with a lot of
women. Administration was where women were, after all, that was
where they had been stashed after being told they couldn't go out into
the fleet. So the combat exclusion had the unintended effect of placing a lot of smart, professional women on the staffs of admirals and
Pentagon movers and shakers—exactly the type of men who could get
policy changed. The women wound up behind the men who mattered.

As commander of the Atlantic fleet, Kelso had witnessed firsthand the degree of resistance men had to women serving alongside
them on ships. But he also saw again and again that women could do
the job. A commander at Norfolk told Kelso that women couldn't
work in a certain dry dock, because, he said, they couldn't handle the
sandbags that held the sand used in air guns. Kelso sent in a woman
worker incognito, "dressed in blue jeans," and found out that the men
picked up the sandbags in teams of two. Kelso subsequently overruled
the commander and opened up the dry dock to women.

"Most of the jobs we do in the Navy are not strength-related,"

Kelso said. "There are some, but what we do is use two or three people. Normally they'd ask the big guy, but the big guy usually breaks more things than he fixes. So in my thinking, if a female wants to be in a dirty ol' engine room, and she can do it, why should I stand in her way?"

Something else that crystallized Kelso's thinking was the Anita Hill/Clarence Thomas hearings. "They told me something that I didn't appreciate previously, that this was a matter of a lady who was very unhappy in her workplace. And I thought about it, and I said, it must be a real jungle out there." Kelso had two daughters and two sons. The sons were both naval officers, one a submarine engineer and one a doctor. Mary, his older daughter, was married to a naval officer, and she was outspoken in her views on women in the workplace. This was in part due to some less-than-positive experiences of her own in that area. "She was not harassed in the sense Anita Hill claimed she was," said Kelso, "but she felt she didn't have the same opportunity to advance, to make the same wages."

Tailhook, of course, served to pound the lessons home. Even Kelso's wife, confronted by the news reports of anarchy on the third deck, asked him, "What is it about the Navy?" Kelso presented himself as being "shocked that naval officers would engage in that kind of behavior." He had seen the infamous ball-walking photographs that had been broadcast on "A Current Affair." According to his longtime special assistant for public affairs, Commander Deborah Burnette, Kelso during this period would pace around his office, saying, "I just cannot get over it."

Was Frank Kelso crying crocodile tears over Tailhook? Was this view of him—an old salt shocked by aviator misconduct—merely convenient historical revisionism? Part of the Kelso's response to Tailhook was, indeed, politically expedient. But the fact remained that the incident changed his idea about just how fair the Navy was being in its treatment of women. As long as women were locked out of certain positions, Kelso now believed, they would continue to be accorded less respect.

A remarkable set of circumstances, both personal and political, had converged to change Frank Kelso's mind about the combat ban. The Navy was downsizing, eliminating many of the billets available to women. "In order to give these women that we had in the Navy a fair shot, we really needed to open up more positions to them, and as the other types of ship started going away, then the combatants were about the only way we had to do that."

In February 1993, Kelso signed off on a memorandum titled "It's Time," which recommended lifting the combat exclusion on Navy ships. He forwarded the plan to Clinton's new Secretary of Defense, former Wisconsin congressman Les Aspin. Aspin was immediately concerned, because he was witnessing an exact opposite movement on the part of the Air Force. General McPeak had informed him that the Air Force was shutting down opportunities for women in its jet-pilot pipeline, concluding that with the combat exclusion in place, there was no logical reason for them to be there. Faced with the prospect of two of his service branches pulling in opposite directions, Aspin felt he had to act. "Consistency," Aspin said. "That's got to happen."

The actual announcement was timed so that it just squeaked in as an achievement of the Clinton administration's first 100 days in office. On April 28, Aspin issued the order that Kara Hultgreen, Loree Draude, Rosemary Mariner and thousands of other women had been waiting for. "The services shall permit women to compete for assignments in aircraft," read the memorandum, "including aircraft engaged in combat missions." Aspin also directed the Navy to "develop a legislative proposal, which I will forward to Congress, to repeal the existing combat exclusion law and permit the assignment of women to ships that are engaged in combat missions."

At the press conference announcing the change, the Navy suffered the indignity of being trumped by the Air Force, ironically the service branch slowest to adopt new roles for women. It was the Air Force, not the Navy, who supplied the media that day with what they clearly had to have: living, breathing, female fighter pilots. There stood Kelso, announcing that the Navy was, in aviation-speak, "good to go"—ready to implement the changes. But McPeak, the same man who had pronounced to the DACOWITS only days before his implacable bias against female fliers, didn't talk much. He merely produced Lieutenant Jeannie Flynn and Captain Sharon Preszler. Flynn was, predictably enough, a pretty twenty-six-year-old. Preszler, described by *Time* as "a soft-spoken strawberry blonde," made the assembled media hearts beat faster when she announced, "I can be a killer. I can and will kill in defense of my country." The press ate it up. It would be Flynn who would be profiled in *People,* not the long-suffering Navy women who had flown long and lobbied hard for the right to fly in combat.

It didn't matter. The mood at the naval air stations was euphoric. "This is sort of like being able to vote," Kara Hultgreen crowed. "This is historic. I feel super, I'm ecstatic, I'm thrilled." Rosemary Mariner said, "It's something that I've been looking forward to for 20 years. I knew it would happen. I envy the young ones." Loree Draude said she was, in a word, "stoked."

Chapter Nine

———

THE TROGLODYTES

WHAT HAD BEEN BILLED AS THE "FIRST ANNUAL *GAUNTLET* BACCHA-nalia" was a disappointment to its organizer, a Navy flight officer named Michael Kitchen. *The Gauntlet* was his baby, an eight-page satirical newsletter edited and largely written by him. He had started it in the fall of 1992, in the prop wash of the Tailhook scandal, laboriously typing out the first issue even though he didn't have a word processor. "The last thing I ever wrote was a paper in my senior year of college," Kitchen said. A pastiche of opinion, anecdotes, broad satire and rude jokes, *The Gauntlet* was, by Kitchen's lights, a modest success. He had advertised three or four times, small ads in the *Navy Times*. There were now, in May 1993, over 100 subscribers paying twelve dollars a year for monthly issues. Given the nature of the new Navy, and the nature of *The Gauntlet,* Kitchen felt it all had to be kept carefully anonymous. He usually used the *nom de guerre* "Richard Fitzwell" ("One lieutenant commander in my squadron, I literally had to say it to him very slowly—Dick . . . Fitzwell—before he got it").

The conference, announced as a "no-host" affair for the friends of *The Gauntlet,* was Kitchen's attempt to lengthen the new publication's political reach. He decided to hold the event at the Crystal

Gateway Marriott, in Arlington, Virginia—close by the shadow of the
Pentagon, in a bloodless precinct that boasted a sprawling maze of an
underground mall. He wanted to meet all the people he had been
talking to over the phone in the last few months, *Gauntlet* interviewees like Phyllis Schlafly and Brian Mitchell. Kitchen booked May 21
for the conference, which he envisioned as a sort of combination bull
session and pep rally. Get the ball rolling on opposing some of the
ridiculous changes that seemed to be coming for the Navy. Show the
colors. Alert the forces of political correctness that they were there. So
Kitchen loaded his extra copies of *The Gauntlet* into his car and drove
with his wife Jennifer from their home in Virginia Beach.

Kitchen, eager to greet conventioneers, stood in the hotel's forn
deoked Atrium Lounge, wearing his bomber jacket with its Bart Simpson "I wasn't there" flight patch, waiting to greet the throngs who
never quite materialized. By five, the lobby of the Crystal Gateway
was still nearly empty. Oh, there were a few of the faithful. Bruce
Herbert, introduced by Kitchen as a former Navy commander, was
much in evidence, a mustachioed Donald Pleasance–type who kept
referring to Kitchen's wife as "Jennifer, our charming host-*ess*," inexplicably accenting the second syllable. There was something spooklike
—in the Langley sense—about his demeanor. A reporter from the
Navy Times sat in for a few moments, then left.

The mood was one of forced buoyancy, with all the no-shows laid
to dark political purposes. "People are afraid to subscribe to my newsletter, much less show up when the NIS might be there with a camera," Kitchen explained. "Political correctness is really becoming a
beast. It's really overkill. I just shake my head." Later on that night he
journeyed down from his room to the hotel bar and tried to distribute
copies of *The Gauntlet* to a trio of Marines. They declined.

Kitchen was raised in the Midwest, and fell in love with flying
when he went up in a glider during college. It was that love, rather
than his father's experience as a Navy man, that led him to enlist.
"About that age, I found out I needed glasses. I thought I wanted to
fly fighters. And the only service that allowed people who wanted to fly

fighters to wear glasses was the Navy." His plan was to have the Navy pay for his college, and then get a commission to fly. He wound up about as far from fighters as you could get, as a blue-shirt electronics technician on submarines, but stuck it out and eventually graduated from Aviation Officer Candidate School.

The Gauntlet was published out of Kitchen's home outside of Virginia Beach. He and Jennifer had two kids, Dawn and Christopher, and a Doberman they'd trained to fetch cans of beer. Jennifer kept a quarter horse. ("Gives me a chance to pass sugar cubes over a fence.") In the brutal hierarchy of naval air, Kitchen was a perpetual wannabe. He was prior enlisted, a "backseater" (naval flight officer) not a pilot, flying an E-2, not an F-14, in the Reserves, not the regular Navy. During Desert Storm, he was flying drug interdiction in Panama, living in a converted tool shed. "It was disheartening, having trained for that, to be in Central America, being bored to death. Like every other American, I watched it on TV."

The Gauntlet attempted to be as politically incorrect as it possibly could. It announced itself as "a journal for the politically correct and sensitive military person." The statement of purpose printed in each issue then continued: "Drunken debauchery of the kind recently displayed (you know where and you know who) is not tolerated but will be graded." Early issues also identified the publication as "a JOPA production"—meaning the Junior Officers Protection Association. Kitchen identified JOPA as "an unofficial official organization," and in fact its existence was more or less openly acknowledged throughout the Navy. "It doesn't matter if you went to the academy or ROTC or AOCS," Kitchen said. "They teach you that the guy next to you is your buddy. The guy who flies next to you is your wingman. You're going to take care of him no matter what. There's no special handshake. There's just some things that the junior officers take care of among themselves that they don't want anybody to know about it. They taught us to take care of ourselves, so we do."

Although Kitchen called JOPA "rank-specific, not gender-specific" and said that women can freely join, there was not much evidence of that. *The Gauntlet*'s namesake, of course—the men in the hallway on the Las Vegas Hilton's third deck—could itself be called "a JOPA production."

Kitchen had also watched the Tailhook scandal unfold on television. "Although I wasn't at Tailhook '91, I probably would have gone if I had not been at sea. I did go in 1990. I do not condone what happened to the women, let me say that, first and foremost. But having been there and been in that same area before, from the elevator bank to the hallway, where the rooms are, let me tell you this about when I was there in 1990. The general public thinks that these women walked down the hallway and these guys were standing at parade rest, one row on one side and one row down the other and they came to attention, reached out and grabbed their favorite body part. Well, it's not that way. In that hallway, it's crammed. Imagine trying to get to the front of a Rolling Stones concert. You're pushing and shoving. It wasn't that anybody was just able to walk freely down that thing."

The Gauntlet also featured a monthly hand-wringing column by "Pat Shredder." And in February 1993, a few months prior to the Crystal City Marriott get-together, Bruce Herbert penned a pasquinade supposedly from the "National Legislative Director" of something calling itself the Animal Lovers League (ALL). Now that gays were getting into the military, Herbert wrote, ALL was demanding parity for its members. "Congresswoman Patricia Schroeder assures us that animal lovers will be as welcome in all the services as gays, lesbians or any other heretofore disenfranchised practitioners of unconventional sexuality." There were also interviews with sympathetic politicians such as Eagle Forum chairwoman Phyllis Schlafly ("I sent her a copy [of the interview] and after that she stopped sending me any kind of information at all," Kitchen said. "I think I was a little bit too salty.") Later issues of the newsletter took a more serious bent, including pleas for donations to the defense funds of Tailhook defendants.

But as broad as *The Gauntlet* could be, at its heart lay an essential question. Congress could decree overreaching changes in the makeup of the Navy, but no law on the books could possibly dictate every nuance of a new Navy culture. Who would be responsible for that? By which agency, human or bureaucratic, would it be done? By whose standard? So far, Kitchen was openly disdainful of the attempts. "There was a guy named Ben. Normally call signs come up from something stupid you did, or some physical attribute. He didn't really do anything, but his name was Ben, so his call sign became 'Benny' and then 'Ben Wa.' There's very few people that that really means anything to. But it came down to our chain of command to review every person's call sign to make sure that it's not offensive. He used to have a name tag that said 'Ben Wa.' No more. Another fellow, his nickname was Bung. Right when he got into the squadron, he had surgery on his anus. So he got that nickname. It's kind of innocuous, really. But guess what?—that call sign 'Bung' went away. I'll give you another example: the guy's last name was Cherry. James Cherry. He got the nickname 'Buster.' Guess what? 'No, no, no, you won't use Buster.' I mean, Bung and Ben Wa at least had some kind of offensive context, but this guy's name tag just said Buster."

After the full dimensions of the failure of *The Gauntlet* conference had sunk in, the small circle of believers tightened around itself and relaxed. Michael Kitchen finally sat himself down. Jennifer Kitchen, demure in a cream-colored sweater, her hair carefully styled, followed her white wine with a White Russian. Bruce Herbert, *The Gauntlet*'s reigning *éminence grise,* wore an emerald hankie scissor-folded in the pocket of his blazer. He was snapping photos with his Olympus. "To memorialize the occasion," he explained, but it seemed to make everyone a little nervous.

While the others stared at their drinks, Herbert held forth, very much *honi soit que mal y pense.* "I think this is an evil time," Herbert said. "The lunacy of gays, the lunacy of women in combat. I think they're very sad times, today. You have a Judeo-Christian ethic of women having a protected role and a civilizing role. That's a respected, not a denigrating role. Roles have turned upside down. The epitome of political correctness is homosexuals—and also women being thrown into the front lines."

A retired Annapolis aviator with chipped teeth and black eyes sat next to his chunky Filipino wife, who wore a gold brooch representing a jet inside a gold circle. He reminisced about SERE School in the sixties, where he got his eardrums busted. "Are there any women going to SERE school now?" Kitchen asked. The pilot said there were. "Are the standards the same for them?" asked the pilot's wife "because at the [Naval] Academy I know they're not."

Throughout the cocktail hour, there was an eerie *Stepford Wives* atmosphere hanging over the group. The women present wordlessly sought their husbands' permission before making decisions on such trivial matters as whether to move into the cocktail lounge for the free happy-hour buffet. Roles here were anything but "upside down." For Michael Kitchen, and for a lot of people, the question still remained: What sort of Navy were women joining? If the old days of rum, sodomy and the lash had been struck down, what would take their place?

"IF WOMEN ARE NOW EXPECTED TO KILL AND BE KILLED," SAID KATE Walsh O'Beirne of the ultra-conservative Heritage Foundation, "the feminists [will] have achieved their gender-blind Nirvana." According to Elaine Donnelly, along with O'Beirne a former member of the Presidential Commission on the Assignment of Women in the Armed Forces, Bill Clinton was preparing "to order the nation's daughters into killing zones and rape motels which he himself avoided."

Although there would be no equality for military women without the lifting of the combat ban, the lifting of the ban did not automatically mean equality either. There were too many gray areas. There were too many issues that Congress could not legislate. And the Navy was just too large—like an aircraft carrier steaming at full power—to be able to turn on a dime. It needed a lot of ocean.

It was not just a question of paronomastic call signs. Would it no longer be permissible to "cuss like a sailor?" And if not, where were the Free Speech guarantees (always a slippery commodity in the military) of the sailors who felt themselves curtailed? The question of call signs, for instance, and of "cussing like a sailor," are both small and large. How any tribe describes itself or communicates is indicative of its moral tenor, self-esteem and regard for others. In the Navy, the language was juicy, in the sense of being colorful, and in the sense of furnishing rich opportunity for analysis.

There were the cadence calls or "jodies," which sometimes graphically mixed sex and violence. Since the time the Navy had first put planes in the air there had been "nose art"—painting on the nose cones or fuselages of Navy planes—which was oftentimes X- or at least R-rated. Crossing-the-line traditions had been traced all the way back to tenth-century Nordic ships crossing the forty-fifth parallel. Were these now all to be swept away in the name of protecting female sensibilities? Or, perhaps more radically, could they be modified in a way that would allow female expression as well?

The military was, of course, still a predominantly male preserve. Before the Aspin memorandum of April 28, a full 60 percent of the jobs in the armed forces were closed to women. And Aspin's executive action was by no means a clean sweep. There were still exceptions, exclusions and quid pro quos—no hand-to-hand combat, for example, no ground fighting. Aspin asked that the service chiefs give a rationale for any jobs they deemed inappropriate for women still, but he did not require they open all jobs. After the memo took effect, 40 percent of the military was still closed to women. An absolutist might ask just what the female fliers were celebrating. Another partial victory, and one which depended upon the whim of an electorate which had sent a Republican into the White House in five of the last seven elections?

For the Navy and the Air Force, though, the lifting of the legislative ban on women in warplanes and on combatants was much more than a symbolic victory. Planes and ships constituted the core of their business. Neither service had many of the front-line, foot-soldier jobs that the Pentagon and most of the American public still believed should be off-limits to female military members. Navy personnel planners were promising a "gender-free" organization in five years' time. Still, for the present, both branches remained overwhelmingly male in both tenor and substance, meaning that the very people expected to transform the Navy were themselves products of the old environment. These were men sent to do a woman's job. The Navy leadership was determined to make the ranks safe for females. But the nuts-and-bolts changes necessary for that process were left to a group of administrators far removed from the ranks themselves—in Washington, mostly, or in fleet headquarters. There was a hint of the chivalric code here, of the knight making the world safe for milady. In the spring of 1993 it looked as if there was no crusading fervor in the world more terrible than a man who felt he was performing service in the name of a woman.

It was all well and good for a woman like Marty Evans to dismiss age-old traditions wholesale. ("What do they contribute? Nobody's ever convinced me. I'm sure there are people that will tell you the Navy is going to hell in a handbasket because we don't do this stuff anymore, but nobody's presented a rational argument. I don't buy it.") The sentiment in the ranks—for both men and women—was far less certain. Many women on the *Cape Cod*, for example, were actively looking forward to their crossing-the-line initiations, which they felt to be a legitimate (and legitimizing) imprimatur of their status as full-fledged seafarers. If the new Navy was going to be "put through the deflavorizer"—as Woody Allen used to say about his mother's chicken —and if it were all done in the name of women, was this necessarily doing the Navy female a favor?

The problem was there was no longer any middle ground. You were either with the program or you weren't. The zone of overlap in the interests of the saltiest Old Navy male and Kara Hultgreen, say, or Karlene Dent, or even Paula Coughlin—that zone was being ignored. Hultgreen would have liked to "handle" a barroom brawl on her own terms, without necessarily being labeled a victim. Dent wanted to be able to tell a racy joke without it being taken to mean she was open to all comers. Coughlin wanted to party with her cohorts and not get mauled. All three wanted to prove their skills at work, with no special treatment, no coddling, but without any extra hassles, either.

Navy leadership responded only in absolute terms, imposing upon the ranks a high order of rectitude that seemed derived from an old Puritan ideal. All pagan exuberance must be summarily quashed. The whole issue was complicated by the fact there were a good many men who masked their fear and mistrust of women by defending the sacrosanct traditions they felt would be diluted or, worse, completely dissolved in the new Navy.

SARA MCGANN STARED WIDE-EYED THROUGH THE OPEN DOORWAY OF the cavernous "barber area" in Alumni Hall at the U.S. Naval Academy in Annapolis. Soft mounds of hair were piled onto the concrete floor between the old-fashioned, ocher-colored barber chairs. In the chairs sat young women or men, shrouded up to the neck in blue plastic, getting their hair cut to regulation academy length.

"Holy cow," McGann murmured. It was the first day of July 1993. The skies were lowering and closed. The hazy Southern weather seemed to have drifted in on the campus from the Severn River. This was "I-Day," Induction Day at the academy for the Class of 1997: Sara McGann and 1,189 of her classmates, 167 of whom were women. The whole place had been taken over by plebes, as first-year midshipmen are called, and families of plebes. Pretty much everything was worth a "holy cow."

There was the immaculate, almost unearthly beauty of the yard, the emerald lawns punctuated with overarching gingkoes and elms, studded with handsome, sepulchral naval monuments. "Those who expect to reap the blessings of freedom must, like men, undergo the fatigue of supporting it," read a plaque beneath a fountain that stood beside the incoming road from Gate 3. "Given in memory of classmates who have given their lives in service of their country, 1972." There was the immensity of the tradition, but there was also the immensity of actually taking the plunge, of stepping into an experience which would pluck you up and mold you and change you irrevocably and forever. To a seventeen-year-old girl from Groton, Connecticut, it all seemed impossibly portentous.

The haircut actually was a big deal. Or had been made into one, in the years since women had entered the academy, in 1976. For the boys, the experience would leave them shaved to the skull. The girls had their hair shorn to the collar; it couldn't stand more than two inches thick from the head. Therein lay the rub. A lot of the traditionalists had seized upon The Haircut as evidence that the Navy was bending its rules to accommodate women. Every single cultural adjustment could be made into a battleground, and no fight was too small. It was symbolic; it was *important.* You didn't need to go back to Samson and Delilah or the shaved heads of female collaborators in World War II to know what people were squabbling about. In 1994, when The Citadel, the publicly supported military school in Charleston, South Carolina, was hassling over admitting Shannon Faulkner, its first female full-time cadet, her lawyers and the school's had to have a judge decide what kind of haircut she would get.

Five of the eighteen barbers employed by the Naval Academy for I-Day knew how to cut women's hair. Over the years, rules for the female plebe cut had drifted. Women used to have to wait until the second semester of their senior year until they could grow it out, and now they could grow it long the second semester of plebe year, though even then they could only do so if they always wore it up. The woman who cut McGann's assured her that even though her locks were thick, she wouldn't have to cut them any shorter—instead she could pull her hair back with a barrette. "All right!" Sara said.

The plebes proceeded in turn through the official I-Day stations: check-in, name tag, baggage drop, eye tests, blood tests, urinalysis, breathalyzer and (for the women) pregnancy tests. McGann stopped at women's uniform issue, where she picked up a laundry bag and, among other items, socks, purple shower shoes, bedroom slippers, "grandma underwear" (cotton jockey briefs, jog bras), blue and yellow Speedo swimsuit, black neckerchief and bayonet belt, a pair of New Balance cross trainers. A couple of years before, mids had stopped being assigned combat boots. They would get a pair later, at the end of their first year, before doing the required summertime stint at Quantico. Finally Sara, in her green shorts and black T-shirt, stood a little bashfully on an old-fashioned wooden stool to get her dimensions taken, the yellow tape measure wielded by a civilian contractor. "Woo hoo!" said Sara, emerging from the dressing room in her too-long white trousers and baggy blouse ("white works echo," the uniform was called).

"Doing the old sea bag drag, eh?" said a male squad leader standing by the doorway.

It was good that Sara was excited about her uniform, since she wouldn't wear civilian clothes for some time. In four years, when she was a midshipman first-class, a "firsty," she would have liberty every night until midnight—"Cinderella liberty," it was called—and she would be allowed to come and go in civilian clothes. For now she lined up with the other plebes in her starched whites and "Dixie cup" hat against the white wall of the loading dock, to form up for the bus that would take her back to Bancroft Hall to unpack and put away her new belongings.

McGann was born near the sub base in Groton, where her father was stationed, and had lived there all her life. Her high school, St. Bernard's in Uncasville, had been small, private, Catholic. These weren't kids who bucked the system. One of her girlfriends was taking the next year off, but the rest were going on to good schools, like Wellesley or Holy Cross. One of McGann's best friends, Josh, had signed up for the Air Force Academy, another was accepted at the Coast Guard Academy, but chose Bucknell instead. McGann herself had had a choice of schools, including Cornell, Villanova, and Notre Dame, where her father had graduated, but she "didn't get pushed at all" in that direction. She knew she wanted to study biochemistry, and "Notre Dame has an entire building devoted to it, and Cornell has a new biochemistry major and an emphasis on environmental and life sciences."

Annapolis didn't offer a biochemistry major, so she would study chemistry. She knew she wanted a military career. "I've always wanted to do something to serve my country. When I was little I used to think about the Peace Corps, but that was just a childhood fantasy." An

ROTC commander she spoke with at Notre Dame "had gone to the Naval Academy and he said the best naval officers come from there, and that there's a strong connection between academy graduates— they look out for each other." At the academy they emphasized discipline and structure, which she knew she wanted. So the decision was made.

Both McGann's parents had come with her for I-Day. Her dad had retired from the Navy a year ago as a commander after serving twenty-six years with the submarine force. Sara could rattle off the names of both the ships he'd served on—the *Skipjack*, the *Marshall*, the *George Washington*—and the numbered battle squadrons to which they belonged. Bill McGann strolled the academy grounds dressed for retirement in a pastel polo shirt, waiting to say good-bye to his daughter. His skin tone was somewhat gray, as if it had not yet recovered from a career of submarine dives. Sheila McGann, Sara's mother, had been worried at first about whether Annapolis would be safe for her daughter to attend. "When the whole Tailhook thing exploded," Sara recalled, "she cautioned me about things that might happen there. If anything like the Tailhook scandal happened—any sexual harassment—she said to call her or tell people about it. I said it would probably be okay."

Sara had dedicated the month before she became a midshipman to the wholesome pursuits of girlhood, driving to the beaches of Massachusetts with friends or staying out late at a Spin Doctors concert. The theme of Sara's senior prom had been "This Is the Time." It was held in the O Club at the sub base, with a dj rather than a live band, and afterward all McGann's friends went over to Kristin Hellberger's house to play Ping-Pong and, later, fall asleep in front of the TV. With her deep pink nails and blond-gold hair, her innocent, open face and calico sundress, it was difficult to imagine McGann surviving the rigors of plebe summer, let alone a career in the Navy.

But her mother could envision it. Sara, said Sheila, is "academically capable and strong-willed enough" to succeed at Annapolis. "We've always said you can be anything you want. Then, when she says I want to be *this,* you can't say 'No!' Of course, I had reservations. After Tailhook, it would be foolish and inane not to. Just because there are policies or courses, you can't change things overnight. There are a lot of people that don't know what's right and what's not, what's kidding around." But she said she'd never seen any conduct "remotely approaching" that of the Tailhook incident in the submarine community she'd been part of for a quarter of a century.

Sara McGann had visited the academy from June 7–12, 1992, through a special program the Navy arranges for promising candidates. During the summer program, she and the other academy candidates attended an "information session," at which school officials talked about the Gwen Dreyer case, the hazing scandal that had broken into the headlines in 1990. "They said they were aware of it and were trying to fix it. They'd installed counseling courses for men and women to prevent further occurrences." That made McGann feel more secure.

But there were mixed messages about the Dreyer case from midshipmen McGann spent time with in the summer session. Gwen Dreyer had been given to horseplay, it was rumored, she had been trying to get out of the Navy, it was all a case of sour grapes. There had been seemingly random but repeated efforts to recast the Dreyer case in a light more sympathetic to the men in the incident. Even neighbors of McGann's, both of whom had graduated from the Naval Academy—the wife in the first class with women, in 1980—concurred with the party line. "The girl who was chained to the urinal was an admiral's daughter and didn't stick to regulations all that much. She was a troublemaker." Sara's neighbors said the girl had most likely brought some of her treatment on herself, "though obviously not all of it."

When Sheila and Bill McGann visited college campuses with their daughter, they went out of their way to ask about campus security. While most of the schools provided general answers, the academy was specific. The head of recruiting, Captain Ashbury "Sandy" Coward, gave them explicit background on the Dreyer case and its legacy for the school. He, too, stressed a side of the story that hadn't appeared in the media. Dreyer, he said, was planning to leave Annapolis anyway and "was perhaps not cooperating fully with the spirit of the academy."

"This was not just a case of hazing at all," Gwen Dreyer had said in 1989, after she left the Naval Academy. "It has to do with being a woman. Women are integrated into the Academy, but they are not accepted . . . After the whole thing was over, one of the guys told my roommate that this kind of thing was going to keep happening until we, the female midshipmen, got a sense of humor."

There had indeed been changes at Annapolis over the four years since Dreyer announced herself as a victim of sexual harassment and left the academy. That scandal had come to be known by staff as "our own mini-Tailhook." There were four separate reviews and assessments. The studies had all determined, much like the study group conducted by Marty Evans in 1987, that after more than a decade as a coed environment, the academy was not doing that well integrating women. General Order I-90 had forbidden any physical touching of plebes "for any reason except for their own safety or during approved athletic contests," and prohibited "horseplay or any other contact" when it involved "involuntary participation"—effectively outlawing rougher, invasive forms of hazing. Gone (at least officially) were academy hazing traditions such as full-body latherings with shaving cream, hosings or toilet head-dunkings. The academy had also increased the number of female commanders in leadership roles.

Navy leadership, determined to make the ranks safe for women, had asserted itself over the U.S. Naval Academy. The new Navy had, in fact, taken the academy by the scruff of its neck and shaken it like a terrier might shake a rat. A leadership professor and retired U.S. Marine Corps colonel named Paul E. Roush produced classes, speeches and position papers featuring a thoroughgoing rejection of the "profoundly disturbing sense of arrogance in the various facets of the Tailhook phenomenon." The Navy felt moved to hire people like Maureen Sullivan, a perceptive lieutenant commander who was another leadership instructor at Annapolis. "We need to get away from lecturing and into dialogue," Sullivan said. "People need to say, 'This is what happened to me. Is this or is this not sexual harassment? Did I do the right thing? If I didn't do the right thing, you're not going to kill me right now or send me away. You're going to forgive me and help me learn what I need to do so I won't do this again and I'll be a better leader.' "

But the terrier could not shake out all of the Old Navy. There were still stubborn pockets at the academy both opposed to and, to some extent, untouched by change. Some midshipmen proudly declared themselves "Webb-ites," in honor of former Secretary of the Navy James Webb. Webb, a Reagan appointee, was famous at the academy for a polemic published in *The Washingtonian* in 1979 entitled "Women Can't Fight." "We would go months without bathing," began the article, "except when we could stand naked among each other next to a village well or in a stream or in the muddy water of a bomb crater." The article drew on Webb's Vietnam Marine foot-soldier experience to blast "Washington society, which seems to view service in the combat arms as something akin to a commute to the Pentagon." Webb wrote, "We became vicious and aggressive and debased, and reveled in it, because combat is all of those things and we were surviving." After an explicit description of the misery inflicted upon him as a plebe by academy upperclassmen, Webb's article jumped to Vietnam, where fifty-one of his platoon members had been killed in a seven-week stretch. "When I sat down next to fifty-one and cried like a baby, I'd been there before," Webb wrote, "and by then I was not merely Jim Webb, plebe, trying to survive a morning of a malicious upperclassman: I was a Marine platoon commander."

Organized mayhem, wrote Webb, was the mission of the U.S. military, and that mission was being eroded as women were "pushed toward the battlefield." More specifically, the arenas where warriors were groomed to conduct organized mayhem, the service academies, were being destroyed by the introduction of women into their ranks. "There is a place for women in our military," he wrote, "but not in combat. And their presence at institutions dedicated to the preparation of men for combat command is poisoning that preparation. By attempting to sexually sterilize the Naval Academy environment in the name of equality, this country has sterilized the whole process of combat leadership training, and our military forces are doomed to suffer the consequences." Men fight better than women, stated Webb. It was a biological fact that men were more aggressive than women. Furthermore, he wrote, men fight better without women around.

In writing the article, Webb drew on his recent experience as a visiting professor returning to the academy, from which he himself had graduated in 1968. He bemoaned the changes from the time when he and his plebe classmates were "pushed deep inside ourselves for that entire year, punished physically and mentally, stressed to the point that virtually every one of us completely broke down at least once." Now, he wrote, "you cannot physically punish a plebe. You cannot unduly harass a plebe. God forbid that you should use abusive language to a plebe." The system in general "has been objectified and neutered to the point it can no longer develop or measure leadership."

What arguably had a longer-lasting impact than Webb's rhetorical screeds was the portrait he drew of the 300 women he had seen during his recent academy visit. Over a decade after he wrote, in 1993, there could still be found barely closeted Webb-ites on campus who subscribed to Webb's analysis of female mids. "Many women appear to be having problems with their sexuality. . . . It is no secret that sex is commonplace in Bancroft Hall. The Hall, which houses 4,000 males and 300 females, is a horny woman's dream."

Even with the "softening" Webb decried, academy life was still harsh, especially for plebes. "Plebe funk," a combination of vinegar, formaldehyde and sweat, was the inescapable smell of that first summer, according to one recent graduate, and an odor an Annapolis grad never forgets. "You never stop sweating," she explained. Plebes were still required to "chop" wherever they went, to go at a trot, and it was explained by a midshipman first-class as "a pretty good idea because then the squad leaders can't get ahold of you." Plebes still "squared corners," pivoting at a ninety-degree angle, were forbidden to speak in hallways unless spoken to by an officer or upperclassman, and were expected to recite on command something called "plebe rates," which consisted of bits and pieces of naval history, nautical terms and trivia such as daily menus and TV schedules. Sara McGann's plebe summer would be one long nightmare of shouting and shoeshining and push-ups. "You have to scare the people at the beginning so you have that total respect," said one new ensign. "To have total obedience, you need that kind of shock treatment."

Carol Burke, a professor who had since left Annapolis, published a scathing review of academy traditions in the late August 1992 *New Republic*, at the height of the Tailhook furor. In her seven years with the academy's English department, she had collected a wealth of material. "As a folklorist," she explained in a later article on the same subject, "I was fascinated by the wealth of folk tradition I found when I started looking at the Academy at Annapolis—both from the general military lore passed on from service to service and war to war, and the folklore and folk practices peculiar to the Naval Academy." Soon students and faculty learned of her interest. "They brought me jokes scribbled on sheets of lined paper; lyrics to bawdy marching chants; latrinalia; legends; accounts of pranks, rituals and rites of passage; stories of Academy anti-heroes; and personal narratives of life among the Brigade of Midshipmen."

In her article in the *New Republic*, Burke noted that while the recently instituted "no touching" rule had dramatically curtailed instances of physical abuse, various forms of verbal egregiousness still were commonplace. She remembered a "lovely cool September morning" during the first semester of her tenure at the academy, when she crossed the yard and heard a group of midshipmen, running in formation and chanting: "Rape, Maim, Kill Babies. Rape, Maim, Kill Babies, Oorah!" She quoted a parody song (to the tune of "The Candy Man") sung by members of the Male Glee Club on bus trips home:

> Who can take a chain saw
> Cut the bitch in two
> Fuck the bottom half

And give the upper half to you?
The S&M Man, the S&M Man,
The S&M Man 'cause he mixes it with love
and makes the hurt feel good . . .

There was a "Hog Log" listing of unattractive females, examples of sexist E-mail, the prize of a brick given to the midshipman with the ugliest date. Burke also drew on her collection of WUBA jokes. The acronym, which originally referred to the academy's first uniforms for female plebes ("Working Uniform Blue Alpha") was widely applied to the plebes themselves, reworked in slang to mean "Woman Used By All."

What do you call a mid who fucks a WUBA?
    Too lazy to beat off.
What's the difference between a WUBA and a warthog?
    About 200 pounds, but the WUBA has more hair.

Burke noted that the common thread here was "to stigmatize women midshipmen as overweight and promiscuous," even though the academy's rigorous physical requirements actually made fat midshipmen (male or female) relatively rare.

Students and faculty alike were bitter about what they perceived as Burke's distortion of the school's culture through deliberate inaccuracies and exaggeration. One female ensign, a recent academy graduate, said about the *New Republic* story: "She took things out of context and took things from boot camp and stuff to make us look bad. The harassment now is more subtle. There are guys that feel that way, but they just don't talk to you. Is that harassment, or is that their personal option?" But Burke's true sin was telling tales out of school. She had violated the code of silence of the tribe. In any case, the academy had made a specific effort in the aftermath of Burke's *New Republic* article to clean up the cadence calls used by the mids. For Sara McGann's plebe summer, a Xeroxed booklet spelled out which jodies were now acceptable ("I had a girl in New Orleans/I left her to join the Marines/ I said choose me or civilian life/Now this girl's my lovely wife/Now we're having a lot of fun/She joins me on my 10-mile run").

Many of the cultural questions faced by new female recruits, especially those that seemed almost trivial on the surface, were not so clear-cut. Since 1976, for example, the academy had faced the thorny dilemma of what to do about the "ring dance," the school's annual spring cotillon—namely, what to do about females in military uniform at a big formal dance. On the one hand, the academy was rigorous in its requirements that a uniform be worn at all times, at least until midshipmen were in their senior year and on liberty. On the other hand, the sight of two uniformed mids who happened to be dating each other embracing on the floor of the academy ballroom was just too uncomfortable an image. At first glance, it might seem that two men were dancing together. But if the females could go to the dance in civilian clothing, why not the males? Didn't it violate the standard of one rule for all? "The problem is," one female academy grad said, "the formal uniform needs to be updated." Another young woman agreed: "It makes us look like the Liberty bell." So when some of the women, (especially the ones who were dating male midshipmen, which made it easier to get away with) did what they wanted to do and went in a formal gown, they were perceived by their peers as "having guts." Others snuck in their long dresses to get their photographs taken with their uniformed dates before the dance, then changed into their own uniforms to attend.

And then there was "Herndon" to consider—that academy tradition which requires that the whole raucous plebe class try to scale the twenty-one-foot, lard-smeared Herndon obelisk and snatch a Dixie cup hat from its summit, replacing it with the naval officer's "cover," a feat which legend claimed would make you the first in the class to become an admiral. A female mid had never yet reached the top, and rumor had it that women were forcibly blocked from the pinnacle.

Sara McGann had prepared herself mentally and physically for the ordeal of her plebe year. She had read *A Sense of Honor,* a book that detailed daily life at Annapolis—ironically enough, a book written by James Webb. Academically, she felt "pretty well prepared" since she had "had some good teachers" during her high school years. She was most nervous about "the physical stuff," even though she'd been on her high school's track and swim teams and made it a point to "do lots of crunches and leg lifts every day." She'd been running and mountain biking over the summer to stay in shape. In fact, the weekend before I-Day, she was cheering on her boyfriend, Dan, in a mountain bike race. When she learned he had flipped himself over his handlebars, she raced the two and a half miles up a rugged trail, reaching him before the emergency crew.

At 6 P.M. on that first day of July, in Tecumseh Court, the midshipmen took their oath of office. "Thank you, Lord," said the chaplain, "for listening to the stirring of all our hearts and all of our minds at this moment." Everyone raised their heads to watch a thunderous fly-by of A-6 Intruders. Rear Admiral Tom Lynch, the superintendent of the academy, stood between the two green copper cannons and spoke about "the art of followership, which is the first step of leadership." In the audience, the blue skulls of the newly shorn glowed beneath their Dixie cups. In unison, the plebes raised their right hands and pledged an oath of office that was all but inaudible to the onlookers and family members crowded behind them.

The vast and far-flung apparatus of the U.S. Navy waited to accept Sara McGann and her classmates, an ancient church welcoming acolytes into the fold. It wasn't quite as if she were dedicating her life to Christ, but it was as close as the secular world offered. Like a nun, McGann would be cloistered, with stiff restrictions on her communication with the outside world. What other job required a seventeen-year-old woman to swear an oath? For better or worse, she was to be fed into the military maw. If the Navy had made any progress on gender issues since Tailhook, it would be tested by people like McGann, class of '97. Ironically, recent changes in the Navy would not only attempt to protect Sara McGann and her female classmates from day-to-day harassment, but would also expose them to combat, to life-threatening conditions that were more dangerous than their predecessors ever experienced.

After the ceremony, on the red brick walks of the yard, amid families posing for group portraits, Sara found her parents. "I have only four girls in my platoon!" she told them. There were seventy male plebes with them. Sheila said firmly, "It's all right, Sara. That's life. You can do it." Sara introduced her parents to her roommate, Maureen Moroney from Chicago, whose parents couldn't come with her for I-Day. Tonight, Sara and Maureen said, they would be required to memorize every platoon member's name, hometown and room number.

Bill McGann said, "This ex-military man thinks she'll do fine."

"I'm kinda nervous," Sara said. "You don't have any Tylenol, do you?"

The question earned a short lecture from her mother as she rummaged in her purse. "I'm fairly sure they won't allow you to have any unauthorized medications, so be very careful, even with aspirin." She handed her daughter the analgesic. Sara's father said to the new roommates, "You two look after each other."

Her mother said, "If there's anything we can do, you call."

Sara turned to her father. "Call Dan. Tell him I have a letter all ready to go."

To her mother: "Mom, we really gotta go." Fierce hugs, no tears. Sara was gone.

Mission Valley follows the San Diego River from the sea through a cut in the barren foothills into the desert highlands to the east. In the 1950s, developers fastened upon the area as the main conduit for San Diego's commercial growth, and a linear retail strip incongruously called Hotel Circle grew up along one side of the Ocean Beach Freeway. One of the first arrivals was a restaurateur named Charles H. Brown, who in 1953 built a popular watering hole beside the river and named it the Town and Country Hotel.

As the city sprawled, the Town and Country did too, adding a convention center in 1970, until finally the whole package wound up, by the summer of 1993, a thirty-two-acre business-oriented "resort," replete with banks of yellow roses and birds of paradise, kidney-shaped pools and a Tiki Hut. If you didn't count the golf course to the west, the "country" in Town and Country had long since been paved over. The hotel was wedged between an oftentimes clogged freeway artery and the parking lot of the Fashion Valley Center mall. There remained about Hotel Circle in general and Town and Country in particular a rather forlorn air of fifties materialism, bypassed and gone to seed. What seemed modern then did not quite qualify as quaint four decades later.

The Town and Country was where the chastened and decimated ranks of the Tailhook Association reassembled, in October 1993, for its first convention since the debacle at Las Vegas in 1991. The previous year's convention had been canceled altogether, and this current one was much scaled down from previous incarnations. Gone were the promotional teams for Lockheed and Grumman. Two hundred display booths had shrunk to twelve. Vendors of T-shirts, old unit patches and the ubiquitous carved wooden plaques had replaced jet engine cutaways and smart bomb exhibits on the floor of the Town and Country's Atlas Ballroom. A bus trip to Ensenada had been canceled for lack of interest.

Active-duty personnel had been warned off the convention, forbidden to speak or wear uniforms, allowed to attend only on their own time. The people who assembled that early October were mostly older, mostly retired members of the Navy aviation community. There were 700 preregistered guests, down from 7,000 attendees at Las Vegas two years earlier, and a minuscule percentage of the association's nearly 14,000 members. The media mop-up crews were there in earnest, however, and as the convention kicked off there was some danger that the press would outnumber attendees. CBS, ABC, NBC, CNN, newspapers, magazines, local news broadcasters all sent crews or representatives. A reporter from the *Chicago Tribune* originally booked a room at the Marriott, fearing that the actual site of the convention might be "too dangerous." She quickly moved to the Town and Country, realizing the only real threat there was somnolence. Her editors eventually recalled her altogether, saying there was no story.

In the media vacuum, there were still easy shots to be taken. The Mrs. America Pageant was being held concurrently in the Presidio Room, and much was made of Mrs. Florida's statements to the press (she had hired herself a publicist) that she feared for her safety because her husband couldn't be with her. "I assume the naval aviators attending the convention will be perfect gentlemen," Jacqueline Mallery Solomon said. "However, I have expressed my concern to the hotel that the proper supervision and security be carefully maintained." The fifty "mature beauty queens" somehow seemed to fit in well not only with the sclerotic nature of Tailhook '93, but with the conference of podiatrists going on down the hall.

A bit more spritely were the representatives of San Diego's Women's Action Committee (WAC), which picketed the convention on Friday night. Kept from the convention center itself by security guards, about 150 people paraded on the sidewalk outside with torches, whistles and drums, placards that included FIRE ADMIRAL KELSO, WE SALUTE PAULA COUGHLIN, NO EXCUSE FOR SEXUAL ABUSE, BEND OVER TAILHOOK PIECE OF SHIT and MILITARIST-SEXIST-GAUNTLET GOONS GO HOME! and cries of "Shame, shame, shame." "We're exposing their secrets, breaking their code of silence," said one WAC organizer, Tamara Mason. "The thing that patriarchy tries to do is divide women. We try to support actions that bring women together and expose men's sexism and hatred of women."

WAC also rented (for two hours) a room in the convention complex itself. The group's original plan had been to construct a miniature "Tailhook Hall of Horrors," re-creating conditions on the third deck of the Las Vegas Hilton using Barbie and Ken dolls. It instead hired art historian Frances Pohl of Pomona College, who curated "Ritual and Sacrifice at Tailhook: A Documentary Exhibition." The exhibit, mounted in the Council Room, was heavily grounded in the DoD Tailhook report. "It reminded me of anthropological studies of other cultures," Pohl said. "It seemed the perfect text." She illustrated the "squishiness" of the alcohol-soaked carpet in the third deck hallway with a wet sponge glued onto a piece of cardboard.

On Friday night, Brad Taisey took a quick tour of the WAC exhibit in the Council Room, an unlit cigar punctuating his face. An F/A-18 pilot and lieutenant commander stationed at nearby North Island, he was one of the few active-duty personnel attending the 1993 convention. Taisey's call sign was "Sluggo," and he did resemble the Ernie Bushmiller creation: pumped up but compact, a bulldog rather than a mastiff. In spite of the diminished spirit of the gathering (or perhaps because of it), Taisey struck a serenely unrepentent pose. He stared out at the WAC marchers from behind the plate-glass windows of the ballroom lobby. "Deviants," he offered. "I'm hired to kill people and break things," he said, riffing off a standard Rush Limbaugh line. He despised the Somalia mission, and the new "social work" role of the military. He saw himself as a warrior.

There is nothing more Old Navy than a Marine, and Taisey was about as unreconstructed as the new Navy allowed. He was "prior enlisted," meaning he pulled a stint as an enlisted man before becoming an officer. So Taisey was already experienced when he entered the Naval Academy, standing out among the fresh-scrubbed plebes. James Webb had actually referred to Taisey admiringly in his *Washingtonian* article, calling him "intense and direct, the kind of man I would want commanding one of my platoons if I were to take a company into combat again." Webb had singled Taisey out because he had gotten into trouble at the academy for refusing to serve under a female commander. "She couldn't lead a group of men into a latrine," Taisey explained later.

Like Webb, Taisey was a Marine, transferring to the Navy after it offered him a seat in an F/A-18. He had been at Tailhook '91, been put through a grilling by notorious DoD special agent Peter Black, was present (along with his wife) at the gauntlet. Celeste Taisey, Brad said, had wanted to "go in and see what was going on, and we're standing there, and I'm going 'I don't want anything to do with this.' I couldn't go down there and keep them from pinching *my* butt. You've got some debutantes in this situation, going down there, they've seen *Top Gun* too many times, whatever, and they're going 'Uh-oh.'"

Celeste was alongside Brad at the Town and Country Tailhook convention, too. A law student who was about to sit for the bar, she was taller than he was, willowy, not Nancy to his Sluggo but more the look of the modern Cher, liquid-eyed, with black hair all the way down her back. Like her husband, she had been questioned about Tailhook '91 by DoD investigators. They had met cute at the El Toro O Club, both of them plastered, Brad picking up Celeste and physically carrying her to the dance floor before he ever said a word to her. "Now, is that assault?" Brad asked. The two of them were different but well teamed, and enjoyed a mild, riffing sort of banter. They had been together long enough to be able to finish each other's sentences.

Celeste: "Male aviators . . ."

Brad: ". . . are assholes."

Celeste Taisey, however, did not much resemble the little woman standing behind her man. Her feelings about the situation were more measured, more reflective than her husband's. "If we want to carry out this feminist agenda," Celeste said, "you have to be very careful as to where you put yourself. I think it's dangerous to advance an agenda based on something like Tailhook. Women have to have pride. It has to be advancement based on ability."

"When women say you must respect them—why?" Brad asked. "The only people I really respect are people who beat my ass. If you're looking at it from the military standpoint, where do quotas fit into that?"

Celeste said, "We have an agreement: Men and women are basically different creatures."

Brad said, "I'm a traditionalist pig."

"Women are intuitive creatures," said his wife. "Men might have it, but they can't use it."

Brad said, "It's called a hunch, and it's usually faulty as hell. But if I've got a bayonet and you've got a bayonet, who's going to win?"

Taisey stared out at the WAC demonstrators, marching in torchlight like a group of villagers on the trail of Frankenstein's monster.

"You're all shits!" he shouted out at them. A *Los Angeles Times* reporter was close enough to jot the comment down.

"Brad!" Celeste said, rolling her eyes at him.

But Brad was unstoppable. "You don't hear many people talking about women in combat now, when in Somalia people are getting drug through the streets." Taisey talked about his dealings with women at the Marine Basic School at Quantico in July 1980. There were 220 men and 40 women. "That's where I got a bad taste in my mouth about women in combat." The men were organized in four platoons and there was one platoon of women. There were fifteen forced marches, on which the trainees had to carry a 60-pound pack, a 20-pound ready can of ammunition, plus their own mortar plate or another component for the maneuver. "On almost every single march when we were carrying equipment, after five to ten miles, the women would fall out and ride on the truck with sore feet. The guys would get tired too, but we'd have to carry all their equipment in addition to our own. One woman was the best shot in our group, but she was five two and couldn't carry anything. The party line is women are doing great, wonderful. But it just ain't so."

The mood on the part of the association as a whole, while more cautious than Brad Taisey's, was similarly unrepentent. At the annual membership meeting, a retired Navy captain and former A-4 pilot, introduced as "Captain Hook," talked about the write-in balloting process to elect a new president for the organization. "The old indomitable aviator spirit is still going on," he said. "One of the write-in ballots was for a person named Paula." There was a big round of laughter. Retired Navy Captain Bill Knutson, the association's president, revealed that the organization now had 13,618 members, a 15 percent decrease over the past two years. But the attrition rate for all membership organizations, he said, was 12 percent. "In spite of the trauma, the active-duty membership has remained steady at 31 percent. I suggest you give a hand to those men who have hung in there." Odd, old-fashioned cries of "Hear! Hear!" from the audience, and applause.

After informing the membership about the raft of civil lawsuits filed against it in the wake of the Las Vegas convention, the group's attorney drew cheers when he declared, "My personal opinion is the Tailhook Association put on a splendid symposium in '91. And I don't think we are guilty of anything, in a legal or any other sense." The majority of proceedings were taken up with damage assessments ("corporate sponsorship is down 70 percent,") and a debate over whether to change the association's name ("I think that's bullshit!" came voices from the floor. "No change!" "Tailhook forever!").

"We run the risk of becoming another drinking-and-chowder society," said Bill Knutson, the president of the association, pleading for the adoption of a new mission statement. That was exactly the point. By the time members prepared to leave the fifties time-warp of the Town and Country Hotel, it had become clear that the Tailhook Association had come full circle. What had started a few miles south on the beaches of Rosarito had reverted to form. Despite the presence of a few active-duty members like Brad Taisey, the Tailhook Association was once again an old men's drinking society.

TWENTY MILES TO THE NORTH OF THE TOWN AND COUNTRY, IN THE Fightertown U.S.A." of NAS Miramar, Kara Hultgreen was too busy to attend the '93 Tailhook convention and did not send her regrets. She had been transferred out of Key West to Miramar to learn how to fly an F-14 Tomcat. Hultgreen's Navy career, long stuck in neutral, had suddenly gone into overdrive in the aftermath of the lifting of the combat exclusion. "I'm going to be the first woman to fly an F-14!" she crowed. "Hoo-hoo!"

That wasn't entirely accurate. There had been female test pilots who had flown the jet before. But Hultgreen would be the first female to fly the Tomcat tactically, operationally, off the boat over blue water. The F-14 wasn't even her first choice—she would have preferred the newer, sleeker, safer F/A-18 Hornet. But the Navy had assigned her to Miramar. The Top Gun cachet of the Tomcat had its own appeal, and she liked the way the plane drove. "This jet is a very forgiving jet, as complicated as it is. It's very honest." She would train on an older version, the F-14A, designed over thirty years ago. "The computer power in this system is less than that of an Atari video. That's why they call it the F-14-Aging Tomcat. But it's still an extremely viable weapon."

At Key West, Hultgreen had been frustrated by the slow pace at her squadron. But at Miramar, everything was fast, and she liked that. Here there was too much to do, too much to learn. "When they start you off, they just hook up a fire hose to your mouth and say, 'Here, drink this and don't spill any.' It can be overwhelming." But her job was to survive and prosper, so survive and prosper she would. "Every day you go flying you think, today's the day this thing could bite me in the ass. That's why you can't get complacent or lazy, you can't relax. Because that's when it bites you. You're not careless; you're not reckless. We have fun, but it's not reckless, abandoned fun. Being so precise is fun. You have to have that kind of personality that everything has to be perfect—and it could always be better."

A kind of satisfied euphoria floated like a haze over Hultgreen's new life during this period. She had just moved into a condo in La Jolla. There was a copy of *Seinfeld* on a side table. The furniture was all new; her cabinets were, as was usual for her, compulsively organized. The refrigerator magnets were a pair of aviator's wings, a line drawing of the Hornet, a Bicentennial stamp with a portrait of John Paul Jones and the quote, "I have not yet begun to fight." On the kitchen counter, beside her flight manual and a new copy of the *Family Circle Cookbook*, there was a brass key chain given to her by a friend. The inscription read, "Fighter Chick."

Hultgreen was like a woman released from a long period of servitude. She had boundless enthusiasm for her future, when she would be deployed with VF-213 ("the Black Lions," a venerable combat squadron) upon the carrier USS *Abraham Lincoln*. True to form, Hultgreen had developed a funny, very un-PC riff on her new assignment.

"The Babe—the 'Babe-raham Lincoln,' CVN-72. That's the one

we're going to. A great ship. On the East Coast they're going to the *Eisenhower*. The West Coast, the *Lincoln*. 'Abe.' Okay: 'the Babe.' On the East Coast, the *Eisenhower:* the Ike. You know what they're gonna call it: 'the Dyke.' CVN-69. I think it's funny. I'm laughin'. 'Cause *I'm* goin' to the Babe. And they're going to have a coupla qualifying questions before you get assigned. For the Babe, it's 'Okay, have you ever seen a grown man naked? Do you like to watch movies with gladiators, Sylvester Stallone, Arnold Schwarzenegger? Okay, you, you can go to the Babe.' For the *Eisenhower*, it'll be different. 'Okay, have you ever seen a grown woman naked? Do you like to watch movies with Madonna and Sharon Stone? Off you go to the Dyke. Off you go!' "

Hultgreen and Lieutenant Christine Greene had arrived at Miramar in June, the first of what would become a vanguard trio of women aviators. Greene, who had flown with Loree Draude at Lemoore in VAQ-34, was a radar intercept officer, a "RIO," the aircrew member who sat behind the pilot. Over six feet tall, she matched in height the third female Tomcat flier at Miramar, Lieutenant (jg) Carey Lohrenz. "This is the first time I was ever around a group of women that I actually felt petite," said the five-ten Hultgreen. "Don't tell me the Navy didn't think about that." The Adonis image of Top Gun was about to be augmented by a few Amazons.

The women received a carefully modulated reception at Miramar. "When Christine and I first got to the squadron we went to a Welcome Aboard. We're sitting in this room and talking about what the experience would be like. All of a sudden, out of the blue, the instructor gets up and says, 'Well, nobody's said anything about it so I'm gonna go ahead and talk about it. This is the first class with female aircrew and if any of you guys have a problem with that you just come see me afterward. If you've got a problem flying with a woman in your front seat, if you've got a problem with a woman in your backseat, you come talk to me, because that's just the way it is now. If you've got a problem with that, maybe we can find you another job in the Navy, or maybe you don't belong in the Navy. You certainly don't belong in aviation, you don't belong in this community. And we'll just find you somewhere else to go. So you come talk to me afterward . . .' "

Then Hultgreen and Greene met with the skipper of their training squadron. Commander Vita had had difficulty articulating some of his instructions. "He goes, 'You've got to be able to feel free to come to the club and kick back with some brews and talk about flying. We're all on a call-sign basis here at the RAG. But there can't be any hint of impropriety. And you can't be . . . um . . . living with instructors. And you can't be . . . um . . . dating instructors. And you can't be . . . ummm . . .'

"And I go, 'Okay, Skipper, why don't you go ahead and spit it out? No sex with the instructors. Okay, why don't we just go one step further, put it in fighter-pilot terminology, something we can all understand?' And I look over at Chris and I go, 'Chris, don't fuck the help.'

"And this guy goes, 'Well, shit hot!' And he slaps the table. He goes, 'We're all speaking the same language. All right!' All of the sudden he was all at ease."

Kara Hultgreen knew that some of the guys in the squadron still thought she and Chris Greene should be at home being wives and mothers. Others believed the only good thing about females on board was maybe now they could get laid on the boat. Most men couldn't get past the feeling that the fun was over, they couldn't joke around anymore, would have to watch every word. They moaned and groaned about aviation terms that would have to change. But the women of Miramar were hardly stern taskmasters. They would joke around about air combat terms like "Circle around—hard dick," meaning to fly in a circle and fight aggressively. About the only thing Hultgreen wished the guys would do differently was "go outside the ready room when they farted."

For the most part, Kara Hultgreen felt she was treated essentially as just another squadron-mate, unlike at VAQ-33 in Key West, where "everything I did was scrutinized beyond recognition, to the point where it became something it wasn't. I had people lying about me and spreading rumors about me." At Miramar, "even the ones who probably don't agree with me being here because I'm a woman are there to teach someone how to go out and fly an F-14 in a combat

environment. They are not about to slight me in any way in my training because they know that their lives could depend on me as a wingman and so could somebody else's. They're professional enough to put
aside their personal feelings and say, okay, this is what we're gonna do
and this is how we do it."

On her way to Miramar, driving from Florida, Hultgreen had
stopped in Texas for her older sister's wedding and to attend her tenth
high school reunion. At the reunion she'd been voted "most successful" of her graduating class, as well as the person with the "most
unusual career path." She'd almost gotten "most famous" but that title
had been bagged by "a weather girl in San Antonio." It seemed that
everyone at the reunion had seen Kara Hultgreen on "NBC Nightly
News" the previous February. "Believe it or not," she said, "I got sick
of talking about myself. You know how I hate being the center of
attention."

Chapter Ten

AFTERBURN

LIKE THE LONG DERVISH ARC OF A BOOMERANG, THE TAILHOOK AF-
fair finally wound down where it began, by focusing in on the principal
players, the men and women who had been on the third deck of the
Hilton. If the Navy had made a separate (and uneasy) peace with the
women in its ranks, there was still the unsettling issue of apportioning
blame and punishment. This is what the alarms and disruptions of the
previous two years had been working toward. The endgame was a
complex affair, one which both banged and whimpered.

The prosecution of those involved in the Tailhook scandal
stretched over ten months, following a year and a half of bungled and
protracted investigations. When the final verdict came down, it dealt
not so much with individual issues of guilt or innocence, but with a
ringing, blanket and historical statement about ultimate accountability.

The last Tailhook legal proceedings took place in a red brick
building called by the nuts-and-bolts name of Legal Services, set upon
a grassy knoll inside the sprawling Norfolk Naval Base. Everything
about the building seemed to hum with neutrality, down to the muted
gray carpet spread over every inch of floor. Its six courtrooms were
generically lettered "A" through "F." It was in the largest of these,

Courtroom E, on December 17, 1994, that Captain William T. Vest, Jr., a twenty-eight-year Navy veteran and military judge, heard closing arguments in a pretrial motion seeking to throw the cases against the last of the Tailhook defendants out of court.

The legal process had begun nine months before, immediately upon the release of the Department of Defense Inspector General's report in April of 1993—already a year and seven months after the convention. There were files on two separate groups forwarded for possible further judicial action. The larger group was comprised of 140 officers, 20 Marines and 120 Navy. These included the men who, the DoD Inspector General had determined, were suspects in the most severe crimes against Paula Coughlin and the rest of those sexually assaulted at Tailhook. In all, 23 men were cited for indecent assault. Here finally were those who lined the hallway of the Hilton's third floor. Here were the ball-walkers, the butt-biters and those accused of assorted lesser crimes and misdemeanors such as leg-shaving and zapping.

The second group of files generated by the DoD included every single Navy admiral and Marine Corps general who had attended the 1991 Tailhook Association Convention. Given the Navy's ironclad principle of command responsibility—that a senior officer was ultimately liable for everything that happened on his watch—as well as the public's insistence that the higher-ups not escape scot-free, it was fitting that all flag officers, whether directly implicated in misbehavior or not, at least have the details of their involvement in the Tailhook Convention reviewed. There had been thirty-five flag officers at Las Vegas, and the DoD Inspector General carefully took down their testimony, and the testimony of others concerning them, compiling all the information into individual files, some of which were thick as phone books. These files were forwarded to the Acting Secretary of the Navy, CNO Frank Kelso. But since Admiral Kelso's record was itself included as one of those thirty-five files, they gathered dust in Defense Secretary Les Aspin's office from April to late August, when a permanent Secretary of the Navy, John Dalton, was finally named.

So the setup, at least, for the Tailhook adjudication process was fairly clear-cut. One-hundred seventy-five men total, thirty-five of them at the top Navy and Marine hierarchy. Out of this pool of suspects, surely there would come the smaller number of accused, and from them, finally, the convicted and punished. The question was, Who was going to fry?

If the question was going to be resolved, it was going to happen at Legal Services in Norfolk. Throughout the fall of 1993, Judge Vest presided over the pre-court-martial hearings of commanders Thomas Miller and Gregory Tritt, who were charged with violation of Uniform Code of Military Justice (UCMJ) Article 133, conduct unbecoming an officer. The details of the original charges, what the military called "specifications," had included allegations that Miller "on divers occasions" had "wrongfully and dishonorably exposed his genitals to public view"; had upon tossing a set of hotel room keys to a subordinate officer told him to " 'take [a woman] up to the room and fuck her.' " In addition, based on a woman's account that he had grabbed her rear end, Tritt was originally charged with assault for participating in the smaller "cougar gauntlet" set up on the Hilton patio. Miller was also accused of dereliction of duty (Article 92) and obstruction of justice (Article 134) for not stopping buttocks-grabbing by junior officers at Tailhook, and for characterizing the investigation afterward as "bullshit," saying "I'm not going to tell them shit." By December 1994, lawyers for Tritt and Miller had successfully eliminated all but the charge of conduct unbecoming, for failing to stop the misconduct of junior officers under their command.

Miller and Tritt were joined in a pretrial motion for dismissal by Lieutenant David Samples, and charges against him were more serious: he had been one of the men, Navy investigators said, who had helped strip the clothes off the underage girl in the Hilton hallway that night. Officially, Samples was charged with indecent assault and making false official statements. In the interest of "judicial economy," Judge Vest granted the request of Lieutenant Samples to join Miller and Tritt's defense motion to dismiss.

At the time of Tailhook, all of the defendants had been members of the same squadron. VAQ-139, "the Cougars," were an electronic warfare unit which flew EA-6B Prowlers out of Whidbey Island in Washington State. Miller had been the commanding officer, Tritt the executive officer and Samples a pilot. They had been implicated by their squadron-mates, fellow aviators who had been granted immunity for various charges (such as streaking, indecent exposure, etc.) in return for their testimony.

The mood in the courtroom for the pre-holiday session was oddly giddy, with the mix of tension, camaraderie and exhaustion that develops among people—defense, prosecution, media and judge alike —during a long trial. The talk before the one o'clock hearing was of going home for the holidays, Continental's new "peanut" airfares, a new home one of the reporters had bought. *The Gauntlet*'s Michael Kitchen, off active duty now but still wearing his chocolate leather flight jacket with its Bart Simpson flight patch, had been in the front row of the gallery nearly every day for six months. He had been fully credentialed by Navy public affairs as a journalist from *The Gauntlet*. There were other journalists there, too. "Are we going to finish today?" called out the reporter for the *Virginian-Pilot and Ledger-Star* to Robert Rae, defense counsel for Gregory Tritt. "No," Rae said. "Laugh, Bob, say 'April fool's,'" the reporter implored.

Another local reporter described Tritt and Miller as different as "night and day" and it was true. Tritt was drawn, gray-faced and grim. His junior officers used to call him the "bald old man." Miller, his former boss, was gregarious, showy, charismatic, a big man with a puffy, whiskey-soaked sponge of a face and a head of gray-brown bushy hair. A Scotsman given to affecting a lilt, Miller would quote Robert Burns and toss in conversational asides such as "and he was a bonny lad and brave." He wore shiny black boots and a big gold Mickey Mouse wristwatch, bought when he first was called to Norfolk: "I need something for my sense of humor," he said. "Every once in a while when I'm in court I look at it. It puts a smile on my face." Miller's handle was "Tango," one of those call signs that was actually used in place of the proper name. Before and after the hearing, or

during breaks, you would hear someone call out, "Hey, Tango . . ."
Miller's lawyer was Don Marcari, the model for the Tom Cruise character in the movie *A Few Good Men.* Samples, absent during these
proceedings, was young and nervous-looking, out of place next to the
more senior officers.

The scheduled witness this final day of testimony was Barbara
Pope, summoned to substantiate the defense motion that there had
been undue command influence—the military's version of tampering
with due process. With her raven hair and cobalt wool Chanel-styled
suit, her look was incongruous in the generic, glamorless courtroom.
Pope's testimony revolved around the presence of Secretary Lawrence
Garrett and Admiral Frank Kelso at the Tailhook convention. This had
become increasingly crucial because of the end-run strategy that the
defense had adopted in this pretrial motion. It would not argue the
truth or falsity of any of the accusations against the three fliers on trial.
Instead, it would use a legal maneuver called the "accuser motion,"
focusing on Kelso's dual role as both the ultimate Navy authority in
these proceedings, and a participant at the convention itself.

In military law, an "accuser" was defined as "any other person
who has an interest other than an official interest in the prosecution of
the accused." If Kelso was there, he could not act in any capacity to
prosecute others, as he himself was implicated. Kelso, along with the
other admirals, had already received an admonitory letter from the
Secretary of the Navy about standing by while serious misconduct
occurred during Tailhook. In simpler terms, the Tailhook cases had
been polluted from the top down. The accuser motion was the legal
equivalent of the glass houses proverb: if he was a guilty party himself,
Frank Kelso couldn't throw stones.

Believing Frank Kelso. That was what the whole Tailhook prosecution now hinged upon, like a huge inverted pyramid balancing on a
single point. If Kelso had been at the Hilton on Saturday night—he
adamantly denied he was, although a parade of witnesses had placed
him there—then the cases of Miller, Tritt and Samples fell apart on
the basis of the accuser motion.

Vest questioned Pope directly about her knowledge of Kelso's actions at the convention. Were you not concerned afterward, he said, that Secretary Garrett and other senior officers were there? Pope responded in the affirmative, saying that when she queried Garrett and he spoke of visiting the patio "with the other flags," she "made the assumption that Kelso and Secretary Garrett were there together." The prosecution stepped in to try to stanch the damage. Kelso had already been called and appeared at the hearings on November 29, and testified repeatedly that he had not been present at the Hilton the night of the Tailhook gauntlet. Are you sure your memory doesn't fail you? the defense had asked him. I wasn't there, Kelso had answered. Now the prosecution tried to bolster Kelso's credibility by asking Pope how well she knew Admiral Kelso. Pope responded that she had known him for four years and saw him two or three times a week, "plus some social contact." She added, "He's an honorable man of integrity." When the prosecution asked whether she would believe him under oath, her answer was succinct: "I would."

THAT IT HAD ALL COME DOWN, FINALLY, TO MILLER, TRITT AND Samples—alleged to be a ball-walker and a couple of gauntleteers, obviously minor players—was the product of an unlikely concatenation of events, a string of missteps and blunders, justice not so much denied as derailed. Watching the huge, creaking bureaucracy of the U.S. military attempt to bring the Tailhook miscreants to justice was like watching a large, ham-handed man trying to put together a miniature jigsaw puzzle.

In the abstract, it was fairly easy to determine what the punishments should have been, in order that justice be served in the Tailhook scandal. The wrongdoers in the gauntlet, the men who physically assaulted women, clearly deserved to go to jail. Their commanding officers, by Navy tradition ultimately responsible for what happened, should have received various levels of censure and, in more egregious cases, been relieved of duty. This was what, by common-sense consensus, should have happened. There were wolves out there howling for more, of course, people who said the entire Navy had been proven corrupt and incapable of policing itself.

Tracing the course of the Tailhook adjudication process, it was difficult to seize on any one point and say, *this* was where it all went wrong. Perhaps the fault lay in the Navy's judicial system, which differed from nonmilitary criminal law in subtle but crucial ways. Or perhaps the Tailhook court cases represented an object lesson on how following the letter of the law sometimes leads to a miscarriage of justice.

The files on the 140 junior officers were sent to something called the Consolidated Disposition Authority (CDA), set up by Acting Secretary Sean O'Keefe in December '92, just before his departure with the rest of the Bush appointees. Designed to be a sort of clearinghouse for all the Tailhook prosecutions, the CDA was headed up by two men, Lieutenant General Charles C. Krulak of the Marines and Vice Admiral Joseph Paul Reason. Krulak was a fast-rising star of the Corps, a deeply religious man known to hold morning prayer meetings in his office. "If you went on a world-wide search," said retired Brigadier General Thomas Draude (Loree's father), "you could not have found a better choice." Reason was an imposing, barrel-chested man who had made admiral after only twenty-one years in the Navy, and was described by insiders as "clean as a hound's tooth." Reason was one of the highest-ranking black men in the service, and common description of him, with a brand of casual, almost unconscious racism that was all too common, was "the Navy's version of Colin Powell." "He's unbelievably smart, intelligent and very, very fair," said one female officer.

Both Krulak and Reason were men of unassailable character, and if you believed that the Navy had the institutional capacity to prosecute the Tailhook offenders (and some on the outside doubted that it did), then they were the ones to do it. They reviewed the 140 DoD files and immediately culled over half of them, dismissing the cases outright for lack of evidence. Sexual assault charges are notoriously difficult to try in court, and the removal of the event in time, plus the chaotic conditions of the nights in question, made it difficult for some cases to proceed.

From May to August, the cases against the sixty-odd remaining officers were pursued through administrative and legal channels. Some were dismissed. Forty-three of the officers went to admiral's mast, a nonjudicial disciplinary procedure one step below a full-blown court-martial. In most cases, they received letters of admonition and had to forfeit anywhere between $500 and $2,000 in pay. For most of these officers, chances for promotion were now thin, and their careers in the Navy were effectively over. Some men received counseling and nonpunitive letters of caution, which did not enter their service records.

Five officers refused to go to admiral's mast, opting instead for public court-martial proceedings, which was their legal right. Along with Marine Captain Gregory J. Bonam, the man Paula Coughlin accused of grabbing her from behind and mauling her breasts, they represented the Tailhook Six: Lieutenant Cole Cowden, who investigators said pressed his face against the chest of a civilian nurse (the nurse said she did not want to see Cowden prosecuted); Lieutenant Rolando "Gandhi" Diaz, Barber of Seville, leg-shaver extraordinaire; plus the three aviators from VAQ-139, Miller, Tritt and Samples.

Six out of one hundred and forty. Less than 5 percent, not a stunning success rate—and this was just the effort of getting cases to trial. Criminal conduct charges could have been filed against aviators under four specifications of the UCMJ: battery (also known as unlawful touching); indecent assault; conduct unbecoming; or dereliction of duty. The maximum sentence for the most extreme of these charges, indecent assault, was five years.

From the start, the Consolidated Disposition Authority appeared to be tripping over itself in its eagerness to pursue additional Tailhook prosecutions. Admiral Reason set up "fact-finding panels," which were in effect star chambers designed to pursue high-profile cases. Commander Robert Stumpf, leader of the Navy's Blue Angels precision flying team, was investigated for allegedly being present while a junior

officer in his squadron received fellatio from a prostitute. Captain
Frederic Ludwig, former president of the Tailhook Association, in and
out of mental hospitals since the scandal began, was being treated for
depression. Stumpf, Ludwig and three others were hauled in front of
the fact-finding panels, but there were never formal charges proffered
against any of them. By the end of October 1993, all five had been
exonerated because there were not sufficient facts to support any
charges.

For the most part, the only aviators whose cases proceeded
toward court-martial were those who demanded that the Navy do so.
There was one exception. He was the highest-profile flier to face criminal charges, and the first Marine in the dock, Captain Gregory
Bonam. The proceedings against him began on a sweltering August
1993 day on the Marine base in Quantico, Virginia, in a tiny courtroom furnished with ancient government-issue wooden office chairs.
Bonam was charged with assault "with intent to gratify his lust," as
well as conduct unbecoming an officer. Prosecutors said he was the
man who had attacked Paula Coughlin in Las Vegas. Here was the
purest drama so far in the Tailhook adjudication process, the one
which would directly pit Coughlin against the man she had ID'd as
one of her principal attackers, Mr. Teeth, who in the crush of bodies
in the gauntlet had repeatedly sexually assaulted her.

It turned out that Gregory Bonam's day in court would also be
Paula Coughlin's. Proceedings began with Bonam's Article 32, the
military justice equivalent of a preliminary hearing to see if there was
sufficient evidence to warrant a trial. Coughlin, in her summer whites,
was the prosecution's sole witness. Marine Corps Major Philip A. Sey-
mour, the prosecutor, walked her slowly through an impassioned account of what had happened in the third-deck hallway that Saturday
night. Coughlin then endured four hours of questioning by Patrick J.
Mackrell, Bonam's civilian attorney. Mackrell's questions included
with whom she ate breakfast, lunch and dinner during the convention,
what slots she played, how many glasses of wine and how many margaritas she drank, how long or short her skirts were.

Coughlin calmly detailed almost every hour of every day of her seventy-two hours in Las Vegas. She also said that when he attacked her, Bonam had worn a burnt-orange T-shirt with his call sign, "Boner," stitched across it. At the end of her testimony, Coughlin said that the gauntlet, and the repeated character assassination she had suffered in the Navy since, had in effect placed her in harm's way. "I felt I had passed through a combat zone, and was through it."

Mackrell's counterassault presented Bonam as a grievously wronged man, a victim himself, mistakenly identified by Coughlin. Mackrell didn't deny that Paula Coughlin had been attacked, but there was no way his client could have done what Coughlin said he had. Bonam was portrayed as a devout Christian, who regularly attended St. Patrick's Catholic Church in Meridian, Mississippi, where he had been stationed as a flight officer. He was the son of one of the storied Tuskegee Airmen, a historic all-black World War II Air Force squadron. Not mentioned in testimony (but surely motivating his character witnesses, who universally described Bonam as an upstanding, flawless individual), was the fact he had been diagnosed with spinal cancer in the winter of 1992.

Well-spoken, polished, handsome and assured, Bonam took the stand to say simply that Coughlin had gotten the wrong man. Had he touched any women? "No, I did not." Seen a hallway gauntlet? "No, I did not." Witnessed any gang-style aggression toward women whatsoever? "No, I did not."

Bonam acknowledged being in the Rhino Suite off the hallway of the third deck. He said he had only "two or three beers" there before leaving for the night. The defense introduced a photo of Bonam, in which he posed with a gag rhino horn around his neck. The photo, Bonam said, "would have been taken on September 7," 1991, the night of Coughlin's assault. The defense cited the fact that the photo showed him wearing a green T-shirt with a zigzag design, while Coughlin had said the man who attacked her had worn burnt orange. The stuffed rubber horn was dutifully entered as evidence in court, as was the photo itself. MacKrell was also able to bring out the fact that Coughlin had at first picked the wrong man from a lineup, a Marine clerk who had not attended the convention. Only on the second try had she been able to identify Bonam, and then, she told investigators at the time, with "this minor shadow of a doubt."

The prosecution could summon no one else but Paula Coughlin who would place Gregory Bonam in the hallway that night. A fellow aviator who had been granted immunity for his own misconduct said specifically that Bonam was not there. A roommate of Bonam's provided an alibi for the time during the assault was taking place.

Colonel Stephen S. Mitchell, the military investigating officer in charge of the Article 32, decided to believe Bonam. The case was reopened in mid-October for testimony of a new witness, a civilian who said that Coughlin's attacker was shorter than the six foot-one Bonam. Mitchell then recommended to Krulak at the CDA that charges against the Marine be dismissed. In late October, Krulak informed Coughlin personally that charges against Bonam were going to be dropped.

"I am disappointed with the decision," stated Coughlin in a press release, "but it is in line with the indignation and pain that I and my family have experienced over the past two years because of my attack. Despite investigations by both the Naval Investigative Service and the Department of Defense, no one has been judicially disciplined for the attack on me or any other victim of 'the gauntlet.' I do not believe that justice has been served."

It was a bitter defeat. The lack of any corroborating witnesses meant, effectively, that the wall of silence in naval air had worked. Off the record, Navy investigators continued to insist that Bonam was guilty. They were just unable to prove it in court.

"We know we got the right guy," Bill Hudson, head of the Criminal Division of the NIS during Tailhook, said of Bonam. "Of course, there wasn't enough to convict him. Because she claims she bit him on the arm. And yet he was awakened three hours later by a good friend of his out of a deep sleep, he was in his underwear, and the friend saw no bite mark on his arm. So my guess is there were several people reaching for her, she bit an arm, but it wasn't his. He flunked the polygraph twice. He flunked it once when we gave it to him, and he flunked it again when the DoD IG gave it to him. There's no question, if you have any confidence in polygraphs, that he is the one. But there just never was enough evidence.

Not all investigators share Hudson's confidence in polygraphs, which, owing to the possibility of false-positive results, are not admissible as evidence in court unless they are accompanied by a sworn confession. Said another senior NIS official, "My own feeling about the polygraph is if you get an admission [of guilt] out of it, it's worthwhile, otherwise it's [. . .] nonproductive." The NIS does allow lie detector results to establish innocence, however: all Tailhook suspects who "cleared" their polygraphs were immediately allowed to walk. Gregory Bonam at no time confessed to any wrongdoing at Tailhook, and the results of any polygraphs administered by the NIS or DoD IG were never publicly disclosed.

Continued Bill Hudson: "What happened [with the lineup] was, because [Bonam] was described as a very light-skinned black, we had difficulties putting together a lineup. Because there weren't that many light-skinned black aviators in the Navy and the Marine Corps. So when we started putting photographic lineups together, we had to go down to Quantico to come up with like-looking individuals. At that time we didn't have him as a possible suspect, but we did have photographs of other light-skinned aviators. The photograph that she picked out was a Marine enlisted that was assigned to Quantico. The agent who was working very closely with her during the entire course of this investigation and really had established strong rapport—had spent many, many hours with her going over the assailant—our agent felt when we subsequently got the guy that they could have been brothers. They looked so similar, it just knocked her out how close. They got somebody that looked too close to him is what happened."

Hudson also addressed the issue of Bonam's character, testified to so ardently by witnesses. "If you get somebody in a party mood, and you include alcohol, you see people out of character. It's not that unusual. To achieve what he had achieved as a pilot, he certainly had a great deal of self-discipline. He was very intelligent. He had all the character traits that it took to be a pilot and an officer, and that's very strong character. But he wasn't in character. He wasn't in uniform. He was in a party atmosphere, he had been drinking, there was this so-called gauntlet, there were a lot of women going through it, some of them according to accounts willingly subjecting themselves to this type of behavior—it wouldn't have surprised me."

The green shirt–orange shirt discrepancy did not bother Hudson, either. "Anybody will tell you eyewitness identification is probably the weakest you can ever have. For example, if you give yourself a test, and you're sitting in a restaurant, and you look at somebody walk by, and then you look away and try to write down what they're wearing, you'll find it a very difficult thing to do. You could probably identify that person if you saw them again, but for you to describe the color shirt, the color pants, is extremely difficult. I've given myself that test, and I consider myself a trained observer. Now she saw this under a great deal of stress. She's being assaulted, the guy's standing behind her, he comes over her, and everybody's putting a lot of emphasis on the fact she couldn't identify the color of that shirt, and yet she's not being interviewed by an investigator until three and a half weeks later, describing this incident that occurred in less than a minute under very stressful conditions."

The case against Cowden, the Norfolk-based pilot who stood accused of licking the chest of a Navy nurse, had already been dismissed after Article 32 proceedings in September 1993. At about the same time that Bonam's case was disposed of, Lieutenant Rolando Diaz ran out of money for his court-martial defense and decided he would take the option of going to admiral's mast for the single charge remaining against him: conduct unbecoming an officer. The specification cited Diaz's shaving of the pubic hair of two unnamed women at Tailhook '91, a charge which Diaz essentially did not dispute (though he claimed they were "bikini cuts"). The major thrust of his defense was that he had been shaving legs for two years straight with the full approval of his chain of command—including, he pointed out, Secretary of the Navy George Garrett.

Diaz received a letter of admonition (a permanent addition to his file, effectively ending his chances for advancement in the Navy) and was fined $1,000. He continued to insist that he had shaved Paula Coughlin's legs twice, once while she was in uniform—an allegation which was made much of in the continuing vilification campaign against Coughlin in the Navy community.

Bonam, case dismissed; Cowden, case dismissed; Diaz, guilty of leg-shaving. And then there were three: Miller, Tritt and Samples. As Barbara Pope wrapped up her testimony that December afternoon, Judge Vest heard closing arguments in the pretrial motion to dismiss the remaining three Tailhook cases. He thanked everyone and wished them all a happy holiday season. They could expect his ruling, he said, sometime in the next few months, after the New Year.

BUT WHAT ABOUT THE *REAL* GUILTY GUYS? WHAT ABOUT THE ONES who did the deeds, organized the gauntlet, assaulted, terrorized, man-handled women that night in Las Vegas? Did they all go free? With Lady Macbeth: "All? Did you say all?—oh, hell-kite!"

Gregory J. Geiss was twenty-seven at the time of Tailhook, round-faced and neatly good-looking, tanned but with a slight touch of crapulence to his features. A Mississippi boy, he had the laconic, stud-ied carelessness to his speech that is standard for the naval aviator. Geiss was the consummate bulletproof JO. He had flown an A-6 In-truder in Desert Storm, and like Miller, Tritt and Samples, had been stationed at Whidbey Island, Washington. He even shared a call sign, "Goose," with one of the lead characters in *Top Gun*.

In January 1993, Geiss made what had turned out to be a devil's pact with Department of Defense investigators, granting him com-plete legal immunity for testifying against his peers. Geiss became a symbol of all that was wrong with the Tailhook prosecution. Three of the Tailhook gauntlet participants, including Geiss and Lieutenant Frank Truong, had been given legal immunity even before the release of the DoD report. Investigators, facing an almost total lack of cooper-ation, were desperate for someone to provide leads. Their deals with

men like Geiss and Truong meant that some of the worst offenders in
the incident never saw a courtroom, much less a jail cell.

But because of his statements to investigators—and because
Geiss had the need of a guilty man to talk, we know more about him
than perhaps any other of the inner circle of Tailhook gauntlet members. He seemed unable to resist; he talked extensively with one reporter from a Norfolk-area newspaper, the *Virginian-Pilot and
Ledger-Star*, and even appeared on "60 Minutes." In protecting himself thoroughly, Geiss exposed himself totally.

"You know, I feel responsible," Geiss told the DoD agents when
they came to see him. "I feel bad about it. But I did it and others did
it. It happened. When you take it away as a snapshot, it doesn't seem
innocent. But at the time, it just seemed funny, like a bunch of frat
boys at a frat party."

Geiss arrived at the convention on Thursday, September 5, after
checking into the Sahara, on the Strip. "I mostly hung out at the
Hilton and the Sahara, gambling, partying and swimming," he told
investigators about his weekend. Thursday afternoon he busied himself with a friend coming up with some gag party favors, "kind of a
cute little card thing." "The 10 Steps of Drunkenness," these read,
with the first step being "witty and charming," and step 9, just before
blackout, reading, "I'm invisible. She won't notice if I reach up and
grab her tits."

It was his second Tailhook, and after the barnburner he had
attended in 1988, he was ready. The party favors were his idea of good
Tailhook icebreakers. "You'd go up to women and they'd read number
9. When they did, you'd goose them a little bit, you know. And they
would generally laugh and thought it was funny." One woman, whom
Geiss remembered as a tall, thin blonde, reacted against being fondled. "I just basically walked up and goosed her," Geiss said.
"Where?" asked the agents. "Just on the breasts," said Goose Geiss.
"Both breasts?" the agents wanted to know. "Uh-huh," Geiss answered. "She just kind of turned around and basically said, 'What are
you doing?' And I went, 'Uh-oh,' and just kind of tried to explain it to

her." Geiss was able to fondle a dozen women that first night, and on Friday graduated to pinching asses.

"It's a gimmick," Geiss said. "It's a prank. It's like a fraternity-type thing. I'm not a pervert or a criminal, you know. It was just part of the funny, liquor, boozing party attitude." Geiss, in some accounts described as "the master of ceremonies" of the Saturday night gauntlet, said he was just one of the guys that night.

"You know, everybody seemed real excited by the whole thing, not excited in a 'This is sexual,' but excited about 'Hey, a good football game.' This was just fun, you know, men stuff." He took charge of the gauntlet, waving men off older women, or women he judged would get too angry or upset.

"One girl I grabbed on the butt seemed a little bit irritated and turned to me and said a few choice words. I just said back to her, 'Hey, I'm sorry. I'm sure my friends down the hall will be much more polite to you.' Well, at this time, the guys down the hallway are beating the walls and all that kind of stuff and she proceeded down the hallway where I'm sure she was grabbed." When some aviators from a nearby hospitality suite delivered the underage teenage girl into the gauntlet, drunk and nearly comatose, Geiss said it looked like they were throwing out garbage. After the girl was stripped, a hotel security guard moved to help her. The aviators in the gauntlet scattered at the sight of the guard's police-style uniform.

"You know, you're in the middle of something that you consider otherwise innocent, but when that happens it's just like the lights come on. You go, wait a minute. I don't necessarily compare myself to a roach, but I was quick, I was out of that hallway fast. At some point the lights were turned back on and cockroaches settled back into the hallway."

Geiss later got into his argument with the pair of flight students who had been warning women off from the hallway. "I then walked out into the hall and confronted them. I can't remember exactly what I said, but it was basically, 'What are you doing and why?' " He later calmed down, he said, told the guys he was sorry, and left the Hilton soon afterward.

In the months that followed, as the Tailhook scandal burgeoned and the various investigations intensified, Geiss said he felt like he was "sitting on an egg." At first he had bragged to friends about his part in the gauntlet. He lied repeatedly to investigators. In 1992, he was transferred to Meridian, Mississippi, where he worked as instructor at a PT-7 squadron. Finally, in January 1993, two things happened. His son was born. Three days later, when he was still in a highly emotional state from that experience, Department of Defense agents approached him. They had information that implicated him in criminal acts at Tailhook, they said. They offered him immunity if he would agree to testify against others.

"It was presented to me, and after consulting with my wife and my lawyer, I accepted it. It appeared to me that it was going to come out in the open one way or another, the whole thing. I got tired of sitting in the shadows."

Geiss had escaped prosecution, but he rated his chances of advancement in the Navy as nil. "I think the whole event is tragic. I think a lot of us exercised poor judgment. I'm sad the whole thing transpired. I feel it's a roller coaster I wish we could all get off of. Everybody's real concerned that I sat back and haven't been punished. My life was trashed. The stress and the havoc I have faced at home with my family is incredible."

He added plaintively, "We're talking about one hour, one night, 754 days ago."

SINCE THE RELEASE OF THE DEPARTMENT OF DEFENSE TAILHOOK report in April 1993, the files of thirty-five admirals and generals had awaited the appointment of a permanent Secretary of the Navy to replace Frank Kelso, who had been acting in that capacity since Clinton was elected. The new administration had been roundly criticized for its lack of alacrity in filling crucial positions, and it was on July 23 that John Dalton, a Texas banker and former submariner, stepped into his Pentagon office. Since that time, he had spent hours reviewing the thick DoD investigative files on the Scrambled Eggs. "I have spent

some time every day since on that issue, sometimes all day," said
Dalton in mid-September. "There's been some days when I've done
nothing else but deal with the Tailhook files. I can spend the whole
day on one file and not get through it all."

The job before John Dalton was to resolve in the fairest way
possible one of the most difficult elements of the Tailhook adjudication process. The successful prosecution of the flag officers not only
would imply that justice was blind to rank, but also align itself neatly
with the inviolable military principle of command responsibility. It
would also satisfy the almost palpable craving of some in Congress and
the press that heads should roll, and heads with some gold braid atop
them, too. But it was just here that the Tailhook investigators had
encountered a finally intractable generational difference which
seemed to send the whole affair into some sort of baffling time warp.
For the most part, the admirals in the files had come of age in the
fifties, and were inculcated with a certain set of values. They were
men who just didn't get it and, no matter how often it was explained to
them or how clearly it was laid out, never really would. Reading the .
testimony in their DoD files, it seemed that they were strangers in
their own land. Their somewhat befuddled attitude was typified by
Rear Admiral Jay Sprague, the Navy's "star wars" expert: "Somewhere
in there I saw a sign about leg shaving. I want to say it was some
Eastern theme, mystic, 'Omar, the shaver,' or some coloration like
that, to indicate that this was unique or something," calling to mind
some absentminded professor who had wandered into a fraternity keg
party. It was not so much that the admirals didn't see anything, but
that they couldn't grok what they were looking at.

The DoD IG had stated of its interviews with these men: "We
find ourselves in a serious dilemma with respect to what the flag officers did not see. Although we obtained significant evidence that misconduct occurred at Tailhook '91 on a widespread basis, flag officers,
according to their testimony, seemed to be relatively unaware of it." A
handful of the admirals, it was true, acknowledged knowing that a
ritual involving leg-shaving was taking place. Two of them said they
had seen the Rhino Suite. One, Vice Admiral Richard Dunleavy

(Ret.), even admitted witnessing the gauntlet: "During the 1991 Tailhook convention, I became aware that a 'gauntlet' was operating on Saturday night in the third-floor hallway. I heard guys yelling, 'Show us your . . . (breasts).'

"When I went into the third floor hallway, I saw that it was crowded with people and that a commotion was occurring down the hall as they hooted and hollered. I didn't attempt to stop the commotion because I would not have been heard above the noise and because it appeared to be in fun rather than molestation.

"It was my impression, from what I saw, that no one was upset and I felt they wouldn't have gone down the hall if they didn't like it."

Other admirals expressed similar sentiments Rear Admiral Robert P. Hickey (Commander Carrier Group 7, North Island, California): "The entire passageway was clogged with wall-to-wall bodies . . . What I did was, just to give you my thoughts . . . 'Why would anybody want to be here? I'm getting too old for this stuff, I mean, it's hot. It's sweaty. It's stale. And, they're not falling down drunk or anything, but they're staying there for some reason.'

"And, in retrospect, I suppose I should have tried to find out why they were staying there. But I didn't. And I made my way through this hot, sticky thing and out to the patio."

Rear Admiral Riley Mixson (Director, Air Warfare Division, Office of the Chief of Naval Operations): "That Saturday evening, when I glanced in there, you know, I saw this crowd around the rhino and a bunch of chanting and stuff. And, I saw a couple of women in there. That's when I saw this thing that they had been talking about, the [rhino] penis that I had not seen on Friday night when I went through there.

"It was some rhino song, or, you know, I don't recall the words from it. I didn't stay around that long."

Vice Admiral Edwin R. Kohn, Jr. (Ret.): "What I saw was a ring of people standing around an activity which apparently was leg shaving and what my glimpse of it was that the leg shaving was on-going . . . My reaction is that the world has changed. Our time has changed, that that is quite a unique activity for men and women to participate in."

Well, yes. "Unique activity," indeed. What was Dalton to do with this, a culpability based not on commission or even omission, but on a gulf of understanding? He wound up issuing nonpunitive "letters of caution" to twenty-nine admirals (including Frank Kelso) and one Marine general. Two admirals who had not attended the nighttime festivities at the convention were totally exonerated. Three received letters of censure. These included Vice Admiral Richard Dunleavy, the former head of naval air, who had already retired. His censure meant that his benefits would be frozen at the two-star rank, at a possible loss of over $100,000 in retirement pay over the years. Rear Admiral Wilson Flagg, one of Dunleavy's deputies, and Rear Admiral Riley Mixson, director of air warfare, also received the greater punishment of censure. Mixson issued a gruff rebuttal of the charges against him, and then submitted a request to retire.

There remained the thornier problem of what to do about Frank Kelso. He, also, was on the verge of retirement. A cartoon in the *Navy Times* about this time showed Kelso, bushy eyebrows and all, being pursued by a dog labeled "Tailhook." "Retirement" was represented by a sunset in the distance. ". . . Six months! . . ." panted the cartoon Kelso. "I only need six more months." Reporters for the publication were snubbed by their Navy sources in reaction to the printing of this cartoon.

Kelso was hanging on by his fingernails. In October, Dalton recommended to Secretary of Defense Les Aspin that the chief of naval operations be fired. At that point, Aspin pulled Kelso's feet from the fire, stating in a letter to Dalton that "an evaluation of [Kelso's] record under the criteria you have offered does not suggest to me that he should be asked to resign." When questioned by the Associated Press as to why he wanted to remain in the job after all this, Kelso said stiffly, "I have a real desire to serve the nation as the uniformed leader of the Navy."

Still, the scent of death hung about Frank Kelso, and there were serious questions as to whether he could continue to function effectively as chief of naval operations. Without quite realizing it, Kelso had entered a new political landscape. In a post–Anita Hill world, no public figure associated with charges of sexual harassment, no matter how remotely, would be able to survive. The irony, here, of course, was that Kelso had been one of the best friends that Navy women ever had. Some said he was motivated to open combat positions to women in a cynical attempt to cushion the effects of Tailhook. However true that might have been, it was also true that Kelso had a fundamental change of heart about women in the Navy predating the scandal. Tailhook threatened to blow past that as if it never happened.

It was the Bob Packwood Syndrome come to life, whereby one of the best friends women ever had in the upper house (politically speaking) had suddenly found himself vilified on the basis of accusations of personal wrongdoing. Or the Teddy Kennedy Syndrome, with another champion of women's rights in the Senate being assailed by feminists over the Willie Smith rape trial. In the brave new landscape Kelso had ventured upon, the personal was the political, and what you had done for anyone lately mattered less than what you had done to them.

FRANK KELSO WAS ALREADY DONE, BUT IT REMAINED FOR JUDGE Vest to stick a fork in him. Vest had taken his time with the arguments presented to him in the last remaining Tailhook cases, those of Miller, Tritt and Samples. It was not until February 8, 1994, that he reconvened in Courtroom E of Norfolk Legal Services.

The room was packed. There were many more active-duty personnel there than had attended previously, either showing the colors or attracted by the sharp scent of victory. Three aviators in green nylon flight jackets sat side by side in the gallery's second row. Hear no evil, see no evil.

"This has been a very difficult motion for this court," Vest began. He said there had been 1,500 pages of court records, plus evidence— and this just for a pretrial motion. "I read everything. I took nothing lightly. And that will be demonstrated in my central findings."

But the court session ended without a real climax, since Vest said that his verdict was "not designed for oral presentation." He recommended that interested parties read his 111 pages of findings—available on hard copy and diskette. "If you have any questions, put it in writing." He did, however, announce the only part of the verdict that mattered.

"Admiral Kelso is an accuser," stated Vest drily. With those words, Thomas Miller, Gregory Tritt and David Samples saw all charges against them effectively dismissed. The three officers, after joining their lawyers for a jubilant press conference on the winter-burned lawn outside Legal Services, were free to resume their Navy careers with no punitive action taken against them for their activities at Tailhook '91.

When the press opened their packets or clicked on their floppies, they discovered one of the most blistering documents of the Tailhook scandal, a thoroughgoing denunciation of the entire adjudication process, the Kelso Navy and the whole chain of command. Starting at the top: "The failure by those responsible to take strong corrective action regarding inappropriate behavior that obviously occurred at past Tailhook symposiums is incomprehensible." Any reasonable person, wrote Vest, and certainly a member of the general public, would agree that high-ranking officers who were present at Tailhook could not fairly accuse the junior officers there of failure to act. "The greatest responsibility," he said, "must lie with the most senior officers, and Adm. Kelso was the most senior military officer present." Kelso was "exposed to, and actually witnessed, incidents of inappropriate decorum and behavior," including leg-shaving and the infamous Rhino Suite dildo. Forty-five pages of Vest's decision were fully devoted to proving this assertion.

The report was explicit about its findings on the question of Kelso's attendance, stating, in bland language, "This court finds Adm. Kelso is in error in his assertion that he did not visit the patio on Saturday evening." But the meaning was clear. Frank Kelso had lied repeatedly under oath when he denied his presence at the Hilton third deck the night Paula Coughlin was assaulted.

The most damning testimony concerning Kelso having personally witnessed misconduct at Tailhook, Vest found, had come from a Navy Reserve captain and commercial airline pilot named Robert Beck. Beck had described a conversation he had with Admiral Kelso while they stood on the pool patio Friday evening. Moments into their conversation, Beck recalled, they heard chanting from several men and women, who soon grew into a crowd that he guessed numbered more than one hundred. Beck told the court that the crowd surrounded a woman, and was "trying to allure the young lady into exposing her breasts because they were shouting 'tits, tits, tits' . . . after about five or six of the chants, the admiral said to me, 'Am I hearing what I think I am hearing?' and I said, 'Well, Admiral, if you think that you are hearing "tits" shouted, yes, you are absolutely right.' About 15 to 20 seconds later . . . the crowd aroused in claps and hurraying, and one person in the center, and we could not see the center of it because we were at the same level, but I did and we could see the girl's top of her bathing suit being held up in the air by someone . . . the admiral turned to me and said, 'Well, I guess that's the end of that,' and I said, 'Well, maybe not, maybe not, admiral.' And subsequent to that, there was then a chorus, the words [sic] 'bush' being used several times, and I was looking at the mass of humanity in front of me. At that time, the admiral started walking away . . . the security of the Hilton came and dispersed the crowd."

Vest did not end his catalog of wrongdoing at the Tailhook Convention itself. The investigation afterward, he ruled, was seriously compromised. "This court specifically finds this inaction [to pursue accountability of flag officers] was part of a calculated effort to minimize the exposure of the involvement and personal conduct of flag officers and senior Department of Navy officials who were present at Tailhook '91." There had been a cover-up, in other words, the Navy's equivalent of Watergate or Iran-Contra.

Vest's scathing decision effectively meant the end of Tailhook judicial proceedings. The CDA, exposed to his scorn as a tool of Navy brass, would be dismantled. Vice Admiral Reason told reporters that some guilty parties would probably go unpunished. "I'm almost certain of it. But what would you have me do about that? Evidence is a requirement."

Kelso's public affairs flack, Commander Deborah Burnette, attempted a positive, if desperate, spin. "It wasn't right that people that barfed on their shoes and dropped their trousers got caught and got punished and people who committed aggravated sexual assault did not. Is that right? No, it isn't right. But the system works."

All that remained was to cut the albatross loose. Frank Kelso fought furiously over the weekend of February 12–13, 1994, to control the terms of his departure. Personally stung by Vest's charges of mendacity, he insisted that newly appointed Secretary of Defense William J. Perry and Secretary of the Navy Dalton issue statements attesting to his unimpeachable character. On Tuesday, February 15, the deal was struck. Perry put forth a statement praising Kelso as a man of "highest integrity and honor." He also noted that Deputy Inspector General Derek Vander Schaaf had found "no credible evidence that Admiral Kelso had specific knowledge of the misconduct" at Tailhook. John Dalton also issued a statement, saying that Kelso "has acted, as he has throughout his thirty-eight-year career, with the best interests of the United States Navy in mind."

Kelso spoke at a news conference, standing in front of a bank of microphones in his Pentagon office. Behind him was a painting of the *Bluefish*, a submarine he had once commanded. He announced that he would leave office at the end of April, two months before his planned retirement date of June 30. "I am not happy about this. I am an honest man. I did not lie or manipulate any investigation." He told reporters that he had always promised he would "not retire until the end of Tailhook. I didn't want somebody else to come along and have to deal with that.

"I clearly have become the lightning rod for Tailhook," he said, "and I think it's in the best interest of the Navy that I proceed on and retire and we can get on with this business . . . I greatly regret that I did not have the foresight to see that Tailhook could occur."

Then, like a defeated ship of the line laying down a parting shot as it withdrew, Kelso referred to the larger issues Tailhook had brought forth. "Clearly, we needed to change our culture as to how we thought [about] and how we treated females . . . It takes a long time to change everybody's beliefs and everybody's behavior, but we are moving out to do that."

He announced that "the first young woman at sea in a combat squadron is doing carrier qualifications on the *Eisenhower* today. We're moving smartly to give women equal opportunity in our Navy, and I'm proud of that."

ONE WOMAN WOULD NOT BE AROUND TO BENEFIT FROM THE CHANGES Kelso promised were coming. In a letter to Navy Secretary John Dalton dated February 7, 1994, and released on February 10, five days before Admiral Kelso's announcement, Paula Coughlin ended her Navy career.

"I feel continued service would be detrimental to my physical, mental and emotional health. The physical attack on me by Naval aviators at the 1991 Tailhook convention, and the covert and overt attacks on me that followed, have stripped me of my ability to serve. The foundation on which I serve my country remains steadfast, but I am unable to continue serving effectively as a United States Naval officer or as a Naval aviator."

In a separate statement released through her attorney, Coughlin said, "My request to resign should not be viewed as a message to other women to refrain from reporting a physical assault."

Epilogue

Nothing is so sweet as to return from the sea and listen to the raindrops on the rooftops at home.

—Sophocles

EPILOGUE

AT THE END OF THE TAILHOOK SCANDAL— OR, IF NOT THE END, since the affair seems to sputter and flare repeatedly, then at some provisional denouement—bodies littered the stage as in some Elizabethan tragedy. Out of all the shield-clashing and breast-beating, though, one question survives, like the pure metal of the smelting process after the dross has been burned away. Is it a good thing, finally, that American women are now legally sanctioned to kill and die in war?

In the late twentieth century, women fighting or being drafted in war is an abstract question, and thankfully so, for the vast majority of the country's populace. Unless a family has a son or daughter in the military, it is unlikely that conversation around the dinner table includes debate over readiness, heads and beds, or the effect of G-forces on small-framed human bodies.

Yet there is no lack of people eager to claim that the presence of women in combat will not only damage the country's ability to respond militarily, but also erode certain ordained dynamics between men and women. They are correct insofar as understanding the importance of the question. What happened on April 28, 1993, when Les Aspin lifted the ban on women in warplanes, was more than just a blip. Measured against virtually any historical or cultural timeline, it signals a fundamental shift in the relations between the sexes.

But the image of a woman in the cockpit of a combat jet does not necessarily displace the image of a woman as nurturer. Women in 1995 are nursing infants while wearing flight suits. It doesn't have to sever men's masculinity, either.

What has been established in the aftermath of Tailhook is a different, more durable formula: the crucial relationship between respect and responsibility. The women of the Navy, whether on the third deck of the Hilton or in the ready room at Miramar, would never be respected by their male peers unless and until they were allowed commensurate responsibilities. Giving American women the right to prove themselves as warfighters establishes them on a new footing, as fully participatory, first-class citizens. It serves to dismantle the divided, hegemonic culture of two classes—the protectors and the protected—and leads the way to what theorist Judith Hicks Stiehm calls "a society of defenders." The old gender norms are not trashed, but enlarged.

The standing of women in the civilian world is not going to be instantly transformed because military women are now flying warplanes. Life does not offer up such simple equations. Of course, any incremental change in the status of women can only be a positive development if it leads away from subordination and toward more options for individuals. The inclusion of women in the combat arena certainly qualifies. But more than that, more than simply multiplying the career choices for women, the reality of women warriors presents society with a new archetype. "The men shall see to the fighting," growls Hector in the *Iliad*. But men today no longer have a monopoly on valor.

Law professor Kenneth Karst, in an article published when the combat exclusion was still in place, argued persuasively that even though today's military is a "separate community" in terms of law and practice, "the armed forces . . . teach lessons to the whole society." He added further that "when the national government excludes servicewomen from combat positions, and purports to exclude gay and lesbian Americans altogether, those exclusions work grievous material and stigmatic harm to servicemembers numbering in the hundreds of thousands. The same exclusions are well advertised in the larger society, and so extend their stigmatic harm to women and to homosexuals generally, thus providing painful evidence of the ways in which military and civilian life are interlaced. These forms of segregation are not the product of considerations peculiar to the military; they grow out of the same cultural and political origins that produce discrimination in civilian society."

Karst concluded: "The exclusion of women from combat positions does not keep women out of harm's way; it keeps women in their place." With the lifting of the combat ban, will the reverse also be true? Will it become more difficult to keep women in their place in the world at large?

Another aspect of the larger question, that of a universal draft, looms in the future. This may be the point at which commitment to total equality between the sexes breaks down. Indeed, the drafting of women was a bugaboo used to scare voters away from the Equal Rights Amendment in the 1970s. In 1981, the Supreme Court invoked the combat exclusion rule to turn away a challenge to the male-only draft. The Court said, in effect, that the draft would be used only when the military needed troops for combat, that women were excluded from combat, and that there was thus no reason to include women in the draft. Now that the exclusion has been lifted, a legal argument can again be made for universal draft registration.

Such a prospect would no doubt have even strong proponents of women's equality running for cover. There is no natural constituency for compelling females to serve in the armed forces, and there is a large and fervent one (on the left as well as the right) opposing such a move. Yet there can be little doubt that taken to its logical conclusion, the argument for equal rights also requires a commitment to equal responsibility.

If the forces of the right are eager to treat the question of women in combat as a burning moral imperative—and ready to declare it as one more transgression against "family values"—the response by the left is more ambivalent. Part of this is due to the large pacifist element that has always inhabited the left wing. Judith Stiehm got at the left's double bind: "This [article] is not addressed to those who have a principled commitment to nonviolence. I have studied that position and I respect it. What I do not respect and what I even fear is a position which accepts violence as effective, as necessary, and as appropriately exercised by men only."

Is it a good thing that women kill in war? It is a question that continues to make some feminists deeply uneasy. To many of them, the question of women at war is, as writer and military affairs analyst Cynthia Enloe puts it, "either . . . trivial or ideologically awkward."

Listen to feminist journalist Ellen Willis on Shannon Faulkner's suit against the Citadel: "Its target is a vicious institution, devoid of redeeming social value, that exists for the sole purpose of transmitting authoritarian brutality from one generation of suckers to the next, and instead of trying to get in on the deal, feminists should blow it up." ("Yes," Willis adds ruefully, "I'm aware that this sentiment falls a tad short of qualifying as reasoned social analysis.") Willis is talking about a military academy, but she could just as well be talking about the Navy. There is, in the response of many feminists, when faced with the extremes of male-dominated culture (pornography, football, the armed services), an irreducible element of revulsion. Willis's jeremiad can be distilled to a more basic human reaction: "Yuck!"

This is unfortunate, since a purely rejectionist stance has the paradoxical ability to reinforce stereotypical images of women as afraid to get their hands dirty, of being daintily removed from the fray. Rejection can resemble mystification, as if the military were better left to those who know it. Adapting Hegelian terminology, historian Jean Elshtain deconstructed the rift between two of our cultural ideals, that of "Just Warrior" and "the Beautiful Soul"—another version of the protectors and protected. Beautiful Souls, Elshtain wrote, are those beings "frequently of great individual goodness and purity, yet . . . cut-off and abstracted from the world of which they were a part."

Women have historically, and especially in most of the classic feminist canon, been cast as society's Beautiful Souls, particularly when it comes to the pursuit of war. Unfortunately, "a rather nasty historic bargain has been struck here: Beautiful Souls may stay 'sweet as they are' while 'the boys will be boys.' This demeaning and destructive pact must be broken. It offers only the deadly still of silence, for the Beautiful Souls and the beasts, by definition, cannot speak to one another."

Finally, the feminist dismissal of the armed forces leaves bereft those women who, like Shannon Faulkner (or Paula Coughlin, Loree Draude, Sara McGann), are drawn to military service and, put simply, want the same opportunities as their male counterparts. These are courageous, capable, patriotic women, all of whom came of age with the belief that they, like American women in every other professional field, could no longer be barred from any job on the basis of gender. They are, in the most basic sense, feminists. To write them all off as some kind of pod creatures co-opted by the world of men does a disservice not only to them but to the idea of womankind as diverse, inclusive and plenary.

OF THE SEVERAL CODAS TO THE TAILHOOK SCANDAL, THE ONE WHICH played itself out most prominently occurred on the floor of the United States Senate on April 19, 1994. The question on the floor that day was straightforward: Should Frank Kelso be allowed to retire as a full four-star admiral or be bounced back to two-star status as penalty for his role in Tailhook?

In other, less nervous times, such a question of retirement benefits would warrant no more than a pro forma discussion by the august body to which it was posed. It was odd that the issue should serve as a referendum on Tailhook, but the female members of the House and Senate were going to take their battles where they found them. Even as the CNO had announced his decision to retire early, there were indications that all might not go smoothly for him. Pat Schroeder, who objected to the deal Kelso had struck, enlisted twenty-one other congresswomen to demand an investigation into just how well the military was doing on the subject of sexual harassment. As Kelso's retirement vote loomed, six of the seven female senators (Kay Hutchison, the Republican from Texas, was the lone holdout) girded their loins and took to the floor.

It was supposed to be only a symbolic protest. The six senators— Barbara Mikulski of Maryland, Carol Moseley-Braun of Illinois, Patty Murray of Washington, Nancy Kassebaum of Kansas, Dianne Feinstein and Barbara Boxer of California—knew they were outnumbered. The fix was already in. A week earlier, the Armed Services Committee (under the chairmanship of Sam Nunn) had voted 20–2 to let Kelso retire with four stars, after the unprecedented summoning of Defense Secretary William Perry, Navy Secretary John Dalton and General John Shalikashvili, chairman of the Joint Chiefs, to make pleas on Kelso's behalf. If his four stars were withheld, he would become the first CNO in history to retire at less than full rank. Bill Clinton stated that the case against Kelso was "not sufficiently compelling to deny him his stars," and that to do so would be "very severe."

Against all this, the six senators recognized they were probably tilting at windmills. Mikulski—who as a member of the Board of Visitors at the Naval Academy had helped investigate the Gwen Dryer case—had plotted out strategy at a Democratic senators' retreat in Williamsburg, Virginia, on the previous weekend. In the aftermath of the Thomas-Hill hearings, a new militancy surrounded the issue of sexual harassment among the women on Capitol Hill. They decided to work as a bloc (ultimately joined by Hutchison) to ensure that Admiral Kelso would not go gently into that good night. Not without a fight. They were going to tell the world that they were mad as hell and weren't going to take it anymore.

If it was a symbolic effort, then symbolism could still make for high drama, even in the bombastic arenas of the Hill. In a reprise of a similar trek they made during the Thomas-Hill hearings, nine female members of the House of Representatives, including Pat Schroeder, linked arms and photo-opped their way across Capitol Plaza, to sit in the Senate chambers as a show of support. The decks were cleared. Majority leader George Mitchell was forced to abandon the day's agenda to allow a six-and-a-half-hour debate on the suddenly burning question of Frank Kelso's pension.

Mikulski led the anti-Kelso forces. She portrayed Tailhook as a "sordid, sleazy stain" on Navy culture, said that the Navy followed "the buddy system more than the honor system," and further ridiculed the Navy's effort to investigate itself. "Here we have a whole U.S. Navy, it equipped itself with night optics, but it has myopia when it goes to investigate this matter. Well, put your goggles on, guys. It is time to look and see what is going on."

Sam Nunn literally rose from his sickbed to come to the Senate and defend the admiral. Kelso, he said, had been willing to "go down with the ship" when he offered to resign in 1992. "Now the question is, do we say to the captain of this ship, you should have been down on the bottom with the ship when it went down? There was a mistake made in 1992. You should have gone down with the ship. So we are going to take a rowboat, put you in the rowboat, tie an anchor to your leg, and throw you down to the ship where you should have been all along. That is what we face here today."

The grand-nephew of Carl Vinson added that "knowing Admiral Kelso as I do . . . I believe he would rather have physical mutilation than for the U.S. Senate to vote, in effect, that he is responsible for Tailhook and that we are holding him absolutely accountable."

The opposition effectively turned the Navy's principle of command responsibility against Kelso. Barbara Boxer quoted the DoD report's assessment of the Navy's "long-term failure of leadership." She continued acidly, "And who, I ask, was the leader of the Navy at that time, the CNO? Admiral Kelso, the highest ranking officer in the Navy. He must shoulder the responsibility for that lack of leadership. I say, if you have pride in the Navy, then you take the heat for Tailhook.

"It happened on Admiral Kelso's watch and . . . the minutes have ticked by and the months have ticked by and the years have ticked by without a price being paid by anyone in the military."

But as much as the debate played superbly as a white-hats-versus-black-hats recapitulation of the Tailhook saga, that was just surface reality. Given the fact that it was Frank Kelso who effectively ushered the Navy into a new era of including women in combat duty, he was an odd straw dog for the she-bears of the Senate to tear apart. Various military women's groups, like the DACOWITS and the Women Officers Professional Association, lined up behind Kelso ("You are the one individual who has done more to further opportunities for women than anyone since Admiral Zumwalt in the early 1970's," the DACOWITS enthused, while WOPA stated "We, the professional women of the Navy, are beyond Tailhook."). Barbara Pope, now gone from the Navy and acting as a consultant on workplace issues, said the Senate debate "helps create a perception within the ranks that says, 'See, [sexual harassment] is just a women's problem.' This is a work force issue, not a gender issue."

At the end of the day, Kelso kept his stars, but just barely. The final tally was 54–43, an astonishing turnaround when just a week before the question probably could have been decided by a voice vote. Uneasy sat the white hats on a few heads that day. Exhibiting the droll sort of strange-bedfellow irony in which politics excels, Arlen Specter, who had been the chief Senate inquisitor against Anita Hill, and Bob Packwood, mired in sexual harassment troubles of his own, both voted against Kelso. If it was a victory for the admiral, it was a Pyrrhic one.

"We have upheld the honor of the United States Senate," said Mikulski after the votes were counted. A symbolic triumph, for what was probably, truth be told, a symbolic honor.

THE PAULA COUGHLIN WHO RETURNED TO LAS VEGAS IN THE AUtumn of 1994 was a far different woman than the one who had last been there three years previously. She was a civilian, for one thing, separated by choice and circumstance from the community she had once felt so much a part of. Diminished, too, in other ways, her weight down by a third, looking frail and gaunt, weepy, her bravado gone. The Elizabethan tragedy had laid waste to both sides.

Coughlin went back to Las Vegas to receive what three years of Tailhook prosecutions had never given her: a full hearing. She knew that no one would go to jail because of these proceedings. The action was civil, not criminal. But her court case would represent the most complete airing by far of Paula Coughlin's complaint against the people who assaulted her at Tailhook 1991. Coughlin had filed civil suits against the Tailhook Association and the Hilton soon after the convention. Her action against the association had been settled out of court.

But the gloves came off in Las Vegas, against the Hilton. Her lawyers charged that the hotel had been negligent in providing security for the convention at which she'd been mauled. The question before the eight-member jury (four women, four men) was whether the Hilton, given its knowledge of past Tailhook conventions, might reasonably have expected this one to get out of hand. If hotel management had such expectation, and failed to provide adequate security, it would constitute actionable negligence.

The Hilton's defense was a doomed and, in terms of long-term public relations for the hotel chain, probably a disastrous effort. The hotel's lawyers portrayed Coughlin as a hard-drinking party-girl who had eagerly engaged in the same kinds of improprieties for which the Navy's junior officers had been disciplined. The Hilton had placed ads in San Diego papers looking for additional witnesses to discredit Coughlin, and they found them: one claimed to have seen her getting her legs shaved while in uniform, another two said they'd seen her falling-down drunk that night. Lieutenant Rolando "Gandhi" Diaz served as a star witness, testifying that he had twice given Coughlin's legs "the works"—once while she was wearing her dress whites—on Friday night, the night before she said her assaults took place. They didn't have much of a conversation, Diaz maintained, saying, "I was concentrating on the task to be done." Coughlin, said Diaz, had even signed his "Free Leg Shaves" poster: "You made me see God. The Paulster." Winking and leering from the witness stand, Gandhi explained his role at the party: "I created miracles with legs."

"Goose" Geiss also appeared as an anti-Coughlin witness, testifying via videotape that he saw no hotel security guards anywhere near the gauntlet. He added his own appraisal of Paula Coughlin. She had, he said, "done more in American history to destroy a fine institution" than anyone else.

The Hilton defense called numerous women to the stand to downplay the misconduct of aviators at Tailhook. One, an insurance claims supervisor from Laguna Hills, likened the gauntlet to "walking by a construction site, except it was a little closer." She continued, "But I felt more safe than at many other functions . . . I honestly felt as if I was treated like a lady the entire weekend." A Las Vegas woman acknowledged the convention "wasn't a Sunday school gathering," but "they're neat guys, they treat you like gentlemen." She complained about the aftermath of Tailhook: "You don't generally slap all the babies because one baby is crying," she said. It was a rote victimizing-the-victim defense, and it was seriously out of date.

Arguing negligence, the lawyers for Coughlin stated that the Hilton Corporation was well aware, based on twenty-two years' previous experience, that Tailhook conventions were out of control, but chose to ignore the situation out of a classic profit motive. Witnesses testified that the Hilton's own female employees had been warned against Tailhook's hospitality suites. Coughlin's attorneys presented a handwriting expert who spent hours on the stand explaining about "reversals of motion" and "fluidity of pen strokes," concluding that the writing on Gandhi's poster was not that of Lieutenant Coughlin. The lawyers also introduced the fact that the association was a favorite of corporate chairman Barron Hilton, which might explain why the annual convention received deluxe treatment at the hotel, and why misbehavior might have been condoned.

Finally, Paula Coughlin took the stand herself, to tell her full story in a courtroom for the first time since the scandal started. With her mother, Rena, sitting in the gallery, Coughlin outlined the basic facts of her original complaint, editing only to follow her attorney's request she leave out "the excruciating details." She confronted head-on the accusation that she'd gotten her legs shaved the night before the assault, saying she'd jogged and then gone to sleep early in her hotel room.

Coughlin's father, Paul, a career aviator, also testified, saying that he himself had attended Tailhook conventions, once in 1963, then in 1969 or 1970. The last time he went, "there was a lot more drinking, and people made asses of themselves and I made a mental note not to go again," he said.

Coughlin's injury, her lawyers took pains to point out, did not end with the convention. She took the stand for a second day to tell the court about the resentment of her fellow aviators, the sense she had that the chain of command wanted her out of the Navy. "Most of the people in the Navy, whether I worked for them or not," she said, "were afraid to talk to me. I was shunned." Asked why she decided to resign, she said that anxiety had been "eating me up."

"You're not supposed to think about killing yourself over your job," she told the court.

It took the jury less than three hours to return a verdict in Coughlin's favor. On October 28, they awarded $1.7 million in compensatory damages for the emotional distress Coughlin had suffered as a result of Tailhook. Three days later they awarded $5 million in punitive damages as well. None of Coughlin's former Navy colleagues contacted her upon hearing the verdict. She remained persona non grata.

"There are so many misconceptions of who I am and what I am," Coughlin said. "As much as I wish it weren't true, I don't see how I could ever go back [to the Navy]. The Paula Coughlin Hate Club is still out there."

As Coughlin's attorneys and those of the Hilton Corporation squared off in Las Vegas, the Tailhook Association sponsored its 1994 convention, once more in San Diego. Four hundred mostly retired pilots attended, with no military contractors and no active-duty Navy speakers. "The crowd will come back," predicted one attendee.

After a two-year battle to retire with his third star despite disciplinary measures taken against him, Jack Fetterman prevailed. On March 4, 1994, Fetterman was nominated for retirement with three stars by Secretary of the Navy John Dalton, who simultaneously removed from the admiral's service record the letter of censure placed there by the previous secretary, Sean O'Keefe. "I feel pretty good about it," said Fetterman.

MICHAEL KITCHEN CONTINUES TO WAGE HIS JOPA WAR, THOUGH HE has ceased *The Gauntlet*'s monthly publication and brought out the Summer 1994 issue in November.

USS *CAPE COD* RETURNED TO SAN DIEGO HARBOR FROM ITS SIX-month Western Pacific deployment. For reasons unrelated to having women on board, Captain Hooper's first mixed-gender command had evidently been conducted under some evil star. During the cruise, a crew member hung himself in a berthing area soon after the ship left Pier 7 (the body was stored in a meat locker until the next port of call). A sailor jogging by the ship as it was moored in Jabal 'Ali dropped dead of a heart attack. By the time another *Cape Cod* enlisted man hung himself in a remote workspace far below decks, a psychological counseling team was being flown overseas to treat the shell-shocked crew. Finally, as it was about to return home, the ship ran aground leaving port, damaging the propeller so badly that it could not be repaired, and a new one had to be shipped from the States to replace it. Problems with the integration of women on board were not prominently mentioned in the catalog of the ship's Westpac woes.

THE NAVY CONTINUES TO MOVE METHODICALLY IN IMPLEMENTING the new rules on women in combat. Official policies on recruitment, retention, training and selection of occupational fields are "gender-neutral to the maximum extent possible." Women can now serve in all Navy combat positions except SEAL commando units or on submarines and minesweepers. Ratings such as "gunner's mate, missiles" and "aviation warfare system operator" are now open to both women and men. But while the opportunities are available immediately, actually putting women on ships in the fleet is a much slower process.

Beginning in the summer of 1994, women were assigned as permanent members on a total of eight combat vessels, including four destroyers, two amphibious ships and two aircraft carriers, divided evenly between the Atlantic and Pacific fleets. On each ship, women still represented only 10 to 20 percent of the crew. Two carrier air wings were scheduled as the first to include female pilots in their squadrons. In the short term, ironically, women would actually lose sea billets, because of the high number of destroyer and submarine tenders being decommissioned. By the end of the century, there would be 10,000 women serving at sea—nearly the same number as today, but with a crucial difference in the types of ships on which they would serve.

Part of the reason the Navy has moved so slowly is so that the sailors and officers on board ships and in air squadrons—and their spouses—can receive mandatory training (in equal opportunity, fraternization, responsible sexual behavior) that will "orient" them to having women in their midst. The Navy was careful to assign enough senior-ranking women, both enlisted and officers, who quickly came to be known by the honorific "Grandma."

Admiral Jeremy Boorda, the CNO who replaced Frank Kelso, was a "mustang," or sailor who had risen through the enlisted ranks to receive his commission. Boorda placed no limits on women's participation in the Navy. "The goal is all. The goal is everything," he said a year after his confirmation. That included the submarine force, he said. Future submarine designs would include accommodations for sailors of both sexes. At an appearance before the DACOWITS in late October 1994, Admiral Boorda speculated that the organization might eventually be rendered obsolete. "One of these days, people will wonder what all the fuss was about. Some day the CNO will stand up here, and *she* will say, 'Why do we need a DACOWITS?' "

ON OCTOBER 20, 1994, THE USS *EISENHOWER* BECAME THE FIRST carrier to deploy with women permanently assigned as crew members. There were about 500 women out of 5,500 on board as the carrier left Pier 12 in Norfolk for a six-month Mediterranean cruise. Despite dire predictions of a decline in readiness that having women on board would engender, the Ike left Norfolk on time.

LIEUTENANT LOREE DRAUDE APPLIED FOR A TRANSITION TO TACTICAL aviation. She didn't get her first choice, F/A-18's, but retrained to fly S-3's, and is now stationed with the USS *Abraham Lincoln*'s air wing.

SARA MCGANN REMAINS AT THE NAVAL ACADEMY AT ANNAPOLIS, where she is now a "third-classman," a sophomore, and sings with the Women's Glee Club and the Academy Choir. Last year she ran the Navy-Marine Corps Marathon, and she is considering becoming a Marine.

IN EARLY NOVEMBER 1994, *NEWSWEEK* REPORTED A NEW NAVY SEXual harassment scandal at a training command in San Diego, where seven male instructors were accused of sexually harassing sixteen female recruits over a period of eighteen months. No charges had been filed. Navy officials said they were having difficulty ascertaining the veracity of the complaints, as so many of the victims had dispersed to new duty stations.

THE PREVIOUS WEEK, SEVERAL MEMBERS OF THE ARMY FOOTBALL team at the U.S. military academy at West Point were suspended from the team for the remainder of the season. They had been found guilty of touching the breasts of female cadets while participating in a gauntlet-like "spirit run" during a pep rally.

And in that same week, a twenty-two-year-old Israeli pilot named Alice Miller sued for the chance to be a combat pilot. "The fact that men go to combat and women keep the home fires burning has a deep impact on the way our society views women," she said. "Society will look at them differently if they have a chance to participate as men do in what is viewed as one of the most important tasks here: risking your life in defense of your country."

In Bosnia, women are being trained for front-line combat positions. Women had previously held noncombat posts in the Bosnian Army.

On November 12, 1994, Rosemary Mariner gave birth to a six-pound, ten-ounce baby girl, the first child for Mariner and her husband, Tom. In June 1995, the family will move from Washington, D.C., to Meridian, Mississippi, where Captain Mariner will become the first woman to command a naval air station.

Finally, on November 15, 1994, two female F/A-18 pilots became the first U.S. women to fly combat sorties. The Dyke had beat the Babe. Flying off the USS *Eisenhower* in the Persian Gulf, they patrolled the no-fly zone in the skies over southern Iraq.

Kara Hultgreen did indeed become the first woman to carrier qualify in a combat-ready F-14 Tomcat, the famed Top Gun fighter jet, and previously the exclusive purlieu of the jet bubba. She then joined the Black Lions of VF-213, who were getting ready to deploy for the Persian Gulf. On Tuesday, October 25, 1994, she was approaching the flight deck of the USS *Abraham Lincoln*. It was a clear day and visibility was good. As she was lining up the aircraft for a landing on the deck, the Tomcat suddenly lost altitude. Hultgreen's radar intercept officer, Lieutenant Matthew Klemish, successfully ejected, 200 feet above the ocean and less than half a mile from the deck. He was rescued with minor bruises. Hultgreen ejected a moment later, but by that time the jet had rolled sharply. Hultgreen hurtled sideways. After an extensive search failed to recover the plane or her body, the Navy declared her lost at sea.

Hultgreen's death was accorded full honors, but no extraordinary measures were taken to mark her passing. She was celebrated not as the first female Tomcat pilot, but as a fallen aviator. For the Navy to single her out might somehow lessen the sacrifice of other downed pilots (ten F-14 pilots had died since 1992). In the brutal calculus of naval aviation, the death of the first female Tomcat pilot could not be in any way romanticized or drawn out. "She was a smart girl. I know she knew the chances she was taking," said Hultgreen's grandmother, and the same quiet stoicism seemed to characterize much of the Navy's response to her death.

But there was an ugliness, too, which attended Hultgreen's death, a series of anonymous faxes sent from somewhere within the Navy impugning (falsely, as it turned out) Hultgreen's flight record. In its efforts to desegregate naval aviation, stated the authors of the fax, the Navy was rushing unqualified personnel onto the flight lines. The faxes were an unpleasant reminder of the depth of enmity toward women in naval aviation. How easy it seemed to abandon the Navy's vaunted code of honor, its chatterings about "officers and gentlemen," when the painful question of women in uniform arose. It was an unheard of breach of naval aviation etiquette to question the flight record of a pilot who had gone down. It was just not done. Except with Kara Hultgreen.

Against this slander, the Navy maintained its stoic silence, refusing (as was policy) to release the flight records of the deceased, stating only that Hultgreen was "average to above average" as an F-14 pilot. Hultgreen's mother, Sally Spears, provided the records to the media herself, showing her daughter was ranked third of the seven pilots in her class. "The way I look at it is," Spears said, "being a slightly above average F-14 pilot is like being a slightly above average Phi Beta Kappa."

Because of the controversy, the Navy was forced to perform a salvage operation (at a cost of $100,000) to bring up Hultgreen's Tomcat, in order to analyze what went wrong with the flight. A four-month investigation concluded that the crash was caused by technical malfunction, not pilot error, that when the left engine stalled on approach to the ship, virtually no pilot on earth would have been able to save the plane. Hultgreen's body was recovered also, still strapped to the ejector seat.

In hindsight, the crash rendered Kara Hultgreen's concerted efforts to fly front-line jets in tragic high relief—all those days spent in congressional hearings, all those requests for transfer to combat aircraft, all that striding through the corridors at DACOWITS conferences in her flight suit, as if she had spent the last four years of her young life committing slow-motion suicide by idealism, lobbying for her right to die. Hultgreen was, of course, after something else: the right to live her life on her own terms. What was especially bitter was that every person has to fight to be in her line of work, but nobody had to fight as hard as she did. Her death might have placed her activities in a light both ironic and cruel, but it cannot detract from the essential dignity of that effort.

Notes

CHAPTER ONE: LIGHTING YOUR HAIR ON FIRE

p. 3   Gandhi, like his namesake . . . Section based on author interviews with Rolando Diaz, 9/3/93, 10/5/93.

p. 6   "The Tailhook Association started as an old man's drinking club" Author interview with James D. Ramage, 12/28/92.

p. 6   "flying and hell-raising . . ." Chuck Yeager and Leo Janos, *Yeager: An Autobiography*. Bantam Books (New York: 1986), p. 173.

p. 8   The first thing that happened to Kara Hultgreen . . . Author interviews with Kara Hultgreen, 4/18/93, 9/9/93, 10/6/93.

p. 12   "It's like having the Berlin Wall come down" Quoted in Deborah Schmidt, "Women aviators feel thrill of victory," *Navy Times*, August 12, 1991. In the article, Lieutenant Coughlin voiced her frustration about the combat exclusion: "I wish I could have participated in the Persian Gulf in the capacity I am capable of."

p. 15   Afterward, what happened . . . that Saturday night . . . Author interview with Lisa Reagan and Marie Weston, 1/15/93.

CHAPTER TWO: SIERRA HOTEL

p. 21   "We put up $20,000 prior to getting there . . ." Department of Defense, Office of the Inspector General, Sworn statement by Lieutenant John J. Loguidice, March 10, 1993, pp. 16–17.

p. 21   The Las Vegas Hilton had been the Tailhook convention's home . . . since 1968. *Department of Defense Inspector General, Report of Inves-*

tigation: Tailhook 91, Part 2: Events at the 35th Annual Tailhook Symposium, February 1993, Section V, "Squadron Hospitality Suites," pp. V-3–V-8.

p. 21   Saturday night . . . after returning to their room, Lisa Reagan and Marie Weston . . . Author interview with Lisa Reagan and Marie Weston, 1/15/93.

p. 22   That same Sunday morning, a thirty-year-old Navy lieutenant named Paula Coughlin . . . Author interview with Lieutenant Paula Coughlin, 3/17/93. Additional Coughlin material: Naval Investigative Service Sworn Statement by Captain Bob Parkinson, 10/31/91. U.S. Naval Investigative Service Results of Interview with Captain Parkinson, 10/31/91. Naval Investigative Service Results of Interview with Pax River Staffer, 11/4/91 (Exhibit 132). Naval Investigative Service Sworn Statement by NAS North Island helicopter pilot, 10/18/91. U.S. Naval Investigative Service Sworn Statement by Paula Coughlin, 11/1/91. Naval Investigative Service interview with John Snyder, 11/1/91. John Lancaster, "Eight Years in the Navy, and 'Treated Like Trash,'" *Washington Post National Weekly Edition,* June 29–July 5, 1992. Tom Philpott, "Her Story," *Navy Times,* June 1992. Stephanie Saul, "Tailhook Fallout," *New York Newsday,* August 10, 1992. Linda Bird Francke, "Paula Coughlin: The Woman Who Changed the U.S. Navy," *Glamour,* June 1993.

p. 29   "There are few caste systems as elaborate . . ." Ehud Yonay, "Top Guns," *California Magazine,* May 1983.

p. 30   "It's like in the old days . . ." *Ibid.*

p. 30   "I opened this page," Bruckheimer recalled . . . Alexander Cockburn, "The Selling of the Pentagon? Watching a few good men be all that they can be on the set of *Top Gun,*" *American Film,* June 1986.

p. 30   "This looks like Star Wars on earth" Quoted in R. Serge Denisoff and William D. Romanowski, "The Pentagon's Top Guns: Movies and Music," *Journal of American Culture,* vol. 12, No. 3, 1989.

p. 32   "an excellent opportunity to tell about the pride . . ." *Ibid.*

p. 32   Paramount, the producers' studio . . . *Ibid.*

p. 32   "After a brief calculation . . ." Alexander Cockburn, *op. cit.*

p. 32   "I didn't feel the military pressured me . . ." Quoted in R. Serge Denisoff and William D. Romanowski, *op. cit.*

p. 33   "The script was no good . . ." Author interview with Edward H. Martin, 12/23/93.

p. 33   The domestic box-office gross . . . R. Serge Denisoff and William D. Romanowski, *op. cit.*

p. 36   "We always saw the pilots as rock 'n' roll stars . . ." Quoted in *Ibid.*

p. 36   "We said it would be the 'Mother of all Hooks . . ." October 11, 1991, letter from F. G. Ludwig, Jr., Captain, USN, President, Tailhook Association, addressed "Dear Skipper."

p. 37   "late-night gang mentality" August 15, 1991, letter from F. G. Ludwig, Jr., Captain, USN, President, Tailhook Association, addressed "Dear Tailhook Representative."

p. 37   "like partial lobotomies" Author interview with Ron Thomas, Executive Director, Tailhook Association, 9/10/93.

p. 40   For five weeks . . . See Coughlin sources cited previously.

CHAPTER THREE: IN THE COMPANY OF INTELLIGENT ANIMALS

p. 44   "like a wine-skin from which the wine is drawn" Kenneth J. Hagan, *This People's Navy: The Making of American Sea Power.* The Free Press (New York: 1991), p. 15.

p. 44   "The rising business classes in the cities had been steering their sons . . ." Tom Wolfe, *The Right Stuff.* Bantam Books (New York: 1980), p. 31.

p. 45   "Everyone hates the warrior when there's no war going on . . ." Author interview with Bill Hoover, 1/5/93.

p. 46   "War is delicious . . ." and "in the company of intelligent animals . . ." Martin Gilbert, *Churchill: A Life.* Henry Holt and Company (New York: 1991).

p. 47   "lost in its unshored, harborless immensities" Herman Melville, *The Best of Herman Melville. Moby Dick,* Chapter 32. Castle (Secaucus, N.J.: 1983), p. 96.

p. 47   "I don't know how many birthdays I've spent . . ." Author interview with Gloria Skillerman, 7/3/93.

pp. 48–   The deck of a Navy ship is a place still informed by . . . "greatest
49   rambler in Christendom" Vice Admiral William P. Mack (Ret.) and Lieutenant Commander Royal W. Connell, *Naval Ceremonies, Customs, and Traditions.* Naval Institute Press (Annapolis: 1980), pp. 19–32, 298.

p. 51   "As long as you didn't cause an international incident . . ." Author interview with Craig King, 4/28/93.

p. 51   "They'd proceed to destroy the place . . ." Author interview with not-for-attribution source, 2/5/93.

p. 52   "Everyone wants to fly something that goes fast . . ." Author interview with Don Ring, 12/15/92.

p. 52   "All *Top Gun* did was walk in to Miramar O Club . . ." Author interview with not-for-attribution source, 2/5/93.

p. 52   A Navy commander who was stationed at the Pentagon in 1989 . . . Author interview with Richard Wright, 3/19/93.

p. 53   "The honor and the glory were in many cases . . ." Tom Wolfe, *op. cit.*, p. 103.

p. 53   "invite a girl over and show her your 'snake'" Robert K. Wilcox, *Scream of Eagles: The Creation of Top Gun—And the U.S. Air Victory in Vietnam.* John Wiley & Sons (New York: 1990), p. 17.

p. 54   "Nothing in it was breakable—no glass . . ." Quoted in *Ibid.,* p. 172.

p. 54   "Naval aviation, to an extent, shaped . . ." Department of Defense, Office of the Inspector General, Sworn statement by Lieutenant John J. Loguidice, March 10, 1993, p. 67.

p. 56   For R&R, Gulf war troops had to make do with the Cunard *Princess* . . . Molly Moore, "Pentagon Renting Cruise Ships for R&R in Gulf," *Washington Post,* Friday, December 14, 1990.

p. 56   "Little Brown Fucking Machines . . ." Saundra Pollock Sturdevant and Brenda Stoltzfus, *Let the Good Times Roll: Prostitution and the U.S. Military in Asia.* The New Press (New York, 1993), p. 326.

p. 56   According to Ninotchka Rosca . . . Coco Fusco, "Army Rules," *The Village Voice,* August 11, 1992.

p. 57   "The last extended conflict we had ended in 1972 . . ." Author interview with Bill Hoover, *op. cit.*

p. 58   "the post-Vietnam mind-set, which was just a continuation . . ." Author interview with Ward Carroll, 3/18/93.

p. 58   "It's like a frenzy . . ." Author interview with Suzanne Parker, 4/27/93.

CHAPTER FOUR: THE END OF THE WORLD

p. 61   They all saw nothing . . . Author interview with Barbara Pope, 2/18/93; and Barbara Pope, Women Officers Professional Association Luncheon Address, Washington, D.C., 2/18/93.

p. 62   270 field agents involved, 2,193 interviews . . . Author interview with NIS Special Agent Ron Benefield, Naval Criminal Investigative Service, 3/24/94.

p. 70   "We were first informed of this case more than 30 days after it occurred . . ." Supplemental Statement of RADM(L) D. M. Williams, Jr., Concerning Department of Defense Inspector General, *Report of Investigation: Tailhook 91—Part 1,* September 1992, pp. 6–7.

p. 70   "a fart's chance in a whirlwind" Department of Defense Inspector General, *Tailhook 91, Part 1—Review of the Navy Investigations,* September 1992, p. 18.

p. 70   "As soon as it came to our attention, we jumped into it . . ." Author interview with Bill Hudson, 1/20/94.

p. 71   "Rabbits and trees" Author interview with Loree Draude, 5/18/93.

p. 72   "classic SERE school garbage . . ." Author interview with Kirby Miller, 4/29/93.

p. 74   "No, we didn't put out a big PR thing" Bill Hudson interview, *op. cit.*

p. 74   Witnesses described the flier wrapping his "crank" . . . U.S. Naval
             Investigative Service, Results of Interview, December 17, 1991, p.
             1189.

p. 74   the minor "left on the floor at the location where she was stripped . . .
             totally naked" U.S. Naval Investigative Service, Interview, December 4,
             1991, pp. 713–14.

p. 74   a woman who was "visibly upset and her clothes were stretched and
             torn" U.S. Naval Investigative Service, Results of Interview, November
             1, 1991, p. 1870.

p. 74   "not constant but more a flowing thing" U.S. Naval Investigative Ser-
             vice, Sworn Statement, November 1, 1991, pp. 1994–95.

p. 74   "a good-natured, fun practice which was conducted with a jocular-like
             attitude" U.S. Naval Investigative Service, Results of Interview, p.
             2055.

p. 74   "marked absence of moral courage and personal integrity   ." Naval
             Inspector General, Report of Investigation: Personal Conduct Sur-
             rounding Tailhook '91 Symposium, April 29, 1992, pp. 4–6.

p 75   "A Navy investigation into sexual abuse at a convention of naval aviators
             last September   . ." Eric Schmitt, "Navy Says Dozens of Women
             Were Harassed at Pilots' Convention," New York Times, May 1, 1992.

p. 75   "When investigators questioned the pilots, they ran into a stone
             wall . . ." "CBS Evening News with Dan Rather," April 29, 1992.

p. 76   "If you read through the statements, you can find that they described
             approximately fifty women . . ." Bill Hudson interview, op. cit.

p. 77   "were carrying beer in their hands as they walked down the hall-
             way . . ." U.S. Naval Investigative Service, Results of Interview, No-
             vember 13, 1991, pp. 533–34.

p. 77   "She said that a few comments were made but she said that they were
             regular comments . . ." U.S. Naval Investigative Service, Results of
             Interview, November 1, 1991, pp. 1659–60.

p. 78   a female who "strutted" through the gauntlet "wearing only a USN
             member's white hat . . ." U.S. Naval Investigative Service, Interview,
             November 1, 1991, p. 2015.

p. 78   a groupie who "stripped to her thong"; others who "wear enticing
             dress, and readily go down the gauntlet whooping and hollering . . ."
             U.S. Naval Investigative Service, Results of Interview, December 10,
             1991, p. 1049.

p. 78   "about 10 feet from where the guys [had] organized themselves" U.S.
             Naval Investigative Service Sworn Statement, December 18, 1991, pp.
             1188–91.

p. 79   "Like a big catfight—meowr! . . ." Author interview with Kara Hult-
             green, 9/8/93.

p. 83   "for appropriate action" H. Lawrence Garrett, III, Memorandum for the Chief of Naval Operations/Commandant of the Marine Corps, Subject: Behavior and Attitudes Towards Women, June 2, 1992.

CHAPTER FIVE: SEASON OF THE WITCH

p. 90   A Naval Investigative Service agent named Laney Spigener . . . At the end of November, Coughlin complained to NIS officials, and Spigener was removed from the case. Five months later, after an inquiry, a hearing and a review by his supervisors, the agent was suspended without pay for three days.

p. 90   "Little Miss Paula Coughlin . . ." Author interview with former Miramar F-14 squadron commander, 12/28/92.

p. 90   Rumors about her spread through the Navy . . . "player" Author interview with Bill Hoover, 1/5/93.

p. 90   "teased" the men in the hallway . . . U.S. NIS Results of Interview, November 12, 1991, p. 520.

p. 90   "body shots" Author interview with Craig King, 4/28/93.

p. 90   "red tight dress" and "was doing . . . guys" U.S. NIS, Results of Interview, November 2, 1991, pp. 2064–65.

p. 90   "leather miniskirt" Author interview with Lieutenant Ann Hannegan, 4/28/93.

p. 90   "mini leather skirt and halter top" Bill Hoover interview, op. cit.

p. 90   "short miniskirt that doesn't cover much and a very low-cut shirt" Author interview with Janine Palmer, 1/7/93.

p. 91   They were "saying, 'It's fixed, it's fixed, it's fixed.' " Quoted in Linda Bird Francke, "Paula Coughlin: The Woman Who Changed the U.S. Navy," Glamour, June 1993.

p. 91   "It was the most frightened I've ever been in my life" Quoted in John Lancaster, "Eight Years in the Navy, and 'Treated Like Trash,' " Washington Post National Weekly Edition, June 29–July 5, 1992.

p. 93   "Historically, it's been just the guys . . ." Quoted in Gregory Vistica, "2 Navy Officers Face the Music Over Lewd Verse," San Diego Union-Tribune, July 2, 1992.

p. 93   "In aviation, nothing's sacred" Author interview with Craig King, 4/28/93.

pp. 94–95   "They started playing music and five guys came out . . ." and "It could stand for clock . . ." and "the senior guys there rolled their eyes . . ." Former Miramar F-14 squadron commander interview, op. cit.

p. 95   That evening, June 18, a retired Navy Nurse Corps captain . . . Information drawn from Merrill W. Ruck, "Investigation to Inquire into the Events Which Occurred at the NAS Miramar Officers Club 18 June 1992," July 11, 1992.

p. 95   "I was really amazed . . ." Quoted in Eric Schmitt, "Navy Punishes 2 Officers Because of Lewd Banner," New York Times, July 3, 1992.

p. 96   "to dismantle a decaying culture" and other excerpts from Howard's speech quoted in Lieutenant (jg) John M. Wallach, "No More!" *All Hands*, August 1992.

p. 98   "What it tells you . . ." Quoted in Eric Schmitt, "Now at Navy's Bridge, Battling Sexism," *New York Times*, July 4, 1992.

p. 98   "outrageous . . . behavior that is absolutely unacceptable" Quoted in Art Pine, "Fiscal Expert Named Acting Navy Secretary," *Los Angeles Times*, July 8, 1992.

p. 99   "isolated incident that should not reflect . . ." and "I think it would be a mistake to look at these events as somehow indicating . . ." Quoted in John Lancaster, "Close Cheney Aide Appointed as Acting Secretary of Navy," *Washington Post*, July 8, 1992.

p. 99   "a handful of junior officers . . . somehow have forgotten . . ." " 'Handful of Junior Officers' Blamed for Tailhook Scandal," *Los Angeles Times*, July 23, 1992.

p. 100   "We don't want to approve an officer and see him up . . ." Quoted in David S. Steigman, "Officer promotions face delays," *Navy Times*, June 15, 1992.

p. 100   "At the root of sexual harassment . . ." Quoted in Otto Kreisher, "House Panel Opens Dual Probe into Tailhook, Navy's Inquiries," *San Diego Union-Tribune*, July 11, 1992.

p. 102   "21 times with a wooden oar . . ." Gregory Vistica, "Navy Officer Guilty of Sexual Harassment," *San Diego Union-Tribune*, July 18, 1992. Tolan was found guilty of conduct unbecoming an officer, fined $2,000 and was moved to the bottom of the promotion list for captain. He was not booted out of the service, and his punishment appeared to contravene new guidelines providing for automatic discharge of any sailor guilty of aggravated sexual assault. Tolan's replacement at El Toro's Aviation Physiologist Testing Unit was a female lieutenant commander.

p. 103   "fun but outrageous project . . ." "Navy Clerk Says Captain Asked Her to Pose Nude," *New York Times*, September 13, 1992.

p. 103   "invited women in the audience to perform oral sex on stage" AP item, "Comic's Navy-blue humor sparks furor," *New York Post*, September 7, 1992.

p. 104   "With hard times depressing the local hotel industry . . ." Tom Blair, "It's a jumble out there," *San Diego Union-Tribune*, August 4, 1992.

p. 104   "What was playing there up in the Pentagon scene . . ." and other quotes in this section with sources not identified separately, Author interview with Jack Fetterman, 4/30/93.

p. 106   "absence of firmly founded goals," "no self-respect" . . . John Burlage and Mark Faram, " 'Core values' enter spotlight," *Navy Times*, July 6, 1992.

p. 107   "We went up there and took the Admiral's dog . . ." Office of the

Naval Inspector General, *Report of Investigation (Case Number: 920414)*, Subj: Fetterman, John H., Jr., Vice Admiral, USN, Chief of Naval Education and Training (CNET); Alleged Abuse of Position and Fraternization. June 12, 1992.

p. 109   "rise above the current climate . . ." Quoted in Gregory Vistica, "Ex-vice admiral drills Navy over 'innuendo,' " *San Diego Union-Tribune,* July 26, 1992.

p. 109   "He always tried to do the reasonable thing . . ." Quoted in Eric Schmitt, " 'People's Admiral' Is Buffeted in Storm Over Ethics," *New York Times,* August 1, 1992.

p. 109   "They are going after the wrong admiral" Quoted in "Ex-vice admiral drills Navy over 'innuendo,' " *op. cit.*

p. 109   "The whole purpose of what the taxpayer invests in . . ." Jack Fetterman interview, *op. cit.*

p. 111   "Valvoline and Snap-on calendars . . ." Mark A. Peterman, GMM1 (SW), USS *Lewis B. Puller.* Letter to the Editor: "Vague policies threaten rights," *Navy Times,* September 7, 1992.

p. 111   "Betrayed," "misunderstood" . . . A sample expression of this sense of betrayal: "Dan Howard, Barbara Pope, nobody knows who they are, all of a sudden come out and they're speaking for the Navy. They're saying heads will roll, and meanwhile, where are the admirals? And when the admirals finally do make a stand, it's 'sexual harassment will not be tolerated, it's a zero tolerance policy.' And these were the same guys who when they were CO's and XO's in the ready rooms were telling us about the nutty things they did when they were JO's associated with interfacing with females. Overnight the zeitgeist of naval aviation changed. And that seemed like a breach of trust to the junior officer corps." Author interview with Lieutenant Commander Ward Carroll, 3/18/93.

p. 111   "Woman is God's finest creation . . ." Anthony Peyou, Commander, USN (Ret.), Vista, California. Letter to the Editor, *San Diego Union-Tribune,* July 31, 1992.

p. 112   "Smart people" . . . "don't go to a hotel . . ." Celia Collier, Naval Air Station Patuxent River, Maryland. Letter to the Editor, *Navy Times,* July 20, 1992. Another typical statement: One female officer at Lemoore Naval Air Station told an NIS agent in November 1991 that women at Tailhook had "put themselves in a vulnerable position by their 'stupid decisions.' " U.S. NIS, Results of Interview, November 1, 1991, p. 1291.

p. 112   "Paula Coughlin is empirically right . . ." Author interview with Ward Carroll, 3/18/93, *op. cit.*

p. 112   "Now it is the fashion to 'unman' the Navy . . ." Gordon Houghton,

Spring Valley, California. Letter to the Editor, *San Diego Union-Tribune,* July 31, 1992.

p. 113   "a bunch of 'pantywaists,' sailing around . . ." Karl T. Clarkson, La Mesa, California. Letter to the Editor: *San Diego Union-Tribune,* July 11, 1992.

p. 113   "Congratulations to Rep. Pat Schroeder . . ." Richard S. Caylor, Carlsbad, California. Letter to the Editor, *San Diego Union-Tribune,* July 31, 1992.

p. 113   "The success of any operation . . ." Billy F. Martin, San Diego, California. Letter to the Editor, *San Diego Union-Tribune,* July 11, 1992.

p. 113   "In times better than these—I think . . ." Patrick Groff, San Diego, California. Letter to the Editor, *San Diego Union-Tribune,* July 11, 1992.

p. 114   "I wish to have no Connection with any ship . . ." Quoted in Kenneth J. Hagan, *This People's Navy: The Making of American Sea Power* (New York: The Free Press, 1991). *op. cit.*

CHAPTER SIX: CHIMNEYS IN SUMMER

p. 115   "Being female is not an excuse to be a coward" Rosemary Mariner, Draft Remarks, Zonta International Amelia Earhart Luncheon, January 23, 1993.

p. 116   "had had the time of her life" and other unattributed quotes in this section . . . Author interview with Rosemary Mariner, 2/17/93.

p. 118   "The most vicious, ruthless . . ." Quoted in Anthony Astrachan, *How Men Feel.* Anchor Press/Doubleday (New York: 1986).

p. 119   "established a task force to look at all laws . . ." Cited in Major General Jeanne Holm, USAF (Ret.), *Women in the Military: An Unfinished Revolution* (Revised Edition). Presidio Press (Novato, Calif.: 1992), Appendix 2.

pp. 119–   "There is nothing like watching the Johnny Carson show . . ."; "While
20   the newspapers were making heroines of us . . ."; "One commander told me that women were physically incapable . . ." Rosemary Mariner, Speech at Zonta International Amelia Earhart Banquet, Washington, D.C., January 1983.

p. 127   "That's the meat of the syllabus . . ." This and all other unattributed quotes in this section from author interviews with Loree Draude, 1/7/93, 5/18/93, 5/19/93.

p. 133   "on a regular basis would welcome this kind of activity," "screaming match," "made comments to the effect that a lot of female Navy pilots . . ." Department of Defense Inspector General, *Tailhook 91—Part 1: Review of the Navy Investigations.* September 1992.

p. 133   "I need to emphasize a very important message . . ." Quoted in Eric

Schmitt, "Senior Navy Officers Suppressed Sex Investigation, Pentagon Says," *New York Times,* September 25, 1992.

p. 134   "It's difficult for me to visualize a woman being on my wing going into combat . . ." Author interview with source not for attribution, 1/6/93.

p. 138   "the only remaining official restrictions on women in American life" D'Ann Campbell, "Combating the Gender Gulf," *Minerva: Quarterly Report on Women and the Military,* Vol. 10, Nos. 3 & 4, Fall/Winter 1992.

p. 139   "As a military historian and as a Christian . . ." Quoted in Grant Willis, "Some on women-in-combat panel want report ignored," *Navy Times,* November 30, 1992.

p. 139   "My service on the Commission was . . . one of the most challenging . . ." Captain Mimi Finch, U.S. Army, "Women in Combat: One Commissioner Reports," *Minerva: Quarterly Report on Women and the Military,* Vol. 12, November 1, Spring 1994.

p. 139   "Gender norming" . . . "Quotas," "different standards of training . . ." Quoted in William Matthews, "Don't expect sweeping changes for women," *Navy Times,* November 2, 1992.

p. 140   "a daughter who was a jet-pilot" Presidential Commission on the Assignment of Women in the Armed Forces, *Report to the President.* U.S. Government Printing Office (Washington, D.C.: November 15, 1992).

p. 141   "Of the 23 instructors we have at Top Gun . . ." Presidential Commission on the Assignment of Women in the Armed Forces, *Excerpts from Hearings,* Prepared by R. Cort Kirkwood, Media Liaison, Department of Communications and Congressional Affairs," 1992.

p. 142   "It was the first time I've heard such open hatred . . ." Author interview with Brenda Scheufle, 1/6/93.

p. 143   "If you can do everything the plane asks of you . . ." and other quotes in this section, *Ibid.*

p. 143   "What would this country do if we had a female being raped . . ." Author interview with source not for attribution, *op. cit.*

p. 144   "The whole flavor of the ship would change . . ." Author interview with Craig King, 4/28/93.

p. 144   "I wanted to tell him . . ." Author interview with Pam Lyons, 1/6/93.

p. 146   "it was more lawful and convenient . . . since she was among men . . ." Quoted in *Joan of Arc,* Jackdaw No. 10, Jackdaw Publications Ltd. (London: 1972).

pp. 147–48   "Lily had always shown the sort of aggression . . ." and "bursting with good humor . . ." Quoted in Bruce Myles, *Night Witches,* Presidio Press (Novado, Calif.: 1981).

p. 149   "If the woman was a good soldier . . ." Linda Grant De Pauw, "Women in Combat: The Revolutionary War Experience," *Armed Forces and Society,* Vol. 7, No. 2, Winter 1981, pp. 209–26.

p. 150   "what men and women are arguing about in the twentieth . . ."
           C. Kay Larson, "Bonny Yank and Ginny Reb," *Minerva: Quarterly Report on Women and the Military,* Vol. 8, No. 1, Spring 1990.

p. 150   "No man on the field that day . . ." Quoted in *Ibid.*

CHAPTER SEVEN: LEAVING THE BEACH

p. 153   "Being a commanding officer is a lot like being a super-parent" News Release, USS *Cape Cod* (AD-43), FPO San Francisco, 96649-2535.

p. 153   "like a big Dad, just a lovable person" Author interview with Gloria Skillman, 7/4/94.

p. 153   "I made my decision when I was seven years old . . ." Author interview with James Hooper, 7/3/94.

p. 155   "the finest television set money could buy" "Ceremony in Honor of Hon. Carl Vinson, Chairman, Committee on Armed Services, U.S. House of Representatives," House of Representatives, Committee on Armed Services, August 19, 1964.

p. 157   "If the Navy could possibly have used dogs or ducks or monkeys . . ." Dean Gildersleeve quoted in Joy Bright Hancock, *Lady in the Navy.* Naval Institute Press (Annapolis, Md.: 1972), p. 50.

p. 157   "Office of the Judge Advocate General. 'No use for the services of the Women's Auxiliary is seen at this time . . .'" *Ibid.,* p. 51.

p. 158   "I realized that there were two letters which had to be in it: 'W' for women and 'V' for volunteer . . ." Quoted in Hancock, *op. cit.,* p. 61. "Appointed" was later changed to "Accepted."

p. 158   "When this project was proposed in the beginning of the war . . ." "Subcommittee Hearings on S. 1641, to Establish the Women's Army Corps in the Regular Army, to Authorize the Enlistment and Appointment of Women in the Regular Navy and Marine Corps and the Naval and Marine Corps Reserve, and for Other Purposes," House of Representatives, Committee on Armed Services, Subcommittee No. 3, Organization and Mobilization, February 18, 1948.

p. 159   "To the amazement of senior officers . . ." D'Ann Campbell, "Combating the Gender Gulf," *Minerva: Quarterly Report on Women and the Military,* Vol. 10, Nos. 3 & 4, Fall/Winter, 1992, pp. 13–41.

p. 159   "Enormous offices and record headquarters must be run . . ." Subcommittee Hearings on S. 1641, *op. cit.*

p. 159   "I hope that there would be a few [women] coming in young . . ." *Ibid.*

p. 160   "be given rank not commensurate with responsibility" *Ibid.*

p. 160   "I should like to say this, sir . . ." *Ibid.*

p. 160   "I can see no objections to the bill." *Ibid.*

p. 160   "When the house is on fire . . ." *Ibid.*

p. 160   "No business, no governmental organization . . ." *Ibid.*

At times, the spirited discussions of the legislators took on a slightly surreal, blind-leading-the-blind flavor. Testimony by Bradley, who claimed that women had proved themselves capable in hundreds of Army Air Force job categories, prompted the following exchange:

Johnson (D. California): General Bradley, I think it was 406 categories that you had that women were, you said, peculiarly well-fitted for. Was there included the matter of cooks and waiters?

General Bradley: I did not say "peculiarly" well fitted. I said capable of carrying out. That would be included, of course, but normally they are not used for that, except in their own barracks.

Johnson: I never could understand why you continued to use the men for cooks.

Vinson: Women can only cook small meals.

p. 161   "a long, loud, and lonely proponent of a big Navy" *Current Biography,* Vol. 3, No. 4., H. W. Wilson (New York: 1942).

p. 161   "Vinson: I propose an amendment, if somebody will draft it . . ." Subcommittee Hearings on S. 1641, *op. cit.*

p. 162   "The ship is a reflection of the captain . . ." Author interview with James Hooper, 12/7/92.

p. 163   "I was concerned about how I would deal with this . . ." *Ibid.*

p. 164   "People behave better . . ." *Ibid.*

p. 164   "There are no technical schools for this rating" *The Bluejackets' Manual,* Twenty-first Edition, United States Naval Institute (Annapolis, Md.: 1990).

p. 164   "I like being out on the salt" Author interview with Timothy Voelker, 12/8/92.

p. 165   "On a tender, you have to listen to the guys . . ." Author interview with Michelle Albritton, 7/6/93.

p. 166   "The discomfort of a good dousing in the tank . . ." Vice Admiral William P. Mack (Ret.) and Lieutenant Commander Royal W. Connell, *Naval Ceremonies, Customs, and Traditions.* Naval Institute Press (Annapolis, Md.: 1980).

p. 167   "There's no need for any of that crap . . ." Author interview with James Hooper, 7/3/93.

p. 168   "It's a silly little game" Author interview with Brenda Berger, 7/9/93.

pp. 168–69   "One of the reasons I joined the Navy . . ."; "pretty upset"; "saying the wrong thing . . ."; "It got very ugly"; "The crew pulled together . . ."; "Our purpose is to go out and kill people . . ." Author interview with William Breznau, 12/8/92.

p. 170   "somewhere in the neighborhood of twenty-five or so crew members . . ." Author interview with Alice Smith, 12/9/92.

p. 170 "Just about every division has been decimated by . . . pregnancies." Department heads meeting on the *Cape Cod*, 12/8/92.

p. 171 "seek counseling," "must be done at a civilian facility" *Navy Pregnancy Policy*, NAVPERS 15611, United States Navy, October 31, 1990.

p. 171 "But what's worse . . ." and "so that's three disadvantages . . ." Author interview with Sympharosa Williams, 12/7/92.

p. 171 Pregnancy is not only a medical concern . . . Sex on board a Navy ship is a new concept for old-line captains. "There were things that I worry about on a day-to-day basis that I wouldn't have to worry about if I were still on a submarine," said Jim Suhr, commanding officer of the *Emory S. Land*, a submarine tender based in Norfolk. "Such as the chief engineman telling me that she's going to have to change the locks on my gig because they found some pillows and used condoms in it. I never had that problem on a submarine." The captain's gig, a small motorboat kept on the weather deck, was sacrosanct, making the violation all the more egregious. Author interview with Jim Suhr, 3/16/93.

p. 171 "During the actual hostilities period we had women manning gun mounts . . ." Author interview with L. L. King, 12/4/92.

p. 172 "Deploying and leaving my daughter is the hardest thing . . ." Author interview with Julie Robbins, 12/8/92.

p. 172 "But all it would take is one person" Sympharosa Williams interview, *op. cit.*

p. 172 "The first two weeks of deployment, you have an entire ship that's grieving." Author interview with Deb Mariyah, 12/8/92.

p. 173 "absolutely striking blond woman with a huge diamond ring . . ." Author interview with Marsha Evans, 4/15/93.

p. 175 "We'll dress her up in sailor clothes . . ." Reginald Hargreaves, *Women-at-Arms: Their Famous Exploits Throughout the Ages*. Hutchinson & Co., Ltd. (London: undated).

p. 176 "It is surprising that the ships did not sink more often . . ." Linda Grant De Pauw, *Seafaring Women*, Houghton Mifflin (Boston: 1982), p. 65.

p. 176 "This day the surgeon informed me . . ." Quoted in *Ibid*, p. 74.

p. 177 "rouged challenge" Quoted in John Costello, *Virtue Under Fire: How World War II Changed Our Social and Sexual Activities*. Little, Brown (New York: 1985), p. 86.

p. 177 It started in 1942 . . . One letter, sent to Reverend James MacKrell of Little Rock, began, "I am a Christian . . . and hate sin as bad as anyone." Signed by a nurse, it alleged that women auxiliary members were "inspected" at training centers by male medical officers. The doctors, she wrote, showed the women pictures of nude men, pictures of men sitting on toilets. "Christ loves these girls, and I know he does not like for them to have to line up naked and it is embarrassing for our girls every month. Please send me your book," the letter writer plaintively signed off, *"The Truth About the Mark of the Beast,* also *Satan's Children."* An Inspector General investigation turned up nothing unusual, apart from the precarious mental condition of the nurse who wrote the letter. Quoted in Mattie E. Treadwell, *The Women's Army Corps.* United States Army in World War II Special Studies, Office of the Chief of Military History, Department of the Army (Washington, D.C.: 1954).

p. 178   "enough to stop an engine in no time" Quoted in Marianne Verges, *On Silver Wings: The Women Airforce Service Pilots of World War II 1942–1944.* Ballantine Books (New York: 1991). The death toll for the WASPs has been little acknowledged: twenty-six in air mishaps after flight school, eleven in training, and one in a non-air accident.

p. 178   "according to a supersecret agreement . . ." *Ibid.*

pp. 179–   "a monastic type of place . . ."; "I just wish it would happen this
81   week"; "The root of discriminatory behaviors . . ."; "the best thing that could happen to the Naval Academy . . ."; "When I got there in August . . ." Author interview with Marsha Evans, 2/17/93.

p. 182   "happy to go, mentally exhausted . . ." *Ibid.*

p. 182,   "that is at best inappropriate and at worst morally repugnant . . .";
184   "public sex, attempts to 'sell' female sailors . . ."; "'peso-parties' . . ." Memo from Jacquelyn K. Davis to Secretary Caspar Weinberger, Re: Summary of Findings of 1987 DACOWITS Westpac Trip, August 26, 1987.

p. 183   "We expect counsel from this group to help us evolve policies . . ." Anna Rosenberg, quoted in Mary Fainsod Katzenstein, "Feminism Within American Institutions: Unobtrusive Mobilization in the 1980s," *Signs: Journal of Women in Culture and Society,* 1990, Vol. 16, No. 1. The source cited for the quote is: Anna Rosenberg Hoffman papers, Schlesinger Library, Radcliffe College, 83-M162-84-M65, Carton 4.

p. 184   "was known, prior to the trip, to have dismissed such issues as sexual harassment as a problem that women themselves invited" Katzenstein, *Ibid.*

p. 185   "the feminist thought-control brigade . . ." Quoted in Mary Fainsod Katzenstein, "The Spectacle as Political Resistance: Feminist and Gay/Lesbian Politics in the Military," *Minerva: Quarterly Report on Women and the Military,* Vol. 11, No. 1, Spring 1993, pp. 1–16.

p. 185   "I don't view this as a women's rights organization . . ." Jacquelyn Davis quoted in Mary Fainsod Katzenstein, "Feminism Within American Institutions: Unobtrusive Mobilization in the 1980s," *op. cit.* Source cited for the quote is: "DACOWITS Expects to Retain Strong Voice," *Air Force Times,* December 7, 1987.

p. 186   "There is no doubt that this legislative provision . . ." and "the Navy institutional character . . ." *Update Report on the Progress of Women in the Navy.* Prepared by the 1990 Navy Women's Study Group (Washington, D.C.: 1990).

p. 186   "were not aggressively carried out . . ." Marsha Evans interview, 4/15/93, *op. cit.*

p. 187   "The Presidential Commission that reported out in late November . . ." "The Alpha and the Omega," Remarks Prepared for Delivery by The Honorable Sean O'Keefe, Secretary of the Navy. USNA Address to the Brigade of Midshipmen, Annapolis, Maryland, January 6, 1993.

CHAPTER EIGHT: GOOD TO GO

pp. 191–   "paddle wheels and 'dozers and backhoes . . ." Author interview with
92   Karlene Dent, 1/12/93.

p. 192   "They tried to rip me a new one" Author interview with Karlene Dent, 2/10/93.

p. 192   "I just about went home in a pine box a couple of times" Author interview with Karlene Dent, 1/12/93.

pp. 192–   "He's gone through all the hard-knocks" . . . "I've been watching you
93   for a while and I find that you're very mature . . ." . . . "a sympathy fuck" . . . "I certainly will if you undo your coveralls and let me touch your breasts." . . . "We were kind of numbed . . ." Author interview with Karlene Dent, 2/10/93.

p. 195   "Since the court-martial . . ." *Ibid.*

p. 196   "there [is] no real evidence that homosexual status, per se, disable[s] people from distinguished service in the military" Clinton's August 20 remark quoted in Jeffrey Schmalz, "Difficult First Step," *New York Times,* November 15, 1992.

p. 196   "blow the lid off the Capitol" Bob Dole on "Meet the Press," NBC, Sunday, November 15, 1992.

p. 196   "The way it was reported and the way it was talked about . . ." Quoted in Gustav Niebuhr, "Clinton Talks About Religion as His Anchor," *New York Times,* October 4, 1994.

p. 197   "composed of pederastic lovers and their boys" Plato, *Symposium.*

p. 197   "A band that is held together by erotic love is indissoluble and unbreakable . . ." Plutarch, cited in David Cohen, "Notes on a Grecian Yearn: Pederasty in Thebes and Sparta," *New York Times,* March 31, 1993.

p. 198   "How I wish I were in their shoes!" Commander Lin Hutton, "Women Flying High!" *Newsweek,* May 10, 1993. Also, Author interview With Lin Hutton, 3/17/93.

p. 198   "Here we are spending all this time on a small percentage of people who are very vocal" Hutton quoted in Kerry DeRochi, "At hearing, little common ground, but most witnesses said they support the military's ban on homosexuals," *Virginian-Pilot and Ledger-Star,* May 11, 1993.

p. 199   "Obviously, the issue of gays in the military is going to be impor-tant . . ." Barbara Pope, Address to the Women Officers Professional Association, Washington, D.C., February 18, 1993.

p. 200   "Many men still don't think women belong in the military . . ." Colo-nel Cammermeyer quoted in "Lesbians, Long Overlooked, Are Central to Debate on Military Ban," *New York Times,* May 4, 1993.

p. 200–2   "We fought long and hard to not be characterized as whores or lesbi-ans . . ." Author interview with Donna Scrivener, 12/4/92.

p. 200   At Parris Island, South Carolina, where all women Marines received basic training, a 1988 investigation targeted seventy suspected lesbians . . . Information from Jacob Weisberg, "Gays in Arms," *New Republic,* February 19, 1990.

p. 200   In the same year, thirty women (including every black woman on board) were investigated . . . eight were discharged. Information from Michelle M. Benecke and Kirstin S. Dodge, "Military Women in Nontraditional Job Fields: Casualties of the Armed Forces' War on Homosexuals," *Harvard Women's Law Journal,* Vol. 13, 1990.

p. 200   A 1984 congressional report estimated the Pentagon spent an astound-ing $336 million . . . Jim Lynch, "Witch Hunt at Parris Island," *The Progressive,* March 1989.

p. 200   three . . . times as likely . . . Jacob Weisberg put the figure at three in "Gays in Arms"; *op. cit.* Pat Schroeder estimated it was eight times as often in Richard Sisk, "Servicewomen allege 'lesbian-baiting,' " *San Diego Union-Tribune,* August 24, 1992.

p. 200   "a way of fighting back . . ." Schroeder quote from "Servicewomen allege 'lesbian-baiting,' " *Ibid.*

pp. 200–201   "Males are an experiment toward 'the masculine' . . . The sky will not fall." Robert Bly, "What the Mayans Could Teach the Joint Chiefs," *New York Times,* July 23, 1993.

p. 201   "The belief that power rightfully belongs to the masculine . . . no spectre is more terrifying than our own negative identity." Kenneth L. Karst, "The Pursuit of Manhood and the Desegregation of the Armed Forces," *UCLA Law Review,* Vol. 38:499, 1991.

p. 202   "the specific location is not relevant to the subject of this book . . . in all settings we associate with the term 'stag party' " Peggy Reeves Sanday, *Fraternity Gang Rape: Sex, Brotherhood, and Privilege on Campus.* New York University Press (New York and London: 1990), p. 4.

p. 203   "It is absolutely senseless for someone to die because of who he is . . ." Letter from Jim Jennings cited in Pamela Wilson, "Sailor

Claims Navy Coverup in Slaying of Gay Roommate," *San Diego Daily Transcript*, January, 1993.

p. 203   "The only thing left of his face . . ." Dorothy Hajdys quoted in "Sailor Claims Navy Coverup in Slaying of Gay Roommate," *Ibid.*

pp. 205–6   "The CO of one of the A-6 squadrons that was there came over . . . And then I'd leave and I wouldn't come back." Author interview with Kara Hultgreen, 9/9/93.

p. 209   "I have no easy answers for the new secretary . . ." Remarks prepared for delivery by The Honorable Sean O'Keefe, Secretary of the Navy, USNA Address to the Brigade of Midshipmen, Annapolis, Maryland, January 6, 1992.

p. 209   "sexual harassment poster child of the year" Author interview with Ward Carroll, 3/18/93.

pp. 210–12   "What goes on det stays on det . . . But my fears are founded on something concrete, something bad that happened to me." Author interview with Paula Coughlin, 3/17/93.

p. 212   "I hurt for them because their reputations have been damaged" . . . "very much a celebration . . . not a twenty-four-hour sex orgy for five days" . . . "a disgrace to the Navy" Beth Rudd on "Hard Copy," segment aired 2/23/93.

p. 212   "delaying the release of the final report . . ." Quoted in Patrick Pexton, "Decision delayed: Tailhook cloud still hangs over Navy," *Navy Times*, March 8, 1993.

pp. 212–13   "We do not need . . . to know which lieutenant pinched which women . . ." Stansfield Turner, "Big Fish Escape the Tailhook," *Arizona Republic*, January 31, 1993 (Reprinted from *Washington Post*).

p. 213   "like an X-rated novel" Quoted in Linda Bird Francke, "Paula Coughlin: The Woman Who Changed the U.S. Navy," *Glamour*, June 1993.

p. 215   "[Schwarzkopf] said that changes in this area must be made in the interest of military effectiveness . . ." *Hearing of the Manpower and Personnel Subcommittee of the Senate Armed Services Committee on the Subject of Females in Combat*, 102nd Congress, June 18, 1991.

p. 215   "I guess I was looking at it from the standpoint of people being together . . . were less of an evil than the other" Author interview with Frank Kelso, 3/4/94.

p. 215   "It's my personal view that the law should remain as it stands . . ." . . . "worry about the young woman . . ." *Hearing of the Manpower and Personnel Subcommittee of the Senate Armed Services Committee on the Subject of Females in Combat, op. cit.*

p. 216   "of superior intelligence, great physical conditioning . . . that's the way I feel about it" *Ibid.*

p. 216   "I don't think there's any one day lightning struck . . . women working under me or working with me" Frank Kelso interview, *op. cit.*

pp. 216–   "dressed in blue jeans" . . . "Most of the jobs we do in the Navy are
17   not strength-related . . . why should I stand in her way?" *Ibid.*

p. 217   "They told me something that I didn't appreciate previously . . . to
           make the same wages" *Ibid.*

p. 217   "What is it about the Navy?" Quoted in Melissa Healy, "Top Admiral
           Seeks End to Navy Sex Abuse," *Los Angeles Times,* June 6, 1992.

p. 217   "shocked that naval officers . . ." . . . "I just cannot get over it." Au-
           thor interview with Deborah Burnette, 2/28/94.

p. 218   "In order to give these women that we had . . ." Frank Kelso inter-
           view, *op. cit.*

p. 218   "Consistency . . ." "Greater Combat Roles for Women Are Likely,"
           Los Angeles Times, April 8, 1993.

p. 218   "The services shall permit women to compete for assignments in air-
           craft . . ." Secretary of Defense Les Aspin, *Memorandum for the Sec-
           retary of the Army, Secretary of the Navy, Secretary of the Air Force,
           Chairman, Joint Chiefs of Staff, Assistant Secretary of Defense (Force
           Management and Personnel), Assistant Secretary of Defense (Reserve
           Affairs),* Subject: Policy on the Assignment of Women in the Armed
           Forces, April 28, 1993.

p. 219   "a soft-spoken strawberry blonde" . . . "I can be a killer. I can and
           will kill in defense of my country." Bruce W. Nelan, "Annie Get Your
           Gun," *Time,* May 10, 1993.

p. 219   "This is sort of like being able to vote" . . . "I feel super, I'm ecstatic,
           I'm thrilled." Quoted in Patrick Pexton and John Burlage, *Navy Times,*
           May 10, 1993.

p. 219   "It's something that I've been looking forward to for 20 years . . ."
           Rosemary Mariner quoted in Pexton and Burlage, *Ibid.*

p. 219   "stoked" Author interview with Loree Draude, 5/18/93.

CHAPTER NINE: THE TROGLODYTES

p. 220   "The last thing I ever wrote was a paper in my senior year . . ." Au-
           thor interview with Michael Kitchen, 2/24/93.

p. 220   "One lieutenant commander . . ." *Ibid.*

p. 221   "People are afraid to subscribe . . ." Author interview with Michael
           Kitchen, 6/3/93.

pp. 221–   "About that age . . ." Author interview with Michael Kitchen, 2/24/93.
22

p. 222   "Gives me a chance to pass sugar cubes . . ." Author interview with
           Jennifer Kitchen, 3/19/93.

p. 222   "It was disheartening, having trained for that . . ." Author interview
           with Michael Kitchen, 2/24/93.

p. 222   "a journal for the politically correct and sensitive military person" *The
           Gauntlet,* Vol. 1, September 1992.

pp. 222–23   "an unofficial official organization" . . . "rank-specific, not gender-specific" . . . "Although I wasn't at Tailhook '91 . . ." Author interview with Michael Kitchen, 2/24/93.

p. 223   "Congresswoman Patricia Schroeder assures us that animal lovers will be as welcome . . ." *The Gauntlet,* February 1993.

p. 223   "I sent her a copy [of the interview] . . ." Author interview with Michael Kitchen, 2/24/94.

p. 224   "There was a guy named Ben . . ." *Ibid.*

p. 225   "If women are now expected to kill and be killed . . ." Quoted in Barbara Vobejda and Thomas Heath, "Combat Role for Women Seen Likely to Have Wider Social Impact," *Washington Post,* April 29, 1993.

p. 225   "to order the nation's daughters into killing zones . . ." Quoted in Bruce W. Nelan, "Annie Get Your Gun," *Time,* May 10, 1993.

p. 227   "What do they contribute? . . ." Author interview with Marsha Evans, 2/17/93.

pp. 230–31   "didn't get pushed at all" . . . "Notre Dame has an entire building . . ." . . . "I've always wanted to do something to serve my country . . ." . . . "had gone to the Naval Academy . . ." Author interview with Sara McGann, 6/25/93.

p. 231   "When the whole Tailhook thing exploded . . ." *Ibid.*

pp. 231–32   "academically capable and strong-willed enough" . . . "remotely approaching" Author interview with Sheila McGann, 6/25/93.

p. 232   "They said they were aware of it and were trying to fix it . . ." Sara McGann interview, *op. cit.*

p. 232   "The girl who was chained to the urinal . . ." *Ibid.*

p. 233   "was perhaps not cooperating fully with the spirit of the academy" Author interview with Bill McGann, 6/25/93.

p. 233   "This was not just a case of hazing at all" . . . "got a sense of humor" Quoted in John M. Glionna, "Southland Woman Tells of Her Annapolis Ordeal," *Los Angeles Times,* Wednesday, May 23, 1990.

p. 233   "our own mini-Tailhook" Author phone conversation with Karen Myers, 3/10/93.

p. 233   "for any reason except for their own safety or during approved athletic contests" . . . "horseplay or any other contact" "involuntary participation" . . . "Synopsis of Action Taken Subsequent to the Naval Academy Handcuffing Incident," three-page release issued by the Naval Academy, Annapolis, Maryland, undated.

p. 233   "profoundly disturbing sense of arrogance . . ." "Tailhook: Aberrant Behavior or Navy Culture?" Comments provided by Paul E. Roush at the Joint Services Conference on Professional Ethics, Washington, D.C., January 29, 1993.

p. 234   "We need to get away from lecturing and into dialogue" Author interview with Maureen Sullivan, 4/21/93.

p. 234   "We would go months without bathing . . ." James Webb, "Women
           Can't Fight," *The Washingtonian,* 1979.

p. 235   "Plebe funk . . ." Author interview with Andrea Larson, 7/1/93.

p. 235   "a pretty good idea because then the squad leaders . . ." Author inter-
           view with Anthony Arzu, 7/1/93.

p. 236   "You have to scare the people at the beginning . . ." Andrea Larson
           interview, *op. cit.*

p. 236   "As a folklorist . . ." Carol Burke, "Inside the Clubhouse," *The
           Women's Review of Books,* Vol. 10, No. 5, February 1993.

p. 236   "a lovely cool September morning . . ." Carol Burke, "Dames at Sea,"
           New Republic, August 17 and August 24, 1992.

p. 237   *"What do you call a mid . . ."* and "to stigmatize women . . ." *Ibid.*

p. 237   "She took things out of context . . ." Andrea Larson interview, *op. cit.*

p. 238   "I had a girl in New Orleans . . ." "USNA Approved Cadences, Plebe
           Summer 1993," U.S. Naval Academy, Annapolis, Maryland, July 1993.

p. 238   "The problem is, the formal uniform . . ." Andrea Larson interview,
           op. cit.

p. 238   "It makes us look like the Liberty bell." Author interview with Kelly
           Hoeft, 4/20/93.

p. 238   "having guts" Andrea Larson interview, *op. cit.*

p. 239   "pretty well prepared . . ." Sara McGann interview, *op. cit.*

p. 242   "I assume the naval aviators attending the convention . . ." Quoted in
           Ed Jahn, "Tailhook Meeting Opens on Pitching Decks," *San Diego
           Union-Tribune,* October 8, 1993.

p. 242   "We're exposing their secrets, breaking their code of silence . . ." Au-
           thor interview with Tamara Mason, 10/8/93.

pp. 242–   "It reminded me of anthropological studies of other cultures . . ."
43   Author interview with Frances Pohl, 10/8/93.

p. 243   "Deviants . . . I'm hired to kill people and break things" Author in-
           terview with Brad Taisey, 10/8/93.

p. 243   "intense and direct, the kind of man . . ." James Webb, *op. cit.*

p. 243   "She couldn't lead a group of men into a latrine" . . . "go in and see
           what was going on . . ." Brad Taisey interview, *op. cit.*

p. 244   "If we want to carry out this feminist agenda . . ." Author interview
           with Celeste and Brad Taisey, 10/8/93.

p. 246   "I'm going to be the first woman to fly an F-14!" Author interview with
           Kara Hultgreen, 9/9/93.

pp. 246–   "This jet is a very forgiving jet . . ." Author interview with Kara Hult-
47   green, 10/6/93.

pp. 247–   "When they start you off, they just hook up . . ." . . . "The
48   Babe . . ." . . . "This is the first time . . ." . . . "When Christine
           and I first got to the squadron . . ." Author interview with Kara Hult-
           green, 9/9/93.

p. 249   "go outside the ready room when they farted" Author interview with
               Kara Hultgreen, 10/6/93.

pp. 249–   "everything I did was scrutinized . . ." . . . "Believe it or not . . ."
50   Author interview with Kara Hultgreen, 9/9/93.

CHAPTER TEN: AFTERBURN

p. 253   "on divers occasions" . . . "wrongfully and dishonorably exposed his
               genitals to public view" . . . "take [a woman] up to the room and
               fuck her.'" . . . "bullshit," . . . "I'm not going to tell them shit."
               Charge Sheet, Commander Thomas V. Miller, June 21, 1993.

p. 254   "I need something for my sense of humor . . ." William H. McMi-
               chael, "Grounded flier awaits Tailhook ruling," *Newport News Daily
               Press*, February 7, 1994.

p 255   "any other person who has an interest other than an official interest in
               the prosecution of the accused" "Essential Findings and Ruling on
               Defense Motion to Dismiss," *United States v. Thomas R. Miller, CDR,
               USN, and v. Gregory E. Tritt, CDR, USN, and v. David Samples, LT,
               USN,* General Court-Martial, United States Navy, Tidewater Judicial
               Circuit, Norfolk, Virginia, February 7, 1994.

p. 257   "If you went on a world-wide search" . . . "clean as a hound's tooth."
               . . . "He's unbelievably smart . . ." Quoted in Patrick Pexton, "No
               questioning integrity of overseers," *Navy Times*, March 3, 1993.

p. 260   "I felt I had passed through a combat zone . . ." Quoted in Patrick
               Pexton, "Coughlin takes the stand," *Navy Times*, August 30, 1993.

p. 260   "No, I did not." Quoted in Richard A. Serrano, "Accuser Faces Ac-
               cused in Tailhook Sex Scandal," *Los Angeles Times*, August 18, 1993.

p. 260   "two or three beers" Quoted in John Lancaster, "Tailhook Prosecution
               Is Clouded," *Washington Post*, August 18, 1993.

p. 260   "would have been taken on September 7" Quoted in Linda Bird
               Francke, "The Legacy of Tailhook," *Glamour*, November 1994.

p. 261   "this minor shadow of a doubt" Quoted in Maureen Dowd, "Testimony
               Conflicts at Military Hearing on Abuse by Fliers," *New York Times*,
               August 18, 1993.

p. 261   "I am disappointed with the decision . . ." Quoted in Patrick Pexton,
               "Bonam is exonerated; Coughlin wants justice," *Navy Times*, Novem-
               ber 1, 1993.

pp. 261–   "We know we got the right guy" . . . "very stressful conditions" Au-
63   thor interview with Bill Hudson, 1/20/94.

p. 262   "My own feeling about the polygraph . . ." Author interview with se-
               nior NIS official (retired), 2/16/95.

p. 265   "You know, I feel responsible . . ." Quoted in Kerry DeRochi, "Flier's
               deal to tell about Tailhook irks lawyers," *Virginian-Pilot and Ledger-
               Star*, October 3, 1993.

p. 265   "I mostly hung out at the Hilton and the Sahara . . ." Statement to the Naval Investigative Service of Gregory Geiss, January 15, 1992.

pp. 265–   "kind of a cute little card thing" . . . "You'd go up to women . . ."
67   . . . "We're talking about one hour, one night, 754 days ago." Kerry DeRochi, "Flier's deal," *op. cit.*

pp. 267–   "I have spent some time every day since on that issue . . ." Quoted in
68   Phyllis W. Jordan, "Tailhook tops to-do list of Navy's new leader," *Virginian-Pilot and Ledger-Star,* September 17, 1993.

pp. 268–   "Somewhere in there I saw a sign about leg shaving . . ." . . . "Dur-
69   ing the 1991 Tailhook convention, I became aware . . ." . . . "The entire passageway . . ." . . . "That Saturday evening, when I glanced . . ." . . . "What I saw was a ring . . ." "Excerpts from Admirals' Statements," *Virginian-Pilot and Ledger-Star,* September 29, 1993.

p. 268   "We find ourselves in a serious dilemma with respect to . . ." Department of Defense Inspector General. *Report of Investigation: Tailhook 91—Part 2: Events at the 35th Annual Tailhook Symposium.* U.S. Government Printing Office (Washington, D.C.: February 1993).

p. 270   ". . . Six months! . . . I only need six more months." McLeod, Cartoon in the *Navy Times,* December 20, 1993.

p. 270   "an evaluation of [Kelso's] record under the criteria you have offered . . ." Quoted in Phyllis Jordan, "Aspin won't force Kelso to retire," *Virginian-Pilot,* October 5, 1993.

p. 270   "I have a real desire to serve . . ." Quoted in *ibid.*

pp. 272–   "The failure by those responsible to take strong corrective action . . ."
73   . . . "This court specifically finds this inaction . . ." "Essential Findings and Ruling on Defense Motion to Dismiss," *United States v. Thomas R. Miller, CDR, USN, and v. Gregory E. Tritt, CDR, USN, and v. David Samples, LT, USN, op. cit.*

pp. 273–   "I'm almost certain of it. But what would you have me do . . ." "Navy
74   ends Tailhook case; charges against fliers not revived," *Arizona Republic,* February 12, 1994.

p. 274   "It wasn't right that people that barfed on their shoes . . ." Author interview with Deborah Burnette, 2/28/94.

p. 274   "highest integrity and honor." . . . "no credible evidence . . ." Secretary of Defense Statement John Dalton on Admiral Frank B. Kelso II, Office of Assistant Secretary of Defense (Public Affairs), Washington, D.C., February 15, 1994.

p. 274   "has acted, as he has throughout his thirty-eight-year career, with the best interests . . ." John Dalton, statement released by the Secretary of the Navy on the forthcoming retirement of Admiral Frank B. Kelso II, February 15, 1994.

p. 274   "I am not happy about this. I am an honest man . . ." Quoted in "I didn't lie, admiral sez of Tailhook," Reuter News Service, February 12, 1993.

p. 274   "not retire until the end of Tailhook . . ." . . . "Clearly, we needed to change our culture . . ." . . . "the first young woman at sea . . ." Admiral Frank B. Kelso II, Chief of Naval Operations, Press Conference Transcript, February 15, 1994.

p. 275   "I feel continued service would be detrimental to my physical, mental and emotional health . . ." Paula Coughlin, letter to Secretary of the Navy John H. Dalton, February 7, 1994.

p. 275   "My request to resign should not be viewed . . ." Statement released on February 10, 1994, on behalf of Navy Lieutenant Paula Coughlin regarding her request to resign from the Navy, Office of Nancy L. Stagg, Esq., Rudick, Platt & Victor, San Diego, California.

EPILOGUE

p. 280   "a society of defenders" Judith Hicks Stiehm, "The Protected, the Protector, the Defender," Women's Studies International Forum, Vol. 5, No. 3–4, 1982.

pp. 280–   "a separate community" . . . "the armed forces . . . teach lessons to
81   the whole society" . . . "when the national government excludes . . ." Kenneth L. Karst, "The Pursuit of Manhood and the Desegregation of the Armed Forces," 38 UCLA Law Rev., 1991.

p. 282   "This [article] is not addressed to those who have a principled commitment to nonviolence . . ." Judith Hicks Stiehm, op. cit.

p. 282   "either . . . trivial or ideologically awkward" Cynthia Enloe, "The Politics of Constructing the American Woman Soldier as a Professionalized 'First Class Citizen': Some Lessons from the Gulf War," Minerva: Quarterly Report on Women and the Military, Vol. 10, No. 1, Spring 1992.

p. 282   "Its target is a vicious institution . . ." Ellen Willis, Media column, The Village Voice, September 13, 1994.

p. 282   "frequently of great individual goodness and purity, yet . . ." Jean Bethke Elshtain, "On Beautiful Souls, Just Warriors and Feminist Consciousness," Women's Studies International Forum, Vol. 5, No. 3–4, 1982.

pp. 285–   "sordid, sleazy stain" . . . and other quotes in this section, up to "This
86   is a work force issue, not a gender issue." Congressional Record, Tuesday, April 19, 1994, Vol. 140, No. 43. U.S. Government Printing Office, Superintendent of Documents, Washington, D.C. 20402.

p. 286   "We have upheld the honor of the United States Senate" Quoted in Maureen Dowd, "Senate Approves a 4-Star Rank for Admiral in Tailhook Affair," New York Times, April 20, 1994.

p. 287   "the works" . . . "I was concentrating on the task to be done" . . . "I created miracles with legs." Quoted in Warren Bates, "Tailhook shaving described," *Las Vegas Review-Journal,* September 29, 1994.

p. 288   "done more in American history to destroy a fine institution" Quoted in *Ibid.*

p. 288   "walking by a construction site . . . like a lady the entire weekend" Quoted in Warren Bates, "Women testify to Tailhook Behavior," *Las Vegas Review-Journal,* October 14, 1994.

p. 288   "wasn't a Sunday school gathering" . . . "one baby is crying" Quoted in Warren Bates, "Woman claims aviators were gentlemen," *Las Vegas Review-Journal,* October 13, 1994.

p. 288   "reversals of motion" . . . "fluidity of pen strokes" Quoted in "Expert: Coughlin signature not on poster," *Las Vegas Review-Journal,* September 30, 1994.

p. 289   "there was a lot more drinking, and people made asses of themselves . . ." Quoted in Warren Bates, "Experts fault security at LV Hilton," *Las Vegas Review-Journal,* October 7, 1994.

p. 289   "Most of the people in the Navy, whether I worked for them or not . . ." Quoted in Kenneth B. Noble, "Woman Tells of Retaliation for Complaint on Tailhook," *New York Times,* October 5, 1994.

p. 289   "There are so many misconceptions of who I am and what I am . . ." Quoted in Pamela Warrick, "Navy days over, ex-officer looks for life after Tailhook," *Arizona Republic,* November 10, 1994.

p. 289   "The crowd will come back" "Tailhook's faithful flock believes it will fly again," *Las Vegas Review-Journal,* October 17, 1994.

p. 290   "gender-neutral to the maximum extent possible" "Status and Plans for Women in the Navy: Enlisted," Bureau of Personnel Public Affairs Office, Department of the Navy, January 21, 1994.

p. 291   "The goal is all. The goal is everything" Quoted in Patrick Pexton, "Boorda's goal: Women in subs," *Navy Times,* May 16, 1994.

p. 291   "One of these days, people will wonder what all the fuss . . ." Quoted in Neff Hudson, "Boorda: 'We have a Navy today that is more ready," *Navy Times,* November 7, 1994.

p. 293   "The fact that men go to combat and women keep the home fires burning . . ." Quoted in Joel Greenberg, "Israeli Woman Sues for Chance to Be a Combat Pilot," *New York Times,* November 3, 1994.

p. 294   "She was a smart girl. I know she knew the chances she was taking" Quoted in Steve Komarow and Gordon Dickson, "Female aviator, a Navy pioneer, killed in crash," *USA Today,* October 27, 1994.

p. 294   "The way I look at it is . . ." Quoted in "Flight Rating of Navy Pilot Who Crashed Is Made Public," *New York Times,* November 21, 1994.

Selected Sources

The primary source material for Tailspin *consisted of the nearly four hundred interviews I conducted with U.S. Navy personnel between June 1992 and December 1994. I also drew on coverage of the Tailhook scandal and its aftermath, especially in the following newspapers:* the Navy Times, *the* New York Times, Washington Post, Los Angeles Times, San Diego Union-Tribune, Virginian-Pilot *and* Ledger-Star *and the* Pensacola News-Journal. *In addition, I found the following selected sources useful.*

BOOKS

Atkinson, Rick. *The Long Gray Line.* New York: Houghton Mifflin, 1989.

Barkalow, Captain Carol, with Andrea Raab. *In the Men's House.* New York: Poseidon Press, 1990.

Berube, Allan. *Coming Out Under Fire: The History of Gay Men and Women in World War Two.* New York: Free Press, 1990.

Brownmiller, Susan. *Against Our Will: Men, Women and Rape.* New York: Fawcett Columbine, 1975.

Campbell, D'Ann. *Women at War with America: Private Lives in a Patriotic Era.* Cambridge, Mass.: Harvard University Press, 1984.

Cochran, Jacqueline, and Maryann Bucknum Brinley. *Jackie Cochran: The Autobiography of the Greatest Woman Pilot in Aviation History.* New York: Bantam Books, 1987.

Coonts, Stephen. *Flight of the Intruder.* Annapolis: Naval Institute Press, 1986.

Cornum, Rhonda, as told to Peter Copeland. *She Went to War: The Rhonda Cornum Story.* Novato, Calif.: Presidio Press, 1992.

De Pauw, Linda Grant. *Seafaring Women.* Boston: Houghton Mifflin, 1982.

Dunnigan, James F., and Albert A. Nofi. *Dirty Little Secrets: Military Information You're Not Supposed to Know.* New York: Quill/William Morrow, 1990.

Ebbert, Jean, and Marie-Beth Hall. *Crossed Currents: Navy Women from WWI to Tailhook*. Washington, New York, London: Brassey's, 1993.

Elshtain, Jean Bethke. *Women and War*. New York: Basic Books, 1987.

Elshtain, Jean Bethke, and Sheila Tobias, eds. *Women, Militarism, and War*. Savage, Md.: Rowman and Littlefield, 1990.

Enloe, Cynthia. *Does Khaki Become You? The Militarization of Women's Lives*. London: Pandora Press, 1988.

Foss, Joe, and Matthew Brennan. *Top Guns: America's Fighter Aces Tell Their Most Daring and Spectacular Stories*. New York: Pocket Books, 1991.

Fraser, Antonia. *The Warrior Queens: The Legends and the Lives of the Women Who Have Led Their Nations in War*. New York: Vintage Books, 1994.

Gillchrist, Rear Admiral Paul T., USN (Ret.). *Feet Wet: Reflections of a Carrier Pilot*. Novato, Calif.: Presidio Press, 1990.

Goldman, Nancy Loring, Ed. *Female Soldiers—Combatants or Noncombatants*. Westport, Conn.: Greenwood Press, 1982.

Hagan, Kenneth J. *This People's Navy: The Making of American Sea Power*. New York: The Free Press, 1992.

Hancock, Captain Joy Bright, USN (Ret.). *Lady in the Navy: A Personal Reminiscence*. Annapolis: Naval Institute Press, 1972.

Hartmann, Susan M. *The Home Front and Beyond: American Women in the 1940s*. Boston: Twayne Publishers, 1982.

Hayton-Keeva, Sally. *Valiant Women in War and Exile*. San Francisco: City Lights Books, 1987.

Holm, Jeanne. *Women in the Military: An Unfinished Revolution*. Novato, Calif.: Presidio Press, 1992.

Hoyt, Edwin P. *Carrier Wars: Naval Aviation from World War II to the Persian Gulf*. New York: McGraw Hill, 1989.

Humphrey, Mary Ann. *My Country, My Right to Serve: Experiences of Gay Men and Women in the Military, World War II to the Present*. New York: HarperCollins Publishers, 1990.

Jeffords, Susan. *The Remasculinization of America, Gender and the Vietnam War*. Bloomington: Indiana University Press, 1989.

Jones, Ann. *Women Who Kill*. New York: Fawcett Crest, 1980.

Keegan, John. *The Face of Battle*. New York: The Viking Press, 1976.

Kiel, Sally Van Wagenen. *Those Wonderful Women and Their Flying Machines: The Unknown Heroines of World War II*. Revised and Expanded Edition. New York: Four Directions Press, 1990.

Knott, Blanche. *Truly Tasteless Military Jokes*. New York: St. Martin's Paperbacks, 1991.

LaBarge, Lieutenant Commander William H., USN (Ret.). *Road to Gold*. New York: HarperPaperbacks, 1993.

Litoff, Judy Barrett, and David C. Smith. *We're in This War, Too: World War II Letters From American Women in Uniform.* New York, Oxford: Oxford University Press, 1994.

Mack, Vice Admiral William P., USN (Ret.), and Rear Admiral Thomas D. Paulsen, USN. *The Naval Officer's Guide.* Tenth Edition. Annapolis: Naval Institute Press, 1991.

Mack, Vice Admiral William P., USN (Ret.), and Lieutenant Commander Royal W. Connell, USN. *Naval Ceremonies, Customs, and Traditions.* Fifth Edition. Annapolis: Naval Institute Press, 1980.

Marcinko, Richard, with John Weisman. *Rogue Warrior.* New York: Pocket Books, 1992.

Mitchell, Brian. *Weak Link: The Feminization of the American Military.* Washington: Regnery Gateway, 1989.

Morgan, Sherm. *Classic Aviation Humor, Book III.* Louisville, Kentucky: A Blue Heron Book, 1992.

Murphy, Lawrence R. *Perverts by Official Order: The Campaign Against Homosexuals by the United States Navy.* New York, London: Harrington Park Press, 1988.

Myers, James E., Ed. *A Treasury of Military Humor.* Springfield, Illinois: Lincoln-Herndon Press, 1990.

Myles, Bruce. *Night Witches: The Untold Story of Soviet Women in Combat.* Novato, Calif.: Presidio Press, 1981.

Noggle, Anne. *A Dance with Death: Soviet Airwomen in World War II.* College Station, Texas: Texas A&M University Press, 1994.

Pollard, Clarice F. *Laugh, Cry and Remember: The Journal of a G.I. Lady.* Phoenix: Journeys Press, 1991.

Pollock, Elizabeth R. *Yes, Ma'am! The Personal Papers of a WAAC Private.* Philadelphia, New York: J.B. Lippincott Company, 1943.

Sanday, Peggy Reeves. *Fraternity Gang Rape: Sex, Brotherhood, and Privilege on Campus.* New York: New York University Press, 1990.

Schneider, Dorothy and Carl J. *Sound Off! American Military Women Speak Out.* New York: Paragon House, 1992.

Shilts, Randy. *Conduct Unbecoming: Lesbians and Gays in the U.S. Military Vietnam to the Persian Gulf.* New York: St. Martin's Press, 1993.

Smith, Joan. *Misogynies: Reflections on Myths and Malice.* London: Faber and Faber, 1993, 1989.

Steffan, Joseph. *Honor Bound: A Gay American Fights for the Right to Serve His Country.* New York: Villard Books, 1992.

Stiehm, Judith. *Arms and the Enlisted Woman.* Philadelphia: Temple University Press, 1989.

Sturdevant, Saundra Pollock, and Brenda Stoltzfus. *Let the Good Times Roll: Prostitution and the U.S. Military in Asia.* New York: The New Press, 1993.

The Bluejackets' Manual. Twenty-First Edition, revised by Bill Bearden. Annapolis: United States Naval Institute, 1990.

Theweleit, Klaus. *Male Fantasies.* Vols. 1 and 2. Minneapolis, Minn.: University of Minnesota Press, 1987.

Treadwell, Mattie E. *The Women's Army Corps.* United States Army in World War II Special Studies. Washington, D.C.: Office of the Chief of Military History, Department of the Army, 1954.

Verges, Marianne. *On Silver Wings: The Women Airforce Service Pilots of World War II 1942–1944.* New York: Ballantine Books, 1991.

Weber, Joe. *Rules of Engagement.* Novato, Calif.: Presidio Press, 1991.

Wilcox, Robert K. *Scream of Eagles.* New York: John Wiley and Sons, 1990.

Williams, Christine L. *Gender Differences at Work: Women and Men in Nontraditional Occupations.* Berkeley and Los Angeles, Calif.: University of California Press, 1989.

Wilson, George C. *Flying the Edge: The Making of Navy Test Pilots.* Annapolis: Naval Institute Press, 1992.

Wolfe, Tom. *The Right Stuff.* New York: Farrar, Straus & Giroux, 1979.

Yeager, General Chuck, and Leo Janos. *Yeager.* New York: Bantam, 1985.

REPORTS

An Update Report on the Progress of Women in the Navy. Prepared by the 1990 Navy Women's Study Group.

Becraft, Carolyn. *Women in the Military 1980–1990.* Washington, D.C.: Women's Research and Education Institute, June 1990.

Board of Visitors, United States Naval Academy. *Report of the Committee on Women's Issues.* October 9, 1990.

Culbertson, Amy L., Paul Rosenfeld, Stephanie Booth-Kewly, and Paul Magnusson. *Assessment of Sexual Harassment in the Navy: Results of the 1989 Navy-wide Survey.* San Diego: Navy Personnel Research and Development Center, March 1992.

Debate over Admiral Frank Kelso's Retirement, *Congressional Record,* Vol. 140, No. 43. Washington, D.C.: U.S. Government Printing Office, Superintendent of Documents, April 19, 1994.

Defense Force Management: DoD's Policy on Homosexuality. United States General Accounting Office Report to Congressional Requesters, June 1992.

Department of Defense Inspector General. *Report of Investigation: Tailhook 91— Part 1: Review of the Navy Investigations.* September 1992.

Department of Defense Inspector General. *Report of Investigation: Tailhook 91— Part 2: Events at the 35th Annual Tailhook Symposium.* Washington, D.C.: U.S. Government Printing Office, February 1993.

DOD Service Academies: More Changes Needed to Eliminate Hazing. United States General Accounting Office Report to Congressional Requesters, November 1992.

Essential Findings and Ruling on Defense Motion to Dismiss, United States v. Thomas R. Miller, Cdr., USN, and United States v. Gregory E. Tritt, Cdr., USN, and United States v. David Samples, Lt., USN, General Court-Martial, United States Navy, Tidewater Judicial Circuit, Norfolk, Virginia, February 7, 1994.

Hearing of the Manpower and Personnel Subcommittee of the Senate Armed Services Committee, Subject: Females in Combat, Senate Hart Office Building, Room 216, June 18, 1991.

Incidence of Pregnancy and Single Parenthood Among Enlisted Personnel in the Navy. San Diego: Navy Personnel Research and Development Center, October 1989.

Marx, Kenneth A. *Issues Relating to the Unique Medical Needs of Women in the Armed Forces,* for the Research Division, Defense Equal Opportunity Management Institute, Patrick Air Force Base, Florida, 1990.

Naval Inspector General, *Report of Investigation: Department of the Navy/Tailhook Association Relationship and Personal Conduct Surrounding Tailhook '91 Symposium.* Case Number 920684. April 29, 1992.

Parenting Issues of Operation Desert Storm. Hearing Before the Military Personnel and Compensation Subcommittee of the Committee on Armed Services, House of Representatives, February 19, 1991. Washington, D.C.: U.S. Government Printing Office, 1991.

Presidential Commission on the Assignment of Women in the Armed Forces, Report to the President. Washington, D.C.: U.S. Government Printing Office, November 15, 1992.

Subcommittee Hearing on S. 1941, to Establish the Women's Army Corps in the Regular Army, to Authorize the Enlistment and Appointment of Women in the Regular Navy and Marine Corps and the Naval and Marine Corps Reserve, and for Other Purposes. House of Representatives, Committee on Armed Services, Subcommittee No. 3, Organization and Mobilization, Washington, D.C., February 18, 1948.

Thomas, Marie D., Patricia J. Thomas, and Virginia McClintock. *Pregnant Enlisted Women in Navy Work Centers.* San Diego: Navy Personnel Research and Development Center, March 1991.

Women in Combat. The Research Division, Defense Equal Opportunity Management Institute, Patrick Air Force Base, Florida, undated.

Women Midshipmen Study Group. *Report to the Superintendent: The Assimilation of Women in the Brigade of Midshipmen.* Annapolis: United States Naval Academy, July 1990.

Women Midshipmen Study Group. *Report to the Superintendent: The Integration of Women in the Brigade of Midshipmen.* Annapolis: United States Naval Academy, November 1987.

Women in the Military: The Tailhook Affair and the Problem of Sexual Harassment. Report of the Military Personnel and Compensation Subcommittee and Defense Policy Panel of the Committee on Armed Services, House of Representatives, September 14, 1992. Washington, D.C.: U.S. Government Printing Office, 1992.

Women in the U.S. Armed Services: The War in the Persian Gulf. Women's Research and Education Institute, Washington, D.C., undated.

ARTICLES AND PAPERS

Arkin, William, and Lynne R. Dobrofsky. "Military Socialization and Masculinity," *Journal of Social Issues*, Vol. 34, No. 1, 1978.

Association of the Bar of the City of New York Committee on Military Affairs and Justice. "The Combat Exclusion Laws: An Idea Whose Time Has Gone," *Minerva: Quarterly Report on Women and the Military*, Vol. 9, No. 4, Winter 1991.

Benecke, Michelle M., and Kirstin S. Dodge. "Military Women in Nontraditional Job Fields: Casualties of the Armed Forces' War on Homosexuals," *Harvard Women's Law Journal*, Vol. 13, Spring 1990.

Bennett, James Gordon. "Shock Waves at the U.S. Naval Academy," *Glamour*, June 1992.

Berube, Allan, and John D'Emilio. "The Military and Lesbians during the McCarthy Years," *Signs: Journal of Women in Culture and Society*, Vol. 9, No. 4, Summer 1984.

Boo, Katherine. "Universal Soldier: What Paula Coughlin can teach American women," *The Washington Monthly*, September 1992.

Broyles, Jr., William. "Why Men Love War," *Esquire*, November 1984.

Burke, Carol. "Dames at Sea," *The New Republic*, August 17 and 24, 1992.

Burke, Carol. "Inside the Clubhouse," *The Women's Review of Books*, Vol. 10, No. 5, February 1993.

Cockburn, Alexander. "The Selling of the Pentagon?" *American Film*, June 1986.

Cohn, Carol. "Sex and Death in the Rational World of Defense Intellectuals," *Signs: Journal of Women in Culture and Society*, Vol. 12, No. 4, 1987.

Cottam, K. Jean. "Yelena Fedorovna Kolesova: Woman Hero of the Soviet Union," *Minerva: Quarterly Report on Women and the Military*, Vol. 9, No. 2, Summer 1991.

"The Combat Exclusion Law: An Idea Whose Time Has Gone." The Association of the Bar of the City of New York Committee on Military Affairs and Justice, *Minerva: Quarterly Report on Women and the Military*, Vol. 9, No. 4, Winter 1991.

D'Amico, Francine. "Women at Arms: The Combat Controversy," *Minerva: Quarterly Report on Women and the Military*, Summer 1990.

Denisoff, R. Serge, and William D. Romanowski, "The Pentagon's Top Guns: Movies and Music," *Journal of American Culture*, Vol. 12, No. 3, 1989.

Devilbliss, M. C. "Gender Integration and Unit Deployment: A Study of GI Jo," *Armed Forces & Society*, Vol. 11, No. 4, Summer 1985.

Donnelly, Elaine. "The Tailhook Scandals," *National Review*, March 7, 1994.

Dubus, Andre. "A Quiet Siege: The Death and Life of a Gay Naval Officer," *Harper's*, June 1993.

Eisenhart, R. Wayne. "You Can't Hack It Little Girl: A Discussion of the Covert Psychological Agenda of Modern Combat Training," *Journal of Social Issues*, Vol. 31, No. 4, 1975.

Elshtain, Jean Bethke. "On Beautiful Souls, Just Warriors and Feminist Consciousness," *Women's Studies International Forum*, Vol. 5, No. 3–4, 1982.

Enloe, Cynthia. "The Politics of Constructing the American Woman Soldier as a Professionalized 'First Class Citizen': Some Lessons from the Gulf War," *Minerva: Quarterly Report on Women and the Military*, Vol. 10, No. 1, Spring 1992.

Francke, Linda Bird. "The legacy of Tailhook," *Glamour*, November 1994.

Francke, Linda Bird. "Paula Coughlin: The woman who changed the U.S. Navy," *Glamour*, June 1993.

Gattuso, Commander J. A., USN. "Out of the Bull's Eye," *Proceedings*, October 1993.

Gemmette, Elizabeth Villiers. "Armed Combat: The Women's Movement Mobilizes Troops in Readiness for the Inevitable Constitutional Attack on the Combat Exclusion for Women in the Military," *Women's Rights Law Reporter*, Vol. 12, No. 2, Summer 1990.

Horowitz, David. "The Feminist Assault on the Military." Studio City, Calif.: The Center for the Study of Popular Culture, 1992.

Horowitz, David, and Michael Kitchon. "Tailhook Witch-Hunt," *Heterodoxy*, October 1993.

Huston, Nancy. "Tales of War and Tears of Women," *Women's Studies International Forum*, Vol. 5, No. 3–4, 1982.

Karst, Kenneth L. "The Pursuit of Manhood and the Desegregation of the Armed Forces," *38 UCLA Law Review*, 1991.

Krohne, Kathleen. *The Effect of Sexual Harassment on Female Naval Officers: A Phenomenological Study*, Ph.D. Thesis, University of San Diego, January 1992.

Lawson, Jacqueline E. " 'She's a Pretty Woman . . . For a Cook': The Misogyny of the Vietnam War," *Journal of American Culture*, Vol. 12, No. 3, 1989.

Luckett, Perry D. "Military Women in Contemporary Film, Television, and Media," *Minerva: Quarterly Report on Women and the Military*, Vol. 7, No. 3, Summer 1989.

Lydenberg, Harry Miller. "Crossing the Line: Tales of the Ceremony During Four Centuries," *Bulletin of The New York Public Library*, Vol. 59, No. 8, August 1955.

Morin, Stephen F., and Ellen M. Garfinkle. "Male Homophobia," *Journal of Social Issues*, Vol. 34, No. 1, 1978.

"Naval Courtesy," *All Hands*, February 1959.

Reeves, Major Connie L., USA. "The Story of 'Yashka': Commander of the Russian Women's Battalion of Death," *Minerva: Quarterly Report on Women and the Military*, Vol. 6, No. 3, Fall 1988.

Roberts, David. "Men didn't have to prove they could fly, but women did," *Smithsonian*, Vol. 25, No. 5, August 1994.

Roush, Paul E. "Combat Exclusion: Military Necessity or Another Name for Bigotry?" *Minerva: Quarterly Report on Women and the Military*, Vol. 8, No. 3, Fall 1990.

Ruddick, Sara. "Pacifying the Forces: Drafting Women in the Interests of Peace," *Signs: Journal of Women in Culture and Society*, Vol. 8, No. 3, 1983.

Stiehm, Judith Hicks. "The Protected, the Protector, the Defender," *Women's Studies International Forum*, Vol. 5., No. 3–4, 1982.

Webb, James. "Women Can't Fight," *The Washingtonian*, November 1979.

Wilds, Nancy G. "Sexual Harassment in the Military," *Minerva: Quarterly Report on Women and the Military*, Vol. 8, No. 4, Winter 1990.

Yarborough, Jean. "The Feminist Mistake: Sexual Equality and the Decline of the American Military," *Policy Review*, Summer 1985.

Yonay, Ehud. "Top Guns," *California Magazine*, May 1983.

INDEX